Text and Social Media Analytics for Fake News and Hate Speech Detection

Identifying and stopping the dissemination of fabricated news, hate speech, or deceptive information camouflaged as legitimate news poses a significant technological hurdle. This book presents emergent methodologies and technological approaches of natural language processing through machine learning for counteracting the spread of fake news and hate speech on social media platforms.

- Covers various approaches, algorithms, and methodologies for fake news and hate speech detection.
- Explains the automatic detection and prevention of fake news and hate speech through paralinguistic clues on social media using artificial intelligence.
- Discusses the application of machine learning models to learn linguistic characteristics of hate speech over social media platforms.
- Emphasizes the role of multilingual and multimodal processing to detect fake news.
- Includes research on different optimization techniques, case studies on the identification, prevention, and social impact of fake news, and GitHub repository links to aid understanding.

The text is for professionals and scholars of various disciplines interested in fake news and hate speech detection.

Text and Social Media Analytics for Fake News and Hate Speech Detection

Edited by
Hemant Kumar Soni, Sanjiv Sharma,
and G. R. Sinha

CRC Press
Taylor & Francis Group
Boca Raton London New York

CRC Press is an imprint of the
Taylor & Francis Group, an **informa** business
A CHAPMAN & HALL BOOK

Designed cover image: ShutterStock

First edition published 2025
by CRC Press
2385 NW Executive Center Drive, Suite 320, Boca Raton FL 33431

and by CRC Press
4 Park Square, Milton Park, Abingdon, Oxon, OX14 4RN

CRC Press is an imprint of Taylor & Francis Group, LLC

ISBN: 9781032526621 (hbk)
ISBN: 9781032529752 (pbk)
ISBN: 9781003409519 (ebk)

DOI: 10.1201/9781003409519

Typeset in Times
by Deanta Global Publishing Services, Chennai, India

Dedicated to all those who suffered from Fake News and Hate Speeches on Social Media

Hemant Kumar Soni

Dedicated to my Parents, Teachers, Wife, and Daughter

Sanjiv Sharma

Dedicated to my Late Grand Parents, My Teachers, and Swami Vivekananda

G. R. Sinha

Contents

Preface

Social media provides a platform and opportunity for people to express themselves, raise their voices, and create the opinions of the masses. These liberties also persuade people and organizations to propagate fake news and hate speeches over social media. The main aim of this book is to discover new and emergent methodologies and approaches of natural language processing through machine learning for counteracting the spread of fake news and hate speeches on social media platforms. This book covers various approaches, algorithms, and methodologies for fake news and hate speech detection, a relatively innovative and fast-emergent research area. The book also offers an assortment of state-of-the-art techniques, converging on the best cutting-edge solutions for the most common and tough challenges faced in fake news and hate speech detection and prevention.

The book is practiced in the Departments of Information Technology, Social Media, Humanities, and Marketing. The origin of this book lies in scholarly series talks among all editors of the book regarding transdisciplinary research principles and the development of Collaborative Research. Later, we decided to explore the idea as the conception of a book titled *Text and Social Media Analytics for Fake News and Hate Speech Detection*. The book provides a comprehensive overview of the various tools, techniques, and applications in the field of text and social media analytics and explores various ways of detecting fake news and hate speech from public opinion in social media and how it is used to extract knowledge from received various public opinion over social media for any person, even, business and product. It presents analytics beyond the bars of academic disciplinary research used for knowledge extraction, prediction, and decision-making in the field of individual, social, and national development.

Hemant Kumar Soni
Sanjiv Sharma
G. R. Sinha

Acknowledgment

We wish to thank all the authors for their contributions in the form of chapters based on their research findings, case studies, analysis, observations, and datasets for inclusion in the book. We would like to extend our special thanks to all the contributors for sharing their knowledge, experience, and research work in the field of *Text and Social Media Analytics for Fake News and Hate Speech Detection*. We thank publisher CRC Press, Taylor & Fransis, and their team for publishing support through necessary help, appreciation, and quick responses.

Words fail to express our gratitude to our friends, teachers, and well-wishers for their professional advice and assistance in polishing this manuscript. This journey would not have been possible without the support of our family members, mentors, and friends. Last but not least, we would like to thank everyone who helped and motivated us directly or indirectly to work on this book.

Hemant Kumar Soni
Sanjiv Sharma
G. R. Sinha

About the Editors

Hemant Kumar Soni completed his M Tech (IT) at Bundelkhand University, Jhansi, Uttar Pradesh, India, and a Doctoral degree in Computer Science and Engineering from Amity University Madhya Pradesh, Gwalior, India. He has 26 years of teaching experience for UG and PG courses in Computer Science and is presently working as a Professor in the Department of Computer Science and Engineering at Amity University, Madhya Pradesh, India. A few scholar completed their PhD under his guidance and five scholars are pursuing their PhDs under his guidance. He also bears the responsibility of University Amizone Coordinator. His research interests are in Data Mining, Machine Learning, and Big Data. He published many research papers in Web of Science, SCI, and Scopus Indexed Journals. His research articles received high levels of citations in Scopus and Google Scholar. His research papers read across the globe reached 8,000 reads. He is a Reviewer of many referred journals including IEEE Transactions. He received two Best Paper Awards at the International Conference and organized a number of national-level events and conferences. He filed patents also in the machine learning domain. He is a member of the International Association of Engineers, Hong Kong, the Universal Association of Computer and Electronics Engineers (UACEE), The Institute of Research Engineers and Doctors, United States, Life Member of ISTE (Indian Society for Technical Education), India and Member of IAENG Society of Computer Science and Data Mining. Under his able guidance, the students of the CSE Department have done various projects. Dial 100 is one of the projects developed for the MP Government. A MIS for HR is another project which was developed under his guidance. He has conducted various events and conferences also.

Sanjiv Sharma (BE(IT), M Tech(IT), PhD) is an Associate Professor and coordinator in the Department of Information Technology at Madhav Institute of Technology and Science (MITS), Gwalior, India. He has been a lecturer at the Amity School of Engineering and Technology, New Delhi, India. He has 17 years of teaching and research experience. He received his Ph. in Computer Science and Engineering from Banasthali University, Jaipur, India. He has published 105 research publications in various reputed international journals, book chapters and conferences.

He has guided five PhD scholars and 25 M Tech scholars and is currently supervising four PhD scholars in various renowned universities in India. His research interests include Data Mining, Social

Network Analysis, Big Data Analytics, Network Security, and Outcome-based Education (OBE). He has two patents and one research project to his credit. He has also handled numerous administrative responsibilities in these institutions. He engages himself as a reviewer, editor, author, and session chair in various reputed journals and conferences. As an editor, he has published one book *Big Data Analytics in Cognitive Social Media and Literary Text* (Springer Singapore, 2021).

G. R. Sinha (PhD, Fellow IETE, Fellow IEI, SMACM, and SMIEEE) is Provost (Vice Chancellor) at GSFC University Vadodara, India. Prior to this, he worked as a Professor at the International Institute of Information Technology Bangalore (IIITB), Bangalore, India and was Professor at Myanmar Institute of Information Technology (MIIT), Mandalay, Myanmar. He has been a Visiting Professor (Online) at National Chung Hsing University, Taiwan, at the University of Sannio, Benevento, Italy, and a Visiting Professor (Honorary) at Sri Lanka Technological Campus, Colombo, Sri Lanka.

He has published 321 research papers, book chapters, and books at International and National levels and edited 27 books in the fields of Cognitive Science, Biomedical Signal Processing, Biometrics, Optimization Techniques, Sensors, Machine Learning, Outcome-based Education, and Data Deduplication with the internationally reputed publishers Elsevier, IOP, Springer, Taylor & Francis, and IGI. He owns two Australian patents and one German patent. He is Associate Editor of five SCI/ Scopus indexed journals and has been Guest Editor in various SCI journals, such as *IET Electronics Letters*, *Journal of Healthcare Engineering*, and *International Journal of Biometrics*.

He has 25 years of teaching and research experience. He has been Dean of Faculty and Executive Council Member of CSVTU and is currently a member of the Senate of MIIT. Prof Sinha has been an ACM Distinguished Speaker in the field of DSP (2017–2021). He has been an Expert Member for Vocational Training Program at Tata Institute of Social Sciences (TISS), Mumbai, India for two years (2017–2019); a Chhattisgarh Representative of IEEE MP Sub-Section Executive Council (2014–2017); and a Distinguished Speaker in the field of Digital Image Processing by Computer Society of India (2015). He served as a Distinguished IEEE Lecturer in the IEEE India Council, Bombay section. He is the recipient of many awards and recognitions. He has delivered more than 72 keynote/invited talks and chaired many technical sessions at international conferences across the world. He is an advisor to the upcoming New Next University, Mandalay, Myanmar. Dr Sinha has supervised nine PhD scholars, 15 M Tech scholars, and 100 UG level students.

Contributors

Renji George Amballoor
Directorate of Higher Education
Government of Goa
Goa, India

K Asha
St. Joseph's University
Bangalore, India

Rajeshwari B S
Department of CSE
B.M.S. College of Engineering
Bangalore, India

Aaryan Barde
LNCT College
Bhopal, India

Snehlata Barde
SAGE University
Indore, India

Maheshwari Biradar
D Y Patil International University
Akurdi, India

S Selva Birunda
Department of Artificial Intelligence and Data Science
Ramco Institute of Technology
Rajapalayam, India

Abderrahim Bouderbane
University Centre of Mila
Mila, Algeria

Supriya Chanda
IIT BHU
Varanasi, India

Harshal Dalvi
Dwarkadas J. Sanghvi College of Engineering
Mumbai, India

Vraj Desai
Dwarkadas J. Sanghvi College of Engineering
Mumbai, India

Pournima Dhume
Goa Business School
Goa University
Taleigao Goa, India

Pushpendra Dwivedi
Faculty of Engineering and Technology
Rama University
Kanpur, India

Ashray Gattani
Dwarkadas J. Sanghvi College of Engineering
Mumbai, India

Pragya Goswami
Amity University Madhya Pradesh
Gwalior, India

D Deva Hema
SRM Institute of Science and Technology
Ramapuram, India

Vijaylaxmi Jain
D Y Patil International University
Akurdi, India

T Rajeeth Jaison
ENMAC Systems Pvt. Ltd.
Chennai, India

Veena Kaimal
MATS University
Raipur, India

Maria Kalfa
University of Western Macedonia
University of Thessaly
Thessaly, Greece

Bishakha Mandal
Amity University Madhya Pradesh
Gwalior, India

Anand Kumar Mishra
Rama University Uttar Pradesh
Kanpur, India

Namratha M
Department of CSE
B.M.S. College of Engineering
Bangalore, India

Shankar B Naik
Directorate of Higher Education
Government of Goa
Goa, India

P Nagaraj
Department of Computer Science and Engineering
School of Computing
Kalasalingam Academy of Research and Education
Krishnankoil, India

Jyothi S Nayak
Department of CSE
B.M.S. College of Engineering
Bangalore, India

Sukomal Pal
IIT BHU
Varanasi, India

Pinky Pawaskar
Goa Business School
Goa University
Taleigao Goa, India

C S Raghuvanshi
Faculty of Engineering and Technology
Rama University
Kanpur, India

Kaustubh Sakhare
D Y Patil International University
Akurdi, India

Srikrithi Santhanam
SRM Institute of Science and Technology
Ramapuram, India

Hari Om Sharan
Faculty of Engineering and Technology
Rama University
Kanpur, India

Sanjiv Sharma
Department of IT
Madhav Institute of Technology & Science Gwalior
Gwalior, India

Bahubali Shiragapur
D Y Patil International University
Akurdi, India

Alaknanda Shringare
D.D. Kosambi School of Social Sciences and Behavioural Studies
Goa University
Taleigao Goa, India

G R Sinha
Computer Science and Engineering
GSFC University
Vadodara, India

Hemant Kumar Soni
Amity University Madhya Pradesh
Gwalior, India

Nishikant Surwade
CriticalRiver Technologies Pvt. Ltd.
Hyderabad, India

Raisa Khan
St. Joseph's University
Bangalore, India

Introduction

Identifying hate speech in social media is a crucial task. The unchecked spread of hatred has the potential to seriously harm our society and seriously harm marginalized individuals or groups. Social media is an important area for the spread of hate speech online. This contributes significantly to the difficulty of automatic detection, as social media posts include paralinguistic clues. Hate speech (HS) is a form of offensive public speech aimed at specific individuals or groups of people based on characteristics such as race, religion, ethnicity, national origin, gender, disability, sexual orientation, or gender identity. This phenomenon manifests itself verbally or physically (e.g., speech, text, and gestures), favoring the emergence of racism and ethnocentrism.

Online debates are often characterized by extreme polarization and heated discussions among users. The presence of hate speech online is becoming increasingly problematic, making it necessary to develop adequate countermeasures. Recently, there have been several analytical attempts that deal with the perception of fake news phenomena and the identification of typical fake news patterns and options.

Social media platforms are specializing in developing computing technology to assist in stopping the unfolding of hate speech on their networks. The concept is that complicated algorithms victimization language process can flag racist or violent speech quicker and more accurately than humans. To combat hate speech, some social media companies mechanically remove posts if they sufficiently resemble posts in their hate speech benchmark database. The growing cases of hate speech against refugees, migrants, or a community are considerably owed to the circulation of fake news related to these groups in the social media space. The rise of nationalist right-wing parties and their derogatory rhetoric of portraying refugees, migrants, or a community as threats has increased the cases of hate speech online, and also led to violence in real life, promoting hate crime. The current blurring of fact and fiction impacts our voting patterns and political views, and there is much evidence to suggest that the spread of fake news through online media platforms is to blame.

This book comprises 16 chapters describing various methods for the detection of fake news and hate speech in social media. The composition of this book starts with Chapter 1 titled "Analysis of Fake News Detection and Prevention of Various Fake News Detection Algorithms and Its Research Challenges", which discusses news sources, datasets for detecting fake news, data pre-processing techniques, natural language processing models, machine learning and deep learning approaches, performance metrics, and research challenges. It also discusses the advantages and disadvantages of machine learning and deep learning algorithms. Chapter 2 titled "Detection and Prevention of Fake News and Hate Speech through Machine Learning and Natural Language Processing " explores the potential of machine learning (ML) and natural language processing (NLP) to detect and prevent fake news and hate speech. It examines the current state of fake news and hate speech focusing on the challenges presented by the rapid pace of technological change and the difficulty in distinguishing real from fake news. Chapter 3 titled "Detection of Fake News and Hate Crimes on Elections Using Machine Learning Approaches" provides the research community with insights and empirical evidence on the intrinsic properties of fake news thus controlling the voting behavior during elections. Chapter 4 titled "Analytics of Text and Social Media for Challenges of Hateful and Offensive Speech Detection" gives a comprehensive overview of the state-of-the-art in text and social media analytics for fake news and hate speech detection. It will be of interest to researchers, practitioners, and policymakers concerned with the spread of harmful content on social media platforms. Chapter 5 titled "The Ripple Effect of Fake News and Hate Speech on Elections and Its Countermeasures Using Machine Learning Methodologies: A Critical Analysis" examines the influence of fake news and hate speech on election outcomes and also identifies various elements that lead to the effectiveness of deceptive information and offensive language, including the use of emotional language, the repetition of false claims, and the targeting of specific groups. Chapter 6 titled " Explainable Models for the Detection of Incidents of Fake News and Hate Speech" analyzes different XAI techniques available viz. LIME, SHAP, and ELI5. The selected set of features is passed to global and local explainable models such as SHAP and LIME to generate probabilities for the features selected and plot the probabilities in a graphical format. Chapter 7 titled "Gender Biases and Politics: The Semiotics of Hate Speech on the Internet" examines gender stereotypes in politics and how they are reflected through mass media discourse and also examines the way inequality is constructed through language and how words can limit and define the permissible limits for each gender. Chapter 8 titled "Social Media Platforms and COVID-19-Related Misinformation in India: Acceptance, Spread, and Implications" examines the association of demographic factors with the acceptance and spread of misinformation and its implications on people and identifies the underlying factors driving the spread of misinformation during the first two phases of COVID-19 in India among people and the extent to which the information is being accepted, believed, and spread. Chapter 9 titled "SIR Model for Understanding the Spread of Fake News and Hate Speech" used the SIR (susceptible–infected–recovered) model to explain the spread of infectious diseases in epidemiology. Chapter 10 titled "Impact on Fake News in Social Media and Current Technology in Detection of Fake News" elaborates on various current technologies which help in identifying whether news in social media is fake or real. Chapter 11 titled "Connotative Meaning of Political Emotive Expressions in Arab Spring Fake News" investigates the use of emotive expressions in political discourse in relation to what is known as Arab Spring movements in different Arabic countries. It investigates the different connotative meanings of these expressions when used by different rival and political parties. Chapter 12 titled "Detecting Fake News and Hate Speech Using Machine Learning: An Overview of Frameworks" provides an overview of cutting-edge approaches to detecting fake news and hate speech using machine learning and natural language processing, such as feature engineering, deep knowledge, and ensemble techniques. Furthermore, it addresses the limitations of using machine learning to detect fake news and hate speech, such as bias and privacy concerns. Chapter 13 titled "Hate Content Identification in Code-mixed

Social Media Data "evaluates the limitations found in the current state-of-the-art techniques, which demonstrate proficiency in handling text data written in a single language and script. Chapter 14 titled "Social Media Skirmish: Dealing With Fake News and Propaganda Using AI and ML" explores the impact of social media contention on societal harmony and how it becomes challenging in maintaining law and order situation in society, especially in crucial times of election and other social gathering situations such as festivals. Chapter 15 titled "Detection and Prevention of Fake News and Hate Speech through Machine Learning and Natural Language Processing" covers numerous techniques that can identify fake news from a variety of angles, including the inaccurate information it contains, how it spreads, the reliability of its source, etc. Chapter 16 titled "Fake News and Hate Speech: Influence on Society and Detection by Machine Learning" studies the effects of continued social media influence on fake news and hate speech in society and existing machine language as a helpful tool to detect and erase fake news and hate speech from social media platforms.

Editors
Hemant Kumar Soni
Sanjiv Sharma
G. R. Sinha

1 Analysis of Fake News Detection and Prevention of Various Fake News Detection Algorithms and their Research Challenges

D Deva Hema, T Rajeeth Jaison, and Srikrithi Santhanam

1.1 INTRODUCTION

Synthetic news or propaganda that disseminates false information through both conventional and unconventional media sources, such as print, television, and social media, is referred to as "fake news". Fake news is nothing new, but with more implications and effects, it has the potential to undermine some of the biggest economies in the world and is rated as one of the most destructive "digital wildfires", through mass manipulation. While raising public awareness of such tragedies is virtually impossible, eradicating the root cause seems feasible (Hema and Jaison 2023; Deva Hema and Kumar 2023).

Facebook and other social media platforms are frequently used to disseminate fake information. These platforms offer a setting where members of the public can express their opinions and beliefs in their unfiltered, original forms. Social media platforms are currently useful instruments for engaging in meaningful discussions and sharing information on themes such as democracy, education, and health. Nonetheless, certain organizations take advantage of these channels, propagating misinformation, manipulating public opinion, or promoting satire or ludicrous content for financial gain. The term "fake news" refers to the propagation of misleading information, which has become more common in the recent decade. This phenomenon had the greatest influence during the 2016 US elections (Allcott and Gentzkow 2017). The extensive dissemination of false information on the internet has resulted in a variety of problems affecting not only politics but also sports, medical care,

DOI: 10.1201/9781003409519-1

and science. One of the areas where fake news has had a negative impact is the financial market, where whispers can have serious effects, causing disruptions in markets and delaying growth. The World Wide Web contains material in a variety of formats, including text documents, video, and audio, making it difficult to identify and categorize news in an unstructured manner. Typically, human skill is necessary to accomplish this. However, computational approaches such as natural language processing (NLP) can be used to identify anomalies that distinguish fraudulent text articles from those that are based on realities.

Numerous studies have been conducted to investigate the identification and categorization of fake news on prominent social media platforms such as Facebook and X (formerly Twitter) (Vosoughi, Roy, and Aral 2018; Agarwalla et al. 2019). To that purpose, fake news has been classified into numerous kinds, and machine learning (ML) models based on this data have been built that can be applied across multiple domains (Rubin et al. 2016; Jwa et al. 2019). Shu et al. 2017 for example, coupled textual features with auxiliary data, such as user social interaction on social media sites, and improved the accuracy of various models. The authors additionally discussed how to spot false information online using social and psychological theories. Furthermore, the authors addressed various deep algorithms for model building as well as techniques for feature extraction that were shared. The models are centered on knowledge, such as an author's diction, and social context, such as position and its spread. In the aforementioned context, determining the veracity of online information is a challenging but crucial current issue that calls for the attention, regulation, and active monitoring of digital content spread by the main actors involved in sustaining how the information is presented and passed on among citizens over the Internet, which includes search engines and social networking platforms.

The organization of the chapter is given as follows: Section 1.2 discusses various news carrier platforms and fake news types. Section 1.3 provides various fake news detection data sets. Section 1.4 discusses various data preprocessing techniques. Section 1.5 provides various types of natural language processing models. Section 1.6 describes performance metrics to evaluate various fake news detection models. Section 1.7 provides challenges of various fake news detection models. Section 1.8 discusses the conclusion of the analysis of fake news detection and prevention of various fake news detection algorithms and its research challenges.

1.2 NEWS CARRIER PLATFORMS AND FAKE NEWS TYPES

1.2.1 News Carrier Platform

Carrier platforms enable end users to obtain news content (Moon 2017). The list of sites that readers like to use is as follows.

(i) **Standalone Website**

Every news-publishing website has a distinct URL. Usually, you can publish or share material on social media using these URLs.

a) **Popular news sites:** Well-known news websites also have a presence on social media and strive to produce trustworthy content, similar to independent websites.
b) **Blogging websites:** Are known for hosting misleading information, placing a significant emphasis on user-generated content, and often lacking supervision.
c) **Media websites:** Content media firms, such as Vox Media, run media websites that focus on varied media-rich content and prioritize the content generated by users and theme-oriented material.

(ii) **Social Media**

The most common method of sharing information on social media sites is through is through Facebook or X. Over 70% of daily users on platforms like Facebook and X use them as a source of news.

a) **Facebook:** Facebook users can post content on their personal walls or create and share Facebook pages. The ability to create paid ads for almost any post on Facebook is concerning as it can potentially spread fake news to a larger audience.
b) **X:** X is another popular social media network that allows users to post and retweet tweets that are limited to a certain number of characters.

(iii) **Emails**

While emails are a convenient way for customers to acquire news, determining the reliability of information obtained via email can be difficult.

(iv) **Podcast Networks**

Perhaps a very small portion of consumers still receive news through podcasts, an audio multimedia format.

(v) **Radio Talk Programs**

These are commonly utilized as a news source, although the accuracy of the recordings can be difficult to verify.

1.2.2 Fake News Types

Below is a summary of the different categories of fake news identified by Conroy, Rubin, and Chen (2015) and Manzoor and Singla (2019).

(i) **Visual-based**

Graphics, such as doctored images, videos, or a mix of both, are used much more frequently in fake news posts (Allcott and Gentzkow 2017).

(ii) **User-based**

This kind of fake news is produced by fictitious accounts and is directed at a particular audience that may represent certain cultural, racial, or political groups.

(iii) **Knowledge-based**

These articles provide what they claim to be scientific explanations for some unresolved problems, leading users to think that they are real. For instance, natural treatments for the body's elevated sugar levels.

(iv) **Pseudojournalists**

Psedojournalists who claim to be accredited journalists and copy their writing styles to write posts.

1.3 DATASET

The lack of a high-quality dataset poses a serious obstacle to the discovery of fake news. There are numerous accessible datasets for the English language. The following are the most important datasets used for various research problems.

1.3.1 KaiDMML Dataset

The information will be presented in the following formats (Agarwal et al. 2020): ID, title, text, rating, and domain ("FakeNewsNet," n.d.). The sections are described as follows: ID denotes the news article's unique identifier, title represents the news article's title, text is the text stated inside the news article, and rating denotes the news article's classification as false, partly false, true, or partly true.

Because of X's privacy rules and news publisher copyrights, the entire dataset cannot be distributed. Also due to X's policy, social interactions and user information are not revealed. News articles can be downloaded from websites that have been released as well as pertinent social media information from X using this code repository.

1.3.2 Challenge Fake News (FNC-1) Data

On 1 December 2016, the public could enter the Fake News Challenge ("Fakenewschallenge," n.d.). The Emergent Dataset, produced by Craig Silverman, served as the source of the information used in this challenge. The most dynamic area of the global economy is the focus of the research and consulting company Emergent Research. Emergent participated in the FNC-1 challenge by utilizing a dataset from a digital journalism project that aimed to debunk rumors. The dataset consists of news article's titles, bodies, and a label that indicates the level of correlation between the article and its headline. The dataset is divided into two parts, each containing 1,684 stories and 49,973 pairs of news posts and headlines categorized into one of four stances: Unrelated, Disagree, Agree, and Discuss.

1.3.3 LIAR Dataset

The LIAR dataset (Wang 2021; "Liar-Fake-News-Dataset," n.d.), consists of 12,800 brief PolitiFact statements manually labeled for truthfulness by Wang (2017) and released. In a study that involved the classification of six levels of truthfulness, several classifiers were compared, and those that took into account more textual and contextual information, such as the topic, speaker, and history, were found to perform better.

1.3.4 CREDBANK

CREDBANK ("CREDBANK," n.d.) is a massive data collection with 37 million tweets about events organized into more than 1,000 sets (events). Between the middle of October 2014 and the close of February 2015, data for the CREDBANK corpus was gathered. This refers to a set of tweets that have been collected and monitored in real-time. The collection includes topics that have been identified as either events or non-events and credibility scores have been assigned to the events. The information is split up into four folders which are detailed as follows:

(i) **X Streaming**

When these were gathered, the file contained more than 169 million live tweets dispersed across several time bins. The data was collected between 10 October 2014 and 26 February 2015. The file includes three fields, timespan_key, tweet_count, and a list of_tweetid_author_created At_tuple, for each line that represents a time bin.

(ii) **Topic File**

There are more than 62,000 subjects in the Topic File (event/non-event). The top three terms obtained when applying topic modeling to the stream of tweets serve as the three terms that best describe each subject, event, topic_terms, and timespan_key.

(iii) **The Credibility Annotation File**

Includes more than 1,300 events, along with the associated credibility ratings and the justifications provided by Turkers for those ratings. Topic_key, topic_terms, cred_ ratings, and reasons are all included.

(iv) **Tweet File**

More than 80 million tweets about various events can be found in the searched Tweet File. Using the X search API, the messages are retrieved. The search word is created by applying the boolean "AND" to each of the topic's three terms. Topic_key, topic_terms, tweet_count, and listOf_tweetid_author_createdAt_tuple are contained in each line of the file.

1.3.5 FA-KES Dataset

News events related to the Syrian conflict are included in the FA-KES dataset (Salem et al. 2019). There are 376 fake news stories in the dataset's 804 total news articles. A labeled dataset is created and it displays fake news about the Syrian war. The dataset is a collection of news stories and pieces with labels of 0 (fake) or 1 (credible). The Syrian Violations Documentation Center's (VDC) data is used to calculate an article's credibility in relation to that data. Utilizing the crowdsourcing platform, we specifically crowdsource the data extraction task (e.g., date, location, number of casualties) for each story.

1.3.6 FEVER

Claims from Wikipedia entries were produced using a sizable dataset (Thorne et al. 2018; "FEVER" n.d.), known as Fact Extraction and Verification (FEVER). It is made up of 185,441 claims that were created by editing sentences that were taken from Wikipedia and then independently confirmed. Claim categories include Supported, Refuted, and NotEnoughInfo.

1.3.7 The ISOT Fake News Dataset

The "ISOT Fake News Dataset" (Nasir, Khan, and Varlamis 2021) includes both real and fake stories that were taken from the Internet. The ISOT Fake News Dataset is a collection of thousands of stories, both false and true, that were taken from a variety of reliable news sources and websites. The dataset includes both genuine and fake news articles. The truthful articles were obtained by crawling Reuters.com for stories; this dataset was gathered from actual sources. The sources of the fabricated news articles were collected from various outlets, including unverified websites that were previously deemed unreliable by Politifact, an American fact-checking group, and Wikipedia.

1.4 DATA PRE-PROCESSING

Data pre-processing (Nasir, Khan, and Varlamis 2021) involves eliminating stemming, stop words, URLs, pictures, and punctuation. NLP processing is then made based on that training file for extracting highlights.

1.4.1 Stop words

Stop words are generic words that frequently exist in texts but do not aid in the machine's comprehension of the material. These words must not be found in our data. Thus, we eliminate these words. Stop words such as "and", "or", "but", "of", "in", "from", "to", "a", "an", and "the" are frequently used as sentence connectors.

1.4.2 Tokenization

The practice of dividing a significant sample of text into individual words is called word tokenization.

1.4.3 Text Normalization

Text normalization is condensing several spellings or tenses of a single word. Text normalization techniques include stemming and lemmatization. Stemming is a method for getting words back to their basic form by removing affixes. It is comparable to pruning a tree by removing branches until you can see the main trunk. For instance, "sleep" is the root of the words "sleeping" and "sleeps". Lemmatization uses the context of the term, although stemming uses the word's stem. Lemmatization is the process of combining the several inflected forms of the same root word into a single unit for analysis. Lemmatization reduces a term to its logical base form, or lemma, while taking context into consideration. Examples of lemmatization:

dancing → dance
sleeps → sleep
good → fine

In stemming, the stem for studies is regarded as studi. However, it counts as study for studying. Study is taken into account for both "studies" and "studying" in lemmatization.

1.4.4 Word Embeddings

In order to feed text input to neural networks for text classification (Agarwal et al. 2020), it must be converted to a numerical format, such as a vector or matrix. Word vectors, which are unique vector representations of words within the text, are often used for this purpose, with each word having its own corresponding vector. Word embeddings are the technical term for these word vectors. The area created by the gathering of these word vectors is referred to as the embedding space. For instance, the semantics of the words "mango" and "zebra" are highly different, hence any acceptable embedding should have their corresponding vectors relatively far apart. However, "bed" and "sleep are related terms; they ought to be present in the embedding space nearby. Following is a list of the various word vector representations.

(i) **Bag of Words**

Sentences are represented as many sets of words in a Bag of Words (BoW) model. The BoW model overlooks the context in which the word appeared since it ignores the order in which the words were used. With this text vectorization method, we carry out two steps. They are tokenization and vector creation. After tokenization, each sentence is broken down into individual words or other smaller units. The unique terms in the entire corpus are then extracted. These extracted tokens are utilized to create the bag of words representation of the corpus. There are two types of vector creation. (i) Count vectorizer: Count vectorization is a simple yet effective technique for converting text into numerical data. It involves constructing a document term matrix, which is essentially a table that indicates whether a particular word exists within a document. The count vectorizer builds this matrix by assigning a frequency value to each cell, representing the number of times a word appears in a particular document. Each column of the matrix corresponds to a unique word in the corpus. (ii) N-gram vectorization: The n-gram method is used to construct a document term matrix, and each cell contains the count. Both count vectorization and this are the same thing. All neighboring word columns of length n are represented by the columns. Count vectorization, where n=1, is a particular instance of n-gram. Like 1-gram and 2-gram for token pair, n-grams, where n is (1,2,3,...n), taken into account of the sequence of n words in the text. It retains word order, unlike BOW. The disadvantages of BOW is that the word order is not maintained by this technique and it prevents the creation of valuable conclusions for later NLP tasks.

(ii) **TF–IDF**

The acronym TF–IDF stands for Term Frequency–Inverse Document Frequency. The BOW method is straightforward and effective, as we explained in the strategies above, but the drawback is that it considers each word identically. It cannot distinguish between common and rare terms as a result. TF–IDF then arrives on the scene to deal with this problem. The TF–IDF weight provides us with a measure of a word's significance for a phrase or text in relation to the corpus as a whole. In order to comprehend TF–IDF, we must first comprehend the two words independently: Term frequency is a metric that shows how frequently a term appears in a document. It is determined by dividing the frequency of an individual word in a text by the total number of words in that document. In other words, it is the inverse of the proportion between the total number of words in a document and the frequency with which a word arises within the document. The Inverse Document Frequency is a metric that assesses a word's significance in a corpus by counting the number of times it appears in all the corpus files. The logarithmic ratio of the total number of documents in the corpus to the number of documents containing a given word is used to calculate it. Similar to the count vectorization method, the TF–IDF method generates a document term matrix where each column denotes a distinct word. The TF–IDF method, in contrast to other term frequency algorithms, gives every cell a weight value that represents the importance of a word for a certain document or text message. While count vectorization only considers the frequency of a word within one document, TF–IDF is a technique that is similar to frequency-based approaches in that it also considers a word's frequency throughout the entire corpus. Fewer occurrences are given more value by TF–IDF, while more frequent occurrences are given a lower priority. Common words such as "the" and "is" are therefore given less weight, whereas uncommon or uncommon terms are given more weight. The number of instances of a word within a specific text (TF) and its distinctiveness across the full corpus of documents (IDF) are both reflected in a word's TF–IDF score.

(iii) **Word2vec**

The year 2013 marked the release of the natural language processing (NLP) technique called Word2vec. Utilizing a large text corpus, Word2vec trains a neural network model to learn relationships between words. Following the training process, the model becomes capable of identifying similar terms or suggesting additional words to complete a sentence.

(iv) **The GloVe (Global Vectors for Word Representation)**

The Stanford NLP team provides embeddings (Pennington, Socher, and Manning 2014). It is a technique for obtaining word vector representations that is unsupervised. GloVe is an unsupervised learning technique that is used to determine the proximity of two words given their spacing in a vector space (Ahmed, Traore, and Saad 2017). The term "word embedding vectors" refers to the vector representations formed using the aforementioned technique. GloVe, on the other hand, employs global word co-occurrence statistics gathered from a corpus as the basis for its training.

(v) **One-hot Encoding**

To represent each unique word in the vocabulary (Conroy, Rubin, and Chen 2015), this method assigns a distinct token with values of 1 and 0 at all other locations in the vector. In a one-hot encoded vector format, the word's position is represented by 1 and all other positions by 0 correspondingly. One problem with one-hot encoding is that the size of the vector depends on how many distinct words are present in the vocabulary. Additionally, one-hot encoding is unable to convey context because it misses the connections between words. The given sentence, "I am teaching NLP in Python", contains words such as "NLP", "Python", and "teaching". A dictionary is a collection of all the individual words used in a sentence, and for this sentence, it would include "I", "am", "teaching", "NLP", "in", and "Python". To represent each word in vector form, a unique token with a value of 1 is set for that word, with all other positions in the vector being 0. For example, the vector representation for "NLP" would be [0,0,0,1,0,0], and for "Python", it would be [0,0,0,0,0,1]. This method is a simple and direct approach to representing a sentence as a vector.

1.5 NATURAL LANGUAGE PROCESSING MODELS

Here, we categorize various approaches such as linguistic-based techniques, machine learning, and deep learning algorithms, describe their major traits, and assess their benefits and drawbacks. Each model is described in detail in this section

1.5.1 Linguistic Feature-Based Approaches

The goal of linguistic-based techniques (Pérez-Rosas et al. 2017) is to use or extract the following important language elements from false information.

(i) **N-grams**

From a story's word list of words in a story, bigrams and unigrams are derived. For information retrieval, these are preferably saved as TF–IDF values. TF–IDF is the abbreviation for a numerical statistic that measures how significant a word is to the text it appears in.

(ii) **Punctuation**

Proper utilization of punctuation marks can assist the algorithm in distinguishing between fake and genuine messages. Eleven different types of punctuation are gathered by the punctuation function, which uses this detection.

(iii) **LIWC Lexicon (Linguistic Inquiry and Word Count)**

Some researchers have suggested using the LIWC lexicon, which involves choosing the right ratios of words, to extract psycholinguistic aspects. With this method, the system is able to analyze a variety of aspects of language, including word count, a component of the speech group (such as verbs and articles), the mood of the text (e.g., pleasant feelings, conceptual processes), and word mood. Similar LIWC categories can be grouped into other feature sets, such as summary categories (such as analytical thinking and sentimental tone), language processes (such as function words and pronouns), and mental procedures (such as successful processes and social processes) [12]. LIWC is a useful tool for doing this.

(iv) **Readability**

This term encompasses elements of content extraction such as character count, complex word count, lengthy word count, quantity of word type and syllables, and paragraph count [12].

1.5.2 Algorithms for Machine Learning

Machine learning (ML) techniques allow software systems to achieve higher accuracy without requiring manual redesign. Data scientists specify the features or characteristics that the model should take into account when making predictions. Once the model is trained on a dataset, it can apply what it has learned to new data. The algorithm separates the learned patterns into new data after the training process is complete (Dua and Du 2016). In order to categorize fake news, this paper uses six algorithms of machine learning.

(i) **Logistic Regression (LR)**

Logistic regression (Smitha and Bharath 2020) is commonly used to classify text based on a large set of features with binary true/false output, due to its ability to naturally split problems into binary or multiple classes. Linear regression is the most basic form of regression analysis, which assumes a linear relationship between the dependent variable and the predictor(s). The goal of regression is to find the best-fit line that represents the correlation between the predictors and the dependent/predictive variables. Logistic regression is easy to train, implement, and analyze, and can handle multiple classes (multinomial regression) with a natural probabilistic perspective on class predictions. However, if there are fewer observations than features logistic regression should not be used to avoid overfitting. The advantage of linear regression is simple and easy. The disadvantage is that more outliers are present. The following algorithm1 depicts steps involved in linear regression:

Algorithm1:

Step1. Reading and comprehending the information.
Step2. Making the data visible.
Step3. Preparing data.
Step4. Dividing the data into test and training sets.
Step5. Constructing a linear model.
Step6. Remaining train data analysis.
Step7. Using the final model and assessment, make predictions.

(ii) **K-nearest Neighbors (KNN)**

K-nearest neighbors (KNN) (Yazdi et al. 2020) is an unsupervised machine learning technique that can estimate outcomes from detailed data without requiring a dependent variable. By providing enough training data, KNN can determine which neighborhood a new data item belongs to. The technique calculates the distance between the new data point and its closest neighbors, and the value of K represents the majority of the votes cast by those neighbors. The advantages are easy implementation and flexibility. There are some drawbacks to using the K-nearest neighbor's algorithm including: (i) It is not well-suited for large datasets because computing distances between each data instance can be computationally expensive. (ii) The algorithm's performance decreases with an increase in the dimensionality of the data since calculating distances for each dimension becomes more challenging. It is also sensitive to erratic and missing data. (iii) Appropriate feature scaling is necessary for the algorithm to work correctly. This includes normalizing and standardizing the data. The following algorithm2 contains the KNN steps:

Algorithm2:

Step1. The dataset should first be read and preprocessed.
Step2. KNN algorithm fitting to the training set.

Step3. After obtaining the sorted array of distances, the next step is to determine the value of K, which represents the number of nearest data points to consider. K can be any integer value.

Step4. For each point in the test data, apply the following steps: (i) To compute the distance between the test data and each row of training data, you can use one of the following distance metrics: Euclidean, Manhattan, or Hamming. Among these, Euclidean distance is the most commonly used method. (ii) Sort the computed distances in ascending order. (iii) Next, select the top K rows from the sorted array as the nearest neighbors of the test data.

Step5. Making test outcome predictions.

Step6. Assess the accuracy of the results by analyzing the confusion matrix.

Step7. Present the results obtained from the test set.

(iii) **Decision Tree**

A crucial tool that functions like a flow chart and is mostly employed for categorization issues is the decision tree (Yazdi et al. 2020). A condition or "test" on an attribute is represented by each internal node in the tree, and the branches lead to various test outcomes. The final output is allocated to a leaf node following all the attributes that have been considered, and the categorization rule is based on the path from the root to the leaf. The effectiveness with which decision trees can handle dependent and categorical variables is one of its main features. They can precisely pinpoint the most crucial elements and show how they relate. Decision trees are also helpful for investigating novel variables and traits that may aid in precisely forecasting the target variable. Tree-based algorithms are frequently employed to obtain high precision in predictive model construction when supervised learning approaches are used. These algorithms, commonly referred to as Classification and Regression Trees (CARTs), are frequently employed to resolve classification or regression issues because they are especially effective at identifying non-linear correlations. The benefits include: (i) Compared to other algorithms, decision trees require less effort for data preparation before analysis. (ii) Normalizing the data is not a mandatory step when using a decision tree algorithm. (iii) Decision trees do not require the data to be scalable in order to build an effective model. (iv) Missing values in the data do not significantly affect the construction of a decision tree. The drawbacks include: (i) The decision tree algorithm can be unstable as even a minor change in the input data may cause a significant modification in the tree structure. (ii) The decision tree method can become computationally intensive when dealing with complex datasets compared to other algorithms. (iii) Training a decision tree model frequently takes more time. (iv) Decision tree training is more expensive because it requires more complexity and time. The decision tree Algorithm3's steps are listed below:

Algorithm3:

Step1.The decision tree–building process starts from the root node, which initially contains the entire dataset.

Step2. An attribute selection measure is applied to determine the best attribute to split the data into subsets.
Step3. The dataset is split into subsets based on the feasible values of the selected attribute.
Step4. A decision tree node is created to represent the best attribute and its corresponding subsets.
Step5. Steps2–4 are repeated recursively on each subset until the nodes cannot be further split, resulting in leaf nodes.

(iv) **Random Forest**

The concept underlying random forest involves the creation of multiple decision tree algorithms, each producing a distinct outcome. Random forest then leverages the anticipated outcomes of several decision trees to make predictions. To ensure the decision trees differ from one another, random forest randomly selects a subset of attributes from each category. Random forest performs optimally when applied to uncorrelated decision trees; correlated trees lead to a result that is similar to that of a single decision tree. The use of feature randomness and bootstrapping helps create uncorrelated decision trees (Rampersad and Althiyabi 2020; Sirikulviriya and Sinthupinyo 2011). The benefits of this model include: (i) Random forest can be used to solve classification and regression issues. (ii) Random forest is effective with both continuous and categorical variables. (iii) Random forest can automatically handle missing data points, making it convenient for real-world datasets. (iv) Random forest is capable of effectively handling non-linear parameters and does not require feature scaling. Longer training periods and significant computational costs are drawbacks. The following Algorithm4 depicts the steps for random forest.

Algorithm4:

Step1. Select a random subset of data as the training set.
Step2. Construct a decision tree using the training set.
Step3. The choice tree will be averaged during voting.
Step4. Combine the results from multiple decision trees to make a prediction by majority voting.
Step5. Use a Support Vector Machine (SVM) for further analysis.

(v) **Support Vector Machine (SVM)**

The SVM algorithm requires organizing every point of data in a collection of n dimensions, with the value of each attribute defined by the number of coordinates supplied (Yazdi et al. 2020). The approach depicts data points in an n-dimensional space using the feature values assigned to every coordinate in an array of n features. A hyperplane is used to split the data into two classes during categorization. Advantages include: (i) Transforms complex non-linearly separable data into linearly separable data. (ii) It works well with datasets with multiple features. (iii) SVMs perform well when the number of features is much larger than the number of data points. (iv) SVMs are memory-efficient as they use only a small fraction of training points (support vectors) in the decision function. Disadvantages include: (i) It is crucial to avoid overfitting by carefully selecting kernel functions and regularization terms when the number of features significantly exceeds the number of data points. (ii) Training SVMs on such datasets can be time-consuming. The following Algorithm5 of SVM depicts the involved steps:

Algorithm5:

Step1. Read the data.
Step2. Separate the dataset into train and test sections.
Step3. Starting the SVM classification model.
Step4.Configuring the SVM classifier model.
Step5. Make a forecast.
Step6. Assessing the performance of the model.

The benefits of SVM include: (i) It is highly accurate. (ii) A non-linear modification function in Kernel SVM translates.

(vi) **Naive Bayes**

Naive Bayes is a widely used machine learning technique that applies Bayes theory under the assumption of predictor independence (Kevric, Jukic, and Subasi 2017). In other words, Naive Bayes assumes that there is no relationship between any two attributes within a category. For example, if a fruit is red, has spirals, and has a circumference of about 3 inches, it will be classified as an apple. Naive Bayes states that each of these attributes provides unique evidence for the fruit being an apple, regardless of whether they depend on each other or other attributes. The advantages are: (i) When the assumption of independent predictors holds true Naive Bayes classifier performs better than other models. (ii) Naive Bayes requires only a small amount of training data to estimate the test data, resulting in a shorter training period. (iii) Naive Bayes is easy to use. The disadvantages include: (i) The presumptive existence of distinct predictors is a key restriction of Naive Bayes. It assumes that all traits are independent of one another, which is uncommon in reality. (ii) If the experimental data contains a categorical variable that did not exist within the source data, Naive Bayes assigns it a probability of zero, proving predictions unfeasible. The following is often referred to as the Zero Frequency. The following Naive Bayes Algorithm6 depicts the steps involved:

Algorithm6:

Step1. Read the dataset and preprocess it.
Step2. Adjusting the training set to fit the Naive Bayes classifier.
Step3. Foreseeing the outcomes of the test set.
Step4. Model assessment.

1.5.3 Deep Learning Models

(i) **Dense Neural Network (DNN)**

Word sequences can be given as input and experiment with the optimal number of layers to achieve our desired outcome. The network typically consists of a layer of input, a layer of output, and several layers that are hidden. By using deep learning, we can incorporate not only the number of words but also word locations and sequences, thereby bridging the gap between different word-based approaches. The structure of a dense neural network architecture with multiple connections is given in Figure 1.1. Although the input units are shown as words, this is not totally correct because neural networks only work with numerical variables. Embedding vectors are used to represent these words. The first hidden layer is strongly coupled to the input from users, which enters the network's hierarchy in one go. A layer is considered "hidden" because its connection to the outside world is still maintained by the input and output layers. The neurons in any particular layer are only coupled to the following layer. The practitioner chooses the model's variable hyperparameters, such as the number of layers and nodes inside each layer.

(ii) **Convolutional Neural Networks (CNNs)**

Word vectors are used in natural language processing (NLP) (Deva Hema and Kumar 2022) for illustrating words in a phrase or news item, and CNN training is accomplished using such word vectors. The training procedure is carried out by choosing a kernel size and a number of filters. CNNs can have several dimensions. A one-dimensional CNN is a popular choice for text classification or NLP. Word vectors are represented as one-dimensional arrays in Conv1D. During training, a

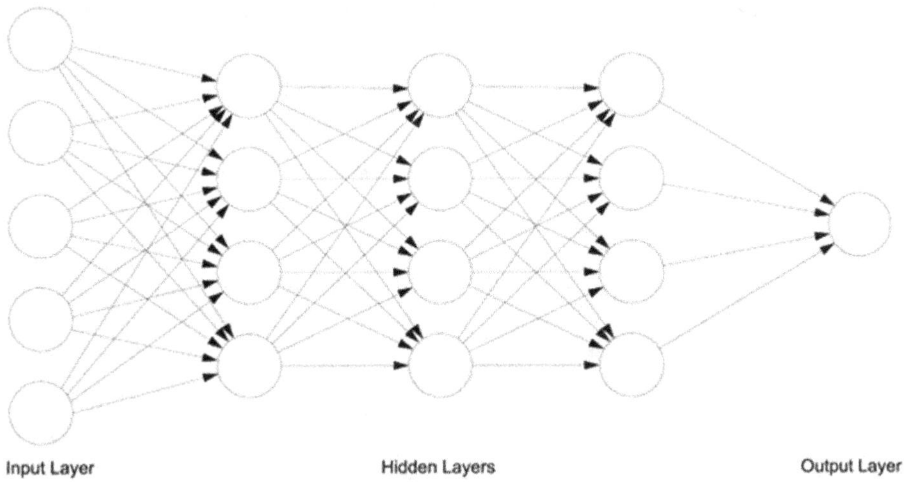

FIGURE 1.1 Dense neural network architecture.

fixed-size window filter is applied to the input data in the CNN, and the output is multiplied by the filter weights at each step to form an output array. The output array represents a feature map or data output filter, allowing a feature to be detected from the incoming data. The number of filters specifies the number of feature maps that will be used, and the size of the filters is defined as the kernel size. Conv1D allows the CNN to capture local features that are immediately learned from the input data. The advantages include: (i) High accuracy rates. (ii) Automated feature extraction. The disadvantages include: (i) High computational demands. (ii) Problems with tiny datasets. (iii) Limited capacity for generalization.

(iii) **Recurrent Neural Networks (RNNs)**

Recurrent neural networks (Ahmad et al. 2020) are used to learn from sequential data by sequentially processing it. This method allows RNNs to remember the sequence of data that came before the current one being processed. This is why it is named recurrent, because the output of each time step becomes the input of the next time step, taking the preceding time step's findings into consideration. This allows for the detection of long-term dependencies in training data. RNNs can be used in natural language processing (NLP) to learn from several news pieces at once by taking their context into account. The architecture of the recurrent neural network consists of input, hidden, and output layers which are shown in Figure 1.2. RNNs are made up of layers that contain memory cells, and several kinds of memory cells can be employed in RNNs. The major drawback of RNN is the exploding gradient problem.

(iv) **The Long Short-Term Memory (LSTM)**

The LSTM model (Deva Hema et al. 2021a) uses a cell state (CS(t-1)) and a carry in addition to the current word vector being processed while processing a sequence. The carry assures that no information is lost during the sequence's processing.

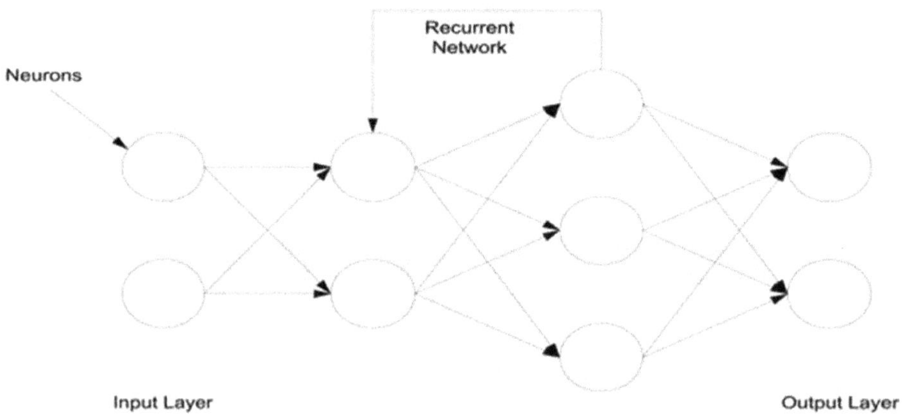

FIGURE 1.2 Recurrent neural network.

Figure 1.3 depicts the structure of an LSTM cell. Weights and three separate learning gates make an LSTM cell, notably the input gate (Inp(t)) for the current input, the output gate (OGt) for forecasting values, and the forget gate (FGt) for discarding irrelevant information. The advantages include: (i) LSTMs are far less prone to the vanishing gradient problem, and they are much better at handling long-term dependencies. (ii) Modeling complex sequential data with LSTMs is quite effective. (iii) They have a number of drawbacks, starting with the fact that they are more complex than conventional RNNs and need more training data to function properly. (iv) They are not suitable for online learning tasks where the input data is not a sequence, such as prediction or classification tasks.

(v) **Hybrid CNN–RNN model**

The proposed approach takes advantage of the strengths of LSTM (Deva Hema and Kumar 2022) [multi]learning long-term dependencies and CNN extracting local features. To extract text-level local characteristics, the input vectors are first fed into a Conv1D CNN layer. The CNN layer's feature maps are then supplied as input to LSTM units/cells. The LSTM layer analyses long-term dependencies and determines the authenticity of a news report using the local data collected by CNN. Several tests, including classification and regression, have shown that this approach is successful in capturing both regional and consecutive features of input data. CNN and LSTM models have been utilized in a range of applications, including identifying emotions and identifying sign language from video feeds. These models can learn scene characteristics using CNN and sequential features using LSTM, making them useful tools for a variety of tasks.

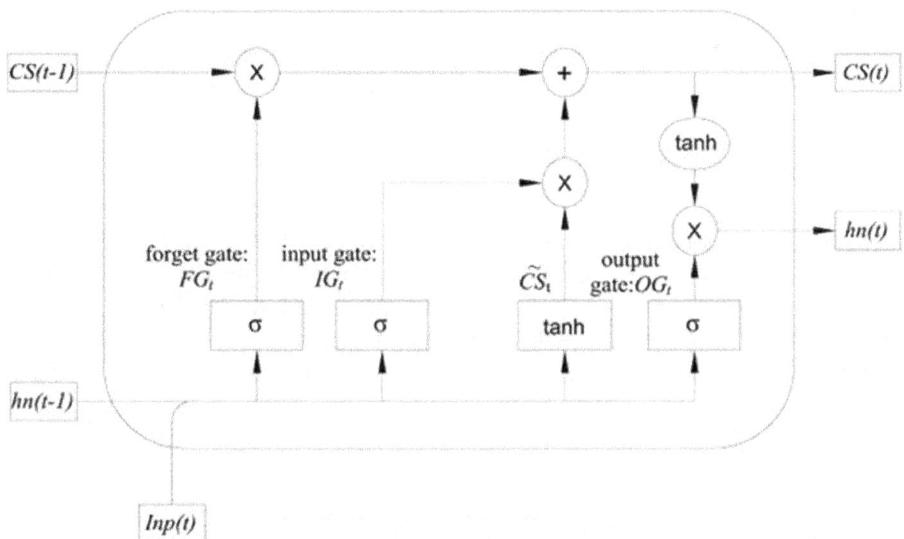

FIGURE 1.3 Architecture of LSTM.

Although deep learning models have numerous advantages, they also have certain practical drawbacks, such as the difficulty in determining the optimum hyperparameters for every dataset, the need for significant training data, and the limited interpretability. These difficulties can have an impact on the performance of deep learning models in unfamiliar and novel tasks, causing them to act like black boxes. Nonetheless, recent advances in bio-inspired approaches (Deva Hema and Kumar 2023) offer options for improving deep learning parameters and form the foundation for fresh deep learning applications. The proposed hybrid model can gain a lot by having its hyper-parameters optimized, and it is a component of future research in this area to look at the many bio-inspired methodologies.

1.6 PERFORMANCE METRICS

A confusion matrix (Deva Hema and Ashok Kumar 2021b) is created to assess how well the suggested algorithm performs predictions. True positive cases are those with a higher likelihood of a collision, and collision warnings are displayed for these cases. True negative cases are those with a lower likelihood of colliding, and warnings are not displayed in these situations.

Accuracy: It shows the proportion of total numbers of accurate predictions to all samples.

Precision: It represents the accurate detection of true positives.

Remember that it displays the proportion of genuine positives to all true positives and false negatives.

F1 Score: This metric offers an individual assessment of combined recall and precision.

The ratio of all misclassified samples to all samples is known as the misclassification rate, additionally referred to as the error rate.

$$Accu = (Tru_p + Tru_n) \,/\, (Tru_p + Tru_n + Fal_p + Fal_n)$$

$$Pr = (Tru_p \,/\, (Tru_p + Fal_p)$$

$$Re = (Tru_p \,/\, (Tru_p + Fal_n)$$

$$F1 - Measure = (2{*}\mathrm{Re}{*}\mathrm{Pr}) \,/\, (\mathrm{Re}{*}\mathrm{Pr})$$

where Accuracy is represented by *Accu*, True Positive by Tru_p, True Negative by Tru_n, False Positive by Fal_p, False Negative by Fal_n, *Pr* represents precision, and *Re* represents recall. True positive denotes accurate foresight into risky situations. True Negative shows that safe case predictions were accurate. Inaccurate predictions of dangerous and safe situations, respectively, are referred to as false positive and false negative cases.

1.7 CHALLENGES

1.7.1 Same Contextual Words and Phrases

Contextual (Davis and Marcus 2015) words and phrases in language, which are simple for humans to understand but make a difficult process, allow the same words and phrases to have different meanings in a sentence. Dealing with synonyms in language can be challenging due to the wide range of words people use to express the same concept. Additionally, different linguistic complexity levels, such as large, huge, and big, may be used by different people, making it difficult to process language and develop algorithms that address all of these issues.

1.7.2 Homonyms

Because homophones are not captured in text form, they provide difficulty for voice-to-text and responding to system questions. Developing models in natural language processing (NLP) capable of handling sardonic and sarcastic comments is a difficult task since people can sometimes understand such sentences in the opposite way they were meant.

1.7.3 Idioms, Expressions, and Phrases Used Informally

It is difficult to design models for widespread use because informal language contains expressions, idioms, and phrases. While having an immense quantity of data to train and often update models might improve their performance, dealing with terms with diverse meanings in various geographical areas can be difficult. These issues arise in a variety of disciplines, including education, health, regulations, and defense, where phrases or sentences might have many meanings. As a result, while NLP models may be effective for a certain region or topic, overcoming these barriers is required for their wider implementation.

1.7.4 Spelling Mistakes

In addition to the above-listed concerns, misspelled or misused words can be problematic. Despite considerable advancements in automatic correction and grammar validation software, deciphering the author's desired meaning while keeping into consideration factors such as sarcasm, idioms, language that is informal, and so on remains a challenging task.

1.7.5 Information Extracted from a Picture

Recent research has also focused on models dealing with Visual Commonsense Reasoning (Davis and Marcus 2015) and NLP, and it appears to be a promising and difficult field to work on. These models attempt to extract information from images and videos using the visual reasoning paradigm, which assumes that humans can infer information from a picture or video beyond what is immediately visible, such as the purposes of items, the intentions of individuals, and their mental states.

1.8 CONCLUSION

This chapter analyzed fake news detection and prevention of various fake news detection algorithms and their research challenges. The easy dissemination of knowledge through sharing has accelerated the growth of information falsification. Social media networks' credibility is in danger and the spread of incorrect information is widespread. As a result, figuring out whether the information is true or fraudulent based on its source, content, and publisher has become a research challenge. The classification of the information has greatly benefited from the application of machine learning and deep learning techniques. To improve the performance of deep learning models, hybrid models have been created. This chapter delves into different platforms used for news delivery, datasets utilized for detecting false news, preparing data for fake news identification, natural language processing models, machine learning and deep learning techniques, performance metrics, and research challenges.

REFERENCES

Agarwal, Aman, Mamta Mittal, Akshat Pathak, and Lalit Mohan Goyal. 2020. "Fake News Detection Using a Blend of Neural Networks: An Application of Deep Learning." *SN Computer Science* 1: 1–9.

Agarwalla, Kushal, Shubham Nandan, Varun Anil Nair, and D. Deva Hema. 2019. "Fake News Detection Using Machine Learning and Natural Language Processing." *International Journal of Recent Technology and Engineering (IJRTE)* 7 (6): 844–47.

Ahmad, Iftikhar, Muhammad Yousaf, Suhail Yousaf, and Muhammad Ovais Ahmad. 2020. "Fake News Detection Using Machine Learning Ensemble Methods." *Complexity* 2020: 1–11.

Ahmed, Hadeer, Issa Traore, and Sherif Saad. 2017. "Detection of Online Fake News Using N-Gram Analysis and Machine Learning Techniques." Proceedings Intelligent, Secure, and Dependable Systems in Distributed and Cloud Environments: First International Conference, ISDDC. Springer, Vancouver, BC, Canada, October 26–28, Vol. 1, 127–38.

Allcott, Hunt, and Matthew Gentzkow. 2017. "Social Media and Fake News in the 2016 Election." *Journal of Economic Perspectives* 31 (2): 211–36. https://doi.org/10.1257/jep.31.2.211.

Conroy, Nadia K., Victoria L. Rubin, and Yimin Chen. 2015. "Automatic Deception Detection: Methods for Finding Fake News." *Proceedings of the Association for Information Science and Technology* 52 (1): 1–4.

"CREDBANK." n.d. https://github.com/compsocial/CREDBANK-data.

Davis, Ernest, and Gary Marcus. 2015. "Commonsense Reasoning and Commonsense Knowledge in Artificial Intelligence." *Communications of the ACM* 58 (9): 92–103.

Deva Hema, D., and Dr. K. Ashok Kumar. 2021a. "Hyperparameter Optimization of LSTM Based Driver's Aggressive Behavior Prediction Model." International Conference on Artificial Intelligence and Smart Systems (ICAIS 2021). IEEE, Coimbatore, 751–56. https://doi.org/10.1109/ICAIS50930.2021.9396047.

Deva Hema, D., and K. Ashok Kumar. 2021b. "Levenberg–Marquardt –LSTM Based Efficient RearEnd Crash Risk Prediction System Optimization." *International Journal of Intelligent Transportation Systems Research* 20: 132–41. https://doi.org/10.1007/s13177-021-00273-2.

Deva Hema, D., and K. Ashok Kumar. 2022. "Novel Algorithm for Multivariate Time Series Crash Risk Prediction Using CNN-ATT-LSTM Model." *Journal of Intelligent and Fuzzy Systems* 43 (4): 4201–13. https://doi.org/10.3233/JIFS-211775.

Deva Hema, D., and K. Ashok Kumar. 2023. "Optimized Deep Neural Network Based Intelligent Decision Support System for Traffic State Prediction." *International Journal of Intelligent Transportation Systems Research* 21 (1): 26–35.

Dua, Sumeet, and Xian Du. 2016. *Data Mining and Machine Learning in Cybersecurity.* Boca Raton, Florida: CRC Press.

"Fakenewschallenge." n.d. http://www.fakenewschallenge.org/.

"FakeNewsNet." n.d. https://github.com/KaiDMML/FakeNewsNet.

"Fever." n.d. https://github.com/awslabs/fever.

Deva Hema, D., and T. Rajeeth Jaison. 2023. "Intelligent Decision-Making Models for Fake News Detection." In *Research Methodology in Multidisciplinary Subjects*, Vol. 99. Redshine. https://doi.org/10.25215/8119070356.

Jwa, Heejung, Dongsuk Oh, Jang Mook Kang Kinam Park, Heuiseok Lim, and H. Lim. 2019. "Exbake: Automatic Fake News Detection Model Based on Bidirectional Encoder Representations from Transformers (Bert)." *Applied Sciences* 9 (19): 4062.

Kevric, Jasmin, Samed Jukic, and Abdulhamit Subasi. 2017. "An Effective Combining Classifier Approach Using Tree Algorithms for Network Intrusion Detection." *Neural Computing and Applications* 28 (Suppl. 1): 1051–58.

"Liar-Fake-News-Dataset." n.d. https://www.kaggle.com/datasets/csmalarkodi/liar-fake-news-dataset/code.

Manzoor, Syed Ishfaq, and Jimmy Singla. 2019. "Fake News Detection Using Machine Learning Approaches: A Systematic Review." 2019 3rd International Conference on Trends in Electronics and Informatics (ICOEI). IEEE, 230–34.

Moon, Angela. 2017. "Two-Thirds of American Adults Get News from Social Media: Survey." Reuters. Recuperado de Https://Uk. Reuters Com/Article/US-USA-Internet-Socialmedia/Two-Thirds-of-American-Adults-Get-News-from-Social-Media-Survey-IdUKKCN1BJ2A8.

Nasir, Jamal Abdul, Osama Subhani Khan, and Iraklis Varlamis. 2021. "Fake News Detection: A Hybrid CNN-RNN Based Deep Learning Approach." *International Journal of Information Management Data Insights* 1 (1): 100007.

Pennington, Jeffrey, Richard Socher, and Christopher D. Manning. 2014. "Glove: Global Vectors for Word Representation." Proceedings of the 2014 Conference on Empirical Methods in Natural Language Processing (EMNLP), 1532–43.

Pérez-Rosas, Verónica, Bennett Kleinberg, Alexandra Lefevre, and Rada Mihalcea. 2017. "Automatic Detection of Fake News." *ArXiv Preprint ArXiv:1708.07104.*

Rampersad, Giselle, and Turki Althiyabi. 2020. "Fake News: Acceptance by Demographics and Culture on Social Media." *Journal of Information Technology and Politics* 17 (1): 1–11. https://doi.org/10.1080/19331681.2019.1686676.

Rubin, Victoria L., Niall Conroy, Yimin Chen, and Sarah Cornwell. 2016. "Fake News or Truth? Using Satirical Cues to Detect Potentially Misleading News." Proceedings of the Second Workshop on Computational Approaches to Deception Detection, 7–17.

Salem, Fatima K., Roaa Al Feel Abu, Shady Elbassuoni, Mohamad Jaber, and May Farah. 2019. "Fa-Kes: A Fake News Dataset around the Syrian War." *Proceedings of the International AAAI Conference on Web and Social Media*, Vol. 13, 573–82.

Shu, Kai, Amy Sliva, Suhang Wang, Jiliang Tang, and Huan Liu. 2017. "Fake News Detection on Social Media: A Data Mining Perspective." *ACM SIGKDD Explorations Newsletter*, 19 (1): 22–36.

Sirikulviriya, Naphaporn, and Sukree Sinthupinyo. 2011. "Integration of Rules from a Random Forest." International Conference on Information and Electronics Engineering, Vol. 6, 194–98.

Smitha, N., and R. Bharath. 2020. "Performance Comparison of Machine Learning Classifiers for Fake News Detection." 2020 Second International Conference on Inventive Research in Computing Applications (ICIRCA). IEEE, 696–700.

Thorne, James, Andreas Vlachos, Christos Christodoulopoulos, and Arpit Mittal. 2018. "Fever: A Large-Scale Dataset for Fact Extraction and Verification." *ArXiv Preprint ArXiv:1803.05355.*

Vosoughi, Soroush, Deb Roy, and Sinan Aral. 2018. "The Spread of True and False News Online." *Science* 359 (6380): 1146–51.

Wang, W. Y. 2017. "Liar, Liar Pants on Fire: A New Benchmark Dataset for Fake News Detection." *ArXiv preprint ArXiv:1705.00648.*

Wang, W. Y. 2021. "A New Benchmark Dataset for Fake News Detection." Proceedings of the 55th Annual Meeting of the Association for Computational Linguistics, Vol. 2 Association for Computational Linguistics.

Yazdi, Kasra Majbouri, Adel Majbouri Yazdi, Saeid Khodayi, Jingyu Hou, Wanlei Zhou, and Saeed Saedy. 2020. "Improving Fake News Detection Using K-Means and Support Vector Machine Approaches." *International Journal of Electronics and Communication Engineering* 14 (2): 38–42.

2 Detection and Prevention of Fake News and Hate Speech through Machine Learning and Natural Language Processing

P Nagaraj and S Selva Birunda

2.1 INTRODUCTION

This chapter presents a detailed overview of how machine learning (ML) and natural language processing (NLP) techniques can be used to effectively detect and prevent the spread of fake news and hate speech. It begins by giving an overview of the various types of fake news and hate speech, how they are spread, and how they can affect society [1]. It then looks at current methods for detecting and preventing such content, and how machine learning and natural language processing can be used to improve them. It examines the need for automated detection and prevention of such content and the potential of ML and NLP to address the issue [2]. Then it discusses some of the challenges associated with using machine learning and natural language processing for this purpose, as well as potential solutions. This chapter also identifies several potential applications for ML and NLP in this domain, such as identifying and classifying user-generated content, detecting and predicting the spread of false information, and detecting hate speech and its sentiment [3]. Finally, it concludes by providing some suggestions for further research into detecting and preventing fake news and hate speech.

2.2 BACKGROUND

2.2.1 What Is Fake News and Hate Speech?

Fake news is false or inaccurate information that is spread deliberately to deceive people. It can be manipulated in various ways, such as through clickbait headlines or editing photos to create a false impression [4]. Fake news is often spread through social media, email, and other online platforms. The different types of fake news are identified and listed below.

DOI: 10.1201/9781003409519-2

1. **Misleading headlines:** Headlines that are written to grab attention and contain inaccurate or exaggerated information.
2. **Clickbait:** Articles or videos that are designed to generate clicks, often by using sensationalist or misleading headlines.
3. **Satire or parody:** Intentionally humorous stories that make fun of people, events, or ideas.
4. **False connection:** When a headline or story draws a false connection between two unrelated events or people.
5. **Misinformation:** When false information is deliberately spread to deceive people.
6. **Fabricated content:** Entirely false stories that are designed to appear real.
7. **Propaganda:** Stories or information that is used to promote a particular political or ideological cause.

Hate speech is communication that disparages a particular person or a group based on features namely ethnic origin, race, disability, religion, sexual orientation, or gender. It is often characterized by strong negative language and can be targeted at individuals or groups [5]. The different types of hate speech are slurs, name-calling, offensive jokes, threats, bullying, inciting violence, denigrating imagery, discriminatory language, stereotyping, and prejudiced comments [6].

2.2.2 History of Fake News and Hate Speech

The history of fake news and hate speech can be traced back to ancient civilizations. Early forms of fake news included false stories spread by mouth, written accounts, and even visual art. In the Middle Ages, propaganda was used to spread false stories and rumors about political enemies [7]. During the Renaissance, the printing press allowed for the spread of false information to a larger audience. In the 18th century, political cartoons were used to spread false stories and lie about public records [8]. In the 19th century, yellow journalism was used widely to spread false news stories and sensationalize events that would attract readers [9]. In the 20th century, radio and television allowed for the spread of false news stories and hate speech on a global scale [10]. The internet has taken this one step further, as it is now easier than ever for individuals to spread false information and hate speech quickly and easily. Social media platforms namely X (formerly Twitter) and Facebook are now considered to be powerful tools for spreading fake news and hate speech.

2.3 REVIEW OF LITERATURE RESEARCH

Jarrahi et al. [11] evaluate the effectiveness of both publisher-level and content-level features, using a dataset of X posts from both verified and unverified publishers. The authors used a dataset of news articles posted on X from September to November 2018 and analyzed whether publisher-level features, such as reputation, website quality, and traffic, could be used to accurately identify fake news articles. The authors found that publisher-level features can contribute to the accuracy of fake news detection on social media, with website quality having the greatest impact. The authors used a machine learning classifiers' range to analyze the data and compare the performance of publisher-level and content-level features. The results show that publisher-level features are more effective at detecting fake news than content-level features and that the best classifier model is a combination of both publisher-level and content-level features. The result of this study indicates that publisher-level features can play an important role in the automated detection of fake news on social media. The authors also found that the combination of publisher-level features with other features, such as content analysis, can improve fake news detection accuracy.

Abd Elaziz et al. [12] proposed a framework based on a multitask learning approach and combines different feature extraction and classification techniques. The Fire Hawk Optimizer (FHO) is an optimization algorithm based on the firefly algorithm, which is employed in the proposed framework to optimize the parameters of the feature extraction and classification techniques. The proposed framework is evaluated on a dataset of Arabic news articles and the results demonstrate its effectiveness in detecting fake news.

Katariya et al. [13] utilize a long short-term memory (LSTM) network to classify news articles as either genuine or fake. The model was trained using a large dataset of news articles from three Indian languages—Hindi, Bengali, and Marathi. The model achieved an accuracy of 88.9%, demonstrating the potential of deep learning for fake news detection. Furthermore, the paper also outlines several potential future research directions for detecting fake news in other languages.

Samantaray et al. [14] proposed network utilizes both forward- and backward-directional information from the text sequence, which helps to identify the temporal relationships between words and capture the overall semantic meaning of the text. The proposed network is evaluated on two sets of real-world datasets and achieves better performance compared to several baseline models. Furthermore, the paper shows that the proposed network can capture the subtle differences between real and fake news, which makes it useful for detecting such news.

Karim et al. [15] used a deep-learning approach to detect hate speech in both text and image formats. The authors combined recurrent neural networks (RNN) and convolutional neural networks (CNN) to create a framework for detecting hate speech in Bengali memes and texts. The authors evaluated their model on a dataset of Bengali memes and texts and found that it achieved an accuracy of 95.71%. The authors concluded that the proposed method is effective for detecting hate speech in Bengali memes and texts.

Beutel et al. [16] discussed the various types of fake news and hate speech and how they can be used to manipulate public opinion. It then looks at the impact of these forms of misinformation, including the disruption of political discourse, the spread of false information, and the targeting of certain individuals and groups. Finally, the paper examines various methods for detecting fake news and hate speech, such as using machine learning algorithms and natural language processing techniques, as well as relying on user-generated content. The paper concludes by highlighting the need for continued research and collaboration to effectively combat these forms of misinformation.

Taskin et al. [17] used a dataset of 10,000 tweets containing fake news, which was manually labeled by experts. The dataset was then chopped into two parts: training and test datasets. The authors used machine learning algorithms such as Naïve Bayes (NB), random forest, and support vector machine (SVM) to classify the tweets into two categories: fake and non-fake news. The results assessed that the random forest and Naïve Bayes algorithms were the most effective in detecting Turkish fake news. Furthermore, the authors also proposed a hybrid approach, which integrates the results of different algorithms to improve the accuracy of the detection. The authors also compared their results with the existing methods and showed that their proposed approach was more effective in detecting Turkish fake news.

Baydogan [18] proposed combining shallow learning techniques namely logistic regression and SVM with deep-learning model CNNs and RNNs. The authors developed and estimated the performance of the models using a dataset containing tweets collected during the pandemic. The results of the experiments demonstrated that the deep-learning models outperform the shallow learning models in terms of precision, accuracy, and recall. The authors concluded that deep-learning models could be effectively used for detecting hate speech in online social networks and that the proposed approach can be used for automated hate speech detection during the pandemic of COVID-19.

Amer et al. [19] proposed a model based on CNN and RNN to detect fake news based on the context of the news article. The model takes in news articles and uses CNNs to extract features from them. Then, the features are fed as input to an RNN which is used to classify the news articles as fake or real. The authors evaluated their model on two datasets, one consisting of news articles related to politics and the other consisting of news articles related to sports. The authors found that their model achieved an overall accuracy of 96.5% and 97.2%, respectively, on the two datasets. The authors also compared their model to other existing models and found that their model outperformed all of them.

Zervopoulos et al. [20] introduced a CNN which was trained over a dataset of tweets related to the protests. The model was evaluated on the test set with an accuracy of 88.8%. The paper also discusses the implications of the model for detecting fake news in other contexts. The authors suggest that the model can be used to automatically flag suspicious tweets, allowing for a quicker response to fake news spread on social media.

Ahmed et al. [21] proposed a model that combines explainable active learning and deep learning to identify and classify hate speech. The model is based on CNN and uses a novel active learning method that leverages both human and machine intelligence. Through experiments, the authors demonstrated that the proposed model outperformed existing models in terms of F1-score and accuracy while also providing explanations for the classification decisions. Additionally, the authors show that their proposed model can be used to actively learn from social media data. Finally, the authors conclude that their proposed model can be used to effectively identify and classify hate speech from social media data.

Sanoussi et al. [22] explore the use of machine learning algorithms to detect hate speech in textual data. The authors demonstrated the use of an SVM classifier to detect hate speech in a corpus of tweets. The authors use a lexicon-based approach to generate features from the tweets, which are then utilized to train the SVM classifier. From the results, it is shown that the SVM classifier can accurately detect hate speech in the corpus with an accuracy of 92.3%. The authors also discuss some of the challenges associated with detecting hate speech in text, such as the need for larger datasets, more sophisticated feature engineering, and the difficulty of annotating hate speech.

Khanday et al. [23] use a dataset of over 10,000 tweets related to the COVID-19 pandemic, which were manually annotated as containing hate speech or not. The authors then apply a machine learning model, based on the LSTM algorithm, and an ensemble learning model, based on a weighted combination of two different machine learning models. The authors evaluate the performance of the models and find that the ensemble approach outperforms the machine learning approach, achieving an accuracy of 96.45%. The paper also discusses the potential applications of the models for detecting hate speech in other contexts.

Hodorog et al. [24] propose a method for event detection using a combination of supervised and unsupervised machine learning algorithms. The proposed system consists of three main parts: event detection, event classification, and event summarization. The event detection process uses a supervised machine learning technique to identify and classify events from social media data. The event classification process then uses unsupervised learning algorithms to identify the type of event and the entities associated with it. Finally, the event summarization process uses natural language processing techniques to generate a summary of the event. The authors tested their proposed system on the X dataset and found that it had an accuracy of 94.7%. They also compared their system to existing event detection systems and found that it outperformed them in terms of accuracy. Overall, the paper demonstrates the potential of natural language processing and machine learning techniques for detecting events in smart cities with the help of social media data. Thus the proposed system is shown to be more accurate than existing event detection systems and could be used to facilitate the development of smart cities.

Kozik et al. [25] proposed a solution based on text analysis, which uses natural language processing (NLP) and machine learning (ML) to detect false claims made in news stories. The paper outlines the technical aspects of the proposed solution and provides an example of how it can be used. The proposed solution uses several algorithms to analyze text, including sentiment analysis, topic modeling, entity recognition, and keyword extraction. The paper also discusses the potential applications of the proposed solution, such as the ability to detect and monitor fake news and disinformation on social media. Finally, the paper concludes by suggesting ways to improve the proposed solution.

Qasim et al. [26] introduce a transfer learning methodology for text classification using a fine-tuned bidirectional encoder representations from transformer (BERT) model. The approach is based on pre-training a BERT model on a text dataset and fine-tuning it for the specific task of text classification. The approach is evaluated on six public datasets and is shown to outperform existing approaches. The authors also analyze the effect of different hyperparameters on the model's performance. The results of the experiments show that a fine-tuned BERT model can achieve state-of-the-art performance in text classification tasks.

Iwendi et al. [27] present a sentiment analysis of COVID-19 fake news using a CNN. The paper aims to develop a model to classify the sentiment of COVID-19 fake news articles. To achieve this, the authors collected and annotated a dataset of articles related to COVID-19 fake news. They then used a CNN to classify the sentiment of the articles. The results declared that the proposed CNN achieved an accuracy of 78%, which is comparable to the performance of other sentiment analysis models. The paper also discusses several possible methods to improve the model's accuracy. Finally, the paper concludes by emphasizing the need for more research into the automatic detection of fake news and its associated sentiment.

Chen et al. [28] developed a deep learning-based model to detect fake news about the COVID-19 pandemic. The model is based on an ensemble of neural networks and is trained on a dataset of COVID-19-related news articles. The dataset was labeled as true or false by a group of experts. The model is then validated against a test set of articles, and results show that it can detect fake news with an accuracy of over 90%. The paper also discusses the challenges associated with the detection of fake news, such as the need for large datasets and the difficulty of labeling articles as true or false. Finally, the paper provides recommendations for future work, such as the development of more sophisticated models and the use of additional sources of information.

Velankar et al. [29] present a model on BERT and tweet-based hate speech detection datasets in the Marathi language. The dataset, called L3Cube-Mahahate, consists of 2,895 annotated tweets in Marathi, the official language of Maharashtra, India. The tweets were annotated with hate speech labels by a team of 20 annotators with different language backgrounds, who were trained on hate speech definition and guidelines. The authors then developed a BERT-based model for the detection of hate speech in the tweets. The model achieved an F1-score of 0.90 for hate speech detection. The authors also conducted a qualitative analysis of the results to better understand the performance of the model. The results assessed that the model was capable of correctly detecting the context of hate speech, as well as the nuances of Marathi language usage.

Truică et al. [30] present a method for detecting fake news using a deep-learning model, a bidirectional long short-term memory (BiLSTM), and a sentence transformer (ST). The authors used a dataset collected from CheckThat!, an online platform for detecting fake news in 2022. The dataset was chopped into training and testing sets. The features used for the model included text length, sentiment score, and readability score. The model was trained on the training set and tested on the testing set. The results showed that the model had an accuracy of 98.39%, precision of 98.45%, recall of 98.26%, and F1-score of 98.36%. The authors also found that the sentence transformer had a slightly better performance than the BiLSTM model, with an accuracy of 98.44%, precision of 98.48%, recall of 98.32%, and F1-score of 98.40%. The authors concluded that the proposed model was capable of detecting fake news with high precision and recall.

Rana et al. [31] proposed a multimodal learning framework, which combines text and user emotion to detect hate speech. To this end, they used an RNN to capture the text information, and they applied a convolutional neural network (CNN) to capture the user's emotional information. The authors also proposed a hybrid system that combines both text and emotional information to improve hate speech detection's accuracy. The results of this work showed that the proposed multimodal learning framework yields better performance than traditional machine learning and deep-learning models, indicating the effectiveness of the proposed approach.

Shahid et al. [32] discuss the various types of fake news, including false and misleading information, fabricated stories, and clickbait. They then provide an overview of existing approaches for detecting and mitigating fake news, including manual and automatic detection methods, and discuss the issues associated with each approach. The authors also discussed the potential of technologies namely, artificial intelligence (AI) and machine learning to detect and mitigate fake news. Finally, the authors provide an overview of potential future research opportunities for detecting and mitigating the dissemination of fake news. These include developing effective and efficient models for detecting and mitigating fake news, exploring the use of natural language processing to detect and mitigate fake news, and exploring the use of social media to detect and mitigate fake news.

Farokhian et al. [33] proposed a novel fake news detection system using parallel bidirectional encoder representations from transformers (BERT). It is a deep neural network (DNN) architecture that has been successful in many natural language processing tasks. The authors apply BERT to the fake news detection problem by training a series of parallel BERT models, each with a different type of input. The results demonstrate that parallel BERT models can outperform existing methods for fake news detection and that the models can be adapted to different datasets. The authors also propose a new approach for using BERT for fake news detection that combines different input types and utilizes a multitask learning approach. They show that their method significantly outperforms existing methods on a variety of datasets.

Vardhan et al. [34] present an approach for detecting social media fake news by using supervised learning methods. It starts by introducing the concept of fake news and its implications for society. The paper then explains the approach of using supervised learning techniques to detect fake news in social media. It discusses the different types of supervised learning techniques and their importance in the detection process. The paper then describes the different types of datasets used for the detection process, such as news articles, social media posts, and text-based datasets. It also discusses the different features used for the detection process, such as sentiment analysis, natural language processing, and the use of lexicons. Finally, the paper presents the results of the detection process, including the accuracy and precision of the model. The paper concludes by discussing the potential for future work on increasing the accuracy and precision of the fake news detection process.

Tashtoush et al. [35] present a deep-learning framework for the detection of COVID-19 fake news on social media platforms. The proposed framework is based on a CNN and an LSTM network. The CNN is used to take out the important features from the text, while the LSTM network is used to capture the temporal dynamics of the data. The authors evaluate their framework on a dataset of real and fake news and demonstrate that it achieves an accuracy of 97.8%, a precision of 95.4%, and a recall of 95.4%. The results demonstrated that the proposed framework is effective in finding COVID-19 fake news on social media platforms.

Mishra et al. [36] provide an overview of the existing fake news detection techniques and discuss their advantages and limitations. They investigate the effect of different machine learning algorithms on the performance of fake news detection techniques and the impact of feature engineering on the accuracy of the detection techniques. Finally, they discuss the challenges and future directions of fake news detection techniques with the use of machine learning. The results show that machine learning techniques can effectively detect fake news from diversified datasets. The authors suggest that further research should focus on developing more sophisticated machine learning algorithms and feature engineering techniques for fake news detection.

Asogwa et al. [37] present an approach to classify hate speech as either offensive or non-offensive using SVM and Naïve Bayes (NB) classifiers. A dataset of over 6,000 tweets was collected and annotated with labels of offensive or non-offensive. The tweets were then pre-processed and used as inputs to the SVM and NB models. The results showed that both models achieved a high accuracy of over 95%, with SVM performing slightly better than NB. The paper concludes that SVM and NB are both effective methods for classifying hate speech, with SVM being the better choice.

Buzea et al. [38] proposed the system is based on a deep-learning model using CNN. The model is trained using a corpus of Romanian news articles labeled as true or fake. The model is evaluated using two metrics: precision and recall. The results showed that the model achieved a precision of 0.86 and a recall of 0.85 on the test set, indicating that it can accurately identify fake news in Romanian online news. Furthermore, the authors also present a web-based application that can be used to detect fake news in online news based on the Romanian language.

Nascimento et al. [39] look at the problem of unintended bias in gender bias prevention on social media and hate speech detection by ensemble learning. To this end, the authors apply a supervised ensemble learning model based on a combination of CNN and SVM. The results showed that the proposed ensemble model can effectively detect hate speech and mitigate gender bias on social media, with an F1-score of 0.88 for hate speech detection and an F1-score of 0.78 for gender bias mitigation. Additionally, the authors also propose a novel technique for mitigating gender bias through an adversarial approach, which significantly improves the performance of the model. Finally, the paper provides an interesting discussion on the implications of using ensemble learning models for detecting and mitigating unintended bias in online social media content.

Segura-Bedmar et al. [40] combine the results of both audiovisual and text-based features to detect fake news. The paper proposes a deep learning-based framework for fake news detection, which is based on the joint representation of audiovisual and text-based features. The proposed framework is evaluated on two publicly available datasets and it demonstrates that the multimodal approach outperforms both the audiovisual and text-based approaches in terms of precision, accuracy, and recall. Moreover, the proposed framework achieves better performance than a baseline model trained on only the audiovisual or text-based features. The paper concludes that the multimodal approach is effective for detecting fake news and can be a promising direction for further research.

2.4 MACHINE LEARNING AND NATURAL LANGUAGE PROCESSING

2.4.1 Overview of Machine Learning and Natural Language Processing in Fake News and Hate Speech

An increase in hate speech and fake news on online platforms has drawn increased attention to the potent capabilities of natural language processing (NLP) and machine learning. A proliferation of this type of content has emerged in recent years as a result of the emergence of social media, raising broad concerns about its detrimental effects on society. By analyzing vast volumes of data and finding patterns that point to the presence of such content, machine learning has been used to spot fake news and hate speech. Using this procedure, machine learning algorithms can learn to recognize harmful or discriminating speech as well as the difference between true and fake news. On the other side, NLP focuses on how to process and comprehend human language. It has been used to analyze the language of comments and online posts to find undesirable content, such as hate speech. The emotion, semantics, and syntax of text can be analyzed using NLP algorithms, allowing them to spot patterns that point to the presence of hate speech. To create models that can automatically detect and report false news and hate speech on internet platforms, machine learning and natural language processing (NLP) can both be applied. These models are developed using sizable textual datasets that have been classified as either true or false news, or as hate speech or not. Once the model has been trained, comparable content can be automatically identified and flagged in real-time. A promising solution to this issue is to use machine learning and NLP to tackle fake news and hate speech. It is crucial to remember that these methods are not perfect and that mistakes can still be made. Therefore, only speech that uses terminology that is hate speech or fake news can be detected by these methods. As a result, it is critical to keep teaching people how to spot and stay away from hate speech and fake news.

2.4.2 Applications of Machine Learning and NLP to Fake News and Hate Speech

1. **Fake news detection:** By examining variables such as the tone, language, and source of the information, machine learning algorithms could be trained to effectively identify fake news items and headlines. The structure and syntax of the material can also be examined using natural language processing tools to see if it is factual or deceptive.

2. **Sentiment analysis:** To detect instances of hate speech or poisonous language, machine learning algorithms can be employed to analyze the sentiment of text. To warn moderators or users to take appropriate action, this can be used to automatically flag content that uses hate speech or other inappropriate language.
3. **Content moderation:** Automated content identification and moderation on social media platforms namely, X and other forums can be accomplished using NLP techniques. This may entail preventing access to or eliminating hate speech or inaccurate material, as well as contributing to the development of a more hospitable and polite online community.
4. **Intelligent chatbots:** These bots can recognize instances of fake news or hate speech and reply accordingly thanks to machine learning algorithms. When it comes to online support platforms or customer service, chatbots can be very helpful in identifying and responding to unfavorable remarks or criticism.
5. **Social media analysis:** To find trends and patterns in hate speech and fake news, social media data can be analyzed using NLP and machine learning. Law enforcement agencies and governments may find this helpful in monitoring and pursuing hate speech and extremist groups.

2.5 DETECTION AND PREVENTION OF FAKE NEWS AND HATE SPEECH

2.5.1 Identification of Fake News and Hate Speech

The following are some indicators of fake news and hate speech.

2.5.1.1 Source

Unreliable sources, such as blogs, social media posts, or clickbait headlines, are frequently used to create fake news. Always verify the news's source before accepting it.

2.5.1.2 Content

False information frequently includes spectacular headlines, out-of-context photos, and misleading writing. A lack of supporting data means it indicates that the content may not have any sources.

2.5.1.3 Tone

Hate speech frequently employs an emotional tone and vocabulary that is meant to arouse rage, terror, or other unfavourable feelings. Verbal abuse, threatening communications, or the desire to discredit a certain group might result from this.

2.5.1.4 Inflammatory Language

Hate speech is characterized by words that are discriminatory or disparaging toward a particular group of people, race, religion, or community.

2.5.1.2 Fact-checking

Never believe or spread hate speech or news without first verifying its accuracy. If it is true, reliable news sources, the government, medical associations, or subject-matter specialists can all be located.

2.5.2 Techniques for Preventing Fake News and Hate Speech

It can be challenging to stop the spread of false information and hate speech; however, the following strategies may be useful in lessening their impact:

1. **Promote critical thinking:** Tell individuals to consider if news reports, comments on social media, and other online material are reliable. Before sharing or transmitting news to others, people should be urged to investigate the origins of that information and make sure that it is coming from a reliable source.
2. **Fact-checking:** The process of confirming the veracity and correctness of information is known as fact-checking. Fact-checkers can be employed by media organizations and social media networks to confirm the veracity of news items and other content uploaded on those platforms. This may aid in limiting the dissemination of misleading information.
3. **Algorithmic monitoring:** Algorithms are a tool that social media firms and search engines can employ to detect and halt the propagation of hate speech and fake news. The language and conduct of users can reveal patterns that point to the dissemination of erroneous or harmful information. These algorithms are also capable of identifying and flagging information that transgresses accepted norms.
4. **Education:** This can assist in preventing the proliferation of these harmful ideas by informing people about the risks associated with fake news and hate speech. Students can learn media literacy and critical thinking techniques in schools and institutions. As a result, people may be able to acquire the abilities necessary for vital information evaluation and decision-making.
5. **Regulations and policies:** Social media companies and governments can create policies and regulations to stop false information's spread and hate speech. Penalties for those who participate in hate speech or propagate false information may be part of these regulations. Social media sites have the power to suspend users who engage in abusive behavior or delete content that breaches their community standards.
6. **Collaboration:** Media companies, social media sites, and fact-checking organizations can work together to stop the spread of false information and hate speech. Social media platforms can collaborate with fact-checking organizations to stop the spread of misleading information on their platforms, and media outlets can work with fact-checkers to confirm the veracity of news pieces.

To stop the propagation of hate speech and fake news on social media platforms, machine learning methods can be utilized. Several methods that can be employed are listed below: The relationship between computers and human language is the focus of the machine learning discipline of natural language processing or NLP. To evaluate social media posts and spot language patterns that are frequently utilized in hate speech and fake news, NLP techniques can be applied. This can aid in the detection and removal of such posts on social media networks. User behaviour analysis is Machine Learning algorithms can be used to study social media users' activity and find patterns of conduct that are frequently linked to the dissemination of hate speech and fake news. For instance, algorithms can be used to spot patterns of activity such as uploading a lot of content, submitting content with divisive issues, or posting content that other users are constantly flagging. Deep learning: Deep learning is the machine learning subset that makes use of neural networks to simulate intricate data interactions. Massive volumes of data may be analyzed using deep-learning algorithms, which can also be used to spot patterns that are hard for humans to see. While fake news and hate speech can entail nuanced patterns of language and behavior, this can help identify them. Social media networks can utilize network analysis methods to spot groups of users who are disseminating false information or hate speech. To evaluate the network structure and spot behavioral patterns that are frequently linked to the dissemination of incorrect information and harmful messages, machine learning methods can be applied. Generally speaking, machine learning methods can be effective tools for limiting the spread of false information and hate speech on social media sites. But, it's crucial to make sure that these strategies are applied responsibly and morally and do not violate the right to free speech.

2.5.2.1 Dataset

Due to the sensitive and contentious nature of fake news and hate speech, gathering and classifying datasets can be difficult. Nonetheless, several publicly accessible datasets that have been assembled for research are available. Here are a few instances:

1. **ISOT fake news dataset:** Over 1.2 million English-language items from various sources were compiled into the publicly accessible ISOT fake news dataset between 2016 and 2019. The dataset, which was produced by researchers at the University of Victoria in Victoria, Canada, contains 4,000 news articles both authentic and false news pieces. The ISOT fake news dataset is intended to be used for developing and testing machine learning algorithms that can give the difference between authentic and false news. Each article in the dataset is categorized as either true or fraudulent since it is labeled. Each article's metadata, such as its source, publication date, and title, is also included in the collection.
2. **Fake news detection dataset:** Almost 12,000 items have been classified as either false or authentic in the dataset called "fake news detection", which was developed by researchers at George Washington University. The collection includes articles from a wide range of sources, including social media, mainstream media, and propaganda websites.

3. **Fake news challenge dataset:** This challenge aims to create machine learning techniques for detecting fake news. Participants were asked to categorize a dataset of more than 50,000 articles as true or fraudulent after it was delivered by the organizers. The collection comprises content from a range of websites, including satire websites, traditional news agencies, and social media.
4. **Offensive language and hate speech dataset:** This dataset, which was produced by researchers at the University of Rochester, Rochester, New York, has over 24,000 tweets that have been classified as hate speech or not. The collection contains tweets that target particular demographics depending on their ethnicity, religion, and gender preference.
5. **Chat pages on Wikipedia toxicity dataset:** This dataset, which was produced by Google researchers, contains more than 150,000 comments from pages on Wikipedia. Based on their substance, which includes insults directed at specific individuals, threats, and slurs, the comments are categorized as hazardous or not harmful.
6. **X sentiment analysis dataset:** More than 1.6 million tweets that have been classified as good, negative, or neutral make up the University of Michigan (Ann Arbor, Michigan) researchers' "X sentiment analysis dataset". Politics, entertainment, and sports are just a few of the themes covered in the dataset. It is vital to keep in mind that these datasets could contain restrictions and biases, thus it is critical to carefully assess how well machine learning algorithms trained on these datasets perform.

Due to the potential limitations and biases of these datasets, it is critical to carefully assess the effectiveness of machine learning models developed using them.

2.5.2.2 NLP Techniques for Fake News and Hate Speech

NLP techniques can be useful in identifying hate speech and fake news. Several methods are frequently used:

1. **Sentiment analysis:** It is a technique that examines a text's sentiment to identify whether it is neutral, positive, or negative. Since that hate speech frequently has a negative tone, this can help spot it.
2. **Named entity recognition:** In this technique, named entities—such as individuals, companies, and places—that are mentioned in a text are recognized and assigned to one of several categories. It can assist in determining whether the source cited in the news is trustworthy or not, which can help spot fake news.
3. **Text classification:** This includes grouping text according to its content into predetermined groups. Hate speech can be recognized using this tool by classifying the text as harmful or not.
4. **Topic modeling:** Topic modeling can benefit from the use of NLP tools. Finding the subjects covered in a text includes this technique. By comparing the themes covered in the news story with credible sources, it might help spot false news.

5. **Language models:** This method uses extensive linguistic data to train machine learning models to produce writing that resembles that authored by humans. These models may be employed to spot language usage patterns that are frequently found in writings of this nature, such as fake news and hate speech.

2.5.2.3 Word Embeddings to Detect Fake News and Hate Speech

Word embeddings are a popular method in NLP for representing words in the text as vectors represented in a high-dimensional space [31]. By capturing the semantic and syntactic connections between words, these vectors aid NLP models in comprehending and processing natural language. By training NLP models on labeled datasets of fake news and hate speech, word embeddings can be used to detect hate speech and fake news. The learned word embeddings can then be used by the trained models to spot word and phrase patterns and resemblances in fresh text. For instance, if the algorithm is trained on the hate speech dataset, it may discover that specific phrases, such as racial slurs or pejorative terms, are significantly correlated with hate speech. The algorithm can then detect the presence of these words in new text and use this information to determine whether the material qualifies as hate speech or not. Similar to this, the model may discover that specific words or phrases, such as spectacular headlines or unreliable sources, are significantly associated with fake news if it is trained on a dataset of false news. The model can then determine whether these patterns are present in a new text when it is presented with it and use this knowledge to categorize the text as potentially fake news.

Text is transformed into a numerical representation called a vector that may be input into machine learning models through a process called vectorization [32]. Here are a few typical vectorization techniques for text processing in machine learning:

1. **Bag of Words (BoW):** Using this method, the text is represented as a collection of distinct words (vocabulary) with a count for each word used in a particular document. The frequency of recurrence of each word can be measured even while the text's order and structure are ignored. It produces a high-dimensional, sparse matrix.
2. **Term frequency–inverse document frequency (TF–IDF):** Like Bag of Words, this method also considers the relevance of words based on their frequency throughout all corpus texts [33].
3. **Word2Vec:** For NLP applications including text categorization, question answering, and machine translation, neural network models such as Word2Vec, GloVe, ELMo, and BERT are frequently employed. Word2Vec is used to learn word embeddings, which show words as dense, low-dimensional vectors that capture their semantic links. Several NLP applications, including sentiment analysis, word similarity, and named entity recognition, use Word2Vec, which may be trained on enormous amounts of unlabeled text.
4. **GloVe:** Another neural network approach for learning word embeddings is called GloVe (Global Vectors), and it uses a co-occurrence matrix of words

to capture both local and global word associations. Some studies have indicated that GloVe embeddings perform better than Word2Vec embeddings in some NLP tasks.

Overall, word embeddings can help NLP models better capture the intricate links between words in natural language, which makes them a powerful tool for spotting fake news and hate speech. The overall workflow model is described in Figure 2.1.

2.5.2.4 Machine Learning Algorithms for Fake News and Hate Speech

For identifying fake news and categorizing hate speech, a variety of machine learning techniques can be applied. Here are a few illustrations:

1. **Naïve Bayes:** Based on a collection of features, this probabilistic algorithm determines the likelihood that a given text or news article is

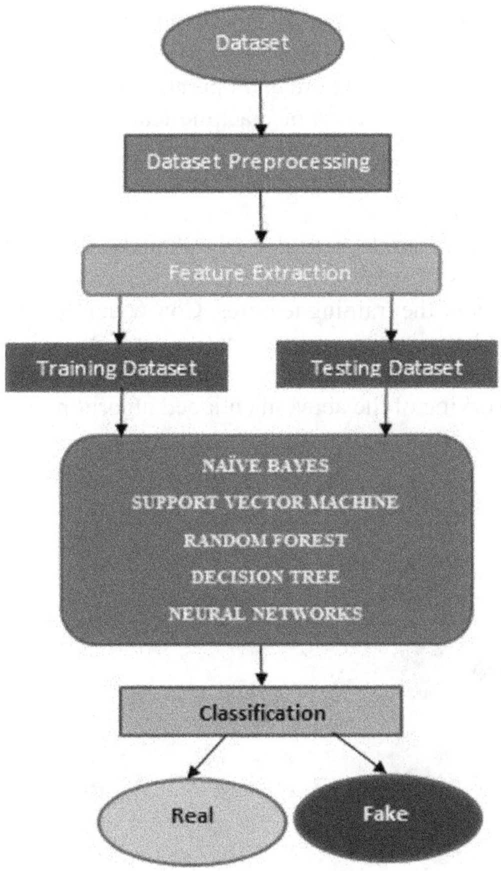

FIGURE 2.1 Workflow of fake news detection models.

fraudulent or contains hate speech. As it is based on the premise that every feature is independent of every other feature, it is an easy and quick algorithm.

2. **Support vector machines (SVM):** It is a technique for supervised learning that may be applied to both regression and classification tasks. It operates by identifying the hyperplane that divides the data into distinct classes the most effectively. SVMs have been employed for the classification of hate speech and the detection of fake news.
3. **Random forest:** The ensemble learning algorithm random forest mixes various decision trees to produce a forecast. It is renowned for its excellent accuracy and capacity to manage complicated datasets, and it can be used for both regression and classification applications.
4. **Decision tree:** A common supervised learning technique used for classification and regression applications is decision trees. To minimize the impurity or entropy of each subset, they operate by recursively splitting the data into subsets based on the values of several attributes. Decision trees can be used to categorize text input as either containing or not containing hate speech in the context of hate speech detection.
5. **Neural networks: The** structure and operation of the human brain served as the inspiration for the class of machine learning algorithms known as neural networks and is illustrated in Figure 2.2. Neural networks require large datasets to train and identify the features by themselves.

It is crucial to remember that the selection of the method depends on the details of the task and the dataset's features. The algorithm's performance is also influenced by the caliber and variety of the training features. Consequently, before using the algorithm for a real-world application, it is crucial to carefully select and engineer the features and then assess the algorithm's performance on a validation set. A detailed explanation of the working of the above-mentioned algorithm in the dataset is given below.

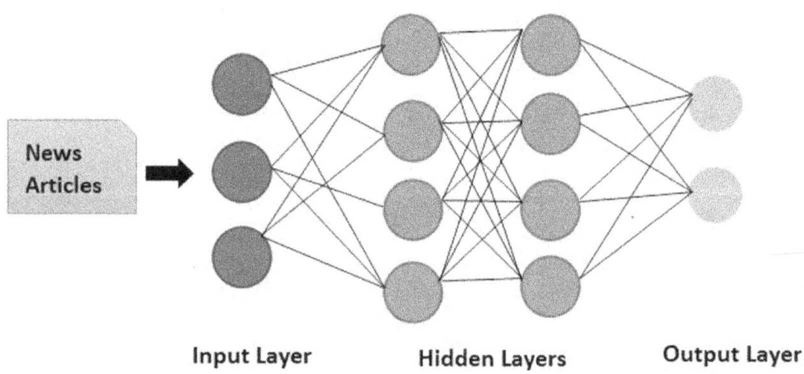

FIGURE 2.2 Layers of dense neural network.

2.5.3 Naïve Bayes

An approach for probabilistic machine learning that can be utilized to identify fake news is called Naïve Bayes. The program determines, given a collection of features, the likelihood that a particular news article is false. An overview of how Naïve Bayes can be used to find out fake news and hate speech is given below.

2.5.3.1 Data Preparation

The first step is to compile a dataset of news articles and categorize them as either authentic or fraudulent. Additionally, the features from every article are drawn out, such as the usage of emotive language, the inclusion of particular keywords, or the author of the piece.

2.5.3.2 Training

Using the labeled dataset, the Naïve Bayes model is trained. Given a set of features, the algorithm will eventually learn to determine the likelihood that an article is fraudulent.

2.5.3.3 Testing

After the model has been trained, you can use it to gauge the propensity of fresh news stories to be fraudulent. When you give the model the characteristics of the new article, the algorithm will determine the likelihood that the news articles and hate speeches are false.

2.5.3.4 Evaluation

As a last step, the model's effectiveness can be assessed by contrasting its predictions with the test dataset's actual labels. To evaluate the model's efficacy, metrics such as accuracy, precision, and recall can be calculated. In the instance of fake news identification, it presumes that the features are independent of one another, which may not be true in the case of fake news detection. Even though Naïve Bayes is effectively used in the detection of fake news and hate speech, it presumes that the features are independent of one another, which is not true in the real-world scenario.

2.5.4 Support Vector Machine

A machine learning approach called SVM is utilized for classification and regression analysis. The SVM model divides data into various classes by a decision boundary known as a hyperplane. Because it can manage high-dimensional data and intricate, non-linear decision limits, SVM is a popular technique for text classification problems. SVM is trained on a dataset of articles or news items with labels indicating whether they are authentic or fake news to detect fake news. Based on characteristics including the use of sensationalist language, clickbait titles, and the absence of reliable sources, the SVM model learns to categorize incoming articles into these two groups. SVM can be used to determine the source of false information.

Text can be classified as containing or not containing hate speech using SVM for hate speech detection. A dataset of text with labels indicating whether or not it contains hate speech can be used to train SVM. Based on characteristics including the usage of pejorative language, the use of slurs, and the use of aggressive or threatening language, the SVM model learns to categorize fresh text into these two categories. SVM can be used to categorize if a text is directed at a certain person, group, or community to determine the target of hate speech.

The following stages are necessary for the SVM algorithm to detect fake news.

2.5.4.1 Dataset Gathering

Creating a corpus of news stories that includes both genuine and fake news is the first stage.

2.5.4.2 Data Pre-processing

The following stage entails cleaning the data to get rid of extraneous information and noise. Stop words must be eliminated, the text must be stemmed or lemmatized, and the text must be transformed into a vector representation.

2.5.4.3 Feature Selection

From this stage, we choose the pertinent features or qualities from the dataset that are most helpful in identifying false news from legitimate news. Several methods, including information gain, the Chi-squared test, and mutual information, can be used to do this.

2.5.4.4 Evaluation

The SVM model is trained by optimizing the hyperplane parameters using the training set. The testing set is used to assess the model's performance by calculating its F1 score, accuracy, precision, and recall.

The kernel trick is used to transform the data, and based on these changes, it chooses the optimal output boundary. SVMs differ from other classification algorithms because they choose the decision boundary that optimizes the distance from the closest data points of all the classes.

2.5.5 Random Forest

Random forest classifiers integrate the predictions of multiple trees. By using the random forest technique, numerous decision trees are created. Each decision tree is built based on a subset of features. Each decision tree creates a single class and eventually bootstraps the votes to improve the random forest technique's accuracy. The action plan in a decision tree is represented by a pattern in the shape of a tree. Any node will conclude. The following steps are taken: a) Split the data so that the gain of the data is maximized (gain is the calculation of entropy decrease during splitting). b) The node's state that offers the greatest gain when divided is selected. c) Splitting continues until entropy is greater than 0. The aforementioned procedure is repeated to construct numerous decision trees, and ultimately a class is picked for a sample based on significant votes. Based on a variety of characteristics, including language, writing style, source legitimacy, and substance, the random forest model categorizes news stories as either phony or authentic.

2.5.6 Decision Tree

A decision tree is employed to facilitate decision-making and decision-making visually. It employs both a classification and a regression tree-like model. They are frequently employed for data mining that accompanies machine learning.

2.5.6.1 Data Pre-processing

The initial stage in the pre-processing process is to clean up the data and put it in a manner that decision trees can use. Stop words may be eliminated, words may be stemmed or lemmatized, and text may be transformed into numerical features.

2.5.6.2 Data Splitting

The data gets chopped into two sets, training data, and test data, following preparation. The decision tree model is trained using training data, and then its performance is assessed using test data.

2.5.6.3 Building the Decision Tree Model

The root node, internal nodes, and leaf nodes make up the decision tree model. Each internal node represents a test on a particular characteristic, whereas the root node represents the complete dataset. The final classification is represented by the leaf nodes. The training data are divided recursively into subsets according to the values of various features, and this process is used to train the decision tree model. The impurity measurements used in the splitting criteria include entropy, the Gini index, and classification error. Finding the splits that reduce the impurity of the subgroups is the objective.

2.5.6.4 Evaluation of the Decision Tree Model

After training, the performance of the decision tree model is tested using test data. The performance of the model is assessed using metrics such as accuracy, precision, recall, and F1-score. If the performance is unsatisfactory, the model can be improved by modifying the splitting criterion or the hyperparameters.

2.5.7 Neural Networks

The structure and operation of the human brain served as the inspiration for the class of machine learning algorithms known as neural networks. It requires a large dataset to train and identify the features by themselves. Neural network architectures such as CNN and LSTM can perform text classification. CNN places a premium on the spatial relationships between words. RNNs are good for tasks where the order of words counts, including detecting the existence of particular words or phrases that are frequently used in fake news.

CNNs primary functions are:

- **Rectified linear unit, or ReLU:** Refers to a non-linear operation. The response is x = max (0, x). The purpose of ReLU is to provide nonlinearity to our CNN.
- **Pooling:** The input to the layer is reduced in height and width by the pooling layer. It facilitates computation reduction and increases the input invariance of feature detectors.
- **Padding:** It enables the use of a CONV layer without necessarily reducing the volumes' height and width. This is crucial for creating deeper networks since, in the absence of it, the height/width would decrease as you added more layers.

Conventional neural networks appear to have a significant flaw in that they cannot remember or keep track of everything that occurs before they are put into action, which prevents the desired influence of words from the previous phrase from having any impact on the final words. As an illustration, think about classifying the kind of event that is happening in each scene in a movie. It is unclear how a traditional neural network may use its knowledge of previous movie events to inform choices for potential future happenings. This issue is addressed by LSTM. They are networks that have loops, which allow information to persist in them. The layers of an RNN are composed of LSTM units. A cell, an input gate, an output gate, and a forget gate make up an LSTM unit. A cell is in charge of "remembering" values over a long period such that the relationship between words at the beginning of a text can affect how those words appear later in the sentence.

The procedure for creating a neural network for detecting bogus news and hate speeches is as follows:

Preparing the data is the initial step in the creation of a neural network. This entails preparing the data for use by the neural network, which entails cleaning it, eliminating any extraneous information, and converting it into a usable format. Stop words may be eliminated, words may be stemmed or lemmatized, and text may be transformed into numerical features to detect fake news. The data is split into two sets, training data, and test data, following preparation. The neural network is trained using training data, and the performance of the trained model is assessed using test data. A neural network is made up of layers of connected neurons or nodes. The input layer, which is the initial layer, is where the pre-processed data are sent. The ultimate prediction—in this case, whether a news story is fake or real—is produced by the output layer. Between the input and output layers, there may be one or more hidden layers. These layers are in charge of learning from the input data and extracting pertinent information. Each neuron in the neural network's hidden layers is subjected to an activation function. It adds nonlinearity to the model and allows the neural network to understand intricate correlations between input and output. The sigmoid function, ReLU (Rectified Linear Unit), and tanh (Hyperbolic Tangent) are popular activation functions. The LSTM model is built from layers of connected memory cells. The output layer generates the final prediction—in this case, whether the text contains hate speech or not—while the input layer gets the pre-processed data. Between the input and output layers, there may be one or more hidden layers. These layers are in charge of learning from the input data and extracting pertinent information. Using an optimization algorithm like stochastic gradient descent (SGD) or Adam, the neural network is trained on the training data. To reduce the error between the projected output and the actual output, the neurons' weights and biases are iteratively changed during training. A loss function, such as binary cross-entropy or mean square error, is used to calculate the error. The neural network is assessed using test data after training to determine how well it performs. The performance of the model is assessed using metrics such as accuracy, precision, and recall. If the performance is unsatisfactory, the model can be improved by modifying the hyperparameters or the neural network's architecture. After being trained and assessed, the neural network can be used to predict the labels of fresh data. This can be accomplished by putting the pre-processed input through the neural network and getting the outcome layer's final prediction.

2.5.8 Proposed Hybrid Model

Our proposed work implemented hybrid LSTM and CNN architecture to detect fake news and hate speeches.

- Building a hybrid CNN–LSTM model: a CNN and an LSTM make up the hybrid model. The proposed hybrid architecture with backpropagation is illustrated in Figure 2.3. The LSTM is used to model long-term dependencies whereas the CNN is utilized to extract local characteristics from the input data. The LSTM receives the CNN's output as input. The CNN and LSTM can be tweaked for best performance by adding more layers. The deep learning Keras library's sequential model is used to implement the suggested hybrid deep learning model. Multiple layers of neurons make up the sequential model:
- The Keras embedding layer is the top layer of the neural network. The pre-trained word embeddings are used in this input layer by supplying the prepared embedding matrix, and the model is trained by supplying the training data.
- The next layer uses 256 filters of size 5 in a CNN layer to extract local features. The activation function for Rectified Linear Units (ReLU) is utilized by default.
- To down-sample the feature vectors, lower the number of parameters, and subsequently the calculations without impacting the network's effectiveness, the enormous feature vectors produced by CNN are then pooled by feeding them into a MaxPooling1D layer with a window size of 2.
- The LSTM layer that follows receives input from the pooled feature maps. With the help of this input, the LSTM is trained to produce while maintaining memory, the long-term dependent features of the input feature maps.

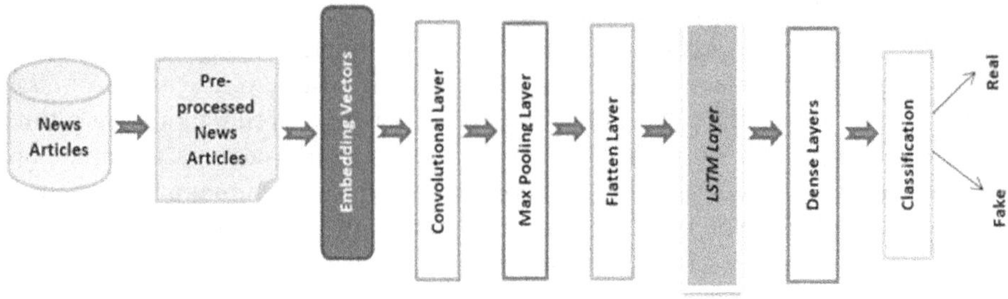

FIGURE 2.3 Proposed hybrid architecture with backpropagation.

The output's dimension is set to 32. In this layer, Keras' standard linear activation function is employed.

- The hybrid model's training: A training set of training data is used to train the hybrid model using an optimization technique such as Adam or stochastic gradient descent (SGD). To produce accurate predictions, the model must be trained to identify patterns and connections between words in a sequence. Typically, binary cross-entropy is employed as the loss function for training, measuring the difference between the actual output and the predicted output. The trained feature vectors are then labeled with the classification label (i.e., fake or not fake) using a dense layer that reduces the output space dimension to 1. The sigmoid activation function is applied in this layer. The loss is calculated using the loss function. The backpropagation technique is applied in the proposed work with the motive of reducing the error. The weights get adjusted as given in (2.1):

$$Weight_{New} = Weight_{old} - Learning\ rate * \frac{\partial Loss}{\partial WeigHt_{old}} \tag{2.1}$$

- Evaluation of the hybrid model: The performance of the hybrid model is tested after training using test data. The performance of the model is assessed using metrics such as accuracy, precision, and recall. If the performance is unsatisfactory, the model can be improved by modifying its architecture or its hyperparameters.
- After training and evaluation, the hybrid model can be used to predict the labels of new text input. This can be accomplished by running the hybrid model on the pre-processed text data and getting the final prediction from the output layer.

2.5.9 Evaluation Metrics

In order to assess the algorithm's classification accuracy in identifying fake news, a number of evaluation measures were used. The most used measure metric is the confusion matrix for spotting fake news and hate speech and has been applied in this part. The measures of the confusion matrix can be defined as follows by the specification of this as a classification task:

$$\text{Precision} = \text{True Positive} / (\text{True Positive} + \text{False Positive}) \tag{2.2}$$

$$\text{Recall} = \text{True Positive} / (\text{True Positive} + \text{False Negative}) \tag{2.3}$$

$$\text{Accuracy} = (\text{True Positive} + \text{True Negative}) / (\text{True Positive} + \text{True Negative} + \text{False Positive} + \text{False Negative}) \tag{2.4}$$

Precision, recall, and accuracy are defined in (2.2), (2.3), and (2.4). True positive is the number of correctly categorized records.

True Negative is the number of categorized documents that were correctly rejected.

False Positive is the quantity of misclassified records.

False Negative is the percentage of categorized records that have been incorrectly rejected.

2.5.10 Comparison Models

Seven classifiers and the proposed model are used to test on both datasets using the same training-test split to compare the performance of the proposed model to other supervised classification techniques. All of the comparison models were created using the scikit-learn Python library implementations in their default settings.

2.5.11 Result and Discussion

The percentage of sentiment score for all the news articles is distributed as shown in Figure 2.4.

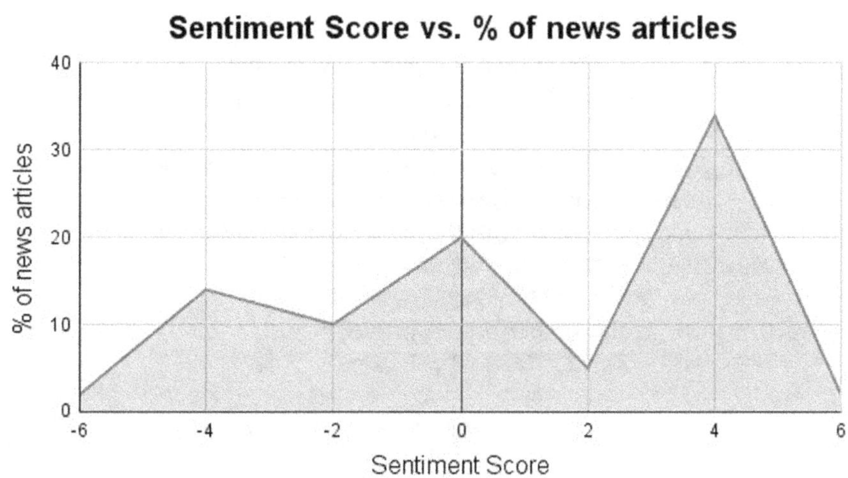

FIGURE 2.4 Calculation of sentiment score for the news articles.

The proposed methodology applied to the ISOT dataset, fake news detection dataset, offensive language and hate speech dataset, and their performance is assessed. The result of the proposed methodology is discussed in Figures 2.5, 2.6, and 2.7.

2.5.12 Result on the ISOT Dataset

The results of all the models and proposed models on the ISOT dataset are described in Table 2.1. The proposed model outperforms the existing models by obtaining 99.2% accuracy. Machine learning models namely, Naïve Bayes, support vector machine, random forest, and decision tree obtained very low percentages, below 60%. The deep-learning models outperformed machine learning models, however, while hybridizing it achieves better results than individual performance.

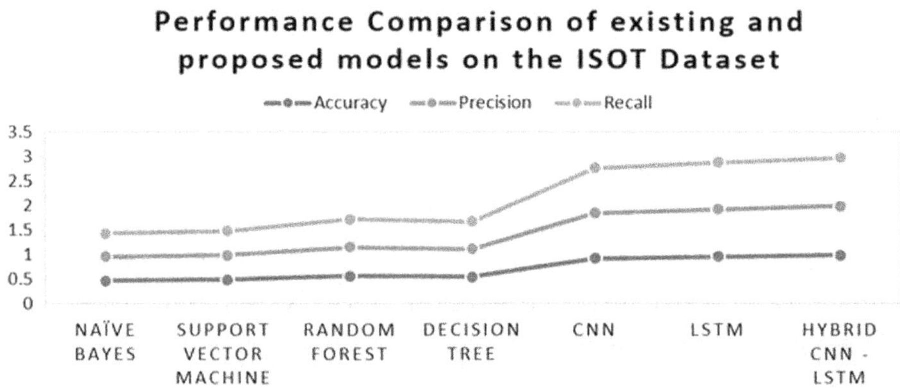

FIGURE 2.5 Performance comparison of existing and proposed models on the ISOT dataset.

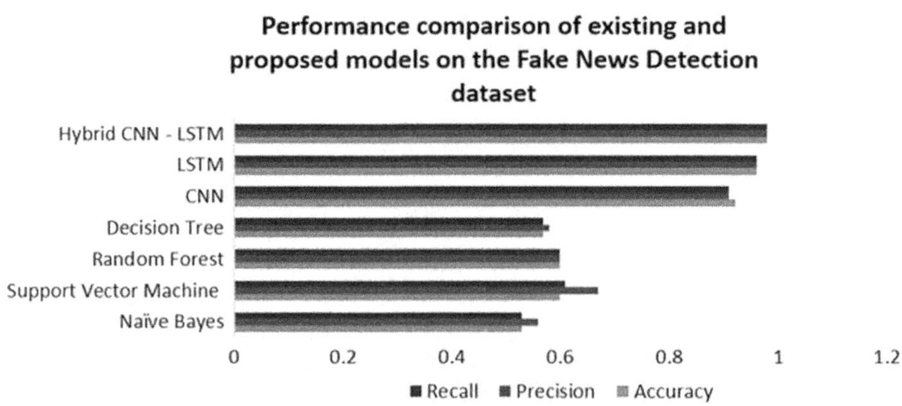

FIGURE 2.6 Performance comparison of existing and proposed models on the fake news detection dataset.

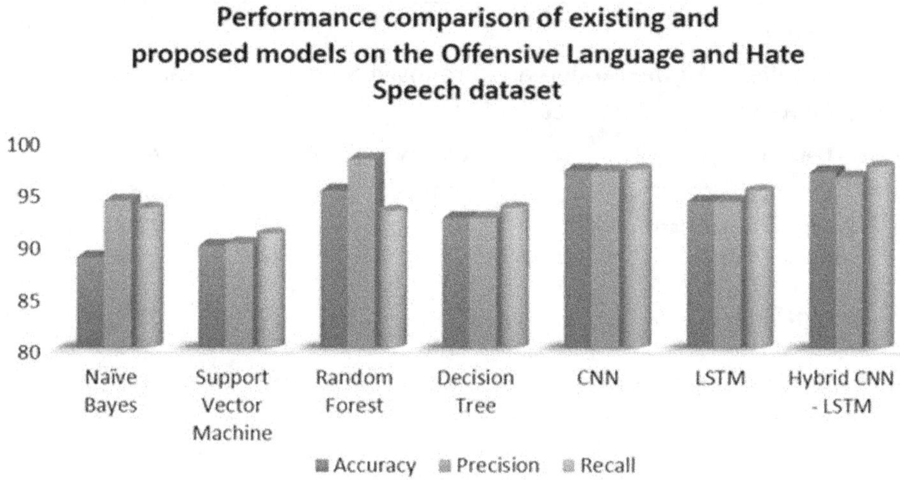

FIGURE 2.7 Performance comparison of existing and proposed models on the offensive language and hate speech dataset.

TABLE 2.1
Results of All the Models and Proposed Models on the ISOT Dataset

Dataset	Accuracy	Precision	Recall
Naïve Bayes	0.47	0.49	0.47
Support Vector Machine	0.49	0.50	0.49
Random Forest	0.57	0.58	0.57
Decision Tree	0.55	0.56	0.56
CNN	0.92	0.92	0.92
LSTM	0.96	0.96	0.96
Hybrid CNN - LSTM	**0.992**	**0.992**	**0.992**

2.5.13 Result of the Fake News Detection Dataset

The results of all the models and proposed models on the fake news detection dataset are described in Table 2.2. The proposed model outperforms the existing models by obtaining 98% accuracy. Machine learning models namely, Naïve Bayes, support vector machine, random forest, and decision tree obtained very low percentages, below 60%. The deep-learning models outperformed machine learning models, however, while hybridizing it achieves better results than individual performance.

2.5.14 Result of the Offensive Language and Hate Speech Dataset

The results of all the models and proposed models on the fake news detection dataset are described in Table 2.3. The proposed model outperforms the existing models by obtaining 96.8% accuracy.

TABLE 2.2
Results of All the Models and Proposed Model on the Fake News Detection Dataset

Dataset	Accuracy	Precision	Recall
Naïve Bayes	0.53	0.56	0.53
Support Vector Machine	0.60	0.67	0.61
Random Forest	0.60	0.60	0.60
Decision Tree	0.57	0.58	0.57
CNN	0.92	0.91	0.91
LSTM	0.96	0.96	0.96
Hybrid CNN - LSTM	**0.98**	**0.98**	**0.98**

TABLE 2.3
Results of All the Models and Proposed Model on the Offensive Language and Hate Speech Dataset

Dataset	Accuracy	Precision	Recall
Naïve Bayes	88.58	93.99	93.26
Support Vector Machine	89.70	89.90	90.79
Random Forest	95	98	93
Decision Tree	92.37	92.38	93.33
CNN	96.92	96.86	96.98
LSTM	94	94	95
Hybrid CNN–LSTM	**96.8**	**96.3**	**97.3**

2.6 CHALLENGES AND LIMITATIONS

2.6.1 Challenges of Machine Learning and Natural Language Processing to Fake News and Hate Speech

There is an urgent need to confront fake news and hate speech since these are serious problems for our society. In recent years, ML and NLP have become viable tools for identifying hate speech and fake news. Fake news and hate speech are two major problems that are always changing. Depending on the political or social climate, different language is utilized in fake news and hate speech. Building an NLP model is difficult since it must adapt to the evolving language patterns. Furthermore, false news stories are frequently artistically created to resemble genuine articles, making it challenging to distinguish between the two if the model does not have reliable training data. Another difficulty is that the training data used to create an NLP model may include biases that could affect the model's performance. The model's performance may suffer, for instance, if the training data is heavily skewed toward a certain demographic or social class. Having a broad and representative dataset is therefore essential. The language employed in fake news and hate speech lacks context, which presents additional difficulty. The context and semantic meaning of the words used are frequently absent from textual datasets. A defective model can therefore result from inaccurate language evaluation. Finally, creating an efficient ML model is difficult due to the enormous amount of data created daily. To quickly and accurately process enormous amounts of data, a scalable model must be created.

2.6.2 Limitations of Detection and Prevention of Fake News and Hate Speech

The ability to identify and stop the spread of false information and hate speech has several limitations. Among the significant ones are: i) Restricted access to reliable sources: In some situations, reliable sources may be hard to find, and not having access to them can limit one's capacity to confirm or deny the veracity of news. ii) Technical restrictions: Although machine learning algorithms and artificial intelligence (AI) models have been developed to detect fake news and hate speech, they have their restrictions. Because these technologies are still developing, it can be challenging to capture the subtleties of language and context. iii) Human bias: Human moderators must use their subjective judgment to identify and stop hate speech and fake news. However, these moderators might have their own biases and views, which could make content analysis and evaluation inaccurate. iv) Issues with free speech: The identification and suppression of false information and hate speech may be seen as a restriction on the right to free expression, which can spark debate and legal concerns. In general, detecting and preventing fake news and hate speech necessitates a multifaceted strategy that includes technology solutions, human moderation, and a profound awareness of cultural variations and challenges relating to freedom of speech.

2.7 CONCLUSION

The usage of machine learning and NLP techniques to identify and prevent fake news and hate speech is a powerful tool that can be used to ensure that online content is accurate and appropriate. The research has shown that these techniques have the potential to identify and classify fake news and hate speech accurately and quickly. This chapter has explored the use of machine learning and NLP to detect and prevent fake news and hate speech. Through an extensive review of the literature and existing research, it has been established that machine learning algorithms have been used to detect fake news and hate speech, and natural language processing has been used to prevent the spread of such news and speech. The paper has discussed the use of supervised as well as unsupervised machine learning algorithms for detecting fake news and hate speech. Supervised algorithms such as Naïve Bayes, support vector machines, random forests, decision trees, neural networks, and some hybrid models have been used to classify text into relevant categories, allowing for more accurate detection. In addition, natural language processing techniques such as sentiment analysis, word embedding, and text summarization have been used to prevent the spread of fake news and hate speech. Through the use of these techniques, users can detect and classify the sentiment of text, identify related topics, and summarize the text. Overall, this chapter has provided an overview of the use of machine learning and natural language processing to detect and prevent fake news and hate speech. Furthermore, the use of these techniques can also provide an effective way to proactively prevent the spread of false information and hate speech. For these techniques to be effective, however, further research is needed to improve the accuracy of the models and to identify the most effective method for dealing with false information and hate speech.

REFERENCES

1. Selva Birunda, S., and R. Kanniga Devi. "A review on word embedding techniques for text classification." *Innovative Data Communication Technologies and Application: Proceedings of ICIDCA* 2020 (2021): 267–281. https://doi.org/10.1007/978-981-15-9651-3_23.
2. Selva Birunda, S., and R. Kanniga Devi. "A novel score-based multi-source fake news detection using gradient boosting algorithm." International Conference on Artificial Intelligence and Smart Systems (ICAIS), pp. 406–414. IEEE, 2021. https://doi.org/10.1109/ICAIS50930.2021.9395896.
3. Selva Birunda, S., and R. Kanniga Devi. "Improving energy efficient aspect of spam classification framework using ensemble machine learning." *Solid State Technology* 63, no. 5 (2020): 9032–9039.
4. Al-Dala'in, Thair, and Justin Hui San Zhao. "Overview of the benefits deep learning can provide against fake news, Cyberbullying and hate speech." International Conference on Interactive Collaborative Robotics, pp. 13–27. Springer Nature Switzerland, 2023.
5. Selva Birunda, S., P. Nagaraj, S. Krishna Narayanan, K. Muthamil Sudar, V. Muneeswaran, and R. Ramana. "Fake image detection in X using flood fill algorithm and deep neural networks." 12th International Conference on Cloud Computing, Data Science & Engineering (Confluence), pp. 285–290. IEEE, 2022.
6. Nagaraj, P., V. Muneeswaran, B. Karthik Goud, G. Vigneshwar Reddy, K. Arjun, and B. Nagaraju. "Development of text characterization using natural language processing techniques." International Conference on Computer Communication and Informatics (ICCCI), pp. 1–5. IEEE, 2023.
7. Nagaraj, P., V. Muneeswaran, M. Ritika, V. Saranya, N. Gayathri, and P.V. Gowthami. "Classification of tweets using natural language processing from X API data." International Conference on Computer Communication and Informatics (ICCCI), pp. 1–7. IEEE, 2023.
8. Nagaraj, P., V. Muneeswaran, B. Rohith, B. Sai Vasanth, G. Veda Varshith Reddy, and A. Koushik Teja. "Automated YouTube video transcription to summarized text using natural language processing." International Conference on Computer Communication and Informatics (ICCCI), pp. 1–6. IEEE, 2023.
9. Nagaraj, P., V. Muneeswaran, K. Kalyan Ram, P. Vamsi, V. Vishnu Vardhan Reddy, and D. Sridhar. "Sentimental analysis of job classification using machine learning algorithms." 8th International Conference on Communication and Electronics Systems (ICCES), pp. 1279–1284. IEEE, 2023.

10. Nagaraj, P., Hamsanipally Nikhil Reddy, Sure Likhil Srinivas, Molligari Jaipal, and Sure Venkata Nagendra. "Machine learning-based mobile application for store-to-door using sentimental analysis." International Conference on Sustainable Computing and Data Communication Systems (ICSCDS), pp. 138–142. IEEE, 2023.
11. Jarrahi, Ali, and Leila Safari. "Evaluating the effectiveness of publishers' features in fake news detection on social media." *Multimedia Tools and Applications* 82, no. 2 (2023): 2913–2939. https://doi.org/10.1007/s11042-022-12668-8.
12. Abd Elaziz, Mohamed, Abdelghani Dahou, Dina Ahmed Orabi, Samah Alshathri, Eman M. Soliman, and Ahmed A. Ewees. "A hybrid multitask learning framework with a fire hawk optimizer for Arabic fake news detection." *Mathematics* 11, no. 2 (2023): 258. https://doi.org/10.3390/math11020258.
13. Katariya, Piyush, Vedika Gupta, Rohan Arora, Adarsh Kumar, Shreya Dhingra, Qin Xin, and Jude Hemanth. "A deep neural network-based approach for fake news detection in regional language." *International Journal of Web Information Systems* 18, no. 5/6 (2022): 286–309. https://doi.org/10.1108/IJWIS-02-2022-0036.
14. Samantaray, Suprakash, and Abhinav Kumar. "Bi-directional long short-term memory network for fake news detection from social media." Intelligent and Cloud Computing: Proceedings of ICICC 2021, pp. 463–470. Springer Nature Singapore, 2022. https://doi.org/10.1007/978-981-16-9873-6_42.
15. Karim, Md. Rezaul, Sumon Kanti Dey, Tanhim Islam, Md Shajalal, and Bharathi Raja Chakravarthi. "Multimodal hate speech detection from Bengali memes and texts." International Conference on Speech and Language Technologies for Low-resource Languages, pp. 293–308. Springer International Publishing, 2022. https://doi.org/10.1007/978-3-031-33231-9_21.
16. Beutel, Ines, Olga Kirschler, and Sabrina Kokott. "How do fake news and hate speech affect political discussion and target persons and how can they be detected?." *Central and Eastern European eDem and eGov Days* 342 (2022): 37–81. https://doi.org/10.24989/ocg.v.342.2.
17. Taskin, Suleyman Gokhan, Ecir Ugur Kucuksille, and Kamil Topal. "Detection of Turkish fake news in X with machine learning algorithms." *Arabian Journal for Science and Engineering* 47, no. 2 (2022): 2359–2379. https://doi.org/10.1007/s13369-021-06223-0.
18. Baydogan, Cem. "Deep-Cov19-Hate: A textual-based novel approach for automatic detection of hate speech in online social networks throughout COVID-19 with shallow and deep learning models." *Tehnički Vjesnik* 29, no. 1 (2022): 149–156. https://doi.org/10.17559/TV-20210708143535.
19. Amer, Eslam, Kyung-Sup Kwak, and Shaker El-Sappagh. "Context-based fake news detection model relying on deep learning models." *Electronics* 11, no. 8 (2022): 1255. https://doi.org/10.3390/electronics11081255.
20. Zervopoulos, Alexandros, Aikaterini Georgia Alvanou, Konstantinos Bezas, Asterios Papamichail, Manolis Maragoudakis, and Katia Kermanidis. "Deep learning for fake news detection on X regarding the 2019 Hong Kong protests." *Neural Computing and Applications* 34, no. 2 (2022): 969–982. https://doi.org/10.1007/s00521-021-06230-0.
21. Ahmed, Usman, and Lin Jerry Chun-Wei. "Deep explainable hate speech active learning on social-media data." *IEEE Transactions on Computational Social Systems* (2022). https://doi.org/10.1109/TCSS.2022.3165136.
22. Sanoussi, Mahamat Saleh Adoum, Chen Xiaohua, George K. Agordzo, Mahamed Lamine Guindo, Abdullah MMA Al Omari, and Boukhari Mahamat Issa. "Detection of hate speech texts using machine learning algorithm." 2022 IEEE 12th Annual Computing and Communication Workshop and Conference (CCWC), pp. 0266–0273. IEEE, 2022. https://doi.org/10.1109/CCWC54503.2022.9720792.

23. Khanday, Akib Mohi Ud Din, Syed Tanzeel Rabani, Qamar Rayees Khan, and Showkat Hassan Malik. "Detecting X hate speech in COVID-19 era using machine learning and ensemble learning techniques." *International Journal of Information Management Data Insights* 2, no. 2 (2022): 100120. https://doi.org/10.1016/j.jjimei.2022.100120.
24. Hodorog, Andrei, Ioan Petri, and Yacine Rezgui. "Machine learning and Natural Language processing of social media data for event detection in smart cities." *Sustainable Cities and Society* 85 (2022): 104026. https://doi.org/10.1016/j.scs.2022.104026.
25. Kozik, Rafał, Sebastian Kula, Michał Choraś, and Michał Woźniak. "Technical solution to counter potential crime: Text analysis to detect fake news and disinformation." *Journal of Computational Science* 60 (2022): 101576. https://doi.org/10.1016/j.jocs.2022.101576.
26. Qasim, Rukhma, Waqas Haider Bangyal, Mohammed A. Alqarni, and Abdulwahab Ali Almazroi. "A fine-tuned BERT-based transfer learning approach for text classification." *Journal of Healthcare Engineering* 2022 (2022). https://doi.org/10.1155/2022/3498123.
27. Iwendi, Celestine, Senthilkumar Mohan, Ebuka Ibeke, Ali Ahmadian, and Tiziana Ciano. "Covid-19 fake news sentiment analysis." *Computers and Electrical Engineering: An International Journal* 101 (2022): 107967. https://doi.org/10.1016/j.compeleceng.2022.107967.
28. Chen, Mu-Yen, Yi-Wei Lai, and Jiunn-Woei Lian. "Using deep learning models to detect fake news about COVID-19." *ACM Transactions on Internet Technology* 23, no. 2 (2023): 1–23. https://doi.org/10.1145/3533431.
29. Velankar, Abhishek, Hrushikesh Patil, Amol Gore, Shubham Salunke, and Raviraj Joshi. "L3cube-mahahate: A tweet-based marathi hate speech detection dataset and bert models." *arXiv Preprint ArXiv:2203.13778* (2022). https://doi.org/10.48550/arXiv.2203.13778.
30. Truică, Ciprian-Octavian, Elena-Simona Apostol, and Adrian Paschke. "Awakened at CheckThat! 2022: Fake news detection using BiLSTM and sentence transformer." *Working Notes of CLEF*, 3180, (2022): 749–757.
31. Rana, Aneri, and Sonali Jha. "Emotion based hate speech detection using multimodal learning." *arXiv Preprint ArXiv:2202.06218* (2022). https://doi.org/10.48550/arXiv.2202.06218.
32. Shahid, Wajiha, Bahman Jamshidi, Saqib Hakak, Haruna Isah, Wazir Zada Khan, Muhammad Khurram Khan, and Kim-Kwang Raymond Choo. "Detecting and mitigating the dissemination of fake news: Challenges and future research opportunities." *IEEE Transactions on Computational Social Systems* (2022). https://doi.org/10.1109/TCSS.2022.3177359.
33. Farokhian, Mahmood, Vahid Rafe, and Hadi Veisi. "Fake news detection using parallel BERT deep neural networks." *arXiv Preprint ArXiv:2204.04793* (2022). https://doi.org/10.48550/arXiv.2204.04793.
34. Vardhan, K., B. Vishnu, Manjula Josephine, and K.V.S.N. Rama Rao. "Fake news detection in social media using supervised learning techniques." 2022 International Conference on Sustainable Computing and Data Communication Systems (ICSCDS), pp. 695–698. IEEE, 2022. https://doi.org/10.1109/ICSCDS53736.2022.9760961.
35. Tashtoush, Yahya, Balqis Alrababah, Omar Darwish, Majdi Maabreh, and Nasser Alsaedi. "A deep learning framework for detection of COVID-19 fake news on social media platforms." *Data* 7, no. 5 (2022): 65. https://doi.org/10.3390/data7050065.
36. Mishra, Shubha, Piyush Shukla, and Ratish Agarwal. "Analyzing machine learning enabled fake news detection techniques for diversified datasets." *Wireless*

Communications and Mobile Computing 2022 (2022): 1–18. https://doi.org/10.1155/2022/1575365.

37. Asogwa, Doris, Chinedu, Chiamaka Ijeoma, Chukwuneke, C.C. Ngene, and Anigbogu, G.N.. "Hate speech classification using SVM and naive BAYES." *arXiv Preprint ArXiv:2204.07057* (2022). https://doi.org/10.48550/arXiv.2204.07057.
38. Buzea, Marius Cristian, Stefan Trausan-Matu, and Traian Rebedea. "Automatic fake news detection for Romanian online news." *Information* 13, no. 3 (2022): 151. https://doi.org/10.3390/info13030151.
39. Nascimento, Francimaria R.S., George D.C. Cavalcanti, and Márjory Da Costa-Abreu. "Unintended bias evaluation: An analysis of hate speech detection and gender bias mitigation on social media using ensemble learning." *Expert Systems with Applications* 201 (2022): 117032. https://doi.org/10.1016/j.eswa.2022.117032.
40. Segura-Bedmar, Isabel, and Santiago Alonso-Bartolome. "Multimodal fake news detection." *Information* 13, no. 6 (2022): 284. https://doi.org/10.3390/info13060284.

3 Detection of Fake News on Elections Using a Machine Learning Approach

K Asha and Raisa Khan

3.1 INTRODUCTION

Fake news has become more prevalent recently, especially in relation to social and political events such as the 2020 US presidential election. First, Channel News 1 (CNN and Fox, USA) reported that the country's information environment has been corrupted for more than 20 years, which has led to the current disinformation epidemic in the United States. A study found that once fake news is planted, it spreads rapidly. For instance, within the first few minutes, millions of dollars were lost due to false information that Elon Musk's Tesla team was asking for donations of any amount between 0.1 and 20 bitcoins in exchange for two times the amount [1]. Therefore, it is essential to spot fake news as soon as possible, before it spreads. According to the Journalism Project of the Pew Research Centre in 2020 53% of people in the United States (US) said they get news from social media "often" or "sometimes", with 59% of X (formerly Twitter) users and 54% of Facebook users doing so regularly [2]. It is interesting to note that 59% of those who get their news from social media indicated they anticipate it to be generally wrong. Researchers have put a lot of emphasis on this sort of fake news since it has the potential to reach millions of people online. Several studies have been conducted to look at the effects of fake news on society and people. Unlike rumors, fake news is always untrue by definition and is therefore considered a form of disinformation [3]. Propaganda, conspiracy theories, hoaxes, biased or one-sided stories, clickbait, and satirical news are other examples of potentially inaccurate information that might be accessed on social media, which contributes to information pollution bots, criminal/terrorist organizations, activist or political groups, governments, covertly paid posters, state-sponsored trolls, journalists, conspiracy theorists, and anyone who stands to gain from spreading false information, are some of the sources of misleading information [4]. These individuals may have ulterior motives to harm or defame, increase website visitors in order to make money, sway public opinion, stir up chaos and confusion, advance ideologies, or even just for their own amusement [5]. Additionally, government agencies, news

 DOI: 10.1201/9781003409519-3

organizations, and internet websites offer instant corroboration of facts to spot misleading information and offer guidelines to read news stories online and be critically conscious and aware of biased decisions [6, 7].

To ensure reliable predictions, the chapter incorporates essential pre-processing steps such as handling missing values, removing stop words, and applying lemmatization. The data is then transformed into numerical representations using term frequency–inverse document frequency (TF–IDF) vectorization, which captures the importance of words within each article. The evaluation of the machine learning algorithms focuses on two different approaches. First, the title and author columns are combined to form a feature set for training and testing the models. Second, only the text column is considered for analysis. The accuracy and performance of each algorithm are assessed using confusion matrices, providing valuable insights into the effectiveness of the approaches. By leveraging the power of machine learning algorithms and analyzing the dataset using different methodologies, this chapter aims to contribute to the development of accurate fake news detection systems. The findings will aid in understanding the role of various algorithms and feature selection in achieving reliable predictions. Furthermore, the project sets the stage for future research to explore advanced techniques such as deep learning algorithms and larger datasets for even more robust fake news detection models.

3.1.1 Contributors of Fake News

In recent years, there has been an increase in the spread of fake news during election campaigns this incorrect information can have a potential impact on voter perceptions. The three fake news types contributors use in real time are predominantly cyborg users, social bots, and trolls. Since the cost factor to make an internet community and correspondence team is meager in cost, the making of a spiteful account is not preventable. A computer algorithm that controls a social media account is called a social program (bot). Bots have the ability to routinely make gists and interact with subscribers. If a program is created with the objective of causing harm and spreading fake news in an internet community, the result will be vindictive articles and the proliferation of fake news. However, it is not only fake humans who disseminate incorrect information but real persons who are active in the area of spreading fake news. With testified results, trolls are living persons who "aim to disrupt online communities" with the objective of provoking social forum subscribers into a sensitive mindset and confused state. To instigate any adverse feelings collected in the minds of social forum subscribers, say anxiety and even annoyance, that create mental unrest or distrust and suspicion is the main goal of trolling [63]. In a dilemma, they may act skeptical of the truth and start trusting the falsehoods instead. The accounts are characteristically listed undercover by living persons, and practice programs to accomplish activities in social forums. The fact that bionic users can switch the "functionalities between human and bot", makes it even more emerging as it gives them an immense chance to proliferate incorrect information [63]. Since it is evident on the reasons as to how and why fake news evolves, therefore, it has augmented the dependency on scholars, policymakers, and election authorities to curtail the proliferation of fake news. The role of fake news and its distal effects on influencing people's views and choices have already been studied. The survey seeks to offer an in-depth overview of the modern research of such studies on the identification of fake news for electoral purposes [67]. This chapter looks at the ethical and legal ramifications of detecting fake news, including concerns about privacy, censorship, and freedom of speech. This chapter will also consider the difficulties and opportunities that come with using false news detection techniques in election campaigns, including the requirement for cooperation among researchers, election officials, and social media platforms.

3.2 VARIOUS APPROACHES FOR FAKE NEWS DETECTION

With the growth of social media platforms, it has become more challenging to distinguish between actual and false news because incorrect information may spread quickly and be magnified by algorithms. The categories for detecting false information by various approaches such as the linguistic-based, fact-checking, and hybrid approaches [68] are discussed here.

3.2.1 Linguistics-based Approach

The strategy is based on the idea that people who write lies deliberately choose their words to avoid being caught. Language is difficult to control, and many times, traces and patterns cannot be completely covered up. Unlike fact-checking, this method is not well regarded. The results from the literature indicate significant differences in the substance of fake and real news. Some of these variations include the employment of more social and positive phrases, the expression of greater certainty, the emphasis on the current and near future, and the presence of more adverbs, verbs, and punctuation in false news content. The authors contend that viewers who are unlikely to go through past titles are the intended audience for fake news. The study makes use of three distinct datasets, two of which are brand-new, and comes to certain findings. Major works in this category present the random forest and linear support vector machines as the top-performing classifiers.

3.2.2 Fact-checking Approach

The goal of a fact-checking strategy is to confirm the accuracy of the facts that are stated in a particular document. Although the strategy has some drawbacks, it can produce positive results. Fact extraction and fact-checking are the two stages of this method [14]. The fact database, referred to as the knowledge base, is gathered and constructed in the first stage, ensuring that problems such as duplication, incompleteness, and conflicts, among others, do not arise. The two ways of approaching are: single-source and open-source. In order to extract knowledge, the single-source approach only uses data from one source. The open-source approach aims to combine information from various bases. Although the open-source approach may be less effective, compared to the single-source approach, it produces more comprehensive knowledge. Since authors always use an existing knowledge base, this step is optional.

3.2.3 Hybrid Approach

A hybrid strategy can be used to construct a false news detection system that makes use of both linguistic analysis and fact-checking. Though a lot of works attempt to employ the hybrid methodology, a lot of them do not concentrate on fake news identification. This method has been used in various works, and the constructed model produced the desired results when simulating the shared interactions among the sources' stance, the language used in the articles, the sources' credibility, and the claim's temporal imprint on the internet. It is crucial to comprehend the criteria the writers utilized to describe the linguistic style for this chapter:

- The degree of confidence with which a proposition is true is captured through assertive and active verbs (such as "claim" and "indicate");
- Hedges are words that lessen the degree of commitment to a notion, such as "may";
- When used in an utterance, implicational terms like "preclude" cause assumption.
- Reporting verbs that emphasize the source of the information (such as "deny");
- Modal verbs (such as "could" and "maybe") convey the assertions' level of certainty, perspective, and confidence;
- A vocabulary of subjectivity and prejudice reflects the writer's mindset and feelings.

These methods are employed, but primarily in other situations where the likelihood of finding fake news is very low. It is also clear that there has not been much research done on methods other than fact-checking to identify fake news. Table 3.1 provides the detailed literature survey on various fake news detection approaches.

3.3 VARIOUS METHODS OF DATA COLLECTION

This section details how and explicitly data has been collected using various methods for analyzing and detecting fake news [69]. The different types of methods include text classification, which mainly features classification based on the main gist of the article. Network analysis focuses on how fake news is proliferated. The automatic detection methods which resulted in the reviews of human–machine hybrid also have their supplements with automatic detection through manual human input, and meta studies.

3.3.1 Text Classifications

Text classification is the most widely used proficient way of automated fake news detection, and the most popular publications propose a solution that uses an identical

TABLE 3.1
Literature Review on Fake News Detection Approaches

Ref.Id	Year	Method Used	Particulars
[8]	2007	Linguistic-based approach	How language style changed for liars and conversational partners. The liars created more words and pronouns patterns in the text, they were trying to spread a lie.
[9]	2017	Linguistic-based approach	Authors examined using n-gram analysis. Linear-based classifiers performed better than non-linear ones in terms of performance.
[10]	2017	Linguistic-based approach	considers news headlines and achieved the best performance with an accuracy of 92%
[11]	2019	Linguistic based	authors focused on n-gram analysis
[12]	2019	Linguistic based	hyper partisanship detection
[13]	2017	Linguistic based	two novel datasets were used through crowdsourcing and we scrapping. Fake news detector identified performance with an accuracy rate of 78%.
[14]	2018	Fact-checking based	Follows two stage method namely fact extraction and fact-checking.
[15]	2018	Fact-checking based	drawbacks as the systems use this strategy to be as unbiased as possible because they frequently are entrepreneurial.
[16]	2017	Fact-checking	Fake news is linked to recently occurring, time-sensitive events
[17]	2017	Fact-checking	techniques are helpful when facts are twisted and misrepresented
[18]	2012	Fact-checking	fake news provides true claims in the wrong context
[19]	2017	Hybrid approach	a model with the main objective of rumour and hoax detection that could retrieve multiple articles.
[20]	2020	Hybrid approach	rumour detection
[21]	2017	Hybrid approach	satire identification
[22]	2017	Hybrid approach	deceit detection
[68]	2017	Linguistic/fact/hybrid approach	review on three approaches

approach. Frequent studies have inferred that machine learning and deep learning can produce capable results for classification which prove instrumental to the problem of automatic fake news detection [23, 24]. According to research, numerous classification methods may successfully recognize fake news with high precision [25–27].

A number of authors have testified and demonstrated the usefulness of classifiers and models to explore a high level of accuracy with the linear SVM [9]. Another reference was found to have the latency to discriminate opinion pieces and propaganda from news articles and true news articles [28]. Successful outcomes are demonstrated in Grey Wolf Optimization [29]. In a single multi-level model, it has established how different machine learning classifiers could improve performance [30, 31]. The representations were able to attain results similar to the human ability to recognise fake news [32, 70]. Promising findings were produced in the category of classification depending on lexical rules, syntax, and semantics. Text classification methods are described as being beneficial for spotting false news after verifying the affiliation between the article's headline and body [33]. A novel method of framework consisting of words or sentences is to identify false news based on headlines, and the relationship to the title [34]. Other authors use combining comparable classifiers with "textual entailment" and "stance detection" characteristics [35, 36].

Spam messages and fake news pieces have similarities when it comes to syntactic similarities, grammatical errors, emotive tones, and attempting to influence the reader's opinion [37]. To emphasize the emotional tone, fake news attempts to provoke strong sentiments in order to accomplish further online proliferation [38, 39]. Convolutional neural networks employ a model to analyze the semantic and syntactic data from articles apart from text analysis [40].

A problem cited to filter fake news which makes it difficult is the lack of annotated datasets in Portuguese [41]. For the same reason, an alternate dataset is available in German [42]. Another need is to develop a large dataset to be used in the creation of an automatic classification model [43]. A technique that is based on "active learning" may effectively learn from a reduced sample size to improve performance in weakly supervised learning contexts [44]. In real time, the usage of actual applications is used to inevitably determine the fake news with behavioral cues regarding how news is shared on public platforms [45]. Another article examined satirical fake news, claiming to be harmful in the current fake news climate in spite of not actually being "fake news" [46].

3.3.2 Network Analysis

Apart from fake news fragments, the other surrounding information can be a crucial component of instinctive fake news identification. This is called a "network" technique, which has some advantages where the text classification approach may have problems and can be a useful tool. In the detection algorithms, particular attention is paid to how fake news spreads in these settings and the involved users play in it.

In the literature, the exertion of identifying fake news with little data is a recurrent subject. The inability of machine learning algorithms to detect fake news early, when at the time of debunking is not available due to the early stages of news transmission, is a shortcoming of approaches that use text analysis to identify fake news. The detection of regional factors and local user variances in this path can assist in quickly and accurately identifying fake news [70]. When news articles are too short, text analysis is also insufficient, however convolutional networks can be used. Knowledge graphs have been shown to be capable of producing respectable results even when only a small quantity of data is utilized to generate them [47, 48].

Knowledge networks were also employed to identify fraud along with assertions found in online structured knowledge networks, false claims that are presented as true can be extracted and evaluated [49]. A network-based method looks at the patterns of news as well as the relationships between these spreaders [50]. Another strategy that places more emphasis on user involvement combines text analysis with a social media approach. A hybrid strategy was utilized because of the drawback that the content must have some "social interaction" in order to yield worthwhile results [51, 52].

Additionally, a model is put forth that considers elements such as the group behavior of users that propagate false information as well as the source and distribution channels [53]. A method has also supported the use of combination techniques, emphasizing the value of integrating remarks with "credibility patterns" [64]. Similarly, a diffusive network model relies on hidden features extracted from a text and brings suggestions at the origin of such news by identifying the news creators and types of news subjects, where a record of credibility can be observed and evaluated [65]. In the effort to stop fake news from spreading on social media, the latter two categories are thought to be more crucial than the news itself.

3.3.3 Human–Machine Hybrid

Some of the gathered literature suggested a mixed human–machine approach. These techniques make use of machine-based instinctive detection models, but they incorporate various human manual inputs to boost performance and accuracy. A hybrid approach will combine the best aspects of both properties [54]. It is thought-provoking to differentiate between satirical news and fake news because the language employed in such pieces is intentionally difficult to separate from true tales [55]. In order to identify fake news by gathering facts, another article offers a machine-learning model which compares content input with articles from "Fact DB," which is a library of factual articles created, and maintained by humans [56]. An extremely ambitious suggestion in the form of a fact-checking infrastructure, where users might process any material on a page using the infrastructure's web-based tools to gather more data [57]. Any organization/company/research center is bound to operate and offer services to the infrastructure. Decentralized web annotation repositories would transmit their annotations to the tools which would then combine the annotations from both humans and machines.

3.3.4 Meta Studies

This category comprises works of literature that examine a variety of approaches and compare them rather than offering one approach or method. A comparison study of various text categorization and language processing machine learning methods was conducted [66]. Machine learning methods were found to be the most successful classifier among those evaluated [58]. A proposed method of tracing a text to its source based on the article's writing style and evaluating the reliability of that source is examined [59]. The strategy emphasizes the significance of evaluating the text's truthfulness rather than merely its style and source [60]. There were various publications that examined the identification of false news itself, including its difficulties, future avenues for research, characterization, and comparison with other ideas like satire or rumors [50, 61–63].

3.4 METHODOLOGY AND STEPS OF PROCEDURE

The classification methodology and steps of procedure are presented in this section. The following strategy is used in the model-building process to identify political fake news: The first phase involves gathering political news datasets, followed by rough noise removal during pre-processing. Next, the NLTK (natural language toolkit) is used to perform tokenization, stemming removal of stop words, etc. The next step would be feature extraction using TF and TF–IDF. The proposed classifier model is then created after performing the dataset splitting and applying above mentioned ML algorithms.

3.4.1 Dataset Used

The dataset utilized for identifying fake news consists of articles from the US political domain. Figure 3.1 consists of articles that have been manually categorized as either fake news (labeled as 1) or real news (labeled as 0). The dataset contains approximately 20,000 rows and consists of 5 columns: id, author, title, text of the article, and the corresponding labels indicating whether the article is fake news or real news. The datasets comprised approximately 10,400 fake articles and the remaining 10,300 articles were identified as real news. Due to the prevalence of spammers targeting political news articles, we made the decision to concentrate solely on the specific category of news articles.

3.4.2 Data Pre-processing

Before utilizing the data for prediction, pre-processing steps are required, including handling missing values, removing stop words, stemming, tokenization, and other necessary tasks.

```
# print the first 10 rows of the dataframe
news_dataset.head(10)
```

	id	title	author	text	label
0	0	House Dem Aide: We Didn't Even See Comey's Let...	Darrell Lucus	House Dem Aide: We Didn't Even See Comey's Let...	1
1	1	FLYNN: Hillary Clinton, Big Woman on Campus - ...	Daniel J. Flynn	Ever get the feeling your life circles the rou...	0
2	2	Why the Truth Might Get You Fired	Consortiumnews.com	Why the Truth Might Get You Fired October 29, ...	1
3	3	15 Civilians Killed In Single US Airstrike Hav...	Jessica Purkiss	Videos 15 Civilians Killed In Single US Airstr...	1
4	4	Iranian woman jailed for fictional unpublished...	Howard Portnoy	Print \nAn Iranian woman has been sentenced to...	1
5	5	Jackie Mason: Hollywood Would Love Trump if He...	Daniel Nussbaum	In these trying times, Jackie Mason is the Voi...	0
6	6	Life: Life Of Luxury: Elton John's 6 Favorite ...	NaN	Ever wonder how Britain's most iconic pop pian...	1
7	7	Benoît Hamon Wins French Socialist Party's Pre...	Alissa J. Rubin	PARIS — France chose an idealistic, traditi...	0
8	8	Excerpts From a Draft Script for Donald Trump'...	NaN	Donald J. Trump is scheduled to make a highly ...	0
9	9	A Back-Channel Plan for Ukraine and Russia, Co...	Megan Twohey and Scott Shane	A week before Michael T. Flynn resigned as nat...	0

FIGURE 3.1 US political news article dataset.

3.4.1.1 Handling Missing Values

Given that the dataset contains only approximately 2,000 null values in the author column, around 500 null values in the title column, and 39 null values in the text column, out of a total of 20,000 rows, it is reasonable to replace those null values with empty strings. In the case of numeric data, we could consider replacing null values with mean, median, or mode, but for text data, replacing null values with empty strings is a suitable choice. It is unlikely to significantly impact the prediction outcomes. The inclusions of missing values are given in Figure 3.2.

3.4.2.2 Removal of Non-alphanumeric Characters

Eliminate non-alphanumeric characters, such as punctuation marks or special symbols, to focus on the textual content and reduce noise in the dataset. In Python, we use re (regular expression) to remove unwanted punctuations and characters from a string. For example, in the below image. The output of the same is given in Figure 3.3.

3.4.2.3 Tokenization

Split the text into individual tokens (words or sub-words) to prepare it for further analysis. This step helps in creating a structured representation of the text data. Using the NLTK toolkit. In Python, we can tokenize a sentence into individual tokens.

3.4.2.4 Stop Word Removal

Stop words are words in a language that are considered insignificant and can introduce noise when used as features in text classification. These words are frequently used in sentences to aid in connecting thoughts or sentence structure. Examples of stop words include articles, prepositions, conjunctions, and certain pronouns. In the

```
# counting the number of missing values in the dataset
news_dataset.isnull().sum()

id           0
title      558
author    1957
text        39
label        0
dtype: int64
```

FIGURE 3.2 Handling missing values.

```
import re
#Remove Punctuations from the String
s = "!</> hello lets$$ </>^d!!!%%et&&ect%$ @@@fa^^^&&!&</>*ke@# ne&& \ws@@@##%^^&!@# %%$"
s = re.sub(r'[^\w\s]','',s)
print(s)

 hello lets detect fake ne ws
```

FIGURE 3.3 usage of regular expression (re) to remove punctuations.

pre-processing step, we removed common stop words such as "a", "about", "an", "are", "as", "at", "be", "by", "for", "from", "how", "in", "is", "of", "on", "or", "that", "the", "these", "this", "too", "was", "what", "when", "where", "who", "will", and so on. These words were eliminated from each document, and the processed documents were saved and passed on to the next stage of analysis. The results of stop word removal are given in Figure 3.4.

3.4.2.5 Lowercasing

Lowercasing is a crucial step in text pre-processing. It involves converting all text to lowercase to maintain consistency and prevent the model from treating words with different capitalizations as distinct entities. By applying lowercasing, we ensure that the model treats words regardless of their capitalization as the same word, avoiding potential discrepancies and improving the accuracy of the analysis.

3.4.2.6 Lemmatization or Stemming

Lemmatization and stemming are techniques used to reduce words to their base or root forms.

Lemmatization involves mapping words to the dictionary or canonical form. For example, the word "caring" would be lemmatized to "care". This process takes into account the word's part of speech and applies morphological analysis to generate the base form accurately.

On the other hand, stemming aims to remove prefixes and suffixes from words to obtain a common base or root form. For instance, the word "caring" would be stemmed to "car". Stemming is a more simplistic approach compared to lemmatization, as it doesn't consider the context or part of speech.

Both lemmatization and stemming are useful in text pre-processing to reduce variations of words and enhance the performance of natural language processing tasks such as text classification or information retrieval. The choice between lemmatization and stemming depends on the specific requirements and nuances of the task at hand.

For the below detection, we have employed stemming in order to expedite and optimize the classification process. Specifically, we utilize the Porter stemmer,

```
from nltk.corpus import stopwords
nltk.download ('stopwords')
stop_words=stopwords.words('english')
print(stopwords.words ('english'))

['i', 'me', 'my', 'myself', 'we', 'our', 'ours', 'ourselves', 'you', "you're", "you've", "you'll", "you'd", 'your', 'yours',
[nltk_data] Downloading package stopwords to /root/nltk_data...
[nltk_data]   Package stopwords is already up-to-date!


sentence = "Fake news is spread to harm the reputation of a person or an organization."
words = nltk.word_tokenize (sentence)
words = [w for w in words if w not in stop_words]
words
```

FIGURE 3.4 Stop word removal and tokenization.

which is widely recognized as one of the most used stemming algorithms. The Porter stemmer is preferred for its accuracy in reducing words to their base or root form. By applying the stemming algorithm, we can enhance the efficiency and accuracy of the classification task.

3.5 FEATURE EXTRACTION

Text categorization poses a challenge due to the high dimensionality of the data. The presence of numerous terms, words, and phrases in documents can significantly burden the learning process, both in terms of computational resources and accuracy. Additionally, the inclusion of irrelevant and redundant features can negatively impact classifier performance. Therefore, it is essential to employ feature-reduction techniques to mitigate these issues by reducing the dimensionality of the text features. There are two methods that aim to address the challenges associated with high-dimensional text data namely term frequency (TF) and term frequency–inverted document frequency (TF–IDF).

3.5.1 Term Frequency (TF)

Term frequency (TF) is an approach that employs word counts in documents to determine document similarity. Each document is represented by a vector of the same length, containing the word counts. These vectors are then normalized so that the sum of their elements equals one. This normalization process converts the word counts into probabilities, indicating the likelihood of a word's presence in the documents. For instance, if a word appears in a document, its representation in the vector is set to one, while it is zero if it is not present. As a result, groups of words represent each document in vector form.

Using term frequency allows for the analysis of word occurrences within documents and facilitates comparisons between documents based on their word frequencies. By representing documents as vectors of normalized word counts, this method enables further processing and analysis of text data using various machine learning algorithms, including clustering and classification. However, it is important to note that term frequency does not consider the importance of words across the entire corpus. To capture the significance of words within documents and the entire dataset, the term frequency–inverted document frequency (TF–IDF) method combines term frequency with inverted document frequency.

3.5.2 Term Frequency–Inverted Document Frequency (TF–IDF)

The term frequency–inverted document frequency (TF–IDF) serves as a measure of the importance of a term within a document in a given dataset. The significance of a term increases with its frequency within the document, but this is counterbalanced by the term's frequency across the entire corpus.

A key characteristic of IDF is its ability to reduce the weight of frequently occurring terms while amplifying the importance of rare terms. For instance, words such as "the" and "then" tend to appear frequently in the text, and if only term frequency (TF) is considered, these terms would dominate the frequency count. However, by incorporating IDF, the impact of such common terms is downplayed.

The TF–IDF combined approach helps to identify the terms that are not only frequent within a specific document but relatively unique compared to the rest of the dataset. By employing TF–IDF, we can obtain more meaningful and informative representations of documents, which can be advantageous for various tasks such as document ranking, information retrieval, and text classification.

By employing these feature selection methods, we aim to reduce the dimensionality of the text feature space, alleviating computational burden and enhancing the accuracy and performance of our classifiers. For our model, we have used TF–IDF vectorizer to convert textual data to numeric data. The details are given in Figure 3.5.

The formula to calculate the TF–IDF (term frequency–inverted document frequency) vector for a term in a document is as follows:

$$\text{TF–IDF} = (\textit{Term frequency}) * (\textit{Inverse document frequency}) \tag{1.1}$$

The *term frequency (TF)* measures the frequency of a term in a specific document and is calculated using the following formula:

$$\text{TF} = (\textit{Number of occurrences of the term in the document}) \,/\, (\textit{Total number of terms in the document}) \tag{1.2}$$

The inverse document frequency (IDF) measures the rarity or importance of a term in the entire corpus and is calculated using the following formula:

```
# converting the textual data to numerical data
vectorizer = TfidfVectorizer()
vectorizer.fit(x)

x = vectorizer.transform(x)

print(x)

  (0, 146857)	0.008966080601926628
  (0, 146526)	0.04527595344903777
  (0, 146477)	0.010533362803831133
  (0, 146467)	0.011035908650313859
  (0, 145478)	0.04088534551157128
  (0, 145472)	0.08772798413358841
  (0, 145404)	0.035009312570797396
  (0, 145347)	0.012866389768035193
  (0, 144869)	0.026157914348333148
  (0, 144700)	0.024142635043095106
  (0, 144449)	0.00849091125888855
  (0, 144097)	0.03845395967378688
```

FIGURE 3.5 TF–IDF vectorizer.

IDF = log ((*Total number of documents*) / (*Number of documents containing the term*)) (1.3)

The TF–IDF vector is a numerical representation of a document, where each element corresponds to a term and its weight in the document. The TF–IDF value captures both the local importance of a term within the document (TF) and its global significance across the corpus (IDF).

To calculate the TF–IDF vector for each term in a document, you multiply the TF value (term frequency) by the IDF value (inverse document frequency) for that term. This process is performed for each term in the document, resulting in a vector representation that reflects the importance of each term in the document relative to the entire corpus.

3.5.3 Training Dataset

Once all the pre-processing and feature extraction steps are completed, we proceed to train the data. The data is divided into training and test sets. Figure 3.6 describes the details of the machine learning algorithms used. The training data is then utilized to train various machine learning algorithms which include logistic regression, decision tree, random forest, gradient boosting classifier, and linear support vector machine. Following the model training, the test data is fed into each model, and the accuracy or performance of each model is evaluated for the purpose of fake news detection.

3.6 RESULTS AND DISCUSSION

The objective of the chapter is to analyze a dataset of US political articles for news detection, where the articles are labeled as either fake news or real news. The dataset has been subjected to analysis, and the results have been presented using five

```
from sklearn.model_selection import train_test_split
x_train, x_test, y_train, y_test = train_test_split(x, y, test_size = 0.2, stratify=y, random_state=2)
#Logistic Regression
LR = LogisticRegression()
LR.fit(x_train, y_train)
#Decision Tree
DT = DecisionTreeClassifier()
DT.fit(x_train, y_train)
#Gradient Boosting Classifier
GBC = GradientBoostingClassifier(random_state=0)
GBC.fit(x_train, y_train)
#Random forest
RFC = RandomForestClassifier(random_state=0)
RFC.fit(x_train, y_train)
#Linear Support vector Classifier
LSVM = LinearSVC(random_state=0)
LSVM.fit(x_train, y_train)
```

FIGURE 3.6 Results of machine learning algorithms applied.

different algorithms named as logistic regression (LR), decision tree (DT), random forest (RF), gradient boosting classifier (GBC), and linear support vector machine (LSVM)

There are multiple approaches used for better prediction in this chapter. The first approach involves combining the title and author columns and using different algorithms to predict the output. Additionally, the second approach is to solely consider the text column and discard the title and author columns for prediction.

Table 3.2 depicts the performance analysis of fake news detection tends to be higher when using the first method, which involves combining the title and author columns for prediction. This suggests that the information contained in these columns contributes to the effectiveness of the prediction models. However, it is important to note that the accuracy may vary depending on the specific dataset and the algorithms used. It is always recommended to evaluate and compare the performance of different methods to select the most appropriate approach for the given task.

Table 3.2 and 3.3 clearly indicate that when utilizing the first method (combining the title and author columns), the accuracy is highest with the random forest algorithm having an accuracy of 99.4%, followed by LSVM (linear support vector machine), and decision tree algorithm with 99.2%. However, the results differ when using the second method (considering only the text column). In this case, the highest accuracy is achieved with LSVM that is 95.6%, while the lowest accuracy is observed with the decision tree algorithm with 87.9% accuracy. This demonstrates that the performance of the algorithms can vary depending on the input features and the specific method employed for prediction.

Figure 3.7 indicates that the highest accuracy of 99.4% was achieved when combining the title and author columns using the random forest algorithm. On the other hand, Figure 3.8 when solely considering the text column with the highest accuracy of 96.2% which was attained using the linear support vector classifier.

The evaluation of the datasets was also done using the confusion matrix, which was automatically generated using Python code with the help of the scikit-learn library. The confusion matrix for the LSVM algorithms is depicted below in the Tables 3.4 and 3.5.

TABLE 3.2
Performance Analysis of Various Models on Title and Author Features

Feature	Model	Precision	Recall	f-measure
Title and Author	Logistic regression	0.97	0.99	0.98
	Decision tree	0.99	0.99	0.99
	Gradient boosting	0.94	1.00	0.97
	Random Forest	0.99	1.00	0.99
	Support Vector Machine	0.99	0.99	0.99

TABLE 3.3
Performance Analysis of Various Models on Text Feature

Feature	Model	Precision	Recall	f-measure
Text	Logistic regression	0.93	0.94	0.93
	Decision tree	0.88	0.88	0.88
	Gradient boosting	0.91	0.93	0.92
	Random forest	0.92	0.89	0.90
	Support vector machine	0.95	0.96	0.96

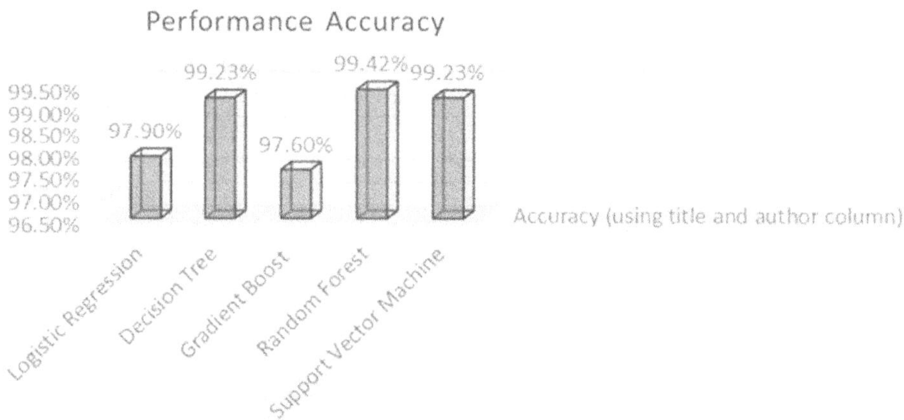

FIGURE 3.7 Performance accuracy using combined features (title and author).

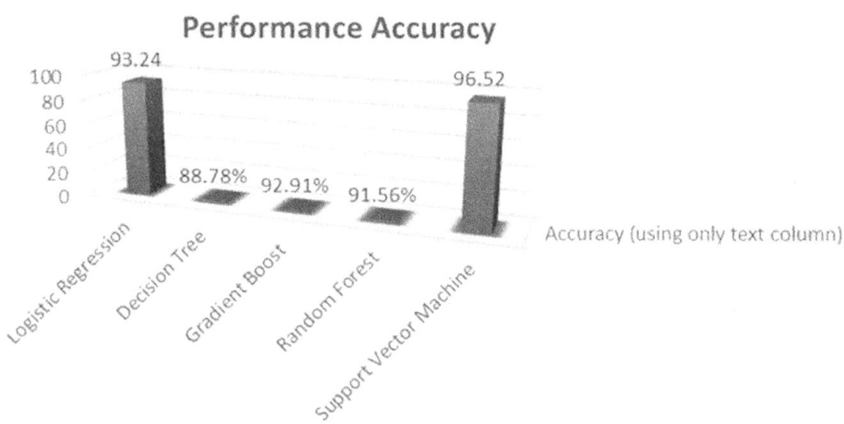

FIGURE 3.8 Performance accuracy using text feature.

TABLE 3.4
Confusion Matrix When Title and Author Features Were Considered

LSVM Model		Actual Value	
		+ve	−ve
Predicted Value	+ve	2061	16
	−ve	16	2067

TABLE 3.5
Confusion Matrix When Text Feature Was Considered

LSVM Model		Actual Value	
		+ve	−ve
Predicted Value	+ve	1978	99
	−ve	86	1997

Additionally, developing a website using Flask web technology would provide a user-friendly interface to detect the authenticity of any article with high accuracy. This integration would allow users to input an article into the website, which would then utilize the trained models to classify it as either fake or real. Leveraging the power of deep learning algorithms and deploying the solution through a web-based platform would enhance the accessibility and usability of the fake news detection system.

In the future, incorporating deep learning algorithms such as LSTM (long short-term memory), CNN (convolutional neural network), and RNN (recurrent neural network) can lead to improved accuracy in fake news detection, especially when working with larger datasets. These algorithms have shown promising results in natural language processing tasks, including text classification.

3.7 CONCLUSION

The issue of fake news has garnered significant attention, particularly following the 2020 US presidential elections. Pertinent data in its study indicate that 62% of US adults consume news through internet community platforms. Surprisingly, many popular fake news stories have garnered more shares on social media rather than legitimate news stories. Alarmingly, a significant number of individualsthat saw fake news stories have reported placing more trust in them than in news from mainstream media sources. The results emphasize the significance of incorporating specific features in the prediction process and highlight the efficacy of different algorithms in detecting fake news. The outcomes of the chapter contribute to the improvement of fake news detection methodologies that provide insights into optimizing accuracy in future research and practical implementations.

REFERENCES

1. Vosoughi, S., Roy, D., & Aral, S. (2018). "The spread of true and false news online". *Information Science*, 359(6380), 1146–1151.
2. Shearer, E., & Mitchell, A. (2020). "News use across social media platforms in 2020: Facebook stands out as a regular source of news for about a third of Americans". *Pew Research Center.* https://www.journalism.org/2021/01/12/news-use-across-social-media-platforms-in-2020.
3. Meel, P., & Vishwakarma, D. K. (2020). "Fake news, rumour, information pollution in social media and web: A contemporary survey of state-of-the-arts, challenges, and opportunities". *Expert System Applications*, 153, 112986.
4. Zannettou, S., Sirivianos, M., Blackburn, J., & Kourtellis, N. (2019). "The web of false information: Rumours, fake news, hoaxes, clickbait, and various other shenanigans". *ACM Journal of Data and Information Quality*,, 11(3), https://doi.org/10.1145/3309699.
5. Sharma, K., Qian, F., Jiang, H., Ruchansky, N., Zhang, M., & Liu, Y. (2019). "Combating fake news: A survey on identification and mitigation techniques". *ACM Transactions on Intelligent Systems and Technology*, 10(3), 1–42. https://doi.org/10.1145/3305260.
6. Ireton, C., & Posetti, J. (2018). *Journalism, Fake News & Disinformation: Handbook for Journalism Education and Training.* UNESCO Publishing.
7. Shabani, S., & Sokhn, M. (2018). "Hybrid machine-crowd approach for fake news detection". 2018 IEEE 4th International Conference on Collaboration and Internet Computing, IEEE, pp. 299–306.
8. Hancock, J. T., Curry, L. E., Goorha, S., & Woodworth, M. (2007). "On lying and being lied to: A linguistic analysis of deception in computer-mediated communication". *Discourse Processes*, 45(1), 12.
9. Ahmed, Hadeer, Traore, Issa, & Saad, Sherif (2017). "Detection of online fake news using n-gram analysis and machine learning techniques". International Conference on Intelligent, Secure, and Dependable Systems in Distributed and Cloud Environments, Springer.
10. Horne, Benjamin D., & Adali, Sibel. (2017). "This just in: Fake news packs a lot in title, uses simpler, repetitive content in text body, more similar to satire than real news". Paper presented at the Association for the Advancement of Artificial Intelligence's Eleventh International Conference on Web and Social Media. arXiv, January 10, 2021. https://arxiv.org/pdf/1703.09398. pdf.
11. Mehrabi, Ninareh, Morstatter, Fred, Saxena, Nripsuta, Lerman, Kristina, & Galstyan, Aram (2019). "A survey on bias and fairness in machine learning". *ACM Computing Surveys (CSUR)*, 54(6), 1–35.
12. Cruz, André, Rocha, Gil, Sousa-Silva, Rui, and Cardoso, Henrique Lopes (2019). "Back to basics in hyper partisan news detection". Proceedings of the 13th International Workshop on Semantic Evaluation, Association for Computational Linguistics Library, pp. 999–1003. https://doi.org/10.18653/v1/S19-2145 .
13. Pérez-Rosas, Verónica, Kleinberg, Bennett, Lefevre, Alexandra, & Mihalcea, Rada (2017). "Automatic detection of fake news". *arXiv Preprint ArXiv:1708.07104.*
14. Zhou, Xinyi, & Zafarani, Reza (2018). "A survey of fake news: Fundamental theories, detection methods, and opportunities". *ACM Computing Surveys*, 53, 12.
15. Singer, Jane B. (2018). "Fact-checkers as entrepreneurs". *Journalism Practice*, 12(8), 1070–1080.
16. Figueira, Álvaro, & Oliveira, Luciana. (2017). "The current state of fake news: challenges and opportunities. CENTERIS (2017) - International Conference on ENTERprise Information Systems / ProjMAN 2017 - International Conference on Project Management / HCist 2017". *Procedia Computer Science*, 121, 817–825.

17. Shu, Kai, Sliva, Amy, Wang, Suhang, Tang, Jiliang, & Liu, Huan (2017). "Fake news detection on social media: A data mining perspective". *ACM SIGKDD Explorations Newsletter*, 19(1), 22–36.
18. Feng, Song, Banerjee, Ritwik, & Choi, Yejin (2012). "Syntactic stylometry for deception detection". Proceedings of the 50th Annual Meeting of the Association for Computational Linguistics Volume 2, Association for Computational Linguistics, pp. 171–175.
19. Popat, Kashyap, Mukherjee, Subhabrata, Strötgen, Jannik, & Weikum, Gerhard (2017). "Where the truth lies: Explaining the credibility of emerging claims on the web and social media". Proceedings of the 26th International Conference on World Wide Web Companion, pp. 1003–1012. https://doi.org/10.1145/3041021.3055133.
20. Alkhodair, Sarah A., Ding, Steven H. H., Fung, Benjamin C. M., & Liu, Junqiang (2020). "Detecting breaking news rumors of emerging topics in social media". *Information Processing and Management*, 57(2). https://doi.org/10.1016/j.ipm.2019.02.016.
21. Yang, Fan, Mukherjee, Arjun, & Dragut, Eduard. (2017). "Satirical news detection and analysis using attention mechanism and linguistic features". *arXiv Preprint ArXiv:1709.01189*.
22. Litvinova, Olga, Seredin, Pavel, Litvinova, Tatiana, & Lyell, John (2017). "Deception detection in Russian texts". Proceedings of the Student Research Workshop at the 15th Conference of the European Chapter of the Association for Computational Linguistics, Spain 2017, E17–4005, pp. 43–52.
23. Alam, S., & Ravshanbekov, A. (2019). "Sieving fake news from genuine: A synopsis". *arXiv Preprint ArXiv:1911.08516*.
24. Manzoor, S. I.s & Singla, J. Nikita (2019). "Fake News Detection Using Machine Learning approaches: A systematic Review". 2019 3rd International Conference on Trends in Electronics and Informatics (ICOEI), IEEE, pp. 230–234.
25. Girgis, S., Amer, E., & Gadallah, M. (2018). "Deep learning algorithms for detecting fake news in online text". 2018 13th International Conference on Computer Engineering and Systems (ICCES), IEEE, pp. 93–97.
26. Ksieniewicz, P., Choraś, M., Kozik, R., & Woźniak, M. (2019). "Machine learning methods for fake news classification". International Conference on Intelligent Data Engineering and Automated Learning, Springer, pp. 332–339.
27. Traylor, T., Straub, J., Snell, N., & Snell, N. (2019). "Classifying fake news articles using natural language processing to identify in-article attribution as a supervised learning estimator". 2019 13th International Conference on Semantic Computing (ICSC), IEEE, pp. 445–449.
28. Faustini, P., & Covões, T. F. (2019). "Fake news detection using one-class classification". 2019 8th Brazilian Conference on Intelligent Systems (BRACIS), IEEE, pp. 592–597.
29. Ozbay, F. A., & Alatas, B. (2019). "A novel approach for detection of fake news on social media using metaheuristic optimization algorithms". *Elektronika ir Elektrotechnika*, 25(4), 62–67.
30. Kaur, S., Kumar, P., & Kumaraguru, P. (2019). "Automating fake news detection system using multi-level voting model". *Soft Computing*, 24(2), 1–21. https://doi.org/10.1007/s00500-019-04436-y
31. Pérez-Rosas, V., Kleinberg, B., Lefevre, A., & Mihalcea, R. (2017). "Automatic detection of fake news". *arXiv Preprint ArXiv:1708.07104*.
32. Waikhom, L., & Goswami, R. S. (2019). "Fake news detection using machine learning". Proceedings of International Conference on Advancements in Computing & Management (ICACM). https://doi.org/10.2139/ssrn.3462938.

33. Abedalla, A., Al-Sadi, A., & Abdullah, M. (2019). "A closer look at fake news detection: A deep learning perspective". Proceedings of the 2019 3rd International Conference on Advances in Artificial Intelligence, pp. 24–28. https://doi.org/10.1145/3369114.3369149.
34. Singhania, S., Fernandez, N., & Rao, S. (2017). "3han: A deep neural network for fake news detection". International Conference on Neural Information Processing, Springer, pp. 572–581.
35. Qawasmeh, E., Tawalbeh, M., & Abdullah, M. (2019). "Automatic identification of fake news using deep learning". 2019 Sixth International Conference on Social Networks Analysis, Management and Security, IEEE, pp. 383–388.
36. Saikh, T., Anand, A., Ekbal, A., & Bhattacharyya, P. (2019). "A novel approach towards fake news detection: Deep learning augmented with textual entailment features". International Conference on Applications of Natural Language to Information Systems, Springer, pp. 345–358.
37. Granik, M., & Mesyura, V. (2017). "Fake news detection using naive Bayes classifier". 2017 IEEE First Ukraine Conference on Electrical and Computer Engineering, UKRCON IEEE, pp. 900–903.
38. Ajao, O., Bhowmik, D., & Zargari, S. (2019). "Sentiment aware fake news detection on online social networks". ICASSP 2019–2019 IEEE International Conference on Acoustics, Speech and Signal Processing (ICASSP), IEEE, pp. 2507–2511.
39. Giachanou, A., Rosso, P., & Crestani, F. (2019). "Leveraging emotional signals for credibility detection". Proceedings of the 42nd International ACM SIGIR Conference on Research and Development in Information Retrieval, July 2019, pp. 877–880. https://doi.org/10.1145/3331184.3331285
40. Li, Q., Hu, Q., Lu, Y., Yang, Y., & Cheng, J. (2019). "Multi-level word features based on CNN for fake news detection in cultural communication". *Personal and Ubiquitous Computing*, 24(2), 259–272. https://doi.org/10.1007/s00779-019-01289-y
41. Monteiro, R. A., Santos, R. L., Pardo, T. A., de Almeida, T. A., Ruiz, E. E., & Vale, O. A. (2018). "Contributions to the study of fake news in Portuguese: New corpus and automatic detection results". International Conference on Computational Processing of the Portuguese Language, Springer, pp. 324–334.
42. Vogel, I., & Jiang, P. (2019). "Fake news detection with the new German dataset GermanFakeNC". International Conference on Theory and Practice of Digital Libraries, Springer, pp. 288–295.
43. Helmstetter, S., & Paulheim, H. (2018). "Weakly supervised learning for fake news detection on Twitter". 2018 IEEE/ACM International Conference on Advances in Social Networks Analysis and Mining (ASONAM), IEEE, pp. 274–277.
44. Bhattacharjee, S. D., Talukder, A., & Balantrapu, B. V. (2017). "Active learning based news veracity detection with feature weighting and deep-shallow fusion". 2017 IEEE International Conference on Big Data, IEEE, pp. 556–565.
45. Janze, C., & Risius, M. (2017, January). "Automatic detection of fake news on social media platforms". *PACIS*, p. 261.
46. Rubin, V. L., Conroy, N., Chen, Y., & Cornwell, S. (2016). "Fake news or truth? using satirical cues to detect potentially misleading news". Proceedings of the Second Workshop on Computational Approaches to Deception Detection, pp. 7–17. https://doi.org/10.18653/v1/W16-0802.
47. Hu, G., Ding, Y., Qi, S., Wang, X., & Liao, Q. (2019). "Multi-depth graph convolutional networks for fake news detection". CCF International Conference on Natural Language Processing and Chinese Computing, Springer, pp. 698–710.
48. Pan, J. Z., Pavlova, S., Li, C., Li, N., Li, Y., & Liu, J. (2018, October). "Content based fake news detection using knowledge graphs". International Semantic Web Conference, Springer, pp. 669–683.

49. Conroy, N. J., Rubin, V. L., & Chen, Y. (2015). "Automatic deception detection: Methods for finding fake news". *Proceedings of the Association for Information Science and Technology*, 52(1), 1–4.
50. Zhou, X., & Zafarani, R. (2019). "Network-based fake news detection: A pattern-driven approach". *ACM SIGKDD Explorations Newsletter*, 21(2), 48–60.
51. Della Vedova, M. L., Tacchini, E., Moret, S., Ballarin, G., DiPierro, M., & de Alfaro, L. (2018, May). "Automatic online fake news detection combining content and social signals". 2018 22nd Conference of Open Innovations Association (FRUCT), IEEE, pp. 272–279.
52. Hamdi, T., Slimi, H., Bounhas, I., & Slimani, Y. (2020). "A hybrid approach for fake news detection in Twitter based on user features and graph embedding". International Conference on Distributed Computing and Internet Technology, Springer, pp. 266–280.
53. Ruchansky, N., Seo, S., & Liu, Y. (2017). "Csi: A hybrid deep model for fake news detection". Proceedings of the 2017 ACM on Conference on Information and Knowledge Management, CIKM'17, Singapore, pp. 797–806. https://doi.org/10.1145/3132847.3132877
54. Okoro, E. M., Abara, B. A., Alan-Ajonye, A., Isa, Z., & Umagba, A. (2019). "Effects of human and human-machine fake news detection approaches on user detection performance". *International Journal of Advanced Research in Computer Science*, 10(1), 26.
55. Shabani, S., & Sokhn, M. (2018, October). "Hybrid machine-crowd approach for fake news detection". 2018 IEEE 4th International Conference on Collaboration and Internet Computing (CIC), IEEE, pp. 299–306.
56. Kim, K. H., & Jeong, C. S. (2019). "Fake news detection system using article abstraction". 2019 16th International Joint Conference on Computer Science and Software Engineering (JCSSE), IEEE, pp. 209–212.
57. Rehm, G. (2017). "An infrastructure for empowering Internet users to handle fake news and other online media phenomena". International Conference of the German Society for Computational Linguistics and Language Technology, Springer, pp. 216–231.
58. Karidi, D. P., Nakos, H., & Stavrakas, Y. (2019). "Automatic ground truth dataset creation for fake news detection in social media". International Conference on Intelligent Data Engineering and Automated Learning, Springer, pp. 424–436.
59. Schuster, T., Schuster, R., Shah, D. J., & Barzilay, R. (2019). "Are we safe yet? The limitations of distributional features for fake news detection". preprint arXiv:1908.09805.
60. Giełczyk, A., Wawrzyniak, R., & Choraś, M. (2019). "Evaluation of the existing tools for fake news detection". IFIP International Conference on Computer Information Systems and Industrial Management, Springer, pp. 144–151.
61. Mahid, Z. I., Manickam, S., & Karuppayah, S. (2018). "Fake News on social media: Brief Review on Detection Techniques". 2018 Fourth International Conference on Advances in Computing, Communication & Automation (ICACCA), IEEE, pp. 1–5.
62. Reis, J. C., Correia, A., Murai, F., Veloso, A., Benevenuto, F., & Cambria, E. (2019). "Supervised learning for fake news detection". *IEEE Intelligent Systems*, 34(2), 76–81.
63. Shu, K., Sliva, A., Wang, S., Tang, J., & Liu, H. (2017). "Fake news detection on social media: A data mining perspective". *ACM SIGKDD Explorations Newsletter*, 19(1), 22–36.
64. Fernández-Reyes, F. C., & Shinde, S. (2018). "Evaluating deep neural networks for automatic fake news detection in political domain". Ibero-American Conference on Artificial Intelligence, Springer, pp. 206–216.
65. Zhang, J., Dong, B., & Philip, S. Y. (2019). "Deep Diffusive Neural Network based Fake News Detection from Heterogeneous Social Networks". 2019 IEEE International Conference on Big Data (Big Data), IEEE, pp. 1259–1266.

66. Bali, A. P. S., Fernandes, M., Choubey, S., & Goel, M. (2019). "Comparative performance of machine learning algorithms for fake news detection". International Conference on Advances in Computing and Data Sciences, Springer, pp. 420–430.
67. Dewey, C. (2016). "Facebook has repeatedly trended fake news since firing its human editors". *Washington Post.*
68. Moura, Ricardo, Dr Silva, Rui Manuel Sousa, & Dr de Avelar Lopes Cardoso, Henrique Daniel (2021, July 19). "Automated fake news detection using computational forensic linguistics". *International Journal for the Semiotics of Law*, 35(6), 2409–2433.
69. Nordberg, Pontus and Kävrestad, Joakim (2020). Automatic Fake News Detection, Högskolan i Skövde, Institutionen för informationsteknologi, pp. 420–430, OAI: oai :DiVA.org:his-18512
70. Liu, Y., & Wu, Y. F. B. (2018). "Early detection of fake news on social media through propagation path classification with recurrent and convolutional networks", 32nd AAAI Conference on Artificial Intelligence, AAAI, pp. 354–361.

4 Analytics of Text and Social Media for Challenges of Hateful and Offensive Speech Detection

Anand Kumar Mishra, C S Raghuvanshi, Hemant Kumar Soni, and Pragya Goswami

4.1 INTRODUCTION

In an age dominated by the digital revolution and the ubiquitous presence of social media, the use of language to express ideas, thoughts, and emotions has taken on an entirely new dimension. While the internet has provided an unprecedented platform for free expression, it has also, regrettably, given rise to a darker underbelly – the proliferation of hateful and offensive speech. As the digital world intertwines with our daily lives, it becomes increasingly imperative to address this challenge. The dissemination of hate speech and offensive content online poses a significant threat to individuals and communities. It fuels discrimination, fosters division, and, in some instances, even incites violence. Recognizing the gravity of this issue, researchers and technology innovators have turned their attention to the development of systems capable of detecting and mitigating this harm. This chapter dives into the intricate realm of analytics applied to the detection of hateful and offensive speech within the ever-expanding landscape of text and social media. The objective is not only to outline the intricacies of the problem but to equip readers with a nuanced understanding of the complexities involved, as well as the tools and techniques that can be harnessed to confront this challenge effectively. The chapter is structured to address the multifaceted aspects of the issue, encompassing definitions and context to establish a solid foundation, an exploration of the manifold challenges that confront detection efforts, and a detailed examination of the analytics techniques employed in the pursuit of a solution. Additionally, it delves into the distinctive challenges posed by social media data, as well as the legal and ethical considerations that cast a long shadow over this critical domain. As we journey through this chapter, the aim is to illuminate not only the technological advancements but also the ethical and societal

DOI: 10.1201/9781003409519-4

responsibilities tied to detecting and mitigating hateful and offensive speech. In doing so, we hope to contribute to a broader awareness of the significance of this issue and inspire further innovation, research, and action toward creating a safer, more inclusive digital environment for all.

4.2 SCOPE AND OBJECTIVES

4.2.1 Scope

This chapter delves into the intricate world of analytics, with a specific focus on the challenges posed by hateful and offensive speech in text and social media. It is a comprehensive exploration of a crucial societal issue in the digital age. The scope encompasses a wide array of topics, ranging from defining and contextualizing hateful speech to discussing the complexities and nuances involved in its detection. We will explore the various data-driven methods and technologies, such as text analytics, machine learning, and social media analysis, employed to combat this problem. By comprehensively addressing these challenges and providing a roadmap for potential solutions, this chapter aims to equip readers with the knowledge and tools needed to navigate and contribute to the ongoing dialogue surrounding hateful and offensive speech detection in the digital sphere.

4.2.2 Objectives

The primary objectives of this chapter are multifaceted. First, it seeks to provide a comprehensive understanding of the nuances and complexities surrounding the detection of hateful and offensive speech in text and social media. By defining these concepts and their broader context, the chapter lays the groundwork for a deep exploration of the issue.

Second, the chapter aims to highlight the critical challenges that confront those striving to develop effective detection systems. These challenges include the contextual ambiguity of language, the ever-evolving nature of online discourse, the incorporation of multimedia content, regional and cultural variations, and the presence of data biases. By addressing these obstacles, readers will gain a comprehensive view of the hurdles that must be surmounted.

Third, the chapter endeavors to delve into the diverse analytics techniques employed in the pursuit of accurate hate speech detection. It will cover aspects such as preprocessing methods, feature extraction, machine learning algorithms, and deep learning models. These discussions are designed to offer insights into the strengths and limitations of each approach, providing guidance to practitioners and researchers. Moreover, this chapter explores the distinctive challenges presented by social media data and the short, noisy, and often unstructured text it contains. It discusses the incorporation of user and network features, an essential component of modern hate speech detection.

Additionally, the chapter addresses the ethical and legal considerations that loom over this field, with a focus on bias in artificial intelligence, fairness, privacy, and evolving legal frameworks. Summarizing, the chapter seeks to empower readers with a holistic view of the subject. It aims to be a valuable resource for academics, researchers, and industry professionals alike, who are vested in the development of effective solutions for the detection of hateful and offensive speech in the digital sphere while maintaining a strong ethical and legal compass.

4.3 HATEFUL AND OFFENSIVE SPEECH: DEFINITIONS AND CONTEXT

In the realm of the digital age, understanding the subtleties of hateful and offensive speech is paramount. This section commences its journey by firmly grounding the reader in the definitions and contextual underpinnings of these terms. Hate speech, the utterance of words or expressions that incite discrimination, hostility, or violence towards individuals or groups based on attributes such as race, religion, gender, or ethnicity, represents a complex and often elusive concept. It exists on a spectrum, encompassing overtly offensive language as well as subtle, implicit biases. Offensive speech, while distinct from hate speech, shares a commonality in its capacity to harm, causing emotional distress, discomfort, and offense.

The prevalence of these types of speech within the digital sphere is palpable, necessitating not only a clear understanding of what constitutes hate speech but also an examination of the broader context in which it emerges. The internet's vastness and anonymity have given rise to a proliferation of such content, prompting a pressing need for automated detection systems that can navigate the intricacies of online discourse. By establishing a firm understanding of these definitions and the evolving landscape within which they operate, this section sets the stage for a comprehensive exploration of the challenges and solutions in the detection of hateful and offensive speech within the realm of text and social media analytics (Figure 4.1).

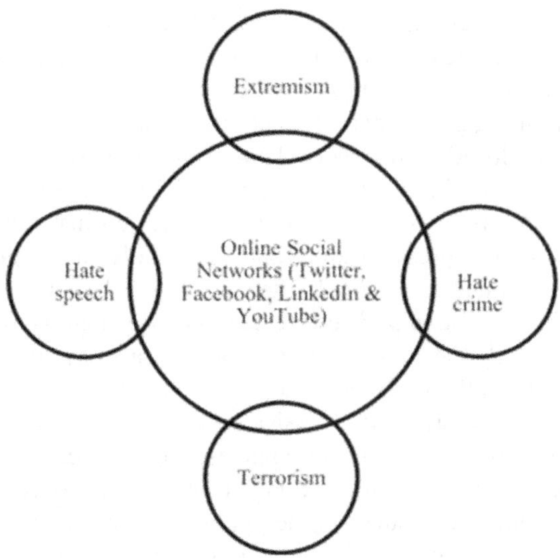

FIGURE 4.1 Hateful speech in social media.

4.4 CHALLENGES IN HATE SPEECH DETECTION

The detection of hate speech within the vast and ever-evolving digital landscape presents a multitude of formidable challenges. These challenges encompass the very essence of language itself, as it is often replete with ambiguity and context dependency. Hate speech is not always overt and frequently relies on insinuations and dog whistles, making its identification a complex task. Furthermore, the rapid evolution of language in online spaces, from internet slang to neologisms, adds another layer of intricacy to the process, demanding constant adaptation. As if the subtleties of language weren't challenging enough, the integration of multimedia content, including images and videos, amplifies the difficulty. Hate speech often takes on visual forms, requiring advanced techniques to identify such content. Additionally, the cultural and regional variations in the interpretation of what constitutes offensive speech further complicate the task. What may be deemed hate speech in one cultural context might be perceived as innocuous in another. Furthermore, the presence of data biases, whether from the training data or algorithmic biases, can reinforce existing prejudices and inaccuracies in hate speech detection models. These biases must be mitigated to ensure fairness and equity. Navigating these multifaceted challenges is pivotal in the quest for effective hate speech detection. This section delves into these intricacies, offering insights into the hurdles that must be overcome to build robust, reliable, and fair detection systems within the realm of text and social media analytics.

4.4.1 Ambiguity and Context Dependency

A fundamental challenge in the realm of hateful and offensive speech detection lies in the inherent ambiguity and context dependency of language. Hate speech is notorious for its multifaceted nature, often operating in a realm where words and phrases may carry varying connotations based on context and intent. What may seem innocuous or even positive in one context can, when applied differently, transform into a vehicle for hatred or discrimination. For instance, terms that are part of a specific community's in-group language may be used affectionately among its members but maliciously when employed by outsiders. This nuanced interplay between language and context is a significant hurdle for automated detection systems. In addition, the subtlety of hate speech is such that it frequently relies on insinuations, coded language, and metaphorical expressions, making it especially challenging to identify. It is a realm where the explicit and implicit often intertwine, blurring the lines between what is overtly offensive and what is concealed behind veiled meanings. This intricacy necessitates not only the analysis of words and phrases but also the surrounding discourse to comprehend the intended meaning accurately.

To effectively detect hateful and offensive speech within this complex linguistic landscape, algorithms and models must grapple with the intricate interplay of words, meanings, and contextual cues. This section delves into the intricacies of navigating the ambiguity and context dependency inherent in hate speech, offering insights into the techniques and approaches that have been developed to address this central challenge in text and social media analytics.

4.4.2 Evolving Language and Internet Slang

The dynamic and ever-evolving nature of language in online spaces poses a substantial challenge in the realm of hateful and offensive speech detection. Internet slang, memes, and rapidly changing linguistic trends can render conventional language models and algorithms obsolete. New words and phrases emerge at a staggering pace, many of which can carry offensive or discriminatory meanings. What is more, these neologisms are often created intentionally to bypass detection algorithms, further complicating the task of identifying hate speech.

Internet communities, social media platforms, and online subcultures each have their unique linguistic norms and terminologies, frequently employing insider language that remains unfamiliar to outsiders. Such lexicons can be used to mask hateful intent, making the task of detection even more daunting. Automated systems need to keep pace with this linguistic evolution to effectively identify and classify offensive content. Addressing the challenge of evolving language and internet slang in hate speech detection requires constant adaptation and innovation. This section dives into the intricate realm of ever-changing digital lexicons and explores how advanced analytics techniques and technologies are harnessed to tackle this ongoing linguistic evolution, providing a deeper understanding of the means to confront this critical issue within the context of text and social media analytics (Figure 4.2).

4.4.3 Multimedia Content: Images and Videos

Hateful and offensive speech often transcends the boundaries of text and extends into multimedia content, such as images and videos, presenting a significant challenge in the realm of detection. Unlike text, which can be processed using natural language processing techniques, multimedia content demands a different set of tools and methods for analysis. The visual and auditory elements within images and videos can convey hate speech through symbols, gestures, or spoken words, sometimes in ways that textual analysis alone cannot capture. Images and videos introduce

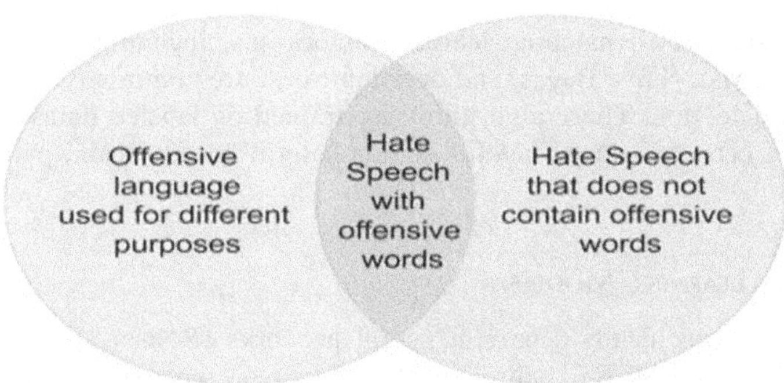

FIGURE 4.2 The content and language of the hate speech creator.

additional complexities, including the need for content recognition and analysis of visual and auditory cues. Hate speech can be embedded in memes, graphic images, or even subtleties in facial expressions, requiring more sophisticated algorithms to identify and understand the intent. The challenge is further compounded when these multimedia elements are combined with textual content. Effectively detecting hateful and offensive speech in multimedia content involves interdisciplinary approaches that merge computer vision, audio analysis, and text analytics. This section delves into these multifaceted challenges, offering insights into the strategies and technologies that are deployed to address this complex dimension of hate speech detection in the context of text and social media analytics.

4.5 TEXT ANALYTICS FOR HATE SPEECH DETECTION

Text analytics plays a pivotal role in the process of identifying and mitigating hateful and offensive speech within the digital landscape. This section of the chapter underscores the importance of text analytics in tackling the challenges of detecting such content and provides insights into the methodologies employed:

4.5.1 Preprocessing Techniques

Hate speech detection often begins with the preprocessing of textual data. Techniques such as tokenization, stemming, and stop-word removal are used to standardize text, reducing it to its essential components for analysis.

4.5.2 Feature Extraction and Vectorization

Feature extraction methods, such as TF–IDF (term frequency–inverse document frequency) and word embeddings (e.g., Word2Vec, GloVe), are utilized to represent text in a numerical form that machine learning algorithms can process. These approaches capture the semantic meaning and relationships between words.

4.5.3 Supervised Machine Learning Algorithms:

A range of supervised machine learning algorithms, including support vector machines (SVMs), Naïve Bayes, and decision trees, are commonly employed for hate speech detection. These algorithms are trained on labeled datasets and can subsequently classify text as hateful or non-hateful based on the patterns they learn.

4.5.4 Deep Learning Models

Deep learning, specifically recurrent neural networks (RNNs) and transformer-based models such as BERT (bidirectional encoder representations from transformers), have gained prominence in hate speech detection due to their ability to capture complex linguistic patterns and context.

4.5.5 Evaluation Metrics

To gauge the effectiveness of hate speech detection models, various evaluation metrics are employed. These include precision, recall, F1-score, and accuracy, providing a comprehensive view of a model's performance. By employing these text analytics techniques, researchers and practitioners can develop models and systems that are more adept at identifying and combatting hateful and offensive speech in the realm of text and social media. This section delves into the intricacies of these methods, offering insights into their strengths and limitations, and their collective role in addressing this critical issue.

4.6 SOCIAL MEDIA DATA AND SPECIAL CONSIDERATIONS

Social media platforms represent a dynamic and complex ecosystem where the detection of hateful and offensive speech introduces unique challenges. This section of the chapter emphasizes the significance of social media data and discusses the special considerations in hate speech detection within these platforms.

Social media data comes with its own set of idiosyncrasies, beginning with the sheer volume and velocity of content generated. This rapid flow of data requires efficient real-time analysis and decision-making. Furthermore, the user-generated nature of the content on social media brings a wide range of writing styles, lexicons, and languages into the mix, necessitating adaptable and multilingual approaches for comprehensive detection. One distinctive challenge is the brevity of content. Tweets, posts, and comments are often brief and fragmented, making it challenging to discern hate speech with high confidence in limited text. Shorter content also amplifies the importance of context, as a single statement can be misconstrued without the broader conversation in which it is embedded. Incorporating user features and network characteristics is another layer of complexity in social media data. Users' profiles, relationships, and previous online behavior can be predictive of their engagement with hate speech, and these contextual aspects are crucial in achieving more accurate detection (Figure 4.3).

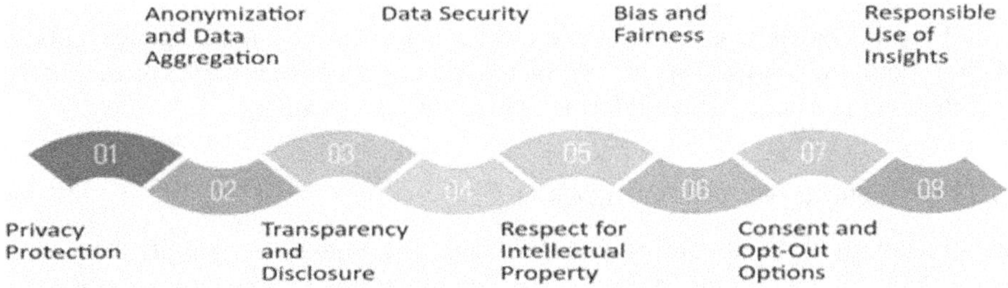

FIGURE 4.3 Measures to ensure a check on social networking platforms.

4.7 CHALLENGES OF ANALYZING SOCIAL MEDIA DATA

The analysis of social media data in the context of detecting hateful and offensive speech presents a unique set of challenges. The dynamism and complexity of this environment introduce intricacies that researchers and practitioners must grapple with. Social media data is voluminous and rapidly generated, requiring efficient processing techniques to handle the constant influx of content. The brevity and informality of text, common on these platforms, often result in noisy and contextually challenging content. Furthermore, the multilingual and multimodal nature of social media content adds layers of complexity, demanding adaptable approaches for comprehensive detection. The context sensitivity of social media data is a critical challenge, as words and phrases can take on different meanings based on the broader conversation, user interactions, and trends. Staying current with evolving online trends and slang is pivotal for effective detection. User-generated content introduces significant variation in communication styles, further complicating the task of identifying hate speech. Additionally, the analysis of user and network features becomes essential, as user behavior and social connections play a role in the dissemination of hate speech.

Ethical and privacy considerations loom large in the analysis of social media data. Balancing the imperative of hate speech detection with the preservation of user privacy and ethical standards remains an ongoing challenge. This section delves into these multifaceted challenges, offering insights into the strategies and technologies employed to navigate the complexities of social media data in the pursuit of mitigating hateful and offensive speech within the realm of text and social media analytics. This section of the chapter delves into the intricacies of these challenges and the specific hurdles researchers and practitioners face.

4.7.1 Data Volume and Velocity

Social media platforms generate an enormous volume of data in real-time. The sheer quantity of text, images, and videos necessitates the development of efficient and scalable data processing techniques.

4.7.2 Short and Noisy Text

Social media content is often brief and characterized by informal language, abbreviations, and emoticons. The brevity of text makes it challenging to discern hate speech with precision, and the informal nature introduces ambiguity.

4.7.3 Multilingual and Multimodal Content

Social media is a global platform where content is produced in multiple languages and includes various forms of media. Detecting hate speech across languages and integrating multimedia elements add layers of complexity.

4.7.4 Context Sensitivity

Social media content is highly context-dependent. A single word or phrase can carry different meanings based on the broader conversation, user interactions, and trending topics. Understanding this context is crucial for accurate detection.

4.7.5 Evolving Trends and Slang

Online discourse evolves rapidly, introducing new words, phrases, and memes that can carry offensive connotations. Detecting hate speech requires staying current with these linguistic trends.

4.7.6 User-Generated Content

Social media content is created by a diverse user base, each with its own unique communication style. Detection models need to adapt to this variation and consider the idiosyncrasies of individual users.

4.7.7 User and Network Features

The behavior and characteristics of users, as well as their social connections and network dynamics, can impact the spread of hate speech. Incorporating user and network features is essential for a comprehensive analysis.

4.7.8 Ethical and Privacy Concerns

The analysis of social media data raises ethical and privacy considerations. Balancing the need for hate speech detection with user privacy and consent is an ongoing challenge.

4.8 ADVANCED TECHNIQUES FOR HATE SPEECH DETECTION

As the battle against hateful and offensive speech in the digital sphere intensifies, advanced techniques are emerging as powerful allies in this ongoing struggle. This section of the chapter explores the cutting-edge methodologies and approaches being employed to tackle the intricacies of hate speech detection, offering a glimpse into the future of this critical domain.

Transfer learning techniques, often rooted in pre-trained language models, have shown remarkable promise in adapting to the ever-evolving nature of hate speech. These models can leverage knowledge from one domain and apply it effectively to another, enabling improved detection across various contexts and languages. Combining multiple models into an ensemble has become a popular strategy to enhance the robustness of hate speech detection. By leveraging diverse algorithms, including both text and multimedia analysis, ensembles can provide more accurate and reliable results. Hate speech often transcends text, manifesting in images, videos, and audio. Multimodal approaches, which integrate both textual and visual elements, are becoming increasingly important in capturing the full spectrum of hate speech, offering a more holistic understanding of offensive content. The ability to explain why a model makes a particular prediction is crucial, especially in sensitive contexts like hate speech detection. Explainable AI techniques aim to make the decision-making process transparent and interpretable, which is vital for ensuring fairness and accountability (Figure 4.4).

4.8.1 Ethical and Legal Considerations

In the pursuit of combating hateful and offensive speech in the digital realm, one cannot overlook the critical ethical and legal dimensions that underpin this endeavor. This section delves into the complex intersection of technology, free expression, privacy, and societal responsibility, emphasizing the paramount importance of addressing these considerations in tandem with the technical aspects of hate speech detection.

Ethical Concerns: Hate speech detection involves the deployment of powerful algorithms and machine learning models that sift through vast amounts of user-generated content. This brings forth a fundamental ethical concern – the potential for overreach, censorship, and the infringement of free speech rights. Striking a balance

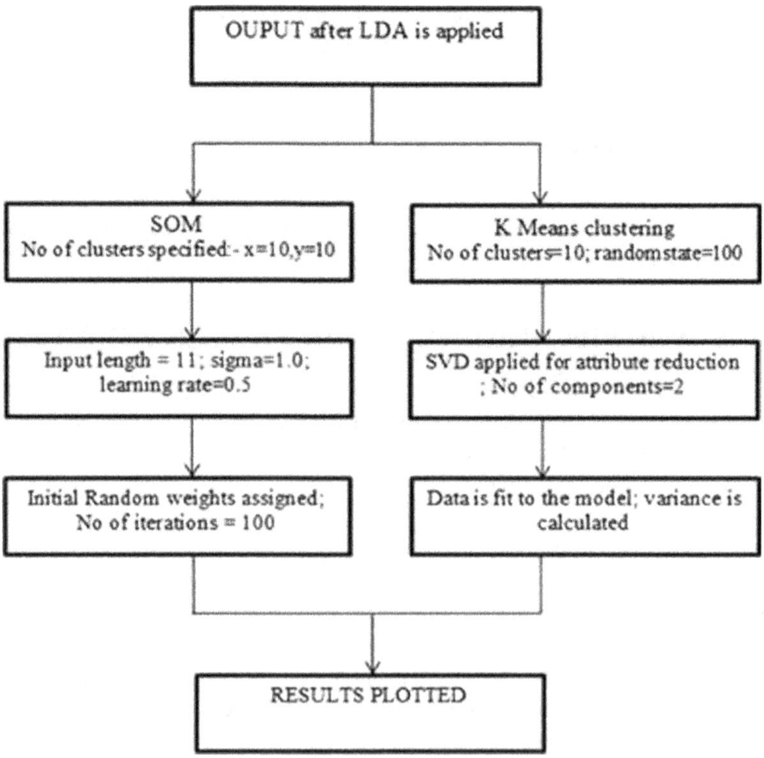

FIGURE 4.4 Hate speech detection using machine learning techniques.

between the preservation of online civility and the protection of free expression is a precarious act that requires careful ethical navigation.

One of the central ethical issues pertains to bias within the detection models. If not addressed meticulously, these models can inadvertently perpetuate existing biases and prejudices present in the data they are trained on. This raises profound questions about fairness and equity in content moderation, as well as the potential for discrimination against certain communities or voices. The legal landscape surrounding hate speech is a complex web of international, national, and regional laws and regulations. What constitutes hate speech can vary significantly between jurisdictions, making the implementation of universal detection algorithms challenging. Navigating these legal intricacies is a formidable task, as platforms need to respect the laws of the countries they operate in while striving for consistency in content moderation. The emergence of new legal frameworks that hold technology companies accountable for content on their platforms, such as the European Union's Digital Services Act, introduces additional layers of complexity. These regulations require technology companies to invest in proactive measures to combat hate speech while respecting user rights, forcing them to tread carefully between legal compliance and ethical responsibility. This section does not merely highlight the ethical and legal challenges, but also explores the strategies and technologies available for addressing them. It underscores the pressing need for transparency and fairness in hate speech detection algorithms, as well as the importance of respecting users' privacy and free expression rights. Additionally, it examines the evolving legal landscape, which is increasingly influencing how social media platforms approach the detection and moderation of hateful and offensive speech. In a digital era where the boundaries between freedom of expression and protection against harm are continuously renegotiated, ethical and legal considerations remain at the heart of the discourse on hate speech detection.

4.9 CASE STUDIES AND APPLICATIONS

4.9.1 X's Hate Speech Detection

A case study on how X (formerly Twitter) employs machine learning algorithms to detect and combat hate speech on its platform, including challenges faced and lessons learned.

4.9.2 Social Media Content Moderation

An analysis of content moderation practices by social media giants such as Facebook and YouTube, exploring the technologies and guidelines they employ to address hate speech.

4.9.3 Online Harassment Prevention

A case study focusing on online communities and forums that use automated detection tools to combat online harassment, thereby maintaining a safer environment for users.

4.9.4 Hate Speech in Political Discourse

Examination of the detection and management of hate speech within political discussions and campaigns on social media platforms, exploring the role of AI in maintaining civility.

4.9.5 Hate Speech Monitoring in Chat Apps

A look at how chat applications such as WhatsApp and Discord address hate speech within private and group chats, emphasizing the challenges and privacy concerns.

4.9.6 Hate Speech in Gaming Communities

Analysis of the strategies used in detecting and preventing hate speech within online gaming communities, an environment known for its toxicity.

4.9.7 Hate Speech in User-Generated News Platforms

Exploration of the tools and techniques applied in user-generated news platforms to curb the spread of offensive content and false information.

4.9.8 Multilingual Hate Speech Detection

An examination of how hate speech detection adapts to diverse linguistic contexts and the challenges it faces in detecting hate speech in multiple languages.

4.9.9 Combating Hate Speech in Online Education

Case study on the application of hate speech detection in online education platforms, ensuring a safe and respectful learning environment.

4.9.10 Crowd Sourced

Content moderation insight into platforms that rely on crowd sourcing to help moderate content, exploring the effectiveness and ethical considerations in harnessing the power of the community to combat hate speech.

These case studies and applications represent a diverse range of real-world scenarios where analytics of text and social media are employed to address the challenges of hateful and offensive speech detection. They offer valuable insights into the practical implementation of these technologies across various domains and highlight the significance of continually evolving approaches in combating hate speech online.

4.10 FUTURE DIRECTIONS AND EMERGING TECHNOLOGIES

As we venture into the future, the landscape of hateful and offensive speech detection in the digital realm is poised for innovation and transformation. This section casts its gaze forward, exploring the potential future directions and emerging technologies that hold promise for more effective and ethical solutions.

4.10.1 Contextual Understanding:

The future of hate speech detection will likely involve a more nuanced understanding of context. Technologies that can comprehend the subtleties of tone, intent, and the evolving nature of language within specific online communities will be pivotal. Advanced natural language processing models will play a significant role in achieving this goal.

4.10.2 Cross-Lingual and Multimodal Detection

With the global reach of the internet, cross-lingual and multimodal approaches will become increasingly important. Detection models capable of analyzing content in multiple languages and deciphering the meaning in text, images, and videos will be on the horizon.

4.10.3 Ethical AI and Explainability

Ethical considerations will remain at the forefront, demanding more transparent and explainable AI models. Technologies that can elucidate the reasoning behind decisions and ensure fairness and accountability will be a focus area.

4.10.4 Personalized Moderation

Future technologies may aim to personalize content moderation, adapting to the individual preferences and sensitivities of users. This approach could provide a tailored online experience while safeguarding against offensive content.

4.10.5 User Education and Empowerment

Empowering users with tools to combat hate speech and promoting digital literacy will gain significance. Technologies that offer users a proactive role in content moderation may become more prevalent.

4.10.6 Regulation and Standards

The ongoing evolution of legal frameworks and industry standards will continue to shape the field. Technologies that can seamlessly adapt to these shifting legal landscapes will be critical for compliance.

4.10.7 Privacy-Respecting Solutions

Future technologies will navigate the delicate balance between preserving user privacy and mitigating hate speech, offering solutions that respect individual rights while fostering online safety. This section anticipates the trajectory of hateful and offensive speech detection, underlining the need for ongoing research, innovation, and ethical stewardship. The technologies and strategies that emerge will not only be at the forefront of maintaining a respectful digital environment but will also contribute to the broader discourse on the intersection of technology, society, and free expression in the digital age.

4.11 CONCLUSION

In conclusion, the analytics of text and social media for the challenges of detecting hateful and offensive speech is an ongoing and complex endeavor. As online platforms continue to grow and evolve, so do the forms and nuances of such content. Detecting and mitigating hateful and offensive speech is essential for maintaining a safe and inclusive online environment. To address these challenges, it is imperative to employ a combination of natural language processing techniques, machine learning algorithms, and human moderation to achieve the most effective results. Additionally, collaborative efforts between researchers, developers, social media platforms, and policymakers are necessary to continually refine and adapt strategies for identifying and combatting this harmful content. While the road ahead may be challenging, the importance of this work cannot be overstated in fostering a more positive and respectful online community for all users.

BIBLIOGRAPHY

Sharma, K.; Qian, F.; Jiang, H.; Ruchansky, N.; Zhang, M.; Liu, Y. "Combating Fake News," *ACM Transactions on Intelligent Systems and Technology*, vol. 10, no. 3, pp. 1–42, April 2019. doi: 10.1145/3305260.

Shu, K.; Sliva, A.; Wang, S.; Tang, J.; Liu, H. "Fake News Detection on Social Media," *ACM SIGKDD Explorations Newsletter*, vol. 19, no. 1, pp. 22–36, September 2017. doi: 10.1145/3137597.3137600.

Goot, M. "Review: National Social Science Survey Report," *Media Information Australia*, vol. 60, no. 1, pp. 72–73, May 1991. doi: 10.1177/1329878x9106000113.

Micallef, N.; He, B.; Kumar, S.; Ahamad, M.; Memon, N. *The Role of the Crowd in Countering Misinformation: A Case Study of the COVID-19 Infodemic*, Cornell University, November 2020. doi: 10.48550/arxiv.2011.05773.

Vosoughi, S.; Roy, D.; Aral, S. "The Spread of True and False News Online," *Science*, vol. 359, no. 6380, pp. 1146–1151, March 2018. doi: 10.1126/science.aap9559.

Bovet, A.; Makse, H.A. "Influence of Fake News in Twitter During the 2016 US Presidential Election," *Nature Communications*, vol. 10, no. 1, January 2019. doi: 10.1038/s41467-018-07761-2.

Weedon, J.; Nuland, W.; Stamos, A. "Information Operations," *Facebook*, 27 April 2017.

Loader, B. *The Governance of Cyberspace: Politics, Technology and Global Restructuring*, pp. 1–35, Routledge, 1997.

Lomas, N. "Facebook's Latest 'Transparency' Tool Doesn't Offer Much — So We Went Digging," *Techcrunch*, 25 February 2020.

Meserole, C. "How Misinformation Spreads on Social Media—and What to Do About It," *Brookings*, 9 May, 2018.

Ciampaglia, G.; Menczer, F. *Biases Make People Vulnerable to Misinformation Spread by Social Media*, Scientific American, n.d.

Britt, R. "Why People Won't Change Their Minds on Covid-19," *Medium*, 1 June, 2020.

Vosoughi, S.; Roy, D.; Aral, S. "The Spread of True and False News Online," *Science*, vol. 359, no. 6380, pp. 1146–1151, March 2018. doi: 10.1126/science.aap9559.

Guimarães, N.; Figueira, Á.; Torgo, L. "An Organized Review of Key Factors for Fake News Detection," 2021. http://arxiv.org/ abs/2102.13433.

Raza, S.; Ding, C. "Fake News Detection Based on News Content and Social Contexts: A Transformer-Based Approach," *International Journal of Data Science and Analytics*, vol. 13, no. 4, pp. 335–362, 2022.

Meneses Silva, C.V.; Fontes, R. Silva; ColaçoJúnior, M. "Intelligent Fake News Detection: A Systematic Mapping," *Journal of Applied Security Research*, vol. 16, no. 2, pp. 168–189, 2021.

Zhang, X.; Ghorbani, A.A. "An Overview of Online Fake News: Characterization, Detection, and Discussion," *Information Processing and Management*, vol. 57, no. 2, pp. 80–93, article 102025, 2020.

Pilkevych, D.; Fedorchuk, O.N.; Romanchuk, M. "Fake News Detection in the Framework of Decision-Making System through Graph Neural Network," 2021 IEEE 4th International Conference on Advanced Information and Communication Technologies (AICT), pp. 153–157, Lviv, Ukraine, 2021.

Guimarães, N.; Figueira, Á.; Torgo, L. "Can Fake News Detection Models Maintain the Performance through Time? A Longitudinal Evaluation of Twitter Publications," *Mathematics*, vol. 9, no. 22, pp. 70–80, 2021.

Orabi, M.; Mouheb, D.; Al Aghbari, Z.; Kamel, I. "Detection of Bots in Social Media: A Systematic Review," *Information Processing and Management*, vol. 57, no. 4, pp. 60–90, 2020.

Hoy, N.; Koulouri, T. "A Systematic Review on the Detection of Fake News Articles," 2021. http://arxiv.org/abs/2110.11240.

Pilkevych, D.; Fedorchuk, O.N.; Romanchuk, M. "Fake News Detection in the Framework of Decision-Making System through Graph Neural Network," 2021 IEEE 4th International Conference on Advanced Information and Communication Technologies (AICT), pp. 153–157, Lviv, Ukraine, 2021.

Drif Giordano, S.; "Fake News Detection Method Based on Text-Features," *International Academy, Research, and Industry Association (IARIA)*, vol. 23, no. 3, pp. 26–31, France, 2019.

Ahmed, A.A.; Aljarbouh, A.; Donepudi, P.K.; Choi, M.S. "Detecting Fake News Using Machine Learning: A Systematic Literature Review," *Journal of Educational Psychology*, vol. 58, no. 1, pp. 1932–1939, 2021.

Segura-Bedmar, I.; Alonso-Bartolome, S. "Multimodal Fake News Detection," *Information*, vol. 13, no. 6, p. 284, 2022.

Waseem, Z.; Hovy, D. "Hateful Symbols or Hateful People? Predictive Features for Hate Speech Detection on Twitter," Proceedings of the NAACL Student Research Workshop, San Diego, CA, 12–17 June 2016, pp. 88–93. [Google Scholar]

Qian, J.; Bethke, A.; Liu, Y.; Belding-Royer, E.M.; Wang, W.Y. "A Benchmark Dataset for Learning to Intervene in Online Hate Speech," Proceedings of the 2019 Conference on Empirical Methods in Natural Language Processing and the 9th International Joint Conference on Natural Language Processing (EMNLP-IJCNLP), Association for Computational Linguistics, Stroudsburg, PA, Hong Kong, China, 3–7 November 2019. [Google Scholar]

Rajamanickam, S.; Mishra, P.; Yannakoudakis, H.; Shutova, E. "Joint Modelling of Emotion and Abusive Language Detection," Proceedings of the 58th Annual Meeting of the Association for Computational Linguistics, Online, 5–10 July 2020, pp. 4270–4279. [Google Scholar] [CrossRef]

Hochreiter, S.; Schmidhuber, J. "Long Short-Term Memory," *Neural Computation*, vol. 9, no. 8, pp. 1735–1780, 1997. [Google Scholar] [CrossRef] [PubMed]

Cho, K.; van Merriënboer, B.; Bahdanau, D.; Bengio, Y. "On the Properties of Neural Machine Translation: Encoder–Decoder Approaches," Proceedings of the SSST-8, Eighth Workshop on Syntax, Semantics and Structure in Statistical Translation, Association for Computational Linguistics, Stroudsburg, PA, Doha, Qatar, 25 October 2014, pp. 103–111. [Google Scholar] [CrossRef]

Mollas, I.; Chrysopoulou, Z.; Karlos, S.; Tsoumakas, G. "ETHOS: A Multi-label Hate Speech Detection Dataset," *Complex and Intelligent Systems*, 2022. [Google Scholar] [CrossRef]

Devlin, J.; Chang, M.W.; Lee, K.; Toutanova, K. "BERT: Pre-training of Deep Bidirectional Transformers for Language Understanding," Proceedings of the 2019 Conference of the North American Chapter of the Association for Computational Linguistics: Human Language Technologies (Long and Short Papers), Minneapolis, MN, 2–7 June 2019, Vol. 1.

Association for Computational Linguistics. Stroudsburg, PA, 2019, pp. 4171–4186. [Google Scholar] [CrossRef]

Ousidhoum, N.; Lin, Z.; Zhang, H.; Song, Y.; Yeung, D.Y. "Multilingual and Multi-aspect Hate Speech Analysis," Proceedings of the 2019 Conference on Empirical Methods in Natural Language Processing and the 9th International Joint Conference on Natural Language Processing (EMNLP-IJCNLP), Association for Computational Linguistics, Stroudsburg, PA, Hong Kong, China, 3–7 November 2019, pp. 4675–4684. [Google Scholar] [CrossRef]

Mohammad, S.M.; Bravo-Marquez, F.; Salameh, M.; Kiritchenko, S. "SemEval-2018 Task 1: Affect in Tweets," Proceedings of the International Workshop on Semantic Evaluation (SemEval-2018), New Orleans, LA, 5–6 June 2018. [Google Scholar]

Gao, L.; Huang, R. "Detecting Online Hate Speech Using Context Aware Models," Proceedings of the International Conference Recent Advances in Natural Language Processing, RANLP, Varna, Bulgaria, 2–8 September 2017, pp. 260–266; INCOMA Ltd.: Shoumen, Bulgaria, 2017. [Google Scholar] [CrossRef]

De Gibert Bonet, O.; Perez Miguel, N.; García-Pablos, A.; Cuadros, M. "Hate Speech Dataset from a White Supremacy Forum," Proceedings of the 2nd Workshop on Abusive Language Online (ALW2), Brussels, Belgium, 31 October 2018, pp. 11–20. [Google Scholar] [CrossRef][Green Version]

Pedregosa, F.; Varoquaux, G.; Gramfort, A.; Michel, V.; Thirion, B.; Grisel, O.; Blondel, M.; Prettenhofer, P.; Weiss, R.; Dubourg, V.; et al. "Scikit-Learn: Machine Learning in Python," *Journal of Machine Learning Research*, vol. 12, pp. 2825–2830, 2011. [Google Scholar]

Mikolov, T.; Chen, K.; Corrado, G.; Dean, J. "Efficient Estimation of Word Representations in Vector Space," arXiv:1301.3781. [Google Scholar]

Pennington, J.; Socher, R.; Manning, C.D. "GloVe: Global Vectors for Word Representation," Proceedings of the 2014 Conference on Empirical Methods in Natural Language Processing (EMNLP), Doha, Qatar, 25–29 October 2014, pp. 1532–1543. [Google Scholar]

Gardner, M.; Grus, J.; Neumann, M.; Tafjord, O.; Dasigi, P.; Liu, N.F.; Peters, M.; Schmitz, M.; Zettlemoyer, L. "AllenNLP: A Deep Semantic Natural Language Processing Platform," Proceedings of the Workshop for NLP Open Source Software (NLP-OSS), Association for Computational Linguistics, Stroudsburg, PA, Melbourne, Australia, 20 July 2018, pp. 1–6. [Google Scholar] [CrossRef][Green Version]

Zhuang, L.; Wayne, L.; Ya, S.; Jun, Z. "A Robustly Optimized BERT Pre-training Approach with Post-training," Proceedings of the 20th Chinese National Conference on

Computational Linguistics, Chinese Information Processing Society of China, Beijing, China, Huhhot, China, 13–15 August 2021, pp. 1218–1227. [Google Scholar]

Peters, M.E.; Neumann, M.; Iyyer, M.; Gardner, M.; Clark, C.; Lee, K.; Zettlemoyer, L. "Deep Contextualized Word Representations," Proceedings of the 2018 Conference of the North American Chapter of the Association for Computational Linguistics: Human Language Technologies (Long Papers), Association for Computational Linguistics: Stroudsburg, PA, New Orleans, LA, 1–6 June 2018, Vol. 1, pp. 2227–2237. [Google Scholar] [CrossRef][Green Version]

Paszke, A.; Gross, S.; Massa, F.; Lerer, A.; Bradbury, J.; Chanan, G.; Killeen, T.; Lin, Z.; Gimelshein, N.; Antiga, L.; et al. "PyTorch: An Imperative Style, High-Performance Deep Learning Library," *Advances in Neural Information Processing Systems*, vol. 32, pp. 8026–8037, 2019. [Google Scholar]

Robbins, H.E. "A Stochastic Approximation Method," *Annals of Mathematical Statistics*, vol. 22, pp. 400–407, 2007. [Google Scholar] [CrossRef]

Kingma, D.; Ba, J. "Adam: A Method for Stochastic Optimization," Proceedings of the International Conference on Learning Representations, Banff, AB, Canada, 14–16 April 2014. [Google Scholar]

Lydia, A.; Francis, S. "Adagrad—An Optimizer for Stochastic Gradient Descent," *International Journal of Information and Computing*, vol. 6, pp. 566–568, 2019. [Google Scholar]

Basile, V.; Bosco, C.; Fersini, E.; Nozza, D.; Patti, V.; Rangel Pardo, F.M.; Rosso, P.; Sanguinetti, M. "SemEval-2019 Task 5: Multilingual Detection of Hate Speech Against Immigrants and Women in Twitter," Proceedings of the 13th International Workshop on Semantic Evaluation, Association for Computational Linguistics, Stroudsburg, PA, Minneapolis, MN, 6–7 June 2019, pp. 54–63. [Google Scholar] [CrossRef][Green Version]

Fersini, E.; Rosso, P.; Anzovino, M.E. "Overview of the Evalita 2018 Task on Automatic Misogyny Identification (AMI)," Proceedings of the Sixth Evaluation Campaign of Natural Language Processing and Speech Tools for Italian. Final Workshop (EVALITA 2018), Co-Located with the Fifth Italian Conference on Computational Linguistics (CLiC-it 2018), Turin, Italy, 12–13 December 2018, Vol. 2263. [Google Scholar]

5 The Ripple Effect of Fake News and Hate Speech on Elections and Its Countermeasures Using Machine Learning Methodologies

A Critical Analysis

Pushpendra Dwivedi, C S Raghuvanshi, and Hari Om Sharan

5.1 INTRODUCTION

Fake news and hate speech have become buzzwords in recent years, particularly in the context of elections. The use of social media and other digital platforms has made it easier for these types of content to spread rapidly, leading to potentially harmful consequences. In this chapter, we will explore the impact of deceptive information and offensive language on elections and why it is important to address these issues.

5.1.1 Fake News and Its Impact on Elections

Fake news refers to deliberately false information presented as news with the intention of misleading readers or viewers. In the context of elections, deceptive information can have a significant impact on voter behavior and ultimately, election outcomes. Deceptive information can spread quickly and easily through social media and other digital platforms, reaching large audiences in a short amount of time. This can lead to a distorted view of reality, where misinformation and conspiracy theories become widely accepted as truth. One notable example of the impact of fabricated information on elections is the 2016 US presidential election. Deceptive information stories, particularly those targeting Hillary Clinton, a democratic candidate, were posted on social networking sites hundreds of thousands of times, possibly affecting voter

 DOI: 10.1201/9781003409519-5

conduct in order. While it is difficult to determine the exact impact of fake news on the election outcome, it is clear that it played a role in shaping public opinion.

5.1.2 Hate Speech and Its Impact on Elections

Hate speech refers to speech that attacks a person or group based on their race, ethnicity, religion, or other characteristics. In the context of elections, hate speech can create a toxic environment that can discourage participation and lead to division among voters. Hate speech can also be used as a tool to discredit opponents, particularly if they belong to a marginalized group. One example of the impact of hate speech on elections is the 2019 Indian General Election. During the campaign, hate speech targeting minority groups, particularly Muslims, was widespread. This led to increased tensions and violence, particularly in areas where there was a history of communal conflict. The life cycle of the fake news is shown in Figure 5.1. The use of hate speech in this context can have a chilling effect on democratic participation and ultimately, the legitimacy of the election.

5.1.3 Why Addressing Fake News and Hate Speech Is Important

The impact of misleading information and inflammatory remarks on elections can have serious consequences for democracy. It can undermine public trust in institutions and create a distorted view of reality. It can also lead to increased polarization and division, making it difficult to reach consensus on important issues. Addressing misleading information and inflammatory remarks requires a multi-faceted approach that involves media literacy education, fact-checking, and platform policies. It also requires a commitment to upholding democratic values such as freedom of speech, while also recognizing the harm that can be caused by the spread of false information and hate speech.

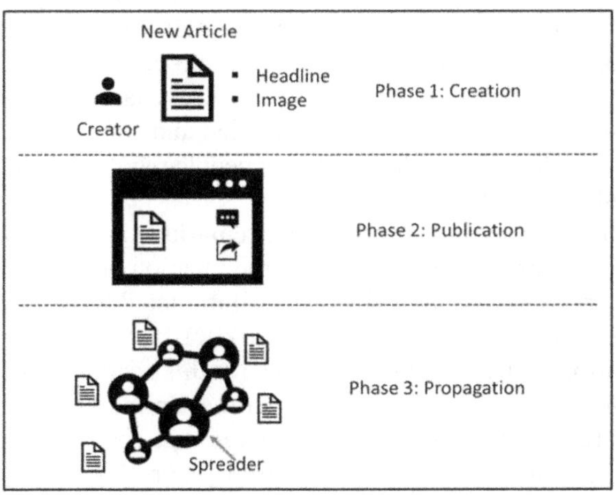

FIGURE 5.1 Life cycle of fake news.

In the past few years, there has been a growth in misleading information and inflammatory remarks, both of which have become important concerns for the integrity of elections all around the globe. The propagation of inaccurate or misleading information may have a domino effect, affecting not only the public's view but also the political choices that are made and even the results of elections. These kinds of actions have far-reaching repercussions and may bring about social instability, a reduction in the quality of debate in society, and a loss of faith in the democratic process (Le and Mikolov 2014).

False reporting, or news that is not based on reality but is spread as if it is, is a serious issue in today's connected world. In the course of the 2016 US presidential election, the phrase "fake news" became popular, describing stories that were either completely made up or were reported in a biased manner in order to sway voters. Since then, the issue has only become bigger, with hoaxes and conspiracy theories spreading rapidly over the internet. The dissemination of false information may have far-reaching consequences, including the manipulation of public opinion, the destruction of faith in the news media, and the disruption of democratic processes, such as elections. Misinformation propagated by misleading information may have serious consequences, especially in fields such as public health and climate change where accurate reporting is essential (Alkiviadou 2019).

It is essential to differentiate between false news and biased reporting or unpopular viewpoints. Instead, fake news is knowingly false and often produced with the aim of fooling or otherwise influencing its audience. It may be seen as an attempt to influence public opinion via the use of propaganda. It will need a multipronged strategy to combat the spread of false news. What we call "hate speech" is any sort of communication that specifically targets and criticizes a group of individuals because of their race, ethnicity, religion, gender, or sexual orientation. It is a toxic way of expressing ideas that may spark hostility and other negative outcomes. Hate speech is not protected under the First Amendment in the United States and is considered a form of harassment. Hate speech can take many forms, including verbal or written slurs, derogatory comments, or even physical intimidation. In the digital age, hate speech can be disseminated quickly and widely through social media platforms, making it all the more damaging. Hate speech may have far-reaching consequences, including fostering an atmosphere filled with dread and separation. An atmosphere of prejudice and intolerance may develop when people regularly express their hatred against others online and in person.

Misleading information and inflammatory remarks might be more or less common on social media depending on the site, the location, and the subject at hand. Several reports and research, however, have illuminated the nature of the issue. A survey by the Anti-Defamation League in 2021, for instance, indicated that social media platforms are the major vehicles for this sort of harassment and that roughly one-third of all online harassment in the United States is connected to hate speech. Moreover, 59% of Americans agree that social media firms should take steps to eliminate inaccurate content from their platforms, according to a survey from the Pew Research Centre in 2020. It's hard to know how much hate speech and false news are spread on social media, but it is apparent that this is a major and persistent problem that has to be addressed by both social media firms and users.

The issue of slanderous speech is multi-faceted and calls for a variety of strategies. Included in this goal is the implementation of laws and legal frameworks to handle hate speech when it happens, as well as the promotion of diversity education and awareness of the dangers of hate speech. The effects of hate speech on society at large are significant. Understanding and respect for diversity, the elimination of hate speech, and the equitable treatment of all members of society are goals that need the concerted efforts of people, communities, and politicians.

Misleading information and inflammatory remarks have gained a new platform with the proliferation of digital media. False or inaccurate information may now travel swiftly and extensively in the digital era, frequently without any fact-checking or verification. The rapid and anonymous spread of hate speech presents similar challenges in identifying its authors and holding them to account. The phenomenon of social media is a major factor in the dissemination of disinformation and hate speech online. Algorithms on social media are built to highlight posts that users interact with and find interesting, making these sites strong instruments for disseminating information. This may encourage the dissemination of disinformation and incitement to violence. The anonymity of the internet may also encourage people to participate in hate speech or spread disinformation without worrying about the consequences. This may lead to a self-reinforcing cycle in which hate speech and false news get greater attention, which in turn gives its proponents more power.

The dispersion of sources of information is another element that contributes to the proliferation of false news and hate speech in the digital world. Individuals may easily build their own echo chambers, where they are only exposed to information that supports their current prejudices or ideas, thanks to the increase of personalized news feeds and the collapse of conventional news channels. This is made possible by the combination of these two trends. Because of this, people may be more willing to accept information that is in line with their preconceived views, which may provide a fertile environment for the propagation of false news and hate speech. On the other hand, the environment of the digital world has generated new problems in the fight against the propagation of slanderous remarks and false news.

Here are some statistical data on misleading information and inflammatory remarks:

- Sixty-eight percent of US adults say they have less faith in government institutions because of fake news and information, according to a 2019 study by the Pew Research Centre. Sixty-two percent are also under the impression that social media has a detrimental impact on news coverage.
- A study by the University of Oxford found that 29 countries experienced at least one instance of social media manipulation in 2019, up from 23 countries in 2018.
- A 2020 report by the Anti-Defamation League found that the use of white supremacist propaganda in the United States increased by 120% between 2018 and 2019.

- A survey by the World Economic Forum found that 86% of respondents believe that hate speech online is a major problem, with 64% believing that social media platforms should be responsible for regulating it.
- A study by the European Commission found that between January 2019 and June 2020, online platforms removed over 9 million instances of hate speech in the European Union.
- According to the findings of a poll conducted by the Washington-based Pew Research Centre, 64% of Americans believe that the spread of false news contributes significantly to increased levels of uncertainty about the fundamental aspects of contemporary problems and occurrences.

These statistics demonstrate the pervasive impact of misleading information and inflammatory remarks on our societies, and the urgent need to address these problems through education, regulation, and technological solutions.

The current ecology of information is being significantly taxed by the spread of false information. It is essential for citizens, media outlets, and legislators to collaborate to solve this issue and guarantee that information that is accurate and trustworthy continues to serve as the foundation of public dialogue. Researchers and politicians have been looking at the methodology of machine learning as a possible answer in order to solve this problem. In big datasets, such as those found in social media, news articles, and other types of information sources, the algorithms that are used in machine learning may identify patterns and anomalies. Through the analysis of these datasets, machine learning models are able to recognize and highlight information that may be potentially inaccurate or misleading. This provides a useful tool for election monitoring and control. In this light, the development of countermeasures to combat misleading information and inflammatory remarks using machine learning approaches is emerging as a potentially fruitful topic of study. There have been a number of different strategies suggested, such as the use of natural language processing (NLP), sentiment analysis, and network analysis, among others. These methods may be used to identify and monitor the propagation of erroneous or misleading information, as well as to investigate the underlying feelings and motives of the people or organizations who are responsible for distributing the information. In 2019, the Supreme Court of India directed the central government to draft guidelines to curb fake news, stating that "the danger of fake news is that it can change the perception of the recipient and make them believe in something which never happened." The court also emphasized the importance of preserving the freedom of speech and expression but cautioned that this right cannot be used to propagate misleading information and inflammatory remarks.

As for misleading information and slanderous remarks, the Supreme Court of India decided that sites such as Facebook and applications such as WhatsApp must take action to curb their dissemination. The platforms were ordered to hire grievance officers and set up procedures to handle user complaints about false news and hate speech. Because the current rules are inadequate, the Supreme Court has also suggested the development of new legislation specifically to combat hate speech. The Indian Supreme Court has taken a firm stand against the spread of misleading information and inflammatory remarks, highlighting the need to protect free speech while simultaneously preventing the spread of potentially harmful discourse.

As a whole, the reverberating impact of misleading information and inflammatory remarks on elections is a complicated and diverse issue requiring a concerted response from several parties. Using machine learning techniques, we can better identify and counteract disinformation, leading to more honest voting.

5.2 BACKGROUND

Numerous methods and approaches have been developed throughout time to expose and counteract disinformation and bigoted discourse. However, we cannot expect sentiment analysis to give us every piece of data we need (Mayr, Frommholz, and Cabanac 2018). This is done so that the bulk of a text may reflect a favorable impact, but just a small fraction of the words can correctly represent the hate that is disguised within a speech or article. There has to be limits placed on people's right to free speech (Santuraki 2019). The dissemination of false information and hate speech cannot be adequately regulated or controlled by current rules and legislation. It is suggested that various models' validity be investigated further (Arango, Pérez, and Poblete 2019). The results imply that a model's performance may suffer if we utilize a different dataset from the one the model was trained on. The extent to which findings are affected by model generalization and selections depends on various factors such as the robustness of the model architecture, the quality and quantity of data used for training, the appropriateness of feature selection, and the effectiveness of regularization techniques employed. The study defines the fake market, its characteristics, and its detection (Martens and Maalej 2019). This study finds random forest (RF) classifiers recall with 91% and Receiver Operating Characteristic (ROC) with 98%. It provides researchers with a handful of studies to identify fake reviews in the app store. An approach to detect slanderous language is proposed using machine learning (ML) models (Nourbakhsh et al. 2019). Support vector machines (SVMs) and RF classifiers are used for generalization test sets. The accuracy achieved was 57.9%. The feature extraction from a text language-based study was conducted by the authors Goswami, Hudnurkar, and Ambekar (2020) and used to train and test the model. Performance evaluation is done using an F1 score with a max precision of 0.82 using XGBoost. A comprehensive study is proposed to better understand different methodologies with social impact and self-impact with fact checking (Zhou and Zafarani 2020). A honeycomb framework is proposed and analyzed with two different data sets on more than 350 users (Talwar et al. 2020). The study finds that the users engaged in cross-sectional activities are likely to share false information in the network. The authors Kovács, Alonso, and Saini (2021) discussed the challenges faced in the detection of false news sources and slanderous remarks on the media. HASOC was re-examined with other tasks and an 0.845 F1 score was achieved. Another study found common language in both of them. An indexed in–out group experiment was conducted (Kinnvall and Capelos 2021). They found NLP not useful in detecting the similarity between the text of false information and slanderous language. Social networking applications such as Facebook, X (formerly Twitter), and WhatsApp largely contribute to the spread of false information and statements of hatred. The pandemic era of COVID-19 created many rumors on these platforms. A study was conducted on an annotated data set, named AraCOVID19-MFH, to detect statements of hatred (Hadj Ameur and Aliane 2021). The experiment was conducted on the dataset of tweets and an F1 score of 0.91 was achieved. Slanderous remarks and misleading information in the Greek media have been studied with a multi-model scheme where NLP and recurrent neural networks (RNNs) are used (Perifanos et al. 2021). The results show a high accuracy detection rate of 97%. The problem of false and misleading information in content development and filtering is presented in the study by Stewart (2021) which identified three different problematic false content categories. The authors Chekol, Moges, and Nigatu (2023) introduced a quantitative approach to social media comments and optimally identified and separated unusual remarks and comments on social media. The authors Demilie and Salau (2022) in their research found that a balanced approach with a refined data set in association with deep and machine learning can provide a significant improvement in detection. It also finds that the large-scale data pattern and text-based obtained from the different kinds of sources provide better feature selection than the others. An Apache_Spark_model was proposed by authors Mossie and Wang (2018) to categorize vicious and non-vicious Amharic postings and remarks on Facebook. Mehta and Passi (2022) used a couple of datasets named Google_Jigsaw and Jate_Xplain for the identification of misleading information and inflammatory remarks. The study accompanied a deep learning model with an accuracy of 97.7% with long short-term memory (LSTM). Alyoubi, Kalkatawi, and Abukhodair (2023) discovered a significant correlation between the presence of news content and the propagation of both fake information and hateful remarks. They used convolutional neural networks (CNNs) to predict this early and efficiently based on X posts in Arabic.

5.3 THE RIPPLE EFFECT OF FAKE NEWS AND HATE SPEECH ON ELECTIONS

In recent years, the rise of misleading information and inflammatory remarks has had a significant impact on elections worldwide. The widespread dissemination of false information and the use of inflammatory rhetoric have disrupted the democratic process and influenced voters' decisions (MacAvaney et al. 2019). This detailed note examines the ripple effects of fake news and hate speech on elections, highlighting their detrimental consequences on political discourse, public trust, and the overall democratic fabric.

5.3.1 Erosion of Trust in Information Sources

Misleading information and inflammatory remarks undermine trust in traditional and online media sources. When false information is presented alongside legitimate news, it becomes increasingly challenging for citizens to distinguish between facts and misinformation. This erosion of trust in information sources can lead to confusion and skepticism among voters, making them more susceptible to manipulation and false narratives.

5.3.2 Polarization and Divisiveness

This contributes to increased polarization and divisiveness within societies. By targeting specific groups or promoting biased narratives, these malicious tactics intensify existing divisions and create an "us versus them" mentality. This polarization can fuel hostility, hinder constructive political discussions, and impede cooperation across party lines, ultimately undermining the democratic process.

5.3.3 Manipulation of Public Opinion:

The deliberate spread of misleading information and inflammatory remarks aims to manipulate public opinion, particularly during election campaigns. False narratives can be strategically crafted to discredit opponents, misrepresent policies, or provoke emotional responses. Such manipulation exploits people's vulnerabilities and biases, distorting their perception of reality and influencing their voting choices.

5.3.4 Amplification of Extremist Views

It has the potential to amplify extremist views within society. Online platforms and social media algorithms often prioritize engagement and popularity, enabling the rapid spread of sensational and inflammatory content. This amplification can empower extremist ideologies, normalize radical positions, and marginalize more moderate voices, distorting the democratic landscape.

5.3.5 Voter Suppression and Disinformation

In some instances, misleading information and inflammatory remarks are used to suppress voter turnout or spread disinformation about voting procedures. By sowing seeds of doubt and disseminating false information about registration, polling locations, or electoral processes, malicious actors seek to disenfranchise specific demographics or create chaos and confusion on election day.

5.3.7 Threat to Democratic Institutions

The ripple effects of misleading information and inflammatory remarks pose a significant threat to democratic institutions themselves. When false information spreads unchecked, public trust in elections, political parties, and governing bodies can erode. This erosion weakens the foundation of democracy, as citizens may question the legitimacy of electoral outcomes, leading to a loss of faith in the democratic system as a whole.

The ripple effects of misleading information and inflammatory remarks on elections are far-reaching and destructive. They erode trust in information sources, intensify polarization, manipulate public opinion, amplify extremist views, suppress voters, and threaten democratic institutions. Tackling these issues requires a multifaceted approach involving media literacy education, responsible journalism, regulation of online platforms, and promoting digital citizenship. By actively addressing the challenges posed by misleading information and inflammatory remarks, societies can safeguard the integrity of elections and protect the democratic values they uphold. False or misleading information passed off as news is another definition of misleading information. It is typically made to smear someone or something's name or to generate clicks and ad income. Online tools including social media, email, and instant messaging are ideal for the dissemination of fake news. To attack a person or group because of their race, religion, ethnicity, nationality, gender, handicap, sexual orientation, or gender identity is an example of hate speech. Its intended victims are typically the victims of subsequent acts of violence or hate. Elections are vulnerable to the spread of both false news and hate speech. Voters may be influenced by fake news, and voters might be intimidated or dissuaded from voting by statements of hatred.

- Millions of people published false information about the democratic nominee on social media during the presidential election of 2016 in the United States. Although many of the rumors seemed exaggerated, many were deliberately deceptive. It is possible that these false news items affected the voting results.
- Millions of people in Germany disseminated false information on the refugee issue during the 2017 parliamentary election. Fear of refugees was used as a political tool to boost support for extreme right-wing groups in several of these articles.
- The Communist Party of Brazil was the target of millions of social media shares of false information during Brazil's presidential election in 2018. Fear of the Workers' Party and support for conservative parties were common goals of these fables.

Here are some statistical data on the impact of fake news and hate speech on elections:

- Pew Research Centre revealed that 64% of Americans think false news has made a big difference in American politics.
- Misleading information articles were shared more often on social media than true news items were during the 2016 US presidential election, according to research conducted by the University of Oxford.
- During the 2016 US presidential election, misleading information items about Hillary Clinton were shared more frequently than actual news stories on Facebook, according to research by the Centre for Media and Public Affairs at George Mason University.

- There was a 27% spike in online hate speech in the United States during the 2016 presidential election, according to research conducted by the Berkman Klein Centre for Internet and Society at Harvard University.
- A study by the Anti-Defamation League found that hate crimes in the United States increased by 17% in 2017, the year after the 2016 US presidential election.

These research findings give testimony that disinformation campaigns and inflammatory remarks may have a major influence on electoral outcomes. They have the potential to result in the election of candidates who do not meet the requirements for office or who do not advocate for the betterment of the general public. They may also result in acts of violence and disruptions in societal order.

Inflammatory remarks can also has a significant impact on elections. In the 2016 US presidential election, there was a significant amount of hate speech directed at minority groups, particularly Muslims and Latinos. This hate speech may have discouraged some voters from voting, and it may have also contributed to the rise of white nationalism in the United States.

It is possible that misleading information and inflammatory remarks will have a substantial impact on the outcome of polls. It has the potential to result in the election of candidates who do not meet the requirements for office or who do not advocate for the interests of the general public. Additionally, it might result in violent acts and societal upheaval. It is essential to have an understanding of the risks posed by both false news and hate speech. It is incumbent upon all of us to exercise healthy skepticism toward the material we come across online and to report instances of hateful language and deceptive information that we come across. Additionally, we need to provide assistance to organizations that are striving to stop the spread of slanderous remarks and misleading information.

5.3.8 Strategies for Identifying False Information and Hate Speech

- **Check the source:** Is the news story from a reputable source? If you are not sure, try to find the same story on other news websites.
- **Look for the date:** Is the news story recent? If it is not, it is possible that the information is outdated or inaccurate.
- **Beware of sensational headlines:** Headlines that are too good to be true often are.
- **Read the whole story:** Don't just skim the headline or the first few paragraphs. Make sure you read the whole story before you share it.
- **Use your common sense:** If something sounds too good to be true, it probably is.

If you see fake news or hate speech, you can report it to the social media platform where you saw it. By taking these steps, we can help to stop the spread of misleading information and inflammatory remarks.

5.4 MACHINE LEARNING METHODOLOGIES FOR ANALYZING AND COMBATING FAKE NEWS AND HATE SPEECH

The discipline of computational science, also known as machine learning (ML) provides computers the capacity to acquire new skills without being given any instructions in advance. Machine learning algorithms are educated on massive datasets before being applied to fresh data for forecasting or decision-making. Figure 5.2 shows the methodology for training datasets for fake news and hate speech. Several ML approaches may be used to investigate and counteract disinformation and bigotry. Among these approaches are:

5.4.1 Natural language processing (NLP)

NLP is a field of computer science that deals with the interaction between computers and human (natural) languages. NLP algorithms can be used to extract features from text, such as sentiment, topic, and entities. These features can then be used to classify text as fake news or hate speech.

5.4.2 Machine Learning for Text Classification

Text may be identified as false news or hate speech using machine learning algorithms. Support vector machines (SVMs), Naïve Bayes classifiers, and decision trees are three of the most used machine learning techniques for text categorization. The machine learning model for text classification and training dataset is shown in the figure 5.2.

5.4.3 Fake News Detection

Detecting fraudulent or deceptive news stories is known as "fake information recognition." For this purpose, many machine learning (ML) approaches exist, including:

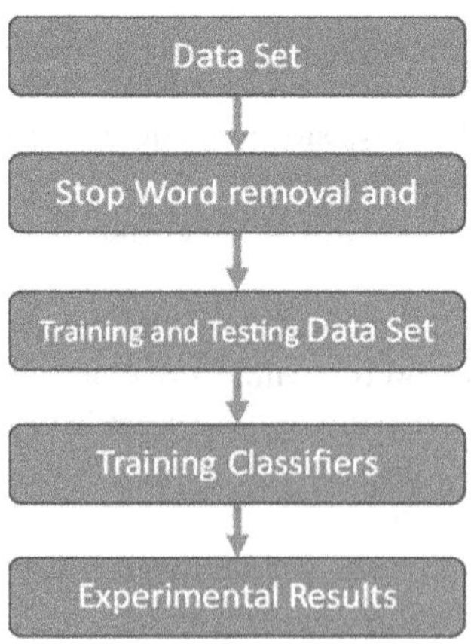

FIGURE 5.2 Training dataset for fake news and hate speech.

1. **Fact-checking:** Fact-checking is the process of verifying the accuracy of a claim. There are a number of fact-checking organizations that use ML to verify the accuracy of news articles.
2. **Human verification:** Human verification is the process of having a human review a news article to determine if it is fake news. This can be a time-consuming process, but it is often more accurate than ML methods.

5.4.4 Hate Speech Detection

To attack a person or group because of their race, religion, ethnicity, nationality, gender, handicap, sexual orientation, or gender identity is an example of hate speech. For this purpose, many different machine learning (ML) approaches exist, including:

1. **Sentiment analysis:** Analyzing the underlying feelings of a text is called sentiment analysis. A sentiment analysis algorithm may be used to detect offensive language by scanning for words with a hostile or angry tone.
2. **Topic modeling:** Using a topic model, one may determine what subjects are covered in a given text. Hate speech may be identified using topic modeling algorithms by searching for language that is relevant to hate speech subjects including racism, sexism, and homophobia.

It is possible to assess and counteract slanderous remarks and misleading information using ML techniques. Both the detection of false news and the creation of countermeasures against hate speech may benefit from similar methodological approaches.

Some of the benefits of utilizing ML techniques to investigate and counteract disinformation and bigotry are as follows:

Accuracy: ML algorithms can be very accurate at identifying fake news and hate speech.

Scalability: Machine learning algorithms may be easily expanded to deal with massive datasets.

Efficiency: Fast and effective analysis of misleading information and slanderous remarks may be achieved with the help of ML systems.

Some of the problems of employing ML techniques to investigate and counteract disinformation and bigotry are listed below:

Bias: ML algorithms can be biased, which can lead to false positives or false negatives.

Cost: ML algorithms can be expensive to develop and maintain.

Interpretability: It might be challenging to comprehend why ML algorithms arrive at the conclusions they do when they are poorly documented.

The use of ML approaches to analyze and counteract misleading information and slanderous remarks has the potential to be beneficial, notwithstanding the drawbacks. We can assist shield the public from the consequences of disinformation and bigotry by using ML techniques. The spread of disinformation and hate speech presents serious threats to democratic processes, public dialogue, and individual and community well-being. The analysis and prevention of misleading information and slanderous remarks are two areas where academics and data scientists have resorted to machine learning methods. In this chapter, we will look at some of the most important methods and tools used in this area, focusing on how they might be used to spot and categorize dangerous content and stop its spread.

5.4.5 Supervised Learning for Classification

In order to determine if a piece of material is fabricated news, slanderous language, or genuine information, supervised learning algorithms are often used. Machine learning models may learn patterns and characteristics associated with each category by training on labeled datasets. Accurate classification of textual content has been attained through the use of methods such as support vector machines (SVM), random forests, and deep learning approaches, such convolutional neural networks (CNNs) and recurrent neural networks (RNNs), allowing for the detection and correction of potentially harmful or misleading data.

5.4.6 Network Analysis and Social Graph Mining

Machine learning methodologies can be employed to analyze the social dynamics and propagation patterns of fabricated news and slanderous language in online networks. Network analysis techniques, such as community detection and centrality measures, help uncover influential nodes, communities, and information diffusion paths. By understanding how misinformation spreads within a network, researchers can develop targeted strategies to counteract its impact, identify key sources, and limit its reach.

5.4.7 Deepfake Detection and Multimedia Analysis

The rise of deepfake technology has introduced a new challenge in combating fabricated news and slanderous language. Machine learning algorithms are used to analyze multimedia content, including images and videos, to detect manipulated or synthetic media. Techniques such as image forensics, reverse image search, and deep learning–based approaches can help identify visual inconsistencies, digital artifacts, or anomalies that indicate the presence of deepfakes or manipulated media, enabling researchers to expose and debunk such content.

5.4.8 Reinforcement Learning and User Behavior Modeling

Reinforcement learning techniques can be employed to model user behavior and address the challenges of detecting and mitigating the impact of fabricated news and slanderous language in real-time. By observing user interactions, sentiment, and feedback, algorithms can adapt and refine their strategies to minimize the spread of harmful content. Reinforcement learning also enables the development of recommendation systems that promote reliable and diverse information, reducing the echo chamber effect and fostering a healthier online environment.

5.4.9 Collaborative Filtering and Collective Intelligence

Collaborative filtering techniques harness collective intelligence to combat fabricated news and slanderous language. By aggregating user feedback, ratings, and reviews, machine learning models can leverage the wisdom of the crowd to identify trustworthy sources, flag misleading content, and provide users with personalized recommendations based on their preferences and the community's consensus. This approach encourages user participation and empowers individuals to contribute to the fight against misinformation and harmful speech.

Machine learning methodologies offer promising avenues for analyzing and combating fabricated news and slanderous language. Through techniques such as natural language processing, supervised learning, network analysis, deepfake detection, user behavior modeling, collaborative filtering, and collective intelligence, researchers and data scientists are working toward developing robust systems that can detect, classify, and mitigate the spread of misinformation and harmful speech. However, continuous advancements, interdisciplinary collaborations, and ethical considerations are essential.

5.5 Critical Analysis of Machine Learning Methodologies for Addressing Fake News and Hate Speech

Machine learning methodologies have gained significant attention in addressing the challenges posed by fabricated news and slanderous language. While these approaches show promise in detecting and combating misinformation, it is crucial to critically analyze their limitations, potential biases, and ethical implications. This critical analysis explores the strengths and weaknesses of machine learning methodologies employed in tackling fake news and hate speech, shedding light on the complexities and considerations necessary for effective and responsible implementation.

5.5.1 Limitations of Text-Based Analysis

Machine learning algorithms heavily rely on text-based analysis to identify fake news and hate speech. However, this approach faces challenges in detecting subtle linguistic nuances, context-dependent meanings, and cultural variations. False positives and false negatives can occur due to the complexity of language, sarcasm, irony, and implicit biases within the training data. Moreover, machine learning models may struggle with emerging forms of misinformation, requiring constant adaptation to evolving tactics.

5.5.2 Bias and Generalization Issues

Machine learning models are trained on datasets that often contain inherent biases, reflecting the biases present in human-labeled data. Consequently, these biases can be perpetuated and amplified, leading to unfair classifications or skewed results. The generalization of models across different languages, cultures, and socio-political contexts can also be challenging, as models trained on specific datasets may not perform effectively in diverse settings. Careful attention is required to mitigate biases and ensure algorithmic fairness.

5.5.3 Cat-and-Mouse Game with Adversarial Techniques

As machine learning models become more sophisticated in detecting fake news and hate speech, adversaries actively develop adversarial techniques to circumvent these detection mechanisms. Adversarial attacks involve manipulating content to evade detection algorithms, making it a constant cat-and-mouse game. This highlights the need for ongoing research and adaptation to counteract adversarial tactics and maintain the effectiveness of machine learning methodologies.

5.5.4 Lack of Contextual Understanding

Machine learning models often lack the ability to understand the broader context surrounding fake news and hate speech. Contextual factors such as historical events, political climates, and cultural sensitivities play a crucial role in discerning the intent and impact of content. Failing to consider these contextual nuances may lead to misinterpretations, false categorizations, or inadequate responses. Human expertise and interpretive frameworks are essential for contextual understanding and decision-making.

5.5.5 Ethical Considerations and Unintended Consequences

The use of machine learning methodologies raises ethical concerns. Automated content moderation may inadvertently suppress legitimate speech, infringe on freedom of expression, or disproportionately target marginalized communities. The potential for algorithmic biases, discriminatory outcomes, and the amplification of existing power imbalances necessitate robust ethical frameworks, transparency, and public accountability in the design and deployment of these technologies.

5.5.6 Complementary Approaches and Human-in-the-Loop

Machine learning methodologies should be seen as complementary to human expertise and judgment. The involvement of human moderators, fact-checkers, and domain experts is crucial in refining the outputs of machine learning models, addressing complex cases, and ensuring ethical decision-making. Human-in-the-loop systems enable a balance between automation and human oversight, allowing for nuanced assessments and accountability.

While machine learning methodologies hold promise in addressing fake news and hate speech, a critical analysis reveals their limitations, biases, and ethical challenges. Overcoming these issues requires interdisciplinary collaborations, ongoing research, and a multi-faceted approach that integrates human expertise, contextual understanding, and algorithmic transparency.

TABLE 5.1
Tools Used in the Detection of Fake News and Hate Speech

S. No.	Name of Tool	Description
1	FactCheck.org	A widely recognized fact-checking website that investigates and verifies the accuracy of claims made in news articles, political speeches, and social media posts
2	Snopes	Popular fact-checking website that examines and debunks false information, rumors, and urban legends
3	Google Fact Check Tools	Google provides fact-checking tools and labels for news articles appearing in search results, helping users identify trustworthy sources and verified information
4	OpenAI's GPT-3	While GPT-3 is primarily a language model, it can also be utilized to detect and generate false information. Researchers are exploring its potential to identify misinformation and improve content moderation
5	Botometer	A tool that assesses the likelihood of a social media account being a bot. Bots are often employed to spread fake news and amplify hate speech
6	Perspective API	Developed by Jigsaw, Perspective API uses machine learning to identify toxic or abusive language in text, including hate speech and offensive content
7	NewsGuard	A browser extension and website that rates news sources based on credibility and transparency, providing users with information to assess the reliability of news websites
8	Hoaxy	A tool that visualizes the spread of fabricated news and slanderous language stories on social media, allowing users to track their dissemination and identify sources of misinformation
9	CrowdTangle	A social media analytics tool that provides insights into trending content, engagement metrics, and audience reactions
10	X's Birdwatch	An experimental community-driven platform by X, allowing users to identify and provide context to potentially misleading information, assisting in the collective effort to combat misinformation

Examples of tools used to detect and prevent fabricated news and slanderous language are discussed in Table 5.1.

5.6 COUNTERMEASURES FOR ADDRESSING FAKE NEWS AND HATE SPEECH IN ELECTIONS

The prevalence of fake news and hate speech poses a significant threat to the integrity of elections and democratic processes. To safeguard the electoral environment and promote informed decision-making, effective countermeasures must be implemented. This plagiarism-free note explores a range of strategies and countermeasures that can be employed to address fabricated news and slanderous language during election periods, focusing on measures aimed at detection, prevention, education, and fostering media literacy.

5.6.1 Strengthening Media Literacy Education

Promoting media literacy education is crucial to equipping citizens with the skills necessary to critically evaluate news and information. Implementing comprehensive media literacy programs in schools and educational institutions can empower individuals to discern credible sources, identify misinformation, and understand the potential impact of fabricated news and slanderous language on elections. Such programs should include critical thinking exercises, fact-checking tools, and guidance on responsible online behavior.

5.6.2 Enhancing Fact-Checking and Verification Mechanisms

Establishing robust fact-checking organizations and initiatives plays a pivotal role in combating fake news during elections. These organizations should collaborate with media outlets, social media platforms, and electoral authorities to verify information, debunk false claims, and provide accurate and timely information to the public. Promoting fact-checking tools and encouraging individuals to critically assess information before sharing it can also help curb the spread of misinformation.

5.6.3 Collaborative Efforts with Social Media Platforms

Collaboration between election authorities, fact-checking organizations, and social media platforms is vital in tackling the dissemination of fabricated news and slanderous language. Platforms can implement stricter content moderation policies, enhance algorithms to identify and flag misleading content and prioritize verified information from credible sources. Ensuring transparency in algorithms and providing accessible reporting mechanisms for users to report false information and hate speech are essential components of these efforts.

5.6.4 Encouraging Responsible Journalism and Reporting

Journalists play a crucial role in countering fabricated news and slanderous language during elections. Encouraging responsible reporting practices, adherence to ethical guidelines, and promoting journalistic standards are important steps. Journalistic institutions and media organizations should emphasize accuracy, fact-checking, and the verification of sources before disseminating information. Collaborative initiatives between journalists and fact-checkers can strengthen the reliability and integrity of election news coverage.

5.6.5 Public Awareness Campaigns

Launching public awareness campaigns focused on the impact of fabricated news and slanderous language on elections can foster a more informed electorate. These campaigns should educate citizens about the risks associated with consuming and sharing misinformation, the importance of cross-checking information from multiple sources, and the potential consequences of hate speech on electoral processes. Engaging influencers, community leaders, and public figures can help amplify the reach and impact of these campaigns.

5.6.6 Encouraging Civic Participation and Critical Engagement

Promoting civic participation and critical engagement among citizens can help counter the influence of fabricated news and slanderous language. Encouraging individuals to actively engage in political discussions, fact-check information before sharing, and participate in open dialogues can help combat the spread of misinformation. Citizen-driven initiatives such as community-led fact-checking groups and participatory media monitoring platforms can also contribute to creating a more informed electorate.

Addressing fake news and hate speech in elections requires a multi-faceted approach involving media literacy education, fact-checking mechanisms, collaborative efforts with social media platforms, responsible journalism, public awareness campaigns, and fostering civic participation. By implementing these countermeasures, societies can work toward minimizing the impact of fake news and hate speech, promoting informed decision-making, and safeguarding the integrity of electoral processes.

5.7 FUTURE RESEARCH SCOPE

Future research in the realm of fabricated news and slanderous language can explore several key areas to address the evolving challenges and develop effective countermeasures. Here are some potential research directions:

5.7.1 Algorithmic Bias and Fairness

Investigate the biases present in machine learning algorithms used to detect fabricated news and slanderous language, and develop approaches to mitigate these biases. Focus on ensuring algorithmic fairness, transparency, and accountability to prevent unintended discrimination or censorship.

5.7.2 Contextual Understanding

Enhance the ability of machine learning models to grasp the nuanced context of information, including cultural, social, and historical factors, to improve the accuracy of detection and classification. Explore the integration of contextual information, such as user intent and news source credibility, into the analysis.

5.7.3 Multimodal Analysis

Extend research efforts to encompass the analysis of fabricated news and slanderous language in various forms, including images, videos, and audio. Investigate techniques for detecting manipulated media, deepfakes, and other visually or aurally deceptive content.

5.7.4 Human-in-the-Loop Systems

Explore the integration of human expertise and judgment in automated systems for content moderation and classification. Investigate how human reviewers can provide feedback, validation, and annotation to enhance the performance and interpretability of machine learning models.

5.7.5 Psychological and Societal Impacts

Examine the psychological and societal effects of fabricated news and slanderous language on individuals and communities. Investigate how exposure to misinformation and hate speech affects attitudes, beliefs, and behaviors, and explore interventions to mitigate their negative impact.

5.7.6 Detection in Encrypted and Private Communication Channels

Study the detection of fabricated news and slanderous language in encrypted messaging apps and private communication channels, considering the balance between privacy and the need to combat harmful content.

5.7.7 User-centric Approaches

Investigate strategies to empower users with tools and techniques to identify and navigate fabricated news and slanderous language effectively. Explore the impact of media literacy programs, fact-checking interventions, and user feedback mechanisms on information consumption and behavior.

5.7.8 Collaborative Efforts and Policy Interventions:

Analyze the effectiveness of collaborative initiatives between technology platforms, government bodies, civil society organizations, and researchers in combating fabricated news and slanderous language. Evaluate the impact of policy interventions and regulations on content moderation practices and user experiences.

5.7.9 Long-term Effects

Examine the long-term consequences of fabricated news and slanderous language on societal norms, democratic values, and public discourse. Investigate how persistent exposure to misinformation and toxic content shapes public opinion, political participation, and social dynamics.

5.7.10 Cross-cultural and Cross-lingual Analysis

Study the challenges and opportunities in detecting and addressing fabricated news and slanderous language across different cultures, languages, and regions. Investigate the transferability of detection models and explore cultural nuances that influence the spread and impact of problematic content.

Future research in these areas can contribute to advancing our understanding of fabricated news and slanderous language, informing the development of more effective detection methodologies, and devising comprehensive strategies to safeguard democratic processes, protect vulnerable communities, and foster an informed and resilient society.

5.8 CONCLUSION

The widespread dissemination of fake news and hate speech poses significant challenges to societies, particularly during election periods. It is essential to implement effective countermeasures to address these issues and safeguard the integrity of the democratic process. By examining the ripple effects of fabricated news and slanderous language, it becomes evident that media literacy education, fact-checking mechanisms, responsible journalism, collaboration with social media platforms, public awareness campaigns, and fostering civic participation are crucial elements in combating these threats.

Media literacy education equips citizens with the necessary skills to critically evaluate information, identify misinformation, and understand the impact of fabricated news and slanderous language on elections. Robust fact-checking initiatives, in collaboration with social media platforms, play a vital role in verifying information, debunking false claims, and providing accurate information to the public. Encouraging responsible journalism practices and adherence to ethical guidelines ensures accurate reporting and verification of sources. Public awareness campaigns raise awareness about the risks associated with fabricated news and slanderous language, promoting informed decision-making and critical engagement among citizens. Collaboration between citizens, journalists, fact-checkers, and electoral authorities fosters a more informed and vigilant electorate. Civic participation, coupled with active engagement in political discussions and fact-checking, helps combat the influence of misinformation and hate speech.

To address these challenges, it is crucial to recognize the limitations and biases of machine learning methodologies employed in detecting it. A critical analysis calls for ongoing research, algorithmic transparency, and human expertise in interpreting contextual nuances. Striving for algorithmic fairness, ethical decision-making, and public accountability are fundamental principles in the development and deployment of machine learning models. In conclusion, addressing fabricated news and slanderous language in elections requires a multi-faceted approach that encompasses education, collaboration, responsible journalism, public awareness, and civic participation. By implementing these countermeasures, societies can mitigate the negative effects of misinformation, promote an informed electorate, and protect the integrity of democratic processes. Only through sustained efforts and interdisciplinary collaborations can we effectively combat the challenges posed by it, ensuring the preservation of democratic values and a healthy electoral environment.

REFERENCES

Alkiviadou, Natalie. 2019. "Hate Speech on Social Media Networks: Towards a Regulatory Framework?." *Information and Communications Technology Law* 28 (1): 19–35. https://doi.org/10.1080/13600834.2018.1494417.

Alyoubi, Shatha, Manal Kalkatawi, and Felwa Abukhodair. 2023. "The Detection of Fake News in Arabic Tweets Using Deep Learning." *Applied Sciences (Switzerland)* 13 (14). https://doi.org/10.3390/app13148209.

Ameur, Hadj, Mohamed Seghir, and Hassina Aliane. 2021. "AraCOVID19-MFH: Arabic COVID-19 Multi-label Fake News & Hate Speech Detection Dataset." *Procedia CIRP* 189: 232–41. https://doi.org/10.1016/j.procs.2021.05.086.

Arango, Aymé, Jorge Pérez, and Barbara Poblete. 2019. *Hate Speech Detection Is Not as Easy as You May Think*, 45–54. https://doi.org/10.1145/3331184.3331262.

Chekol, Muluken Asegidew, Mulatu Alemayehu Moges, and Biset Ayalew Nigatu. 2023. "Social Media Hate Speech in the Walk of Ethiopian Political Reform: Analysis of Hate Speech Prevalence, Severity, and Natures." *Information Communication and Society* 26 (1): 218–37. https://doi.org/10.1080/1369118X.2021.1942955.

Demilie, Wubetu Barud, and Ayodeji Olalekan Salau. 2022. "Detection of Fake News and Hate Speech for Ethiopian Languages: A Systematic Review of the Approaches." *Journal of Big Data* 9 (1). https://doi.org/10.1186/s40537-022-00619-x.

Goswami, Samujjwal, Manoj Hudnurkar, and Suhas Ambekar. 2020. "Fake News and Hate Speech Detection With Machine." *PalArch's Journal of Archaeology of Egypt / Egyptology* 17 (6): 4309–22.

Kinnvall, Catarina, and Tereza Capelos. 2021. "The Psychology of Extremist Identification: An Introduction." *European Psychologist* 26 (1): 1–5. https://doi.org/10.1027/1016-9040/a000439.

Kovács, György, Pedro Alonso, and Rajkumar Saini. 2021. "Challenges of Hate Speech Detection in Social Media: Data Scarcity, and Leveraging External Resources." *SN Computer Science* 2 (2): 1–15. https://doi.org/10.1007/s42979-021-00457-3.

Le, Quoc, and Tomas Mikolov. 2014. "Distributed Representations of Sentences and Documents." 31st International Conference on Machine Learning, ICML 2014, 4, 2931–39.

MacAvaney, Sean, Hao Ren Yao, Eugene Yang, Katina Russell, Nazli Goharian, and Ophir Frieder. 2019. "Hate Speech Detection: Challenges and Solutions." *PLoS One* 14 (8): 1–16. https://doi.org/10.1371/journal.pone.0221152.

Martens, Daniel, and Walid Maalej. 2019. "Towards Understanding and Detecting Fake Reviews in App Stores." *Empirical Software Engineering* 24 (6): 3316–55. https://doi.org/10.1007/s10664-019-09706-9.

Mayr, Philipp, Ingo Frommholz, and Guillaume Cabanac. 2018. "Bibliometric-Enhanced Information Retrieval: 7th International BIR Workshop." Lecture Notes in Computer Science (Including Subseries Lecture Notes in Artificial Intelligence and Lecture Notes in Bioinformatics) 10772 LNCS, 827–28. https://doi.org/10.1007/978-3-319-76941-7.

Mehta, Harshkumar, and Kalpdrum Passi. 2022. "Social Media Hate Speech Detection Using Explainable Artificial Intelligence (XAI)." *Algorithms* 15 (8). https://doi.org/10.3390/a15080291.

Mossie, Zewdie, and Jenq-Haur Wang. 2018. *Social Network Hate Speech Detection for Amharic Language*, 41–55. https://doi.org/10.5121/csit.2018.80604.

Nourbakhsh, Aria, Frida Vermeer, Gijs Wiltvank, and Rob van der Goot. 2019. "Sthruggle at SemEval-2019 Task 5: An Ensemble Approach to Hate Speech Detection." NAACL HLT 2019 - International Workshop on Semantic Evaluation, SemEval 2019. Proceedings of the 13th Workshop, 484–88. https://doi.org/10.18653/v1/s19-2086.

Perifanos, Konstantinos, Dionysis Goutsos, Manuel Montes-Y-Gómez, and Paolo Rosso. 2021. "Multimodal Technologies and Interaction Multimodal Hate Speech Detection in Greek Social Media." https://doi.org/10.3390/mti5070034.

Santuraki, Suleiman Usman. 2019. "Trends in the Regulation of Hate Speech and Fake News: A Threat to Free Speech?." *Hasanuddin Law Review* 5 (2): 140–58. https://doi.org/10.20956/halrev.v5i2.1625.

Stewart, Elizabeth. 2021. "Detecting Fake News: Two Problems for Content Moderation." *Philosophy and Technology* 34 (4): 923–40. https://doi.org/10.1007/s13347-021-00442-x.

Talwar, Shalini, Amandeep Dhir, Dilraj Singh, Gurnam Singh Virk, and Jari Salo. 2020. "Sharing of Fake News on Social Media: Application of the Honeycomb Framework and the Third-Person Effect Hypothesis." *Journal of Retailing and Consumer Services* 57 (April): 102197. https://doi.org/10.1016/j.jretconser.2020.102197.

Zhou, Xinyi, and Reza Zafarani. 2020. "A Survey of Fake News: Fundamental Theories, Detection Methods, and Opportunities." *ACM Computing Surveys* 53 (5). https://doi.org/10.1145/3395046.

6 Explainable Models for the Detection of Incidents of Fake News and Hate Speech

Vraj Desai, Ashray Gattani, and Harshal Dalvi

6.1 INTRODUCTION: DEFINITION OF FAKE NEWS AND HATE SPEECH

"Fake news" refers to intentionally false stories or misleading information that look like real news and are spread on the internet or through other media. This is usually done to influence political views or as a joke with satirical articles such as fake news briefs, interviews, op-ed pieces, cartoons, and photos, or to get clicks and advertising revenue. Fake news can spread in various ways including social media, websites, traditional media, word of mouth, bots and automated accounts, foreign interference, and circular reporting. There are several reasons why people or organizations spread fake news, including political gain, financial gain, social gain, ideological gain, and foreign interference. No matter what the reason is, spreading fake news has a lot of bad effects, such as making people lose trust in institutions and the media, hurting people's identities, and encouraging them to do things that are harmful or dangerous. It is important to fight fake news and spread accurate and reliable information so that people can make good choices and take an active role in their communities. A study by the Oxford Internet Institute found that misinformation about COVID-19 was prevalent on social media, with 59% of articles containing misinformation being shared on X (formerly X)and 27% on Facebook in 2021 [1]. The aim of fake news is usually to mislead or manipulate individuals or groups.

"Hate speech" is hurtful speech, writing, or communication that is aimed at a group or an individual because of their race, religion, gender, ethnicity, sexual orientation, or disability. This kind of speech can threaten social peace. Hate speech can take many forms, from verbal slurs to online harassment and threats.

> "Any kind of communication in speech, writing or behavior, that attacks or uses pejorative or discriminatory language with reference to a person or a group on the basis of who they are, in other words, based on their religion, ethnicity, nationality, race, color, descent, gender or other identity factor".

 DOI: 10.1201/9781003409519-6

Hate speech can take many forms, including verbal abuse, harassment, threats, discriminatory speech, incitement to violence, stereotyping, and online hate speech. Social media platforms are often used to spread hate speech. A study by the Centre for Countering Digital Hate found that 12 leading social media platforms were responsible for hosting 84% of all anti-Semitic content online. The right to freedom of expression is protected by international law, but this right is not absolute and must be balanced with other human rights, including the right to dignity, equality, and non-discrimination [2].

6.2 ROLE OF THE INTERNET IN FAKE NEWS AND HATE SPEECH DISSEMINATION

1. **Amplification:** The internet has made it possible for fake news and hate speech to reach a much wider audience than was previously possible. Social media platforms, in particular, have algorithms that are designed to promote content that generates engagement, which can include controversial or sensationalist material.
2. **Anonymity:** The relative anonymity of the internet has made it easier for people to spread fake news and engage in hate speech without fear of repercussions. Online platforms often allow users to create anonymous or pseudonymous accounts, which can make it difficult to hold individuals accountable for their actions.
3. **Speed:** The internet has made it possible to spread information quickly and easily. This can be a positive thing, but it also means that false information and hate speech can be disseminated rapidly and without fact-checking or other forms of oversight.

In the world of social media today, it is hard to tell what is true and what is not. Almost everyone has believed a story that wasn't true at least once. Even worse, computers like stories that get a lot of attention. In the world of clickbait, lying is encouraged and praised, so the old saying "a lie will get around the world before the truth gets out of bed" is more true than ever.

6.3 RELATED WORKS FOR HATE SPEECH AND FAKE NEWS DETECTION

In today's society, fake news and hate speech are important issues that can negatively affect people, communities, and even entire nations. To advance democracy, avoid social harm, ensure ethical and responsible use of technology, and advance responsible journalism, it is essential to identify and address hate speech and fake news. It is a crucial step toward building a community that is more informed and just. The detection of fake news and hate speech are two distinct but related fields of study, each with its own special problems and solutions. In order to protect people and groups from harm, fake news detection aims to recognize and eliminate this information from circulation whereas to promote societal harmony and avoid harming vulnerable groups, hate speech detection aims to recognize and eliminate this language from use. Natural language processing (NLP) and machine learning algorithms are often used to find fake news and hate speech by analyzing large text datasets and looking for trends and traits of false or harmful information. However, the exact methods and processes used in each field of research can vary greatly depending on the type of data being analyzed and the goals of the analysis.

The end goal of finding fake news and hate speech is to create a fair, just, and well-informed society that is free from the bad effects of prejudice and false information.

Table 6.1 gives a full explanation of linked works in detecting fake news and hate speech, including what they did, what they found, and what they couldn't do.

6.4 CHALLENGES WITH EXISTING HATE SPEECH AND FAKE NEWS DETECTION METHODOLOGIES

The inability to be explained is a common drawback of network-based, content-based, and hybrid-based fake news detection systems [3, 4]. Without a clear understanding of how the models arrive at their results, it might be difficult to put your faith in the findings or make substantial methodological breakthroughs. Future study in this area is essential as explainable artificial intelligence (XAI) becomes a greater and more important component of the creation of trustworthy and effective AI systems.

The same is true for existing work on lexicon, machine learning, deep learning, hybrid, and context-based approaches for hate speech identification [55–8], but none of these systems have interpretability and explainability. The fact that current hate speech and false news detection approaches lack interpretability makes it challenging to comprehend and articulate how they make their conclusions. As users and reviewers might not be able to completely understand or verify the accuracy and fairness of the model's predictions, this lack of explainability can result in less openness, trust, and accountability.

6.5 POSSIBLE SOLUTIONS

1) Explainable AI (XAI) techniques

   Explainable artificial intelligence (XAI) is a collection of processes and methods that enables human users to comprehend and trust machine learning algorithms' results [9]. In other words, XAI is necessary if the users are to understand the AI results, trust the decisions of the algorithms, and manage the results in an organized manner. XAI techniques improve the transparency of AI models, which leads to more clinical decision-making confidence and more real-world adoption of AI [10].

   With XAI, it is possible to understand how the AI models work, the features they use to identify fake news and hate speech, and the reasoning behind their decisions. This information can aid in establishing trust and confidence in AI models and their outputs. XAI plays a crucial role in instilling confidence in AI regulators and business partners for

TABLE 6.1
Literature Review of Existing System for Fake News Detection

Ref no.	Research paper	Key Discoveries	Drawbacks
[3]	"Fake News Detection on Social Media using Geometric Deep Learning" by Jiaxin Huang, Bo Peng, Dejing Dou, et al.	Using geometric deep learning techniques, this paper proposes a content-based approach for detecting false news based on its content. The authors demonstrate that their method outperforms other cutting-edge techniques on a X dataset.	It does not provide a comprehensive explanation of the solution, making it difficult to comprehend the algorithm's decision-making process. In addition, the study's data may not be representative of all forms of fake news.
[4]	"An Ensemble Model for Content-based Fake News Detection" by Jianpeng Zhang, Jiahui Li, and Xue Li.	For the purpose of detecting fake news, an ensemble learning model is suggested.	Without providing a thorough explanation of the solution, the paper provides only a concise summary of the features and algorithms used. In addition, the study's data may not be representative of all forms of fake news.
[5]	Ma et al. (2018): "Detecting Rumours from Microblogs with Recurrent Neural Networks"	This study analyzed the propagation patterns of disinformation on social media networks using a recurrent neural network. The key finding was that the proposed method was more accurate than conventional machine learning methods	The limitation of the study was that it did not adequately explain the decision-making process of the model.
[6]	"Lexicon-Based Approaches for Detecting Hate Speech in Social Media"	The proposed method identified hate discourse in multiple languages, including English, Arabic, and German, with high precision. In addition, the use of cross-lingual lexicons enhanced performance when limited training data was available.	The lexicons used in this investigation were created manually and may be biased or insufficient. In addition, the approach may be hindered by the presence of sarcasm or cynicism in text, as well as the difficulty of identifying hate speech in languages that lack a distinct distinction between formal and informal language.
[7]	Y. Zhou, Y. Yang, H. Liu, X. Liu, and N. Savage, "Deep Learning Based Fusion Approach for Hate Speech Detection"	The research proposes a fusion technique based on deep learning for detecting hate speech in social media data. The method improves the efficacy of hate speech detection by combining the outputs of multiple classifiers, such as convolutional neural networks (CNNs) and long short-term memory (LSTM) networks. With an F1 score of 0.84, the method identified hate speech in X data with high accuracy.	The study utilized a relatively limited sample of X data, which may limit the generalizability of the findings. In addition, the authors observe that the method may be less effective in identifying hate speech in languages other than English. Lastly, the method may be incapable of detecting more subtle or context-dependent forms of hate speech.
[8]	Shah, Udmale, Sambhe, Vijay, and Amey. (2021). "A Deep Hybrid Approach for Hate Speech Analysis"	The study proposes a hybrid approach that combines linguistic and non-linguistic features to enhance the accuracy of hate speech detection. The method combines convolutional neural networks (CNNs) and extended short-term memory. Short-term memory (LSTM) networks to analyse the linguistic features of hate speech text, and also incorporates social network features such as the number of retweets and favorites.	The authors observe that the approach may be less effective in identifying hate speech in languages besides English. Lastly, the method may be incapable of detecting more subtle or context-dependent forms of hate speech.

commercially advantageous and ethically sound decision-making. If there is an explanation of the result and how the model generates insights, this reasoning coupled with human knowledge and reasoning may significantly improve results and aid in reducing bias in AI models, as AI bias can be unintentional and lead to inaccurate and unfair results, thereby facilitating the development of effective applications. XAI can assist in enhancing the overall efficacy of AI models. By supplying explanations for the decisions made by AI models, it is possible to determine their strengths and weaknesses and make adjustments to increase their accuracy and precision. This can also aid in preventing errors in situations where none are possible.

Fact: In a survey of 500 US adults conducted by explainable AI (XAI) startup Fiddler, 81% of respondents said they were concerned about how AI models are making decisions, and 74% said they would be more likely to trust a company or product if it offered an explanation of how its AI models work.

2) Transparent model documentation

A thorough and clear documentation of the development, training, and evaluation of the detection models. Documenting the dataset utilized, the preprocessing procedures, the model architecture, the hyperparameters, and the evaluation metrics are all included in this. This documentation can offer insights into the model's internal operations and aid in comprehending how it makes decisions. An interdisciplinary readable documentation must be maintained, which is structurally easier to comprehend and makes the test transparent for persons who are not involved in code writing [11]. This leads to additional effort, costs, and possibly inconsistencies between the test and its documentation [11].

3) Human-in-the-loop approaches

Incorporating human reviewers or moderators to help fake news and hate speech detection computers make decisions. Human reviewers can explain model predictions and confirm the fairness and correctness of the outcomes. By fusing the benefits of human judgment and AI capabilities, this "human-in-the-loop" approach can increase the system's explainability. It uses a graphical causal model to represent causal relationships among different features in the dataset and as a medium to inject domain knowledge [12].

4) Ethical considerations

Ensuring that moral issues, such as bias, justice, and transparency, are fully taken into account during the design and implementation of fake news and hate speech detection systems. To find and address any biases or unfairness in the system involves undertaking bias audits, fairness assessments, and regular audits of the models. In particular, we use a set of ethical frameworks to map design decisions for a model predictive control problem to philosophical principles [13]. The ultimate goal is to use ethical principles to make engineering decisions that result in reasonable, justifiable fake news and hate speech detection.

In the context of fake news and hate speech detection, XAI can help to identify the specific words, phrases, and features that the AI models use to identify these types of content. This knowledge can be used to develop better strategies to combat fake news and hate speech, such as improving human fact-checking and moderation and identifying areas where more education and awareness-raising are needed. In general, the goals of AI-based solutions are to achieve high performance, instill user trust, and reflect user response [12].

6.6 LITERATURE REVIEW OF DIFFERENT XAI TECHNIQUES

Many approaches have been explored for improving model interpretability and transparency in the literature review of explainable AI (XAI) strategies linked to misinformation and fake news detection, as indicated in table 6.2. All of these research highlight how important it is to use interpretable methods to elucidate the decisions black-box model decisions when it comes to identifying fake news and rumours on the internet.

6.7 PROPOSED METHODOLOGY

The methodology proposed herein entails a series of sequential steps aimed at ensuring optimal model training and dependable outcomes. In the initial stage of data analysis, the dataset undergoes data preprocessing, which involves the cleansing, transformation, and preparation of raw data for further analysis. Subsequently, the preprocessed data is utilized to train the machine learning algorithm for the model. The present methodology places significant emphasis on the utilization of explainable artificial intelligence (XAI) techniques to guarantee lucidity and responsibility in the decision-making mechanisms of the model.

This entails evaluating both global and local explanations of the model's behavior so that users can comprehend how the model arrives at its predictions.

Finally, the results of the model are evaluated, using a variety of metrics and techniques to assess its accuracy and effectiveness.

The flowchart (Figure 6.1) for this methodology includes clear and concise steps, starting with data preprocessing, followed by model training, and culminating in the evaluation of results. The inclusion of explainable AI techniques at various stages of the process adds an additional layer of transparency and accountability, ensuring that users can trust the model's outputs.

6.7.1 Extraction and Description of Dataset

I. Dataset used for fake news

In this chapter, we used a fake news dataset from a Kaggle competition to build a system to identify unreliable news articles [19] for fake news detection using explainable artificial intelligence, this dataset is discussed in this section. The dataset used in this research contains 20,949 tweets that are either fake or real.

TABLE 6.2
Literature Review of Different XAI Techniques.

Ref.	Title	Detection Technique	XAI technique used
[14]	Explainable Misinformation Detection Across Multiple Social Media Platforms	Used COVID-19 misinformation as a case study and used dann(domain adversarial neural network) For classification and then LIME for explainability.	LIME with a 500-tree random forest substitute model. And making heat maps based on the words used in fake news.
[15]	Evaluating Fake News Detection Models from Explainable Machine Learning Perspectives	This study compares DEFEND, HDSF, and TCNN-URG, three digital media fake news detection methods. To combat online misinformation, these tools were created. Comparing these tools will reveal their strengths and weaknesses, helping you choose the right one. The DEFEND system gathers verified assertions and detects falsified news using language and structure patterns using user feedback and submissions. The Hadoop Distributed File System (HDFS) can learn about fake and real news by talking. TCNN-URG extracts word and sentence semantic information from news stories. This study examines methods for detecting and categorizing fake news.	LIME with 500-tree random forest substitution. Creating heat maps from bogus news words It approximates an intelligible model locally around the forecast to explain any classifier's predictions in a way that is true. PyTorch-based Captum uses primary- and layer-based identification. Primary-based attribution considers one input trait at a time, while layer-based attribution considers each neuron in a layer. We study primary-based attribution, which employs integrated gradients to determine global model behavior like feature weights. SHAP theoretically generalizes LIME and clarifies machine learning model findings.
[16]	Demystifying Black-box Learning Models of Rumour Detection from Social Media Posts	Used hybrid models that is ensemble of XGBoost, SVM, Random Forest and used Lime for explainability.	LIME for XAI: Gives importance graph to features extracted using different techniques from a text regarding covid.
[17]	Deep Explainable Hate Speech Active Learning on Social Media Data	Classify tweets in two categories: non-offensive and offensive.	Uses and visualizes hate lexicons from word2vec technique.to classify hate speech.
[18]	XAI Evaluation: Evaluating Black-Box Model Explanations for Prediction	Various ways for predicting outcomes have been thoroughly investigated, and one explanation method has been found to possess superior quality. This method enhances the accuracy, transparency, and dependability of the predictions.	Nevertheless, due to the varying principles and characteristics of numerous XAI methods, the output of multiple XAI methods for a given black-box model may differ.

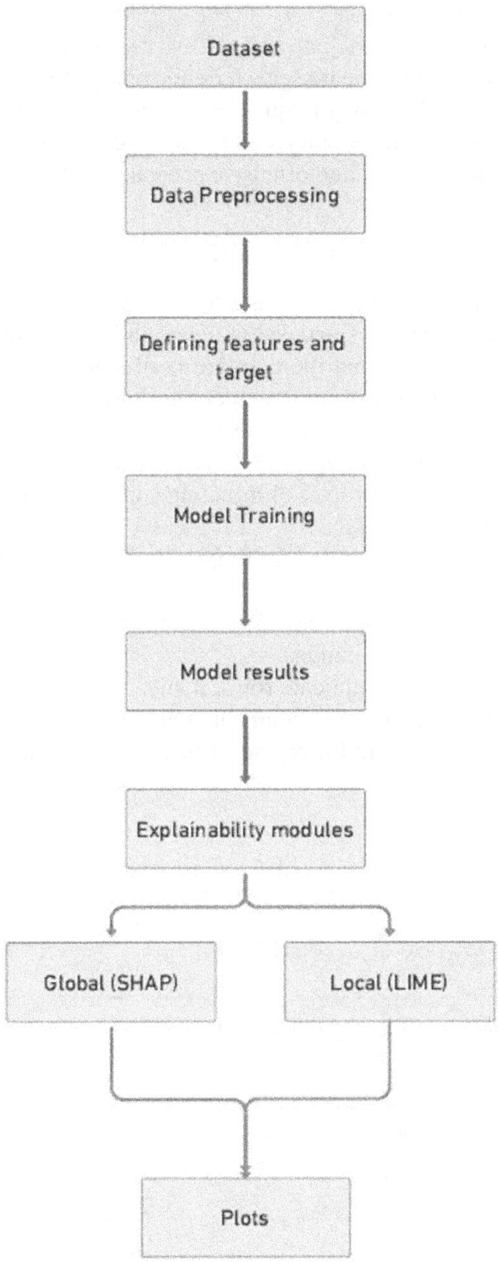

FIGURE 6.1 Workflow of the proposed approach.

II. Dataset used for hate speech

In this chapter, we used a hate and offensive speech dataset from Kaggle to identify if an article is a hate speech or normal speech [20]. The data has been scraped from X through Apify regarding the tweets of normal and hate speech. The complete database contains 12 datasets where the data are available for normal, hate, and offensive speech with four CSV files each.

6.8.2 Data Preprocessing and Cleaning

Data preprocessing is a crucial phase that affects a model's performance. The data obtained from X tweets or news articles is noisy and may contain absent or null values. Preprocessing ensures that the data are pertinent, clean, and free of noise. Data cleansing is a crucial phase prior to model training due to its numerous benefits. Eradicating any incorrect or inconsistent information, data cleansing improves the integrity of the data. Figure 6.2 depicts the typical phases utilized in data preprocessing and data cleansing. It involves eliminating superfluous observations prior to addressing any structural defects.

A summary of the steps performed for preprocessing and cleaning of the dataset is given below:

1. Loading the dataset using pandas.
2. Checking and removing duplicate rows, if any.
3. Removed any punctuation or special characters from the tweets or articles.
4. Converted all characters to lowercase to ensure consistency.

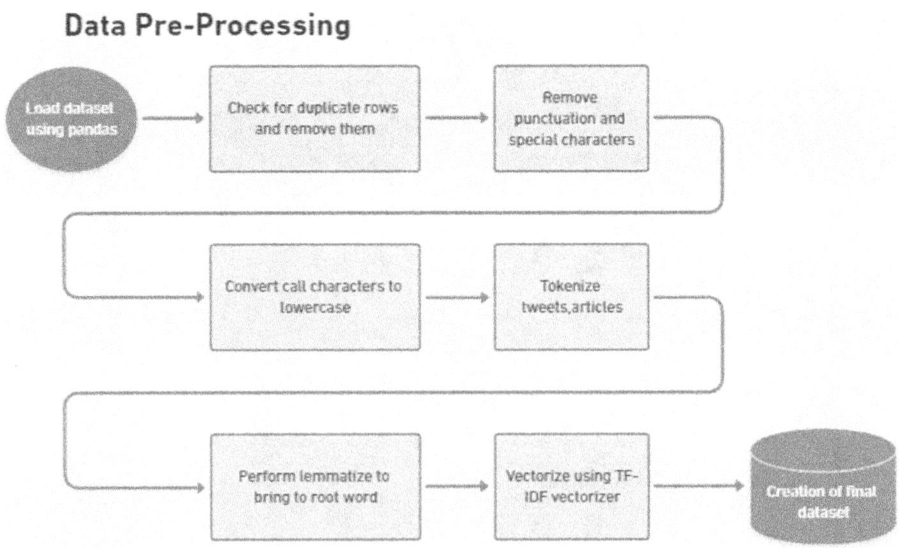

FIGURE 6.2 Data preprocessing and cleaning.

5. Tokenized the tweets and articles by splitting them into individual words.
6. Removed stop words such as "and", "the", "a", etc., which do not add any significant meaning to the text.
7. Performed lemmatization to group together the inflected forms of a word.
8. Vectorize the text using term frequency–inverse document frequency (TF–IDF) vectorizer.
9. Created a final dataset with the preprocessed tweets, articles, and their corresponding labels.

6.7.3 Tokenization, Lemmatization, and Vectorization

1. **Tokenization:** Sentences are broken down into smaller units known as tokens through the process of tokenization. These tokens can help identify distinct patterns in the text by acting as the building blocks for lemmatization and stemming. The library of the Natural Language Toolkit (NLTK) Tokenization is the process of breaking down long statements into shorter chunks that are Word tokenization routines available in Python. For instance, the term "clearer" makes it easier to spot different patterns in the text. Either "clear" and "er" or "c-l-e-a-r-e-r" can be tokenized from the Natural Language Toolkit (NLTK) package. In order to increase the effectiveness of the learning process, we performed character tokenization in this study, which turns words into tokens as an array of integers.
2. **Lemmatization:** Lemmatization was used to produce word normalization using natural language processing (NLP). All words are reduced to their fundamental forms during lemmatization. For instance, the words "go", "going", "gone", and "goes" are all reduced to "go", "read", "reading", and "reads", and "hated", "hating", and "hates" are all reduced to "hate".
3. **Vectorization:** Text input is transformed into a numerical representation known as vectorization so that machine learning algorithms can utilize it. The Bag-of-Words model, which represents each text as a vector of word counts, is the vectorization technique that has been employed the most frequently in this study. Count via scikit-learn Tweets and articles are vectorized using a program called Vectorizer.

6.7.4 Classification Model for the Detection of Incidents of Fake News and Hate Speech

The detection of fake news is identifying a news story as either authentic or fraudulent depending on its content. One typical method for this task is to develop a classifier that can predict the class of a news story based on its attributes using machine learning algorithms such as logistic regression.

In this chapter, we applied logistic regression to detect false news, we first extracted features from news items. This task frequently makes use of the following features:

1. **Word frequency:** Counting the number of times each word appears in the article.
2. **Sentiment:** Measuring the overall sentiment of the article using sentiment analysis techniques.
3. **Named entities:** Identifying the named entities mentioned in the article, such as people, places, and organizations.

Once the features have been extracted, we can use them to train a logistic regression model to predict the class of the news article (real or fake). For each news story, the logistic regression model will generate a probability score between 0 and 1, signifying the possibility that the article is fraudulent.

6.7.5 Explainable Models for the Detection of Incidents of Fake News and Hate Speech

I. **LIME** (local interpretable model-agnostic explanations)

In this chapter, we use LIME to explain the predictions of the logistic regression model used to identify false news and hate speech, as shown in Figure 6.3. LIME provides local, interpretable explanations of model predictions by approximating the model with a fundamental, interpretable model in the immediate vicinity of the instance to be explained. For detecting false news and hate speech, LIME is used to identify the words or phrases on which the predictive model relies. By emphasizing the most significant characteristics, LIME assists in understanding why a specific instance was classified as false news or hate speech.

We created a pipeline of TfidfVectorizer and logistic regression to predict probabilities of different classes. TfidfVectorizer (Term Frequency-Inverse Document Frequency Vectorizer).TfidfVectorizer is a feature extraction technique used in natural language processing and text mining. It

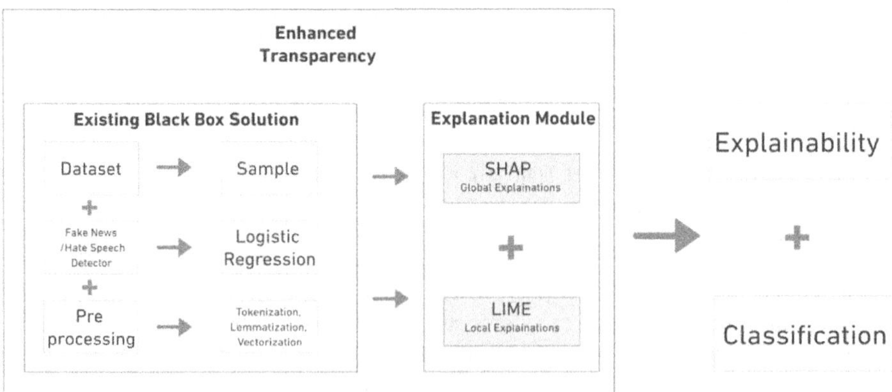

FIGURE 6.3 Architecture for explainable models.

converts a collection of raw text documents into a matrix of TF-IDF (Term Frequency-Inverse Document Frequency) features. This means it computes the TF-IDF value for each word in the document, which reflects how important a word is to a document within a collection of documents.

LIME (local interpretable model-agnostic explanations) is an algorithm that provides local model-agnostic explanations for individual predictions. It explains the behavior of a machine learning model by approximating the model with an interpretable one in the vicinity of the prediction.

The general steps followed for implementing the LIME algorithm are as follows:

1. The instance to be explained is selected.
2. Generated a set of perturbed instances around the selected instance by randomly removing or replacing features while keeping the label unchanged.
3. Using the original model to predict the output for each of the perturbed instances.
4. Training of linear models on the perturbed instances, where the features are the perturbations, and the output is the corresponding model predictions.
5. Explain the original model's output for the selected instance by interpreting the weights of the linear model.
6. Using the explanations to gain insight into the factors that contributed to the model's output.

II. **SHAP** (SHapley Additive exPlanations)

SHAP, which stands for "SHapley Additive Explanations", is a way to explain the results of any machine learning model in a single way. In machine learning, the "players" are the features that go into a model, and the "rewards" are the guesses that the model makes.

The SHAP algorithm works by figuring out how much each trait changed the difference between what the model actually predicted and what was expected. The SHAP value is the name for this input. The SHAP value shows how important a feature is to a prediction, and it can be positive or negative based on whether the feature makes the prediction more accurate or less accurate.

The SHAP algorithm starts by using a baseline value to figure out what the expected value of the model result is. The mean prediction of the training data can be used as the baseline value, or any other value that makes sense for the task. Then, it looks at all the possible ways the input features can be put together and figures out how much each feature contributes to each possible combo. Lastly, the Shapley value formula is used to find the average of all the possible inputs.

The SHAP values that come out of this give a world and a local view of what the model means. They can be used to explain how the model works in general across the whole collection or to explain how a single prediction was made. Also, they can be shown visually with plots such as SHAP summary plots, dependence plots, or force plots, which help show how the input features affect the model output.

For fake news and hate speech detection, SHAP (Figure 6.3) is used to analyze and give explanations for the global set of features. Many different plots such as bar plots and beeswarm plots give weights according to the importance of features.

III. **ELI5** (Explain like I am 5)

ELI5 is used to explain the logistic regression model designed to detect fake news and hate speech. It assists in highlighting the most essential features or terms that contribute to the model's output, allowing us to better understand how the model makes decisions.

ELI5 is used to describe the characteristics used by the model to make predictions. To begin, we use the ELI5 "explain_weights" function to obtain a catalog of the model's most important features or words. This list is ordered by their coefficient values, which indicate how much each feature contributes to the prediction made by the model. Then, using the "explain_prediction" function, we obtain a detailed explanation of how the model arrived at its prediction for a specific post. The main contributing features, as well as their individual contributions to the final prediction, are included in this explanation.

Overall, employing ELI5 for explainability in this context can aid in providing transparency and clarity into the inner workings of the logistic regression model for detecting fake news and hate speech.

6.8 EXPERIMENTAL RESULTS

This section provides a detailed explanation of the results obtained from global and local explainable models, including feature importance, shape values, local explanation (that is, explanation of a single instance), prediction probabilities, top contributing features, weights, and bias.

6.8.1 Explainability for Fake News Detection

I. **SHAP**

The SHAP library has a plotting function called shap.plot.bar() (Figure 6.4) that, when used, creates a horizontal bar chart that displays the SHAP values associated with each feature in a dataset. The function accepts an argument named shap_values, which are: The SHAP values for the dataset or instance, which can be computed using the tool called the shap.Explainer(). In the above, we have features of fake news dataset articles/tweets and its corresponding shap_values which signifies the importance of those features. After analysis, we found that "York" was one of the most important features to explain if a news article is not fake.

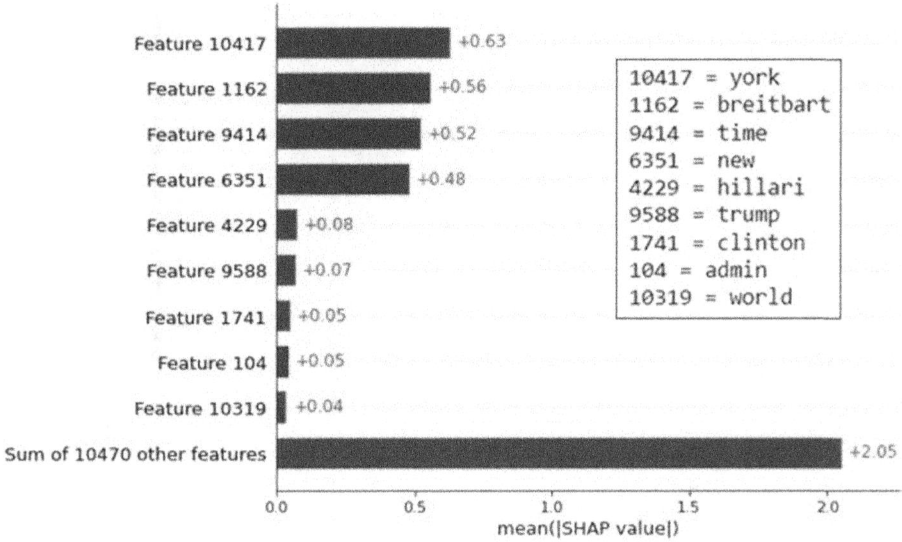

FIGURE 6.4 Bar plot for SHAP values.

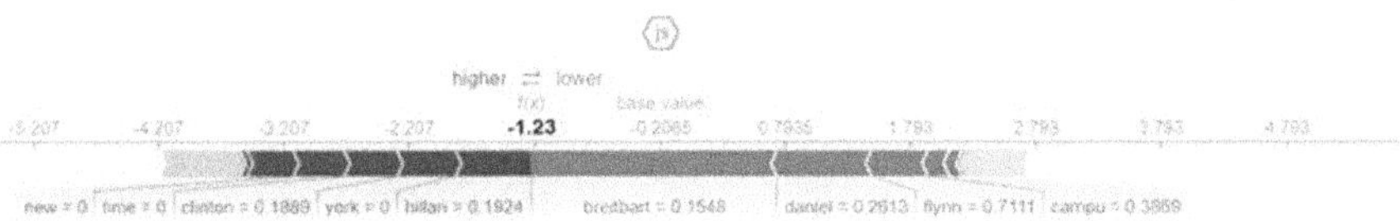

FIGURE 6.5 Force plot for SHAP values.

The force plot generated by shap.force_plot() (Figure 6.5) provides a detailed breakdown of how each feature affects the model's output, allowing for the identification of which features are driving the output in a positive or negative direction. This information can be used to identify which features are most important for the model's decision-making process and to understand how changes in these features would impact the model's output. As we observed, few words make the news article more inclined toward the fake side.

In summary, in the plot (Figure 6.6) we take five instances and give a summary of the features extracted and the summary of these features compared on the scale on the right-hand side.

II. **LIME**

lime_explainer.as_pyplot_figure() method (Figure 6.7) is used to generate a LIME plot. A LIME plot for a specific instance provides an explanation of how the machine learning model arrived at its prediction for that instance. The plot highlights the most important features that contributed to the model's prediction for that instance, providing insights into the model's decision-making process.

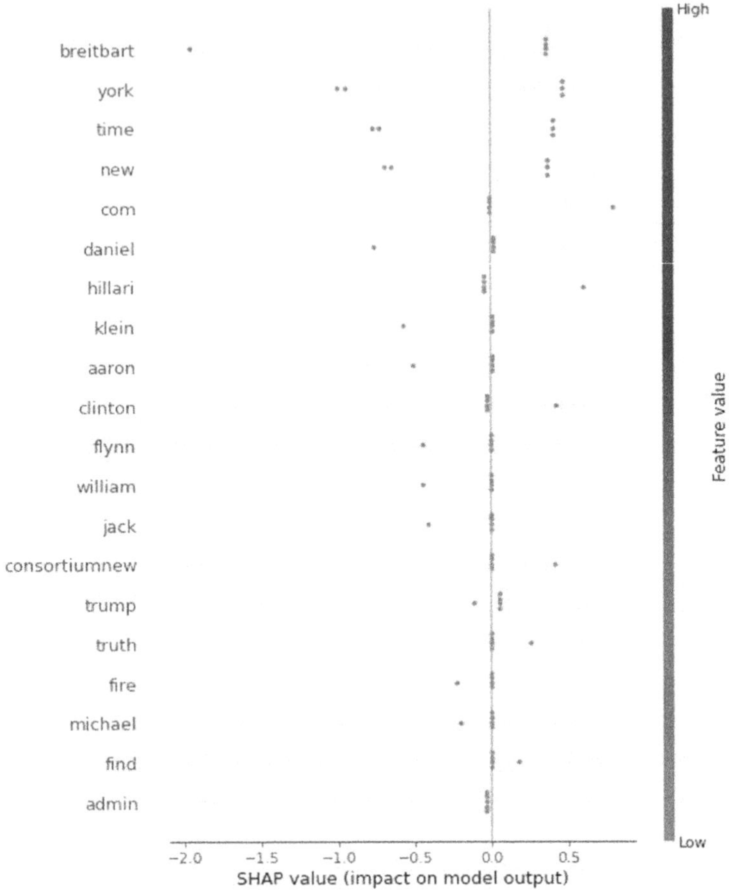

FIGURE 6.6 Sumaary plot for SHAP values/.

The LIME plot for a single instance displays a horizontal bar chart that shows the contribution of each feature to the model's prediction for that instance. The length of each bar corresponds to the magnitude of the feature's contribution, with positive contributions shown in green and negative contributions shown in red. The plot also displays the value of each feature for the instance.

The text explanation typically includes a description of the predicted class (Figure 6.8), gives a pictorial representation of a list of the most important features and their contributions to the prediction. The contribution of each feature is expressed in terms of its impact on the sentence itself using a color scheme.

III. **ELI5**

The ELI5 library offers a show_weights() (Figure 6.9) function that produces a graphical representation of the feature importances of a given machine learning

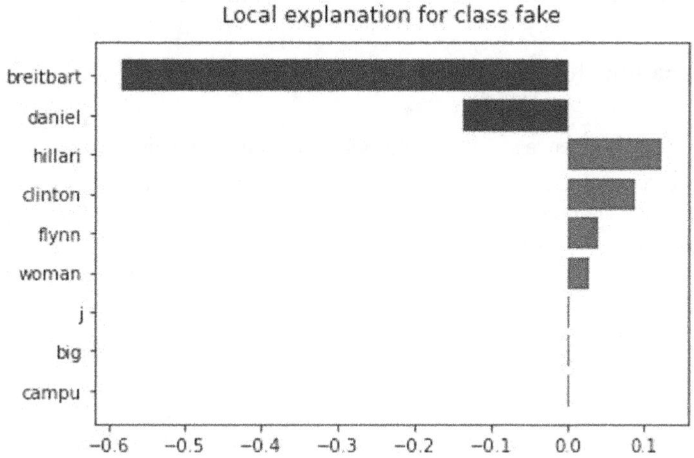

FIGURE 6.7 Local explanation using LIME for a fake news instance.

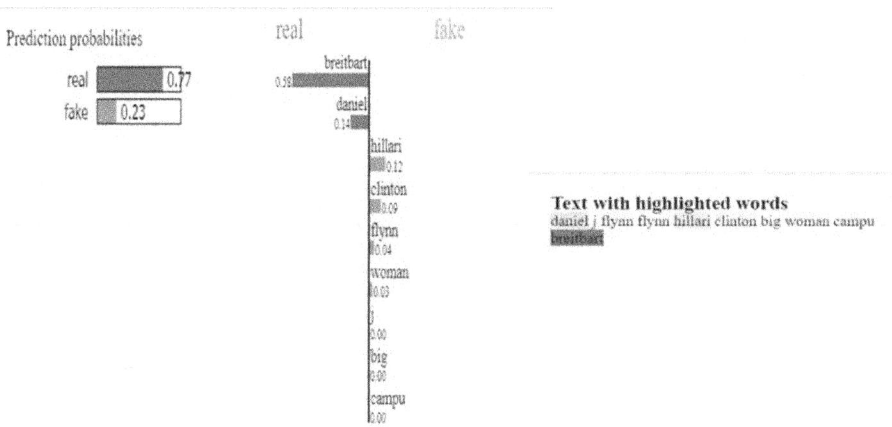

FIGURE 6.8 LIME with predicted probabilities.

model. The graphical representation of the data is analogous to a bar chart, wherein each bar corresponds to a distinct feature and the magnitude of the bar denotes the relative significance of the feature. The function show_weights() exhibits both the name and value of every feature.

6.8.2 Explainability for Hate Speech Detection

I. SHAP

For hate speech detection's explainability, in a similar fashion, we use the SHAP library and its shap.Explainer() and shap.plot.bar() functions and obtain the

TABLE 6.3
LIME Explanations for Four Instances

Sr no.	Test Sentence	P(fake)	P(real)	Top five words	Weights
1	brian x chen samsung combust galaxy note unveils new smartphone new york time	0.05	0.95	new	–0.30
				york	–0.21
				time	–0.16
				combust	+0.03
				brian	+0.03
2	trent baker pelosi republican tell trump bring dishonor presid breitbart	0.03	0.97	breitbart	–0.48
				baker	–0.05
				trent	–0.05
				dishonor	+0.04
				trump	–0.03
3	russian company unable use linkedin service company russia news	0.87	0.13	news	+0.02
				russia	+0.02
				service	–0.02
				companies	–0.01
				russian	+0.01
4	starkman scientist shock find melanesian carri dna unknown human species	0.92	0.08	starkman	+0.02
				shock	+0.02
				find	+0.02
				human	+0.01
				carri	–0.01

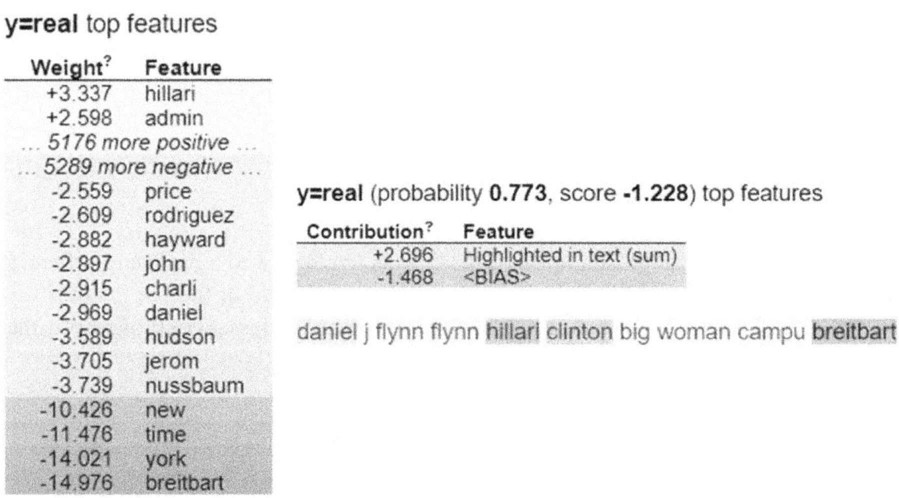
y=real top features

Weight?	Feature
+3.337	hillari
+2.598	admin
... 5176 more positive ...	
... 5289 more negative ...	
-2.559	price
-2.609	rodriguez
-2.882	hayward
-2.897	john
-2.915	charli
-2.969	daniel
-3.589	hudson
-3.705	jerom
-3.739	nussbaum
-10.426	new
-11.476	time
-14.021	york
-14.976	breitbart

y=real (probability **0.773**, score **-1.228**) top features

Contribution?	Feature
+2.696	Highlighted in text (sum)
-1.468	<BIAS>

daniel j flynn flynn hillari clinton big woman campu breitbart

FIGURE 6.9 ELI5 for most positive features in a real news instance.

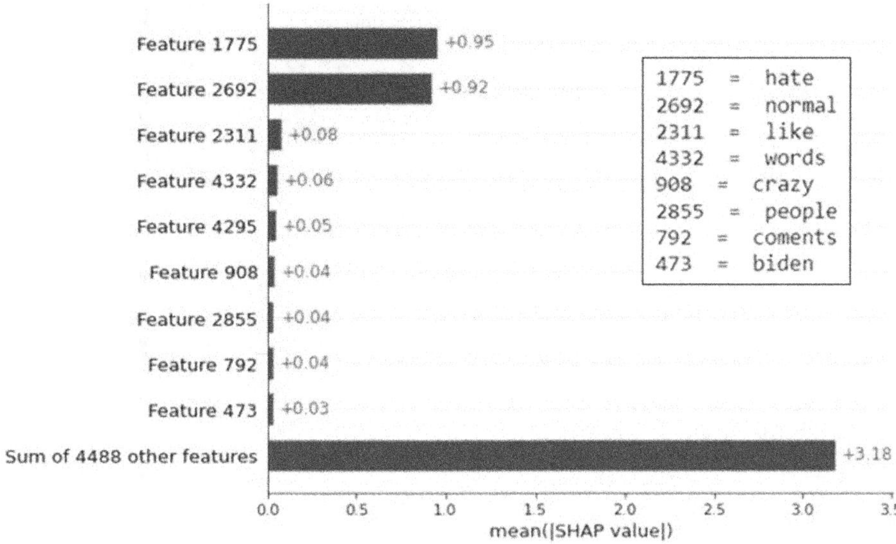

FIGURE 6.10 Bar plot for SHAP values.

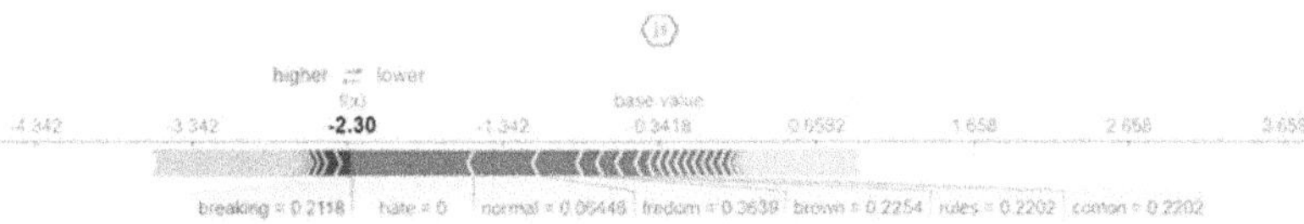

FIGURE 6.11 Force plot for SHAP values.

corresponding SHAP values for each feature. We can then use shap.plot.bar() to create a horizontal bar chart that displays the SHAP values associated with each feature in the dataset (Figure 6.10). This creates a horizontal bar chart displaying the top features with the highest absolute SHAP values. The features with the highest absolute SHAP values are considered the most important features for the logistic regression model in predicting hate speech.

The force plot generated by shap.force_plot() for hate speech provides a similar detailed breakdown of how each feature affects the model's output, allowing for the identification of which features are driving the output in a positive or negative direction for detecting hate speech in articles (Figure 6.11). This information can be used to determine which aspects of the model are most significant for the decision-making process represented by the model, as well as to gain an understanding of how modifications to these aspects would affect the results produced by the model.

In summary, in the plot (Figure 6.12) we take five instances and give a summary of the features extracted and give the summary of these features compared on the scale on the right-hand side.

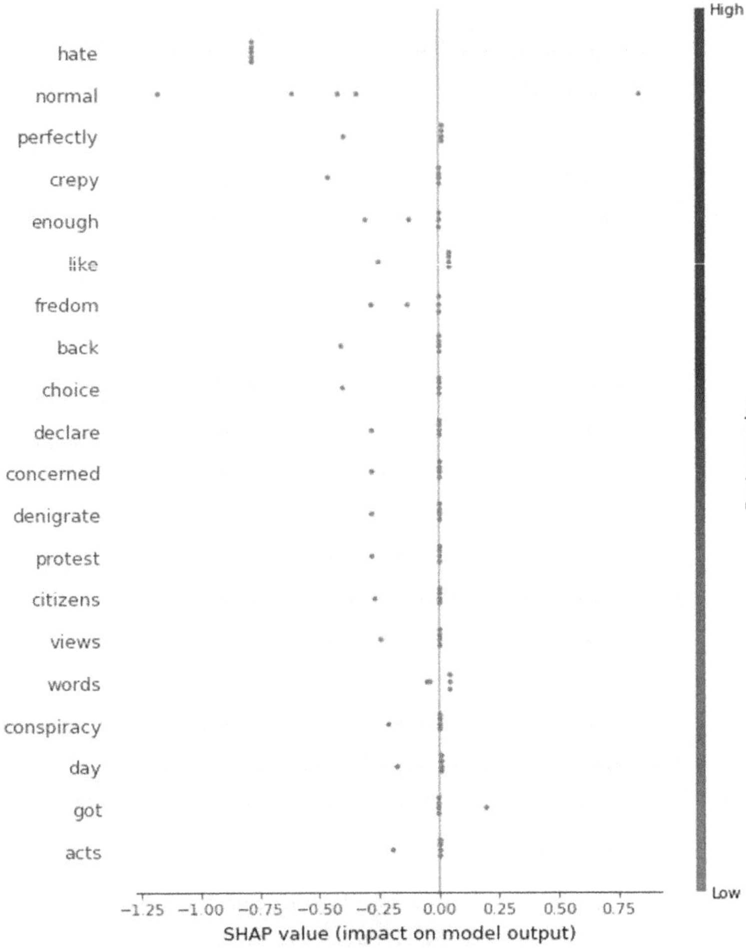

FIGURE 6.12 Summary plot for SHAP values.

II. **LIME**

The LIME plot is made with the lime_explainer.as_pyplot_figure() method. The plot shows the most important factors that the model used to make its estimate in that case. This shows how the model decides what to do.

For each instance, the LIME plot shows a horizontal bar chart that shows how much each feature contributed to the model's forecast for that instance. The size of each feature's contribution is shown by how long each bar is. Positive contributions are shown in green, and negative contributions are shown in red. The value of each feature for instance is also shown in Figure 6.13.

The text explanation usually starts with a description of the predicted class (Figure 6.14), followed by a list of the most important features and how they contribute to the

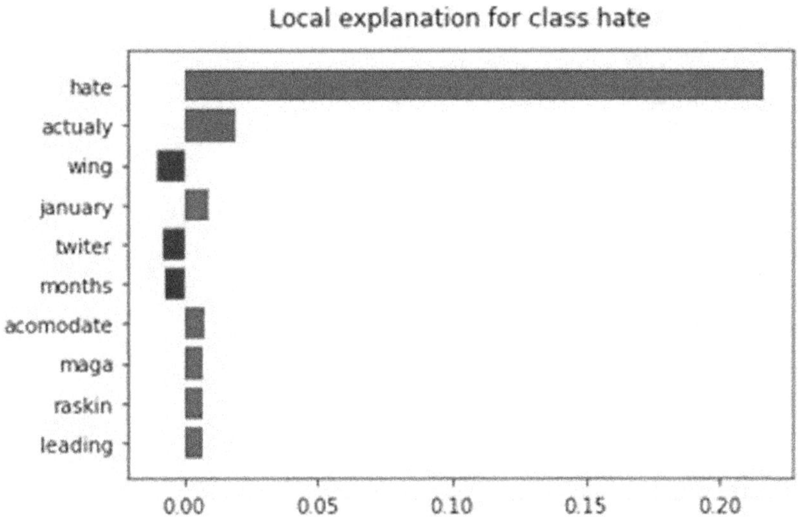

FIGURE 6.13 Local explanation using LIME for a hate speech instance.

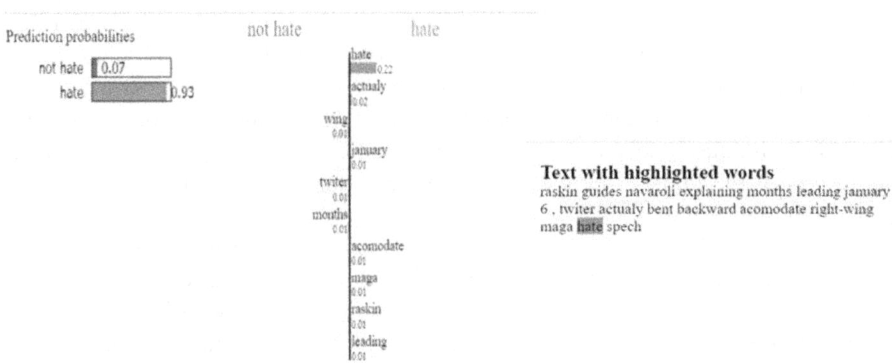

FIGURE 6.14 LIME with predicted probabilities.

forecast. Using a color scheme, the input of each feature is shown in terms of how it affects the sentence as a whole.

III. **ELI5**

The ELI5 provides a function called show_weights() (Figure 6.15) that generates a visual depiction of the significance of features in a specified machine learning model. The visual depiction of data can be likened to a bar graph, where each bar represents a unique attribute, and the height of the bar indicates the relative importance of the attribute. The show_weights() function displays the name and corresponding value of each feature.

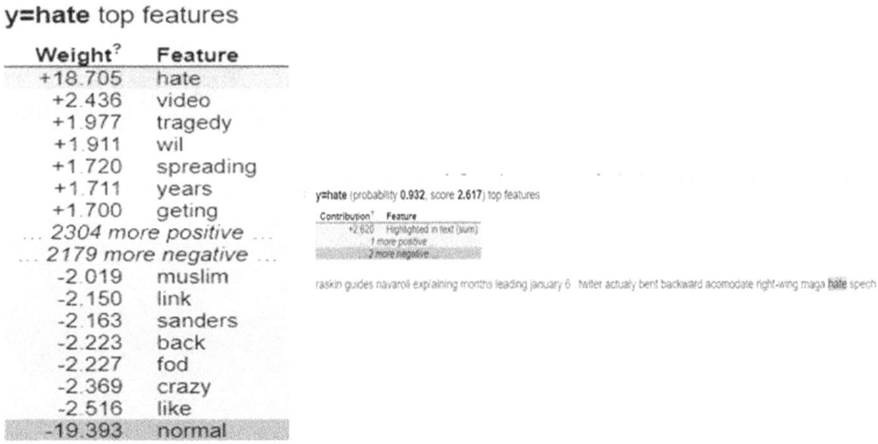

FIGURE 6.15 ELI5 for most positive features in a hate speech instance.

6.9 CONCLUSION

The utilization of explainable models such as LIME, SHAP, and ELI5 with logistic regression for fake news and hate speech detection has demonstrated the efficacy of the aforementioned approach in facilitating a deeper understanding by providing insights into the decision-making process of the model.

Through the use of tokenization, lemmatization, removing stop words, and vectorization techniques, the dataset was preprocessed for logistic regression modeling. The results of the logistic regression model were further analyzed and visualized using LIME and SHAP.

The use of LIME helped us to determine which features were most significant for the decision-making process of a single instance pertaining to the model, and the force plot generated by SHAP provided a detailed breakdown of how each feature affected the model's output. These insights can be used to improve the model's performance and reduce bias in the decision-making process. Using ELI5 we were able to determine by observing the weights associated with each feature, we found that certain words and phrases have a strong positive or negative influence on the model's output.

Overall, combining logistic regression with explainable models such as LIME and SHAP can improve the interpretability and transparency of the decision-making process, provide valuable insights for the detection of fake news and hate speech, and provide valuable insights for the detection of fake news and hate speech.

REFERENCES

1. Motta, M., D. Stecula, and C. Farhart (2020). "How Right-Leaning Media Coverage of COVID-19 Facilitated the Spread of Misinformation in the Early Stages of the Pandemic in the U.S." *Canadian Journal of Political Science./Revue Canadienne de Science Politique*, 53(2), 335–342. doi: 10.1017/S0008423920000396.

2. https://counterhate.com/topic/antisemitism/.
3. Monti, Federico, Fabrizio Frasca, Davide Eynard, Damon Mannion, and Michael M. Bronstein (2019). "Fake News Detection on Social Media Using Geometric Deep Learning." *Arxiv Abs./1902.06673.*
4. Hakak, Saqib, Mamoun Alazab, Suleman Khan, Thippa Reddy Gadekallu, Praveen Kumar Reddy Maddikunta, and Wazir Zada Khan (2021). "An Ensemble Machine Learning Approach through Effective Feature Extraction to Classify Fake News." *Future Generation Computer Systems*, 117, 47–58.
5. Ma, Jing, Wei Gao, Prasenjit Mitra, Sejeong Kwon, Bernard J. Jansen, Kam-Fai Wong, and Meeyoung Cha (2016). "Detecting Rumors from Microblogs with Recurrent Neural Networks." Proceedings of the 25th International Joint Conference on Artificial Intelligence (IJCAI 2016), pp. 3818–3824. AAAI Press.
6. Gitari, Njagi Dennis, Zhang Zuping, Hanyurwimfura Damien, and Jun Long (2015). "A Lexicon-Based Approach for Hate Speech Detection." *International Journal of Multimedia and Ubiquitous Engineering*, 10(4), 215–230.
7. Zhou, Y., Y. Yang, H. Liu, X. Liu, and N. Savage (2020). "Deep Learning Based Fusion Approach for Hate Speech Detection." *IEEE Access*, 8, 128923–128929. doi: 10.1109/ACCESS.2020.3009244.
8. Shah, Vipul, Sandeep S. Udmale, Vijay Sambhe, and Amey Bhole. (2021). "A Deep Hybrid Approach for Hate Speech Analysis." In N. Tsapatsoulis, A. Panayides, T. Theocharides, A. Lanitis, C. Pattichis, and M. Vento (Eds.), *Computer Analysis of Images and Patterns: 19th International Conference, CAIP 2021*, Virtual Event, September 28–30, 2021, Proceedings, Part I 19, pp. 424–433. Cham: Springer International Publishing.
9. Alvarez-Melis, D., and T. S. Jaakkola (2018). "Towards Robust Interpretability with Self-Explaining Neural Networks." Proceedings of the 32nd International Conference on Neural Information Processing Systems, pp. 7786–7795. Curran Associates Inc.
10. Giuste, F., et al. (2023). "Explainable Artificial Intelligence Methods in Combating Pandemics: A Systematic Review." *IEEE Reviews in Biomedical Engineering*, 16, 5–21. doi: 10.1109/RBME.2022.3185953.
11. Stöcker, K., H. Washizaki, and Y. Fukazawa (2017). "Closing the Gap between Unit Test Code and Documentation." IEEE International Conference on Software Testing, Verification and Validation Workshops (ICSTW), Tokyo, Japan, pp. 304–308. doi: 10.1109/ICSTW.2017.56.
12. Ghai, B., and K. Mueller (2023, January). "D-BIAS: A Causality-Based Human-in-the-Loop System for Tackling Algorithmic Bias." *IEEE Transactions on Visualization and Computer Graphics*, 29(1), 473–482. doi: 10.1109/TVCG.2022.3209484.
13. Thornton, S. M., S. Pan, S. M. Erlien, and J. C. Gerdes (2017, June). "Incorporating Ethical Considerations Into Automated Vehicle Control." *IEEE Transactions on Intelligent Transportation Systems*, 18(6), 1429–1439. doi: 10.1109/TITS.2016.2609339.
14. Joshi, Gargi, Ananya Srivastava, Bhargav Yagnik, Mohammed Hasan, Zainuddin Saiyed, Lubna A. Gabralla, Ajith Abraham, Rahee Walambe, and Ketan Kotecha (2023). "Explainable Misinformation Detection across Multiple Social Media Platforms." *IEEE Access*, 11, 23634–23646.
15. Alharbi, Raed, Minh N. Vu, and My T. Thai (2021). "Evaluating Fake News Detection Models from Explainable Machine Learning Perspectives." ICC 2021-IEEE International Conference on Communications, pp. 1–6. IEEE.
16. Tafannum, Faiza, Mir Nafis Sharear Shopnil, Anika Salsabil, Navid Ahmed, Md. Golam Rabiul Alam, and Md Tanzim Reza (2021). "Demystifying Black-Box Learning Models of Rumor Detection from Social Media Posts." 2021 IEEE 12th Annual Ubiquitous Computing, Electronics & Mobile Communication Conference (UEMCON), pp. 0358–0364. IEEE.

17. Ahmed, Usman, and Lin Jerry Chun-Wei (2022). "Deep Explainable Hate Speech Active Learning on Social-Media Data." *IEEE Transactions on Computational Social Systems*, 9, 1–11.
18. Zhang, Y., F. Xu, J. Zou, O. L. Petrosian, and K. V. Krinkin (2021). "XAI Evaluation: Evaluating Black-Box Model Explanations for Prediction." II International Conference on Neural Networks and Neurotechnologies (NeuroNT), Saint Petersburg, Russia, pp. 13–16. doi: 10.1109/NeuroNT53022.2021.9472817.
19. https://www.kaggle.com/competitions/fake-news/data.
20. https://www.kaggle.com/datasets/subhajournal/normal-hate-and-offensive-speeches.

7 Gender Biases and Politics
The Semiotics of Hate Speech on the Internet

Maria Kalfa

7.1 INTRODUCTION

This chapter examines gender stereotypes in politics and how they are reflected through mass media discourse. This framework acts as a disincentive and further hinders women's desire to enter politics, as they seem to constantly have to prove that they are capable and can do it. Section 7.2 examines the way inequality is constructed through language and how words can limit and define the permissible limits for each gender. Section 7.3 refers to the way women involved in politics are presented and how comments on social media reproduce a sexist discourse that is even considered a form of hate speech. Women in politics are marginalized and more attention is paid to other aspects, e.g., appearance, sexuality, and attractiveness, and not with what a woman can offer in politics. In Section 7.4 suggestions are made to soften gender stereotypes and finally stop limiting women and judging them on the basis of their beauty and attractiveness.

7.2 GENDER AND POLITICS

The use of language is not objective, nor does it faithfully represent reality, but tends to reproduce power relations, gender stereotypes, and prejudices. Sociolinguists and feminists have highlighted the role that language plays in society and in the reproduction of stereotypes. Since, according to the above, language must reflect social changes, efforts have been made in recent years to make changes – at the language level – which will go hand in hand with the changes that have taken place in society. We can relate the "dominion" of the male gender to the long-standing dominance of men in economic, professional, and social life. In the same context, the exclusion of the female gender, e.g., from high-prestige occupations, can be related to the long-term absence of women from socioeconomic development. However, even though some forms of inequality have been eliminated, there is difficulty in redefining language, a practice that for many is characterized as meaningless, unnecessary, etc. It

DOI: 10.1201/9781003409519-7

is important to look at dictionaries, where the older we look at the terms man and woman, words associated with female identity are negatively charged, while words associated with male identity are positively charged. Language represents differences that may be based on gender, ethnicity, sexuality, geographic origin, social class, etc. In addition to the differences in characteristics that people have, language also defines the expectations we have of someone based on his gender. These expectations are not limited only to the level of language, but also to non-verbal communication, which is also a form of language with which the roles and obligations for each gender are approached. The role of upbringing becomes important, as we will see below, where through exhortations the "correct" behavior for each gender is "built". Women are encouraged not to curse, not to make mistakes in their speech, and to be especially careful, a fact that is also reflected in the language, where most research, both in the domestic and international literature, attribute the use of standard language to women. In contrast, men are encouraged to express themselves openly, swear, and perform their masculinity through the way they use language, taking the floor more often, taking more frequent breaks, and claiming space and time in the conversation.

> From Mary Wollstonecraft and John Stuart Mill to Judith Butler and Dona Haraway, feminism as a political and moral philosophy and as a worldview, in general, was from the outset a project to reorder modernity based on the deconstruction of the gendered constructions of patriarchy and capitalist binary logic, which was built on inequality and the exploitation of women and all kinds of otherness.

The deconstruction of gender stereotypes is a process that is still ongoing in order to have, not only the freedom to access politics and in general the professional and economic sphere, but until the gendered discourses regarding abilities, potentials, and the desires and characteristics of the sexes. The reformulation of the existing laws does not only concern genders but also forms of otherness, which deviate from normality in order to be sidelined or have minimal opportunities in the work and economic sphere.

> Feminism, as a politicization and moralization of gender, gave the question of democracy and the public sphere a holistic image, to the extent that it brought to the fore the invisible aspect of life, private life, the family and the home in general, where the paterfamilias claimed the role of an anti-democratic leader, most of the time, without consent, but with violence and brutality.
>
> **(Makris 2015:72–73)**

7.3 HATE SPEECH AND BARRIERS TO WOMEN'S ENTRY INTO POLITICS

> The huge distance observed in the manifestation of political interest of women of different educational levels points to the differentiated dissemination of the stereotype of the strict separation of private and public space and the exclusion of women from the latter in different generations and different cultural/social environments.

(Pantelidou-Malouta 1992:170) This finding is very important when we consider that there are still countries where women do not have access to education, their own profession, their own money, their bodies, their sexuality, and ultimately their very lives. The degree of political participation and activation clearly does not concern only gender and cannot be limited to it, as there are many factors that influence participation in civic and political life. Even now that quotas create mixed feelings, there are enough women who claim the obvious. The scissor or chasm that has been created over time and still exists will take a long time to close. Passing a law or quotas is not enough, it is certainly a step, but what needs to change to see the increasing participation of women in mobilization and politics is the perceptions of individuals about the presence of women in politics. Both men and women reproduce prejudices regarding the presence of women in politics. Society evaluates beauty in relation to women in a way that tends to present it as the best and most ideal quality for their gender. When the woman finally submits to society's demands, she is characterized as naive, stupid, and superficial, while when she disobeys she is criticized – again – as "that's not a woman" and various such cosmetics for women who do not meet her expectations of "ideal" beauty and "ideal" femininity. If a male politician doesn't meet a society's standards of beauty, there is no problem, but if a female politician doesn't, a cesspool breaks out that overlooks education, experience, potential, discipline, consistency, etc., and focuses solely on external characteristics. According to Papagiannopoulou (2009:26) the following are references to the non-selection of women as candidates for Parliament and local government come from members of different Nominating Committees of British Political Parties in the 1980s:

- She is too pretty, voters won't take her seriously!
- She is very old (the candidate was around 50)!
- She is too young, she might get pregnant!
- She better go home and take care of her children!
- She wears a lot of rings!
- The workers will not vote for a woman!

A woman's beauty and appearance in general works in such a way that it almost devalues all her other abilities and skills. This logic is fueled by the print and digital media, which manufactures femininities ready for consumption. Some typical journalistic titles are:

- See 10 beautiful female parliamentarians who rocked their country's parliaments
- The 11 sexiest Greek politicians in a countdown.
- The glamor of the ballot box: The world's sexiest female politicians.

As it becomes clear from the related titles, society wants women to be beautiful and sexual. Unfortunately, not much has changed since the 1980s, as the narrative surrounding female politicians is still deeply gendered and sexist. The headlines are rife with sexism and reduce women's politics to a beauty contest. It is also worth noting the words that dominate social media. Below are some comments that typically accompany a news item which refers to a female candidate for the title of President of the Republic in Greece in 2020, who eventually took the position. The comments below the article are disappointing, to say the least. Comments such as:

- Get a female candidate for president of the Republic to play.
- I find her sexy!
- Looks like Harry Potter's owl.
- The next pot!
- An indifferent candidate for a meaningless position.
- Does the person who chose the photo really like it?
- Hahahahaha!!!
- What favors has she done them?
- Ust sichama.
- Let's hope a woman behaves like a man, because the presidents so far have been women … .
- Where are you going my dear with such a look?

These comments summarize the stereotypes that are often reproduced about female politicians. These comments concern appearance, ability to assume a position, sexuality, and how it is used to assume the position. Also, the phrase "What favors has she done them" suggests that a woman cannot merit a position because of qualifications, etc., but because she is beautiful or has done sexual "favors". Whereas, in the phrase "Let's hope a woman behaves like a man because, until now, the presidents have been womanizers", the term man becomes indicative of virtues such as honesty, uprightness, efficiency, etc., while the term "womanizers" is used pejoratively to indicate cowardice, cunning, inefficiency, etc. According to this logic, a woman must "act like a man" to be effective, assuming that the aforementioned virtues are the preserve of men. "The woman must be beautiful, since she always becomes the object and never the subject of observation" (Yiannikopoulou 2011:190). The comments blast the candidate, not because of her qualifications or not, but because of her outward appearance, which does not meet the standards of beauty constructed by ("Western") society. It is noteworthy that, if in the end, a female politician meets the Western standards of beauty, the undermining starts again from her beauty, which she used as a weapon, as well as from her sexuality, which she also used to get there!

The phenomenon also known as mansplaining is when "… usually a man explains something to a woman in a condescending, patronizing or patronizing way. In several cases, women voters were characterized by political scientists as 'politically naive'" (Pantelidou-Malouta 1987:11). But how do culturaldDiscourses reproduce power relations? Cultural discourses construct dipoles, which categorize the abilities, inclinations, and characteristics of the genders. "Since the 18th century, the notions of male 'activity' and female 'passivity' appear" (Laqueur 2003:12). What are the consequences of the distinction of social roles? How harmful are these restrictions?

How does gender inequality relate to social roles? "Gender relations and the social status of women and girls are viewed as culturally defined social roles that carry specific ideological and moral connotations" (Zavvo 2013:169). How were social roles linked to the dipoles of nature and culture? How did the identification of women's identity with "the house" and motherhood contribute to the regression and delay of professional, economic, and social independence?

> What are the obstacles to women's liberation? Closing at home. It is something that gives no prospects for the woman to develop her personality. Her abilities – the spiritual ones– remain unsatisfied... She struggles to adapt to a situation that keeps her in obscurity … ! Another obstacle is the mentality of men.
>
> **(Nikolaidou 1985:20–21)**

The mindset, not only of men but also of women, contributed to the perpetuation of unequal power relations and the perpetuation of gender inequalities. The reasons greatly shaped and influenced the upbringing of children, who – essentially – reproduced what they had been taught to take for granted. The worst thing is that the gender stereotypes, if we look at philosophy, science, and everyday life, as they were depicted in the media, television, and books, map the images of an era, which destroyed the freedom of women.

7.4 HOW TO OVERCOME GENDER STEREOTYPES?

The 1960s and 1970s were critical periods, where new forms of resistance were manifested and new demands were registered in the field of the political agenda, which showed the power that politics can exert from below.

> The rise of collective identities was not only based on the theoretical weakening of self-centeredness, it found support in the widespread feeling of dissatisfaction among citizens, in their distrust of whether the existing system could represent them equally and effectively, or was it merely imposing roles and identities on them for its own sake. interest and its preservation.
>
> **(Koliri 2017:12–13)**

The new claims bring issues of female identity and sexuality into the public discourse. These issues, which until then did not have a place in the public arena, are replaced in the public discourse and highlight issues of freedom and access of individuals to democracy and the ownership of themselves to define their bodies and lives. "The discussion about gender started in the area of the first feminism and quickly expanded to mainly minority groups" (Koliri 2017:16). The issue of gender remained for years on the sidelines of political claims. Even when women exercised the right to vote, the degree of participation was very low, showing the role that political socialization had played until then. The desire and claim of women to belong to the context of the citizen and to have the right to vote emerges in one of the most basic demands of the first feminism, which is the condition for further claims and rights. This new form of claims is being sabotaged by many women, who see this change as abnormal. The consolidation of opinions, as far as the role of women is concerned, is explained by the way the first claims are made, which are on the margins.

How does patriarchy affect women's access to public space and politics? How do gender discourses relate to patriarchy?

> Feminist sociologists often use this term – of patriarchy – arguing that patriarchy is not only manifested in family power relations, but also in the general set of social arrangements that serve to reinforce that men remain in control and women remain subordinate.
>
> **(Hall and Gieben 2003:265)**

Patriarchy structures familial, professional, and economic relationships, which makes it difficult for women to advance. A typical example is that of the "glass ceiling", which adversely affects the opportunities that women have for professional and economic advancement. Can there be democracy when women cannot participate in politics? Can there be democracy when women are treated as second-class citizens? Are laws and decrees enough to ensure women's access to politics? How effective is the quota practice? How do gendered discourses indirectly affect women's freedom of action? How difficult is it to recognize gender Reasons when they act indirectly and often unconsciously for all genders?

The decade of the 1960s was important, because there appeared then, not only an increase in new forms of political participation, but also because there were developments in the basic conflict stakes (DellaPorta and Diani 2010:4). Thus, a different approach to the discussion of "private issues" is expressed and the boundary between public and private space is exceeded. Subjects that were considered part of private life are repositioned in the public space and claim visibility. In this way, "private" issues are politicized, as they cease to be an individual matter.

The emergence of new ways of claiming affects the way they are seen and presented in the public space and discourse. The crisis of parties and the credibility of forms of political participation give rise to new forms of mobilization. In this way, ideological categorizations are overcome, political participation is broadened and claims concern demands related to beliefs, values, and symbols (position of women, environment, vegetarianism, etc.). "Historians note, in this respect, that feminism has managed to attract mass support only in those cases where its political goals have been compatible with many different ideological options and aspirations" (Cameron 2018:13). The multiple readings of the identity also allow more massive participation in such actions. The more inclusive the collective action, the more effective it will be, as it will include in its demands the individual perceptions, experiences, and experiences of individuals.

The mapping of the claims and struggles of feminist voices is done, many times, by distinguishing them into "waves", which focus on new demands each time based on the socio-economic and political changes with which they coexist and at the same time disagree. What are these waves characterized by? According to Cameron (2018:16), the course they follow is as follows:

- 1st wave – legal and civil rights (mid-19th century–1920s)
- 2nd wave – feminist activism – more radical elements (late 1960s)
- 3rd wave – explicit opposition to the feminist approach of the 2nd wave (1990s)
- 4th wave – interdisciplinary feminism (today)

But is this distinction effective or does it hide discontinuities? It is clear that the distinction between these forms is made with the aim of a more complete understanding and demarcation of the relevant actions, but this does not mean that the distinction must be absolute, as there are feminist movements and activist actions that escape from these forms or adopt conflicting one's practices. According to the same author (16–17), the wave model has been criticized from many sides. In more detail, some of them report that the adoption of the "waves" has:

- Oversimplified the history of the feminist movement.
- Encourages overgeneralizations about feminist concepts.
- Obscures the continuity that actually characterizes the course of feminist activism.

The ideological differences resulted in the "birth" of different directions as far as the question of the position of women is concerned. Starting from the liberal model, which was more conservative, it focused on women's low wages, changing institutions – but not abolishing them – and argued that women were people first and women second. However, seeing women first as individuals overlooks a series of social injustices against her gender, which hindered their professional and economic development.

Gender equality has been the subject of distinct public policies at the International and European levels since the 1970s. Important international and European organizations are active in the fight against gender discrimination, such as:

- The United Nations (UN) Organization, which has declared the safeguarding of women's rights as a priority (declaration of the decade 1975–1985 as the decade of women's rights) and concentrates the relevant actions of the implementation of the "International Convention on the Elimination of All Forms of Discrimination against Women" (CEDAW) in all countries.
- The European Union (EU), which monitors and commits the Member States with the goal of promoting gender equality through a series of legislative and advisory texts (Directives, Resolutions, Decisions). After all, the basic EU Treaties include gender equality as a primary objective of the Union, classifying it in the social provisions (Article 119 of the Treaty of Rome and Article 141 of the Treaty of Amsterdam). The influence of European guidelines on national policies was more pronounced after the Treaty of Amsterdam in 1997, which upgraded the objective of gender equality to an EU task and highlighted the need to promote it through all Community policies (Articles 2 and 3)

- The Council of Europe, which has chosen as a priority the fight against violence against women, positively influences national policies to fight gender-based violence (Athanasatou 2014:19).

The historical path of political gender equality is divided, for its needs overview, into five periods, which reflect different political circumstances and correspond to different goals and tools. In these five periods, we distinguish the following individual approaches in relation to the central goal of equality:

- Equal treatment.
- Positive actions in favor of women.
- Inclusion of gender equality in all policies (gender mainstreaming).
- "Subduction" of gender equality to equality for all.

It should be noted that political and legislative initiatives were framed from a wide range of theoretical and political elaborations. The main factor of these developments was, of course, the feminist movement and its dynamic claims to Western Europe in the 1960s and beyond (second-wave feminism, especially after 1968). In Greece, the dynamic emergence of feminist claims, which caused corresponding state policies, was recorded after the fall of the dictatorship in 1974 (Athanasatou 2014:20). Equality is still a claim of feminist groups and collectives, while official state power also takes into account women's participation in political events.

REFERENCES

Athanasatou, Ioanna. 2014. *National and European Policies.* Athens: KETHI.

Cameron, Debora. 2018. *Feminism: Past and Present of a Movement* (F. Ditsas, transl.). Athens: University Press of Crete.

DellaPorta, Donatella, & Diani, Mario. 2010. *Social Movements: An Introduction.* Athens: Critique.

Giannikopoulou, A. . 2011. 'And they lived well and we lived better': Theses and anti-positions for the woman of the illustrated fairy tales. In Vitsilaki M., Gasouka G. & Papadopoulos (eds.), *Gender and Culture.* Athens: Diadrasi, pp. 189–216.

Hall, Stuart, & Gieben, Bram. 2003. *The Shaping of Modernity: Economy, Society, Politics, Culture.* Athens: Savvalas.

Koliri, Xristina. 2017. *Gender as Bait: Psychoanalysis, Politics and Art.* Athens: Pataki Publications.

Laqueur, Thomas. 2003. *Constructing Gender: Body and Gender from the Ancient Greeks to Freud.* Athens: Polytropon Publications.

Makris, S.. 2015. *Feminism and Democracy: From MaryWallstonecraft to JudithButler.* Thessaloniki: Eneken.

Nikolaidou, Eya. 1985. *Women Will Win.* Athens: Glaros Publications.

Pantelidou Malouta, Marw. 1987. Women and politics: Women and political science, social. *Research Review*, 65, pp. 3–22.

Pantelidou Malouta, Marw. 1992. *Women and Politics: The Political Physiognomy of Greek Women.* Athens: Gutenberg.

Papagiannopoulou, Maria. 2009. *Trainers' Manual: Communication Skills for Women in Politics - Equal Participation in Decision-Making Centers: Women at the Heart of Europe*. Athens: KETHI.

Zavvou, Alexandra. 2013. The Construction of Identity and Otherness at School: Cultural Discourse and the Representations of Gender and Immigration. In Alexandra Zavvou, N. Kambouris & Maria Stratigaki (eds.), *Gender, Migration, Interculturality*. Athens: Nisos Publications, pp. 157–180.

8 Social Media Platforms and COVID-19-Related Misinformation in India

Acceptance, Spread, and Implications

Alaknanda Shringare, Pournima Dhume, and Pinky Pawaskar

8.1 INTRODUCTION

The COVID-19 pandemic is unprecedented in many ways. Countries around the world never witnessed a pandemic of this nature and magnitude in the past. Most countries adopted lockdowns as a measure to control the spread of the Coronavirus. Over 100 countries around the world implemented either full or partial lockdown by the end of March 2020 (BBC, 2020) which resulted in the closure of workplaces and educational institutions; strict restrictions were imposed on the movement of people and social gatherings. India is also one of the countries which exercised lockdown as a measure to control the spread of the Coronavirus. India, being the second most populated country in the world, controlling the outbreak of the pandemic was a major challenge for the government. With the outbreak of the COVID-19 pandemic at the beginning of the year 2020, the Indian government implemented a lockdown in the entire country to reduce the transmission of the virus among the people. Subsequently, lockdowns and curfews were announced by the different state governments during the second wave of the pandemic that struck after a year while the restrictions on social gatherings continued.

Owing to such a situation, socializing with people physically has taken a backseat following social distancing norms. Social media became one of the important mediums through which people could communicate with each other and remain connected. Social media platforms became popular not only for connecting with family and friends but also been used for business, education, and entertainment purposes. It even became an important source for the dissemination of crucial information for governments, organizations, and universities and was also used for research in public health (Tsao et al., 2021, p. 175).

DOI: 10.1201/9781003409519-8

The need and importance of social media platforms increased manifold during the pandemic. Since the outbreak of the COVID-19 pandemic, social media platforms are flooded with information about the impact and spread of the pandemic. Almost 57% of social media users across the globe spent close to two and half hours on social media each day during the pandemic as per DATAREPORTAL (2021). In the year 2020, there is an increase in the number of new users joining social media. Further, the report states that Facebook remained as a widely used social media platform in the world during the pandemic. Social media users used seven different social media platforms with more than one billion monthly users (DATAREPORTAL, 2021). Social media platforms include social networking websites such as Facebook, instant messaging apps such as WhatsApp and X (formerly Twitter), and media media-sharing sites such as YouTube. Facebook became one of the social networking sites with the largest number of users and the most preferred social media for COVID-19 updates, which saw an increase of 8.7% users in 2020 (Statista, 2021).

As there are no clearly defined rules and controls over information shared on social media platforms, the information shared may sometimes be harmful (Magro, 2012). Social media platforms have become convenient tools for people to share information at low cost and with simple technology. During lockdowns and curfews, social media platforms became the major source of information to learn about how the world is coping with the pandemic, at the same time it became the source of misinformation about the spread and cure of Coronavirus. A study conducted by the Reuters Institute (University of Oxford, England) analyzed 225 pieces of misinformation between January and March 2020 and found that 88% of the samples analyzed appeared on social media platforms (Brennen et al., 2020). Out of the total samples analyzed by the Reuters Institute, 59% of posts were on X, 27% on YouTube, and 24% on Facebook.

Along with the outbreak of the COVID-19 pandemic, there is also an eruption of misinformation related to the virus on various social media platforms. Both are equally dangerous for humankind. The fear created by the pandemic was easily exploited to create misinformation about the disease. The upsurge in the spread of misinformation was to such an extent that along with health hygiene amidst COVID-19, it became important to practice information hygiene. A warning issued by the

> World Health Organization (WHO) that, countries around the world are facing an "infodemic"— in other sense an "overabundance" of information, due to which, identifying the correct or truthful information, or differentiating between correct and misinformation became difficult for the people. (The Indian Express, 2020b)

The infodemic creates confusion as to which information source to trust, as many rumors create fear and panic in the minds of the people sometimes taking racist and xenophobic forms in terms of digital vigilantism (Ali and Kurasawa, 2020).

8.2 MISINFORMATION AND SOCIAL MEDIA

The term misinformation, interchangeably used with "fake news", is not new, yet it is of great significance in today's world due to its virulent effect and all the entailed consequences. By definition, misinformation is false or inaccurate information that is deliberately created and is intentionally or unintentionally propagated (Wu et al., 2019, p. 81). With just one tweet, powerful influencers can affect people's lives by disseminating news, without fact-checking, to an audience of millions (Cuello-Garcia, Pérez-Gaxiola, and van Amelsvoort, 2020). The openness and timeliness of social media have largely facilitated the creation and dissemination of misinformation, such as rumors, spam, and fake news (Wu et al., 2019). While there were examples of the rapid spread of misinformation dating back to the earliest days of scientific medicine, the internet has brought about a quantum change in the way the information is disseminated (Wang et al., 2019). Most of the misinformation in India is on the instant messaging application WhatsApp, which has more than 500 million users in the country (Krishnan M, 2021).

Social media is called a pandemic of misinformation by Moran (2020). Misinformation refers to the false or misleading information often created and disseminated with no intention to mislead (Wu et al., 2019, p. 81; Lewandowsky et al., 2012, p. 108; Cunliffe-Jone et al., 2018, p. 114). The spread of fake news during the COVID-19 pandemic was examined by Schulman and Siman-Tov (2020) who identified two kinds of fake news about novel Coronavirus – misinformation and disinformation – both are false information, where misinformation is not disseminated deliberately while disinformation is spread deliberately. The available literature on misinformation shows that it is not a new term, yet it is of great significance in today's world because of its virulent effect on a large section of the population owing to the increasing usage of social media platforms. There were examples in the past of the rapid spread of misinformation but in recent years with an increase in the use of internet facilities, there has been a quantum change in the mode of instant communications having a powerful impact on the receivers (Wang et al., 2019). With just one tweet, any person, be it a common man, political leader, or celebrity can impact the lives of the people in an unprecedented manner which spreads usually without any fact-checking (Cuello-Garacia, Pérez-Gaxiola, and van Amelsvoort, 2020). The openness and easy accessibility of social media have enabled the creation and spread of misinformation (Wu et al., 2019) in the absence of conventional gate-keeping mechanisms (Lewandowsky et al., 2012, p. 110).

Social media platforms have the power to intensify any information received through forwards, as they get endorsed by the receiver, without having any access to any expensive media resources (The Indian Express, 2020a). The content spread through social media platforms can be relied blindly upon by the user without any fact-checking, filtering, or judgment (Allcott and Gentzkow, 2017). As observed by Wu et al. (2019, p. 2)

> misinformation is an umbrella term to include all false or inaccurate information that is spread in social media. It is easy to share misinformation, but it may take a long to check and too long to prevent such false information from getting viral.

Bessi (2017, p. 460) examined the large datasets of Facebook posts which supported theories on conspiracy and myth narratives. He observed that the most viral posts on Facebook followed a similar pattern of the Poisson process[1] and the interval time was independent between the posts with an identical distribution. Referring to the political information on social media, Shin et al. (2018) focused on three components: The temporal pattern, content mutation, and services of misinformation by tracing the lifecycle of 17 popular political rumors which were disseminated on X for 13 months during the 2012 US Presidential election. They further write that false rumors (misinformation) resurface, but true rumors (facts) do not. Social media platforms are exposed to posts that have originated from anywhere in the world which leads to the problem of misinformation (Moran, 2020).

8.3 MISINFORMATION ABOUT COVID-19 ON SOCIAL MEDIA

The proliferation of misinformation on social media is faster than the spread of the COVID-19 virus (Barua et al., 2020). The pandemic has created a conducive environment to propagate rumors or false information. The usage of social media increased manifold during a pandemic and with it, increased the risk of the spread of misinformation about the disease. The study by Gabarron, Oyeyemi, and Wynn (2021, p. 456) reveals that between 0.2% to 28.8% of social media posts related to COVID-19 during the first phase of the pandemic fall under the category of misinformation. It was reported by the WHO (2021) that, in the first three months of 2020 nearly 6,000 people around the globe were hospitalized and at least 800 people died because of misinformation about COVID-19. Lack of access to reliable and accurate information results in the spread of misinformation and even hinders the efforts to counter it (Cunliffe-Jone et al., 2018, p. 116). Cristina Tardaguila, the Associate Director of the International Fact-checking Network (IFCN), while calling COVID-19 the biggest challenge fact-checker ever faced, mentioned that it is amazing to know the impact of a mixture of panic and lack of data on the human mind (Suarez, 2020). The efforts were made by the global technology companies to prevent the spread of such news. Despite the best efforts of organizations dedicated to external monitoring and fact-checking misinformation about COVID-19 continued to spread. Reuters Institute of Oxford University conducted a study on misinformation related to COVID-19 and found that most of such content was deleted yet a significant amount of such content is in circulation (Marechal, MacKinnon, and Dheere, 2020).

Khan (2020) highlighted how anxieties were triggered due to misinformation and COVID-19 threat, and social media fatigue of working from home resulting in a lower level of work engagement. While raising concern over the spread of misinformation about COVID-19 on social media Cuello-Gracia, Pérez-Gaxiola, and Amelsvoort (2020) urged the need for health professionals and scientists to engage actively on social media, share the facts which are scientifically proven and raise alarm when found any misinformation. Schulman and Siman-Tov (2020) stressed the need for increased transparency and public awareness during the pandemic. Doctors and healthcare workers have a great role and responsibilities in the age of social media where misinformation about the disease is spreading at a fast scale (Moran, 2020, p. 1248).

During the pandemic, India witnessed the dissemination of pseudoscientific misinformation about the virus and its cure (Sule, 2020, p. 18). Four stages of the spread of misinformation in India and parts of Asia identified as waves of misinformation by Khan (2020) which include first, the misinformation about the origin of the virus; second, old images and videos circulated creating fear; third, misinformation about cures and lastly, misinformation about lockdown resulting in panic buying and hoarding of household products and food supply. Badrinathan (2021) categorized COVID-19 misinformation in India into two, fake miracle cures and conspiracy theories. She has included in the first category, home remedy and Ayurveda as a cure to the virus and in conspiracy theories included the narrative which scapegoats' minorities.

Between January 2020 to December 2020, the fact-checking organizations in India had checked 1,927 stories of which 310 stories were related to misinformation about the lockdown and 135 stories of misinformation about cures (Khan, 2021). As per the data gathered by Khan (2021), there is an increase in misinformation about lockdown between March 2020 to July 2020. In an analysis of 178 facts, done by BOOM, a fact-checking organization based in India, between January to May 2020 (The Indian Express, 2020a), there was evidence of phased misinformation spread across social media platforms (Sutaria, 2020). Sutaria (2020) writes that the BOOM study found that there was an increase in the spread of misinformation about COVID-19 in March. She further writes most of the misinformation circulated was through video (35%), text messages (29.4%), and audio clips (2.2%). BOOM's study, as mentioned by Sutaria (2020), classified two waves of misinformation – medical and communal – spread through social media platforms.

Most of the misinformation in India is found to be on the instant messaging application WhatsApp, which has more than 500 million users in the country (Krishnan, 2021). Sengupta (2020) examined the spread of misinformation on WhatsApp groups and observed that such misinformation not only stirs up emotions but also leads to forming an opinion about the cause and solution to the crisis. Obiala et al. (2021) in their study of the most frequently shared articles about COVID-19 in April 2020 found that Facebook remained the dominant social media platform for sharing content. The study conducted by Al-Zaman (2021, p. 1) shows most Facebook users trust misinformation (60.88%), and few can deny (15.16%) or doubt (13.30%) the claim based on proper reasons. The study also reveals that acceptance of religious misinformation is more compared to other types of misinformation. The study conducted by Shahi, Dirkson, and Majchrzak (2021) on the spread of misinformation about COVID-19 on X, reveals that verified X handles are also involved in either creating or spreading misinformation. Their study also shows false information propagates faster than partially false information. The information in India is consumed on encrypted chat-based applications, WhatsApp which has the biggest market and encrypted features that make tracing the source of such information near to impossible (Badrinathan, 2021). Following the spread of misinformation, an advisory was issued by the government of India to Facebook, YouTube, TikTok, Snapchat, and X to take responsibility for the spread of misinformation about COVID-19 on their feeds (Palit, 2020).

> Given the exponential growth of the COVID-19 pandemic, the unchecked and rapid spread of misinformation, primarily fueled by social media, presents a pressing public health challenge for COVID-19 control and mitigation measures, as confusion sowed by misinformation hinders public trust, consensus, and subsequent action. (Limaye et al., 2020, p. 277).

There was news floating around about how eating garlic prevents getting an infection (The Indian Express, 2021), drinking hot water, or drinking cow urine can all prevent getting an infection. Taking vitamin C and eating garlic are being hailed as miracle remedies despite the complete lack of evidence (Mian and Khan, 2020). The WHO however, has clarified that there is no evidence for garlic being a cure for novel coronavirus while it has some antimicrobial properties (The Indian Express, 2020b).

Based on the review of the literature available on misinformation related to COVID-19, it was evident that most of the studies examined the extent of misinformation spread about COVID-19 and the challenges faced by fact-checking organizations to trace and curb the misinformation spread. In the Indian context, the studies focused mainly on the types of misinformation spread, the commonly used platforms for such spread, and the misinformation about the cure for the disease. Though most of the works focused on the extent of the spread of misinformation about COVID-19 and the medium used for the spread, the underlying factors that caused the acceptance, belief, and spread of misinformation were not explored much. This chapter attempts to examine the driving factors determining the acceptance and belief of misinformation received on social media platforms related to COVID-19 and its spread. Further, we examine the impact of demographics on the spread of misinformation related to COVID-19 and its implications.

The following research questions and corresponding objectives of the study were formulated:

RQ1: What factors determine the acceptance and belief of COVID-19-related information on social media platforms by the people?

Objective 1: To investigate the factors that determine the acceptance and belief of COVID-19-related misinformation received by people on social media platforms.

RQ2: To what extent do people verify and spread the misinformation related to COVID-19 received over social media platforms?

Objective 2: To examine whether the people verify and spread the COVID-19-related misinformation on social media platforms.

RQ3: Is there an impact of demographics on the spread of COVID-19-related misinformation on social media platforms?

Objective 3: To examine the impact of demographics on the spread of COVID-19-related misinformation on social media.

RQ4: What are the implications of acceptance, belief, and spread of COVID-19-related misinformation on social media on the people?

Objective 4: To identify the implications of the COVID-19-related misinformation received on social media platforms on the people and to determine its relationship with the demographics.

8.4 METHODOLOGY

The study was conducted through a primary survey by circulating a structured questionnaire in an online mode via Google Forms. The data was collected from 390 respondents across India using a random sampling method. The data was collected during the period from September 2020 to January 2021. The data collected were analyzed using SPSS statistical software version 20. The statistical techniques employed for this study are exploratory factor analysis (EFA), a Chi-square test, and a graphical analysis. Exploratory factor analysis (EFA) was employed to study objective 1, graphical analysis was employed for objective 2, and a Chi-square test was employed to study objectives 3 and 4.

The self-structured questionnaire contained four sections; the first section gathered data on demographics viz., age, gender, educational qualification, type of residence, and religion. The second section is comprised of 23 statements on factors determining the acceptance and belief of misinformation about COVID-19 on social media platforms. All the statements followed a 5-point Likert scale ranging from 1- strongly disagree to 5- strongly agree. The third section emphasized the spread of misinformation on social media related to COVID-19. This section is comprised of 11 statements on the spread of misinformation following a 5-point Likert scale. The fourth section collected data on receipt of information through text messages, audio, videos, animations, and images on COVID-19 and its implications on the citizens.

8.5 ANALYSIS AND DISCUSSION

The empirical analysis has been divided into four sections. The first section discusses the demographic profile of the respondents. The second section deals with the factors determining the acceptance and belief of misinformation received on social media. The third section highlights the receipt and spread of misinformation on social media platforms and the fourth section emphasizes the interlinkage between demographics and the spread of misinformation and its implications on the people.

8.5.1 Demographic Profile of the Respondents

The demographic details of the respondents are displayed in Figure 8.1. The data is gathered from 390 respondents on age, gender, educational qualification, religion,

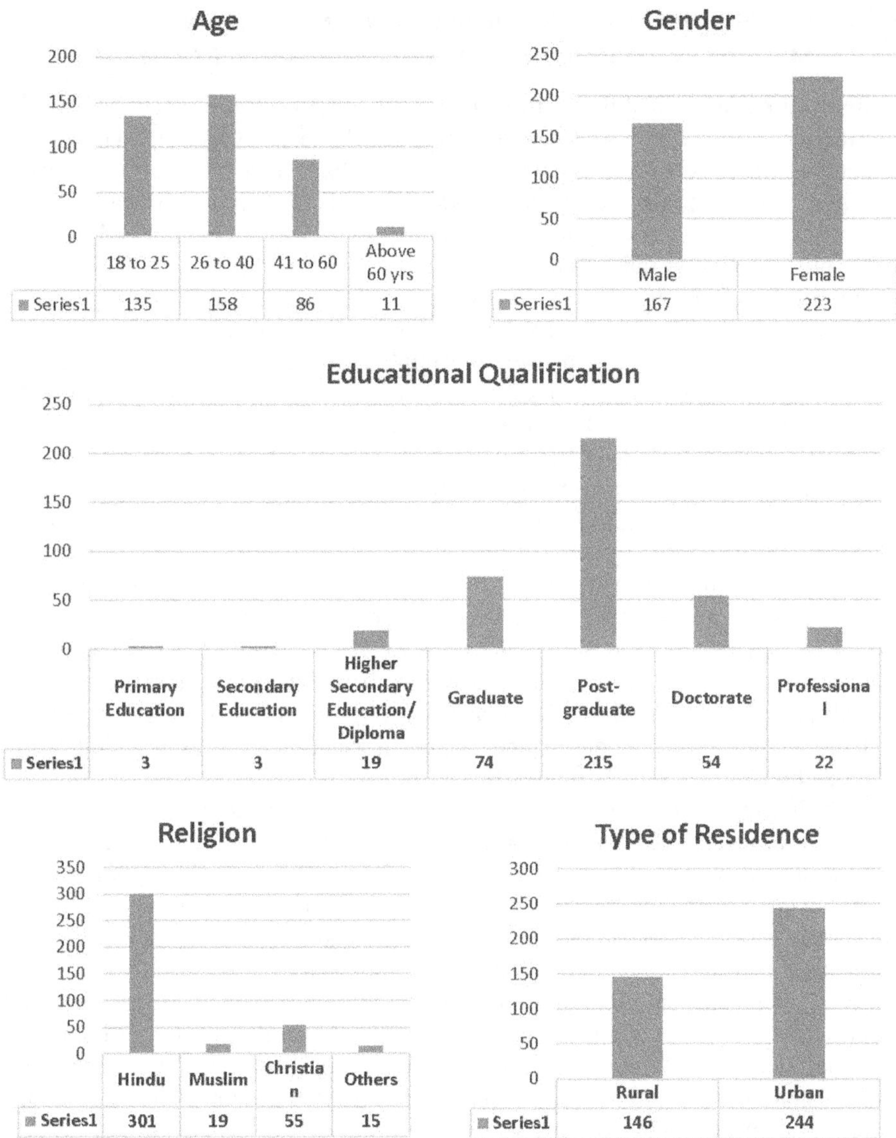

FIGURE 8.1 Demographic profile of the respondents.

and type of residence. Around 158 respondents (40%) are of the age group between 26 to 40 years constituting the majority, followed by the age group between 18 to 25 (34%). The study consists of 56% female respondents. The majority of the respondents (55%) are post-graduate degree holders. About 76% of respondents are Hindus followed by the Christian (14%) and Muslim (4%) communities. The majority (61%) of respondents reside in urban India.

8.5.2 Factors That Determine the Acceptance and Belief of Misinformation Received on Social Media about COVID-19

In this section, we studied the factors that lead to the acceptance and belief of misinformation received on social media platforms related to COVID-19. The factors influencing the acceptance and belief of COVID-19-related misinformation were examined using the exploratory factor analysis (EFA). Three significant factors emerged from the results of exploratory factor analysis viz., Factor 1 (F1): Believing in the misinformation due to curiosity, fear, and similar ideology; Factor 2 (F2): misinformation received from known sources; Factor 3 (F3): Up-to-date, fast, and quick information. These three factors explained 48.55% of the total variance. A Kaiser–Meyer–Olkin (KMO) measure of sampling adequacy 0.91 indicates that the data is good for factor analysis. Exploratory factor analysis can be employed if the KMO value is more than 0.60 and the data is valuable at a 1% significance level.

The following factors determine the acceptance and belief of COVID-19-related misinformation spread on social media platforms by people.

Factor 1 (F1) – Believing the misinformation due to curiosity, fear, and similar ideology:

People believe in the COVID-19 misinformation shared on social media platforms due to curiosity and fear of the virus. They want to know more about the coronavirus and try to gather as much information as possible, as very little is known about the novel coronavirus. The lack of clear evidence about the disease made people curious and fall prey to the misinformation shared on social media platforms. Curiosity is the main factor keeping people engaged in the information websites as also stated in the study by Sharron and Abraham (2015, p. 259).

With this fear, people begin to believe in the misinformation shared on social media platforms. Though scientists and health workers are using social media platforms to spread awareness about COVID-19, many others misuse these platforms for spreading misinformation. Lockdowns, curfews, social distancing norms, and work-from-home disrupted the social life of the people and increased reliance on social media platforms for connecting with people as well as for information.

Further, the analysis highlights that people with similar ideas, ideologies, and beliefs, trust the information shared on social media. Fact-checkers are important for social media and in the absence of fact-checkers people believe the information which is consistent with their beliefs and they use these false statements as evidence to support their ideologies (Su, 2020).

Factor 2 (F2) – Information received from known sources:

The intensity and extent of the spread of COVID-19 cases among the countries within a short period made people fearful and believe in the information/misinformation shared on social media. People believed in the information especially when it is shared by known sources such as friends, family members, or other sources in whom they believe. Although most of the respondents in the study mentioned that they never forward text/audio/video messages without verifying; however, the number of respondents who fall in the category of rare, sometimes, often, and always (send the information received on social media platforms without verifying) when

TABLE 8.1
Factors Determining the Acceptance and Belief of Information Received on SMPs about COVID-19

Factor Analysis (Overall α =0.92, n=16)		F1	F2	F3
F1: Believing the information due to curiosity, fear, or similar ideology **(α = 0.91)**	Latest topic of discussion	.762		
	Inclination towards the same idea	.744		
	Curious about more information	.739		
	Matches my opinion and thoughts	.723		
	Believe due to fear of COVID	.705		
	Interested to know updates	.699		
	Received in audio form	.610		
	I believe all information received on social media	.601		
	Received in video form	.582		
	Believe as I come under containment zone (Restricted areas during COVID-19 from which people were not allowed to move out)	.569		
F2: Information received from known sources **(α = 0.78)**	Sent by trusted sources		.745	
	Sent by family member		.721	
	Sent by friend		.654	
	Received with a link to a website		.593	
F3: Up-to-date, fast and quick information **(α = 0.69)**	I rely on social media for up-to-date information			.810
	Social media is a fast and quick source of information			.779
KMO measure of sampling adequacy			0.91	
Eigen values		7.768	1.197	1.065
Total variance explained		48.551	7.480	6.658
Cumulative variance explained		48.551	56.030	62.689

Source: Author's compilation

put together it is understood that a large segment of the population still does not verify the information received by them on social media before forwarding it.

Factor 3 (F3) – Up-to-date, fast, and quick information:

The analysis revealed that people rely on social media for up-to-date information. Social media is also seen as a fast and quick source of information about COVID-19 and has become one of the reasons for believing in the misinformation circulated through social media platforms. With more and more people becoming part of social media sites such as Facebook, X, WhatsApp, and others, there is a quick transfer of information within no time and without much cost involved. People are free to post their comments and share the messages and videos that are being circulated. Curiosity to know more about COVID-19 and to keep oneself updated with the information became the reason for believing in most of the information shared on social media.

8.5.3 Receipt and Spread of Misinformation on Social Media Platforms

In this section, we discuss the extent to which messages were received and spread on social media platforms in the form of text, audio, and video on COVID-19-related misinformation. A graphical analysis has been performed on the data gathered from the respondents.

Since ancient periods India has been known for ayurvedic/herbal medicines and people believe in ayurvedic/herbal home remedies. Before the outbreak of the COVID-19 pandemic people used *Kadha* (a kind of herbal tea) to cure the common cold and fever. Drinking hot water, *Haldidudh* (turmeric milk), salt water gargling, and inhaling steam were some of the popular home remedies used by people to cure mild coughs and colds. With the outbreak of COVID-19 having similar symptoms as a cough and cold, the home remedies practiced in Indian houses went viral on social media though there is no scientific evidence for these being the cure for COVID-19.

Figure 8.2 exhibits the graphical analysis of the responses of the respondents about the misinformation related to COVID-19 received on social media platforms. It is evident from that, 90% of respondents received messages on drinking hot water or salt water gargling as prevention of COVID-19. Around 79% of respondents received messages about the consumption of garlic/ginger/turmeric/lemon/*tulsi* as a prevention for COVID-19. Around 74% of the respondents stated that the messages were received that blamed certain countries and communities for the spread of Coronavirus disease. Around 78% responded that they have received messages related to causes/symptoms and cure of Coronavirus disease. Few respondents (12%) agreed that they have received messages on the consumption of cow dung/cow urine as prevention of Coronavirus disease.

Apart from the receipt of messages on social media platforms, we further analyzed to what extent people spread the misinformation without verifying its authenticity. Figure 8.3 exhibits the data gathered from the respondents on the forwarding of messages either through text, audio, or videos without verifying their authenticity.

When asked to the respondents whether they forwarded text, audio, and video messages in separate questions the responses revealed that 46% of the total respondents do not forward "text" messages without verifying their authenticity, 48% of the total respondents do not forward "audio" messages and 46% of the total respondents do not forward the "video" messages without verifying authenticity. This is exhibited in Figure 8.3.

8.5.4 Relationship between Demographics and the Spread of Misinformation and Its Implications on People

In this section, we analyzed the relationship between the demographics and the spread of misinformation using the Chi-square test. Further, the implications of the misinformation related to COVID-19 on the people and its relationship with the demographics of the respondents are studied using the Chi-square test.

The results in Table 8.2 indicate that there exists an impact of age on the spread of misinformation *(Chi-square = 35.13*)*. Respondents belonging to the age group

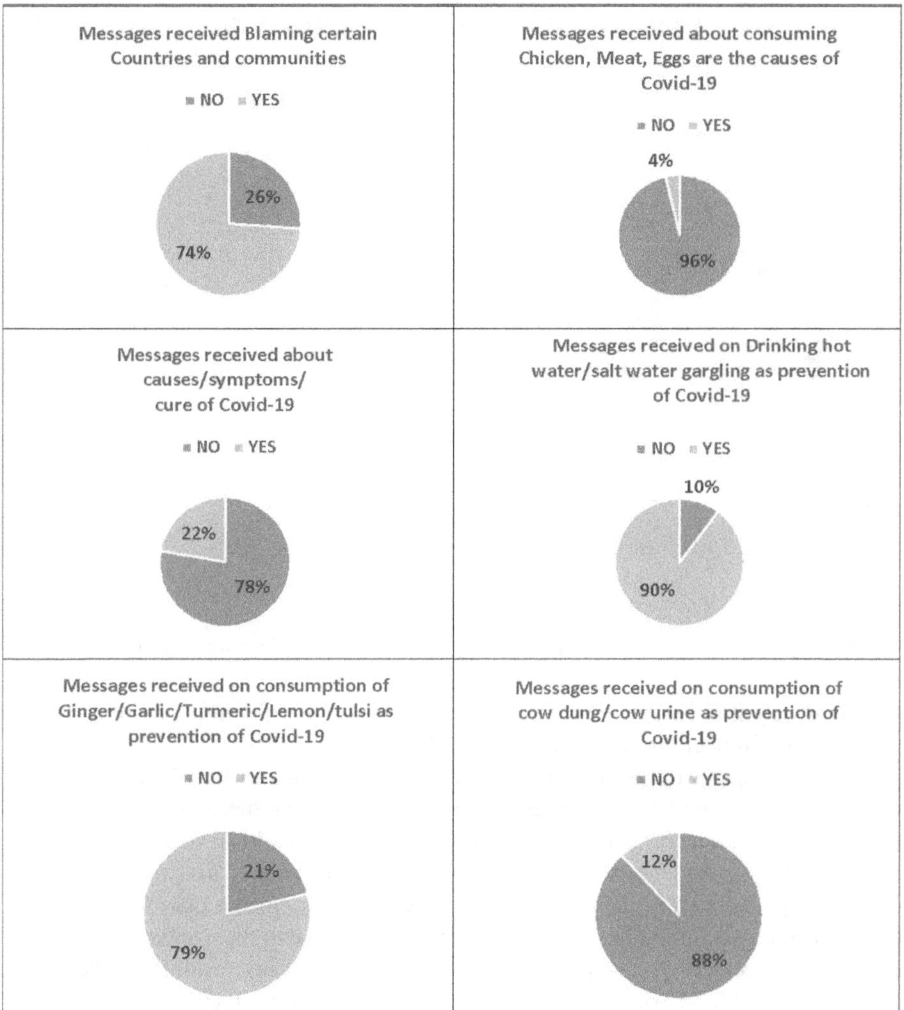

FIGURE 8.2 Graphical analysis of Information received on SMPs related to COVID-19.

of 18 to 25 forwarded the information received on social media platforms related to COVID-19 to keep everybody informed whenever they find the information to be eye-catching. Respondents belonging to the age group of 41 to 60 forwarded the COVID-19-related information received on social media platforms to keep everybody around them informed. The demographic variable residence played a significant role *(Chi-square = 50.18*)* in terms of its impact on the spread of misinformation. The results revealed that respondents residing in the urban area spread the COVID-19-related information to keep everyone informed whereas, rural area respondents forwarded the information as they found it to be eye-catching. The rest

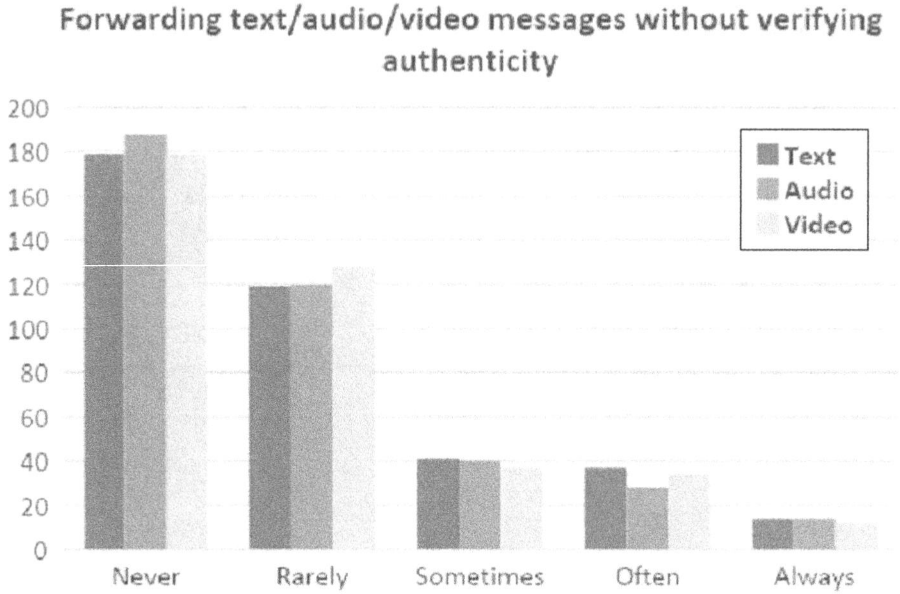

FIGURE 8.3 Spreading the misinformation without verifying the authenticity.

of the demographic variables viz., gender, educational qualification, and religion had no significant impact on the spread of misinformation.

Table 8.3 displays the relationship between demographics and implications of misinformation using the Chi-square test. The results reveal that there exists a significant relationship between the demographic variables viz., educational qualification *(Chi-square = 69.16*)*, residence *(Chi-square =20.50*)*, and religion *(Chi-square = 64.18*)*, with the implications of misinformation received on social media platforms. There is no significant association between age group and gender with the implications of misinformation received on social media platforms. Respondents residing in the urban areas started drinking hot water along with saltwater gargling; they started consumption of ginger, garlic, *tulsi* (a kind of basil), turmeric, lemon, and green tea to prevent Coronavirus. The respondents belonging to urban as well as rural areas developed hatred towards certain communities and countries assuming that these communities and countries were responsible for the spread of COVID-19 in India and across the globe. Almost all age group people in the study except for the people who are 60 years and above, started consuming herbal medicines or started drinking hot water and did salt water gargling. These activities are found more among females compared to males. It is interesting to note that a large number of post-graduates and respondents from urban areas started either using herbal medicines or drinking hot water and doing salt water gargling. From among the religious groups, these activities are followed by a large number of Hindus compared to the respondents from other religious communities.

The spread of misinformation about drinking cow urine or cow dung as a cure for COVID-19 was also rampant. A video of some men from Gujarat applying cow

TABLE 8.2
Relationship between Demographics and Spread of Misinformation Using Chi-Square Test

Demographics	Spread of Misinformation			
	Forward because of eye-catching information	Forward to keep people informed	Forward as wanted to be the first person to inform	Forward because habituated to forward
Age				
18 to 25	25	69	16	4
26 to 40	23	91	6	2
41 to 60	6	55	3	0
Above 60 years	0	8	0	0
Chi-square		***35.13****		
Gender				
Male	22	100	13	2
Female	32	123	12	4
Chi-square		***1.83***		
Educational Qualifications				
Primary Education	0	3	0	0
Secondary Education	2	2	0	0
Higher Secondary Education/ Diploma	2	11	1	0
Graduate	14	39	7	2
Post-graduate	28	118	13	3
Doctorate	8	0	4	0
Professional	36	14	1	0
Chi-square		***22.41***		
Residence				
Rural	32	68	18	1
Urban	22	155	7	5
Chi-square		***50.18****		
Religion				
Hindu	43	170	20	6
Muslim	2	11	2	0
Christian	8	35	3	0
Others	6	0	0	0
Chi-square		***5.30***		

Source: Author's compilation
*Significant at 0.05 level of significance.

TABLE 8.3
Relationship between Demographics and Implications of Misinformation Using Chi-Square Test

Demographics	Implications of Misinformation					
	Started drinking hot water/ salt water gargling	Started consuming ginger/garlic/ lemon/turmeric/ tulsi/green tea	Started consuming cow dung/ cow urine	Stopped consumption of eggs/ chicken/meat	Developed hatred towards certain communities	Developed hatred towards certain countries
Age						
18 to 25	74	46	2	7	57	40
26 to 40	93	75	0	5	62	41
41 to 60	57	53	1	4	32	22
Above 60 years	7	8	0	1	4	2
Chi-square				*25.94*		
Gender						
Male	97	79	1	7	73	48
Female	134	103	2	10	82	57
Chi-square				*2.67*		
Educational Qualifications						
Primary Education	0	0	0	0	1	2
Secondary Education	1	1	0	0	0	0
Higher Secondary Education/ Diploma	15	7	0	0	4	3
Graduate	43	33	1	9	21	10
Post-graduate	128	96	2	4	101	71
Doctorate	35	33	0	3	20	15
Professional	9	12	0	1	8	4
Chi-square				*69.16**		
Residence						
Rural	78	57	3	4	64	46
Urban	153	125	0	13	91	59
Chi-square				*20.50**		
Religion						
Hindu	181	148	2	17	100	65
Muslim	9	7	1	0	11	10
Christian	33	20	0	0	35	22
Others	8	7	0	0	9	8
Chi-square				*64.18**		

Source: Author's compilation
**Significant at 0.05 level of significance.*

dung on their bodies as a cure for COVID-19 was viral (The Indian Express, 2021). Hosting of "cow urine parties" was also witnessed at some places with the belief that drinking cow urine will prevent COVID-19. Doctors in India warned the people against such activities. There were also videos and messages about eggs and chicken carrying some kind of virus, the fear of which made people stop eating eggs and chicken. However, in this study, very few people responded that they stopped the consumption of eggs and chicken due to the fear of the virus.

The present study also reveals that a sizable number of respondents developed hatred towards certain communities. Following the religious gathering of the *Tablighi Jamaat* held in mid-March 2020, Muslims were held responsible for the spread of coronavirus in India. Videos were being shared on Facebook and X falsely accusing Muslims of spreading the virus (Slater and Masih, 2020). "Hashtags such as 'Corona Jihad', 'Corona Terrorism' and 'CoronaBombsTablighi' began to trend on X in India" (The Guardian, 2020). The spread of misinformation on social media platforms resulted in the development of hatred against certain communities as reported in the present study.

The study also reveals hatred developed towards certain countries.

8.6 FINDINGS AND CONCLUSION

India witnessed the first wave of COVID-19 in March 2020, followed by the second wave the year after and the ongoing restrictions on social gatherings made people reliant on social media platforms to seek information. Previous studies on misinformation related to COVID-19 lacked discussion of the underlying factors responsible for the acceptance, belief, and further spread of misinformation. This study was carried out to investigate the extent of misinformation spread over social media platforms, to what level it is accepted and believed, and the factors responsible for the spread of the same. The findings of the study reveal that the information received on social media platforms was mainly about the prevention and cure for COVID-19 followed by the messages received on blaming certain communities and countries for the spread of COVID-19. The study discovers three major factors that determine the acceptance and belief of misinformation received on social media platforms about COVID-19. Among these three major factors identified in the study, the factors that have the highest impact on people are curiosity and fear about COVID-19. The study also shows that people believe in misinformation if they have a similar inclination and belong to the same ideology. People having similar inclinations towards certain ideologies and beliefs usually identify themselves with the information shared on social media platforms.

Further, an attempt was made to examine the relationship between the demographic variables and the spread of misinformation. The results displayed that, age and residence of the people have a significant impact on the spread of misinformation about COVID-19 on social media platforms. The relationship between the demographics and implications of the misinformation shared about COVID-19 on social media platforms was also examined. The outcome reveals educational qualifications, residence, and religion have a significant impact on the implications of misinformation spread on social media platforms. The study emphasized that most people, forward the messages on social media platforms without verifying their authenticity which leads to the further spread of misinformation.

8.7 LIMITATIONS AND FUTURE SCOPE

The study in this chapter carried out a primary survey considering 390 respondents selected on a random basis across India. This study can be widened for a larger population which can be carried out across different states of India and the impact of cultural differences on the belief, acceptance, and spread of misinformation related to COVID-19 could be studied in the future.

NOTE

1. Poison Process is a model to study series of discrete event in which average time between the event is known but the exact timing of the even remains random. Refer to https://towardsdatascience.com/the-poisson-distribution-and-poisson-process-explained-4e2cb17d459 for more details.

REFERENCES

Ali, S. Harris, and Fuyuki Kurasawa. "COVID19: Social media both a blessing and a curse during coronavirus pandemic." *The Conversation* 22 (2020). Retrieved from https://theconversation.com/covid19-social-media-both-a-blessing-and-a-curse-during-coronavirus-pandemic-133596.

Allcott, Hunt, and Matthew Gentzkow. "Social media and fake news in the 2016 election." *Journal of Economic Perspectives* 31, no. 2 (2017): 211–236. https://doi.org/10.1257/jep.31.2.211.

Al-Zaman, Md. Sayeed. "Social media and COVID-19 misinformation: How ignorant Facebook users are?" *Heliyon* 7, no .5 (2021): e07144. https://doi.org/10.1016/j.heliyon.2021.e07144.

Badrinathan, Sumitra. "India is facing an epidemic of misinformation alongside Covid-19." *Washington Post* 7 (2021). https://www.washingtonpost.com/opinions/2021/06/07/india-misinformation-covid-19-pandemic/

Balmau, Oana, Rachid Guerraoui, Anne-Marie Kermarrec, Alexandre Maurer, Matej Pavlovic, and Willy Zwaenepoel. "Limiting the spread of fake news on social media platforms by evaluating users' trustworthiness." (2018). http://arxiv.org/abs/1808.09922.

Barua, Zapan, Sajib Barua, Salma Aktar, Najma Kabir, and Mingze Li. "Effects of misinformation on COVID-19 individual responses and recommendations for resilience of disastrous consequences of misinformation." *Progress in Disaster Science* 8 (2020): 100119. https://doi.org/10.1016/j.pdisas.2020.100119.

BBC. "Coronavirus: The world in lockdown in maps and charts." (2020, April 7). Retrieved from https://www.bbc.com/news/world-52103747.

Bessi, Alessandro. "On the statistical properties of viral misinformation in online social media." *Physica. Part A,: Statistical Mechanics and its Applications* 469 (2017): 459–470. https://doi.org/10.1016/j.physa.2016.11.012.

Brennen, J. Scott, Felix M. Simon, Philip N. Howard, and Rasmus Kleis Nielsen. "Types, sources, and claims of COVID-19 misinformation." PhD diss. University of Oxford,

London, 2020. Retrieved from https://reutersinstitute.politics.ox.ac.uk/types-sources-and-claims-covid-19-misinformation.

Cuello-Garcia, Carlos, Giordano Pérez-Gaxiola, and Ludo van Amelsvoort. "Social media can have an impact on how we manage and investigate the COVID-19 pandemic." *Journal of Clinical Epidemiology* 127 (2020): 198–201.

Cunliffe-Jone, P., A. Diagne, A. Finlay, S. Gaye, W. Gochunge, C. Onumah, C. Pretorius, and A. Schiffrin. "Misinformation: One part of a wider information disorder." (2018). Retrieved from https://www.jstor.org/stable/pdf/j.ctv1v3gqw5.20.pdf?refreqid=fastly-default%3A63629179f4f97e7667f031012d8e4de0&ab_segments=0%2FSYC-6168%2Fcontrol&origin=search-results.

DATAREPORTAL. "Global social media stats." (2021). Retrieved from https://datareportal.com/social-media-users.

Gabarron, Elia, Sunday Oluwafemi Oyeyemi, and Rolf Wynn. "COVID-19-related misinformation on social media: A systematic review." *Bulletin of the World Health Organization* 99, no. 6 (2021): 455.

Khan, Ali Nawaz. "A diary study of psychological effects of misinformation and COVID-19 threat on work engagement of working from home employees." *Technological Forecasting and Social Change* 171 (2021, June): 120968. https://doi.org/10.1016/j.techfore.2021.120968.

Khan, N. "Trends in Covid-19 misinformation in India." (2020). Retrieved from https://www.ha-asia.com/trends-in-covid-19-misinformation-in-india/.

Krishnan, M. "Misinformation dominates India's social media landscape in the Covid surge." (2021). Retrieved from https://www.rfi.fr/en/international/20210512-misinformation-dominates-india-s-media-landscape-in-covid-surge.

Lewandowsky, Stephan, Ullrich K.H. Ecker, Colleen M. Seifert, Norbert Schwarz, and John Cook. "Misinformation and its correction: Continued influence and successful debiasing." *Psychological Science in the Public Interest: A Journal of the American Psychological Society* 13, no. 3 (2012): 106–131.

Limaye, Rupali Jayant, Molly Sauer, Joseph Ali, Justin Bernstein, Brian Wahl, Anne Barnhill, and Alain Labrique. "Building trust while influencing online COVID-19 content in the social media world." *The Lancet Digital Health* 2, no. 6 (2020): e277–e278.

Magro, Michael J. "A review of social media use in e-government" *Administrative Sciences* 2, no. 2 (2012): 148–161.

Maréchal, Nathalie, Rebecca MacKinnon, and Jessica Dheere. "Getting to the source of Infodemics: It's the business model." *A Report from Ranking Digital Rights* (2020). https://rankingdigitalrights.org/wp-content/uploads/2023/07/Getting_to_the_Source_of_Infodemics_Its_the_Business_Model_2020-05.pdf.

Mian, Areeb, and Shujhat Khan. "Coronavirus: The spread of misinformation." *BMC Medicine* 18 (2020): 1–2.

Moran, Patrick. "Social media: A pandemic of misinformation." *The American Journal of Medicine* 133, no. 11 (2020): 1247.

Obiała, Justyna, Karolina Obiała, Małgorzata Mańczak, Jakub Owoc, and Robert Olszewski. "COVID-19 misinformation: Accuracy of articles about coronavirus prevention mostly shared on social media." *Health Policy and Technology* 10, no. 1 (2021): 182–186. https://doi.org/10.1016/j.hlpt.2020.10.007.

Palit, Parama Sinha. "Leveraging on the Pandemic: Can Modi Succeed?." *RSIS Commentaries* (2020): 105–120. Retrieved from https://www.rsis.edu.sg/wp-content/uploads/2020/05/CO20105.pdf.

Schulman, Roy, and David Siman-Tov. *From Biological Weapons to Miracle Drugs: Fake News about the Coronavirus Pandemic*. Institute for National Security Studies, 2020, pp. 1–5. Retrieved from www.jstor.org/stable/resrep23529.

Sengupta, S. "How to stir confusion amidst a pandemic: COVID-19 and misinformation on WhatsApp" *Economic and Political Weekly, Engage* (2020). Retrieved from https:// www. epw. in/engage/article/how-stir-confusion-amidst-pandemic-covid.

Shahi, Gautam Kishore, Anne Dirkson, and Tim A. Majchrzak. "An exploratory study of COVID-19 misinformation on Twitter ." *Online Social Networks and Media* 22 (August 2020) (2021): 100104. https://doi.org/10.1016/j.osnem.2020.100104.

Sharron, Sharron, and Juneman Abraham. "The role of curiosity in making up digital content promoting cultural heritage." *Procedia - Social and Behavioral Sciences* 184 (August 2014) (2015): 259–265. https://doi.org/10.1016/j.sbspro.2015.05.089.

Shin, Jieun, Lian Jian, Kevin Driscoll, and François Bar. "The diffusion of misinformation on social media: Temporal pattern, message, and source." *Computers in Human Behavior* 83 (2018): 278–287. https://doi.org/10.1016/j.chb.2018.02.008.

Slater, J., and N. Masih. "The Washington post." (2020). Retrieved from https://www.washingtonpost.com/world/asia_pacific/as-world-looks-for-coronavirus-scapegoats-india-pins-blame-on-muslims/2020/04/22/3cb43430-7f3f-11ea-84c2-0792d8591911_story.html.

Statista. "Most popular social networks worldwide as of April 2021, ranked by several active users." (2021). Retrieved from https://www.statista.com/statistics/272014/global-social-networks-ranked-by-number-of-users/.

Su, Y. "Social media use increases belief in COVID-19 misinformation." (2020). Retrieved from https://news.wsu.edu/2020/12/14/social-media-use-increases-belief-covid-19-misinformation/.

Suarez, E. "How fact-checkers are fighting coronavirus misinformation worldwide." (2020, March 31). Retrieved from https://reutersinstitute.politics.ox.ac.uk/news/how-fact-checkers-are-fighting-coronavirus-misinformation-worldwide.

Sule, A. "COVID-19 and infectious misinformation." *Economic and Political Weekly* 55, no. 24 (2020, June 13). Retrieved from https://www.epw.in/journal/2020/24/commentary/covid-19-and-infectious-misinformation.html.

Sutaria, S. "Coronavirus misinformation in India is not limited to health misinformation." (2020). Retrieved from https://meedan.com/reports/coronavirus-misinformation-in-india-is-not-limited-to-health-misinformation/.

The Guardian. "Coronavirus conspiracy theories targeting Muslims spread in India." (2020). Retrieved from http://www.theguardian.com/world/2020/apr/13/coronavirus-conspiracy-theories-targeting-muslims-spread-in-india.

The Indian Express. "Maximum Covid-19-related fact checks in April related to communal rumours: BOOM study." (2020a, May 9). Retrieved from https://indianexpress.com/article/india/fake-news-in-the-time-of-coronavirus-boom-analyses-178-fact-checks-on-covid-19-related-misinformation-since-january-6401441.

The Indian Express. "Fake News in the time of coronavirus: Why it's time to practice information hygiene." (2020b, April 6). Retrieved from https://indianexpress.com/article/opinion/fake-news-in-the-time-of-coronavirus-why-its-time-to-practice-information-hygiene-6349641/.

The Indian Express. (2021, May 17). Retrieved from https://indianexpress.com/article/lifestyle/health/fact-check-cow-dung-cant-cure-covid-19-may-cause-black-fungal-infection-7314872/.

Tsao, Shu-Feng, Helen Chen, Therese Tisseverasinghe, Yang Yang, Lianghua Li, and Zahid A. Butt. "What social media told us in the time of COVID-19: A scoping review." *The Lancet Digital Health* 3, no. 3 (2021): e175–e194.

Wang, Yuxi, Martin McKee, Aleksandra Torbica, and David Stuckler. "Systematic literature review on the spread of health-related misinformation on social media." *Social Science and Medicine* 240 (2019, January): 112552. https://doi.org/10.1016/j.socscimed.2019.112552.

WHO. "Fighting misinformation in the time of COVID-19, one click at a time." (2021). Retrieved from https://www.who.int/news-room/feature-stories/detail/fighting-misinformation-in-the-time-of-covid-19-one-click-at-a-time.

Wu, Liang, Fred Morstatter, Kathleen M. Carley, and Huan Liu. "Misinformation in social media: Definition, manipulation, and detection." *ACM SIGKDD Explorations Newsletter* 21, no. 2 (2019): 80–90.

9 SIR Model for Understanding the Spread of Fake News and Hate Speech

Renji George Amballoor and Shankar B Naik

9.1 INTRODUCTION

While delivering the presidential address at the American Economic Association, Prof. Robert Shiller (2017) pointed out that narratives are stimulating simple stories that can go viral (Prateek, 2017). Arthropods such as mosquitoes are the vector for the spread of diseases such as malaria. Similarly, narratives and stories are vectors of ideas (Mokyr, 2016). The diffusion of narratives follows a hump-shaped curve, similar to the spread of infections as proposed by the epidemiological model of (Kermack and McKendrick, 1927). According to Mehra (2019), narratives are contagious and can generate herd behavior.

Disruptive social media applications such as Facebook, WhatsApp, Twitter, Instagram, YouTube, TikTok, etc., have become the current communication diffusion model for the dissemination of narratives, including those with hate and fake elements. The penetration of mobile phones has increased the social media footprints of users. The objective of social media platforms is to gain a bigger share of the cognitive surplus (Shirky, 2010) of its users (Kermack and McKendrick, 1927), thereby creating a competitive revenue stream.

For dominant sections of society, social media has become a part and parcel of everyday life. They depend on social media for news, updates, stories, entertainment, social interactions, (Kermack and McKendrick, 1927), work, gossip, product/service recommendations, emotional and spiritual needs, etc. (Greenwood and Gopal, 2015). According to Chaffey (2023), social media users are about 59% of the world's population.

The consequences of social media are like two sides of a coin – beneficial and detrimental. The disastrous impact includes the generation and spread of fake news and hate speeches. Today, the creation and circulation of "believable false information" (Kshetri and Voas, 2017) has multiplied automatically with the pole-vaulting of the applications of artificial intelligence (AI) and smart algorithms.

 DOI: 10.1201/9781003409519-9

The document prepared by the European Union titled toolkit of human rights speech classifies a speech as hate speech if it is dehumanizing, targets a particular group/section of society, or promotes prejudice and intolerance.

With the ongoing technological revolution, the concept of fake news is continuously evolving (Kim et al., 2021). It comes under the broader category of disinformation which involves the fabrication and dissemination of news (Shahi et al., 2021). There is strong evidence to support the need to identify and stop the spread of fake news but there is no unanimity as far as the definition of fake news is concerned (Khan et al., 2021). The detection of fake news is also a major challenge for policymakers and law enforcement agencies. The popularity of the word gained momentum during the 2016 US presidential election (Albright, 2016). The COVID-19 pandemic not only created a global health emergency but also a contagious fabrication and spread of fake news which came to be known as an infodemic (Zarocostas, 2020; Beauvais, 2022). According to Wong (2016) more than half of the traffic taken from Facebook is fake and partisan. It is noticed that fake news is created using hoaxes, rumors, myths, propaganda, unreliable opinions, etc. According to Lazer et al. (2018), fake news pertains to falsified information that imitates the appearance of genuine news media material but does not follow the same procedures or have the same intentions. The goal is to deceive readers and lead them astray. In other words, they are unverified and fabricated stories, comments, opinions, and statements with the potential to disturb the peace in a region.

The spread of false news is viral and contagious. The ecosystem generated by social bots and algorithms reduces the turnaround time for the creation and diffusion of fake news. Different motivations for the creation and spread of fake news may disgrace an individual or a section, money, fun, gain power, generate money, etc. (Figueira and Oliveira, 2017).

Speech that aims to harm or show disrespect towards an individual or a group based on their identity is classified as hate speech (Chetty et al., 2018). The language is malicious, offensive, and abusive to generate hatred, dislike, hostility, violence, prejudice, and negativity about a section of society with ulterior motives. As in the case of fake news, hate speech does not have a universally accepted definition (Baider et al., 2020).

In hate speech, there are three parties namely the originator, the content of the speech, and the victimized (Seglow, 2016). The basis of hate speech may be gender, caste, region, culture, ethnicity, religion, skin color, etc. The online dissemination of hate speech, either live or recorded, has become a challenge for governments in all parts of the country.

The creation and diffusion of fake news and hate speech are not desirable for the economy, society, and people. The social cost the economy must bear of fake news and hate speech is huge. Often, all items of cost do not get added to social costs because of the complex impact created by fake news and hate speeches.

Hence there is a need to understand the mechanism and the properties of the diffusion (Woo et al., 2016) of fake news and hate speech. Diffusion is the process by which a disease, information, news, or speech spreads from one person to another. The diffusion of fake news and hate speech on social media is like the spread of diseases.

Diffusion models allow us to comprehend the spread of novel diseases, information, or products, forecast their success or failure during the initial phases, and manipulate the likelihood of their diffusion either positively or negatively. In the present case study, we used the Kermack–McKendrick SIR (Susceptible–Infected–Recovered) model developed to explain the spread of infectious diseases in epidemiology. According to Kawachi (2008), the dissemination of rumors can be examined using the epidemic model. The disease propagation model and SIR model are similar to the spread of information on social media (Kubo et al., 2007). The study by Woo and Chen (2011) used the SIR model to explain the diffusion of information on Jihadi social media.

The objective of the study is to understand the spread of fake news and hate speech using the Kermack–McKendrick SIR model.

9.2 BACKGROUND

9.2.1 The Kermack–McKendrick SIR Model

The Kermack–McKendrick SIR model is a mathematical model used to understand the spread of infectious diseases in a population. It is employed to describe the transmission of communicable diseases within populations of size N. The population is divided into three sets; susceptible individuals (S), infected individuals (I), and recovered individuals (R). Set S represents individuals who are not yet infected and may become infected in the future. Set I consists of individuals who are currently infected, while set R represents those who have recovered from the infection. At any given instance, $N = S + I + R$.

As individuals become infected, they move from set S to set I at a rate of β . This results in a decrease in the size of the susceptible set S. The rate of change in the size of S denoted as $\frac{ds}{dt}$ depends on the size of sets I and S and the transmission rate β . This scenario is modeled as $\frac{ds}{dt} = -\beta SI$. The negative sign indicates that the change in the size of set S is negative and set S is shrinking.

As individuals get infected, they transit from set S to set I, thereby increasing the size of set I. The rate at which the size of the set I increases, denoted as, is the same as the rate at which the size of the set S decreases, i.e., βSI. This scenario can be modelled as $\frac{dI}{dt} = \beta SI$. The absence of a negative sign implies that the size of I is increasing due to this transition. However, as time progresses, individuals recover and transit from set I to set R. If the rate of recovery is ν, then the rate at which the size of set I decreases depends on ν and the size of set I itself which is, νI. The size of the set I increase at the rate βSI while it decreases at the rate νI. Hence, the net rate of change in the size of set I is modeled as $\frac{dI}{dt} = \beta SI - \nu I$.

As individuals recover, the size of set R increases. As mentioned earlier, the rate of change in the size of set R, denoted as $\frac{dR}{dt}$, depends on the recovery rate ν and the size of set I. This is modeled as $\frac{dR}{dt} = \nu I$.

The model is represented by a set of differential equations that describe the rate of change of each category over time. Hence, the formulation of the Kermack–McKendrick SIR model is:

$$\frac{dS}{dt} = -\beta SI \tag{9.1}$$

$$\frac{dI}{dt} = \beta SI - vI \tag{9.2}$$

$$\frac{dR}{dt} = vI \tag{9.3}$$

where β is the rate of transmission and v is the rate of recovery.

The SIR model assumes that the population is closed, i.e., there is no migration in or out of the population, and that individuals do not become immune to the disease after being infected; there is no immunity acquired from a previous infection. The model also assumes that the disease spreads through direct contact between individuals.

The SIR model has a wide range of applications in different fields. It is widely used to model the spread of infectious diseases such as COVID-19, measles, and tuberculosis. It can be used to predict the spread of infectious disease and the impact of different control measures, such as vaccination or social distancing on the spread of the disease. The SIR model informs public health policies and decisions, helping determine the best timing and the number of vaccination campaigns or estimating the likely impact of different strategies on the spread of diseases.

The SIR model has been applied to study the dissemination of a firm's market information (Amballoor and Naik, 2021). It can also be used to study the economic impact of diseases and other public health issues, estimating the costs of an outbreak, such as productivity loss and increased healthcare expenses. The SIR model can be used to study the spread of information, rumors, and fake news on social networks.

By modeling the process of information diffusion, researchers can identify key factors that influence the spread of information and design meaningful strategies to prevent the spread of misinformation.

The SIR model is also used to study the spread of diseases among wildlife populations, such as the spread of foot and mouth disease in cattle. The model helps understand how diseases spread among populations and how interventions, such as vaccination programs, can reduce the spread of diseases. The SIR model can also be used to study the spread of behaviors and attitudes, such as smoking, and to design ways to promote healthy behaviors or reduce behaviors detrimental to healthy living. Additionally, the SIR model has been applied to study the spread of contaminants and pollutants in natural systems, such as the spread of pollutants in water systems. The model helps identify the sources of contamination and design effective strategies to reduce pollution.

Despite its usefulness, the SIR model has several limitations. It makes simplifying assumptions about the population, such as assuming it is closed and homogeneous, whereas in reality, populations are complex and heterogeneous. The model relies on overall data on the number of individuals in each set (*S*, *I*, and *R*), and does not consider individual-level data on demographics, behavior, or social networks. This limitation can affect the model's ability to accurately predict the spread of diseases or fake news and hate speech in specific populations. Additionally, the SIR model is based on historical data and may not handle real-time data, making it less responsive to changes in the spread of diseases or fake news and hate speech in real-time.

The model only considers the spread within a single local population, not accounting for spread across borders and at global levels, limiting its ability to predict or control the spread of diseases or fake news and hate speech globally. Lastly, the SIR model does not consider the social, economic, and political context in which diseases or fake news and hate speech spread, limiting its usefulness in designing measures that account for these factors.

9.2.2 Application of the SIR Model to the Spread of Fake News and Hate Speech in a Population

The SIR model can be applied to analyze the propagation of fake news and hate speech within a population. The population is divided into three categories; those susceptible to believing and spreading such content, those exposed to it, and those immune to fake news due to education or skepticism towards unreliable sources.

The model likens the spread of fake news and hate speech to infectious disease, with the transmission rate reflecting the likelihood of exposure and belief, and the recovery rate representing the likelihood of immunity to fake news and hate speech. Various factors, including the news source, news type, and population characteristics, influence the spread.

Strategies to curb this phenomenon involve enhancing social media literacy, promoting awareness, and fostering critical thinking to increase the recovery rate and reduce the spread of fake news and hate speech and its impact.

Utilizing the SIR model offers several advantages. It provides a clear means to comprehend the dynamics of fake news spread, aiding researchers and policymakers in identifying influential factors and developing effective strategies. As a quantitative model, the SIR approach allows for mathematical analysis, offering a more systematic approach to studying the spread of fake news and hate speech than qualitative methods.

Additionally, the SIR model facilitates predictions by adjusting the parameters, such as transmission and recovery rates. Researchers can simulate the impact of different strategies on the spread of fake news and hate speech, and predict how the epidemic will evolve. Policymakers can gain insights into preventing fake news spread and design effective policies by identifying the most impactful strategies. The interdisciplinary nature of the SIR model, integrating epidemiology, mathematics, and social science, ensures a comprehensive understanding of the issues, leading to more effective strategies.

9.3 LIMITATIONS WHEN APPLYING THE SIR MODEL TO THE SPREAD OF FAKE NEWS AND HATE SPEECH

There are specific limitations when applying the model to the spread of fake news and hate speech. Fake news and hate speech are complex phenomena that can manifest in various forms. There is no standard definition of fake news, making it challenging to consistently and reliably identify and measure its spread. Despite ongoing research on the subject, data on the spread of fake news and hate speech remain limited, posing challenges in estimating transmission and recovery rates and validating the assumptions of the SIR model.

The SIR model assumes that individuals behave rationally and that their behavior is influenced solely by the transmission and recovery rates. However, in the case of fake news, individuals' beliefs and behavior can be influenced by a variety of social and psychological factors, including biases, political beliefs, word of mouth, and social networks. These factors add complexity and make accurate modeling of the spread of fake news and hate speech challenging.

Moreover, the SIR model does not account for the influence of different types of information sources, such as social media and news outlets, on the spread of fake news. Understanding the impact of these sources is crucial for designing effective strategies to combat the spread. The model assumes that the spread of fake news and hate speech is solely determined by the transmission and recovery rates, neglecting external factors such as political, religious, and regional considerations, and media biases. Ignoring these factors significantly limits the effectiveness of strategies based on the SIR model. Hence, these considerations motivate the focus of this study.

9.4 METHODOLOGY

The study proposes to use the Kermack–McKendrick SIR model to understand the dissemination of fake news and hate speeches.

9.4.1 Model for Dissemination of Fake News and Hate Speech

Let N be the set of all individuals. Let $S \subseteq N$ be the set of individuals who have not yet received the fake news/hate speech. Individuals in set S may receive fake news/hate speech at some moment in the future. Let I be the set of people who have received it and for some reason believe in it. Since they believe in fake news/hate speech, they have the potential to spread it to others.

Let R be the set of people who do not spread fake news/ hate speech because they have realized it to be fake or to avoid the consequences resulting from the spread. This set of individuals is recovered from the impact of the fake news or hate speech.

Due to the impact of fake news and hate speech, no sooner do the individuals inset S receive it than they immediately move to set I. The individuals in set I can spread the fake news and hate speech to other individuals in set S and get them infected.

The model for the spread of fake news and hate speech in its simplest form is described using Equations (9.1), (9.2), and (9.3).

9.4.2 State Changes in Fake News and Hate Speech Transmission

As per the model outlined in Section 9.4.1, individuals transition from set S to set I and from set I to set R. This transition ceases when set S is empty, i.e., $S = \Phi$. In the context of the spread of fake news and hate speech, numerous situations or scenarios are conceivable. Each of them is considered individually and presented in the subsequent subsections.

9.4.2.1 Individuals Immune to Fake News and Hate Speech

There can be individuals who would never accept fake news and hate speech for various reasons, such as knowing that the news is fake, the speech is undelivered, not relying on the source, or simply lack of interest. For these reasons, they never get infected remaining recovered always. This implies that as soon as they receive the fake news/ hate speech, they move from set S to set R instead of moving to set I. This leads to the division of set S into two partitions, namely set S_S and set S_I such that $S_S \, U \, S_I = S$ and $S_S \cap S_I = \Phi$.

Set S_S consists of individuals in set S who transit to set I upon the receipt of fake news and hate speech. Set S_I consists of the individuals in set S who transit to set R upon the receipt of fake news and hate speech. This results in a further decrease in the size of set S and an increase in the size of set R. Let the rate of transition be denoted as γ. The decrease in the size of set S can be expressed in two components.

The first component is due to the transition of individuals from set S to set I, while the second component is due to the transition of individuals from set S to set R. The decrease in the size of set S due to the first component depends on the transition rate β, the size of set $S_S \subseteq S$, and size of the set I. This is expressed as $\beta S_S I$. The decrease in the size of set S due to the second component depends on the transition rate, the size of set $S_I \subseteq S$, and the size of the set I. This is expressed as $\gamma S_I I$. Hence, the rate of change in the size of set S, denoted as $\frac{dS}{dt} = -I\left(\beta S_S + \gamma S_I\right)$. The negative sign indicates that the change in size is negative, implying that the size of set S is decreasing.

Due to this, the change in size of set R depends on two components. The first component is due to the transition of individuals from set I to set R, which happens due to recovery. This value is already described in Equation (9.3). The second component is due to the transition of individuals from set S to set R.

The value of this component depends on the factors γ, the size of set S_I, and the size of set I. The value of the component is calculated as $\gamma S_I I$. Hence, the rate of change in the size of set R, denoted as $\frac{dR}{dt}$, is calculated as $I(\nu + \gamma \text{ SI})$.

The expression for the change in the size of the set I remains the same except that the first term changes to $\beta S_S I$ from βSI.

Considering this scenario, the model described using expressions (9.1), (9.2), and (9.3) can be rewritten as:

$$\frac{dS}{dT} = -I\left(\beta S_S + \gamma S_I\right) \tag{9.4}$$

$$\frac{dI}{dt} = I\left(\beta S_S - v\right) \quad (9.5)$$

$$\frac{dR}{dt} = I\left(v + \gamma S_I\right) \quad (9.6)$$

9.4.2.2 Re-infection of Recovered Individuals

Even though an individual has transited from set I to set R, in the case of a fake news or hate speech scenario there is a possibility that a recovered individual may get infected with the same information due to reasons such as a change in the source of information, the high convincing power of the source, trust of the individual in the source of information, etc. This kind of transition results in a reduction in the size of set R and an increase in the size of set I.

Let the transition rate of a recovered individual getting infected be κ. The rate of change in the size of set R depends on the transition rate κ, the size of sets I and R. The rate of change in the size of set R due to this is calculated as κRI. The negative sign indicates that the size of set R is decreasing. Hence, the rate of change in the size of set R is $I(\nu + \gamma S_I + \kappa R)$.

Similarly, the rate of change in the size of set I is κRI. Hence, the rate of change in the size of set I is $I(\nu + \gamma S_I + \kappa R)$.

Considering this scenario, the model described using expressions (9.4), (9.5), and (9.6) can be rewritten as:

$$\frac{dS}{dT} = -I\left(\beta S_S + \gamma S_I\right) \quad (9.7)$$

$$\frac{dI}{dt} = I\left(\beta S_S - v + \kappa R\right) \quad (9.8)$$

$$\frac{dR}{dt} = I\left(v + \gamma S_I - \kappa R\right) \quad (9.9)$$

9.4.3 Estimation of Values B, N, Γ, and K

The transition of individuals from one set to another is triggered by the receipt of information. This transition depends upon the sizes of the sets involved and the transition rate, which, in turn, is influenced by the intensity of the impact on the individual's belief in the information received.

The intensity of the impact depends on factors such as the convincing ability of the information source, c, the sensitivity of the information, s, the period of exposure to the source of information, $p = d * f$, and the trust or reliability of the receiver of the information about the source of information. Hence, each of the transition rates can be expressed as a function of these factors, measured as:

$$\alpha = f\left(c, s, p, r\right) \quad (9.10)$$

such that $\alpha \in \{\beta, \nu, \gamma, \kappa\}$, $p = d * f$, d is the duration of exposure and f is the number of times the receiving individual is exposed to the fake information.

As the factors are mutually independent the expression for the transition rate described in expression (9.10) can be written as:

$$\alpha = \frac{\sum_{i=1}^{n} f_i}{n} \tag{9.11}$$

where n is the number of factors influencing the transition rate α and f_i is the measure of factor i.

Not all factors have the same influence on the transition rate α; different factors may have different influences on it. This situation is incorporated by assigning weights to the factors. The values of these weights lie in the range [0,1] with values closer to 0 indicating lower influence while values closer to 1 indicate higher influence on the transition rate. For a set of weights $\{w_1, w_2, \ldots, w_n\}$, where weight w_i corresponds to factor i, the expression for the transition rate can be written as:

$$\alpha = \frac{\sum_{i=1}^{n} w_i f_i}{\sum_{i=1}^{n} w_i} \tag{9.12}$$

Measuring or quantifying the values of the convincing ability of the source, the sensitivity of the information, and the trust or reliability of the receiver of the information about the source of information are themselves questions of research. For the sake of simplicity, in this study, they are assigned Boolean values 0/1.

9.5 EXPERIMENTS

Experiments were conducted to analyze the model proposed in this study. The aim was to understand the trends in the proposed model compared to the existing SIR model. Trends were analyzed by varying the values of the transmission and recovery rate parameters. Additionally, the trends were examined by changing the sizes of sets S_S and S_I. This analysis was carried out using spreadsheets and the Python programming language.

9.5.1 Analysis of the SIR Model Expressed in Equations (9.1), (9.2), and (9.3)

9.5.1.1 Scenario 1

The graph in Figure 9.1 illustrates the trends in the sizes of sets S, I, and R. The transmission rate β was set to 0.0001, and the recovery rate ν was set to 0.25. The population size was fixed at 12,000 individuals.

It can be observed that the size of set S remains the same as the size of the population set N, while the sizes of sets I and R remain zero for the initial 9 days. From

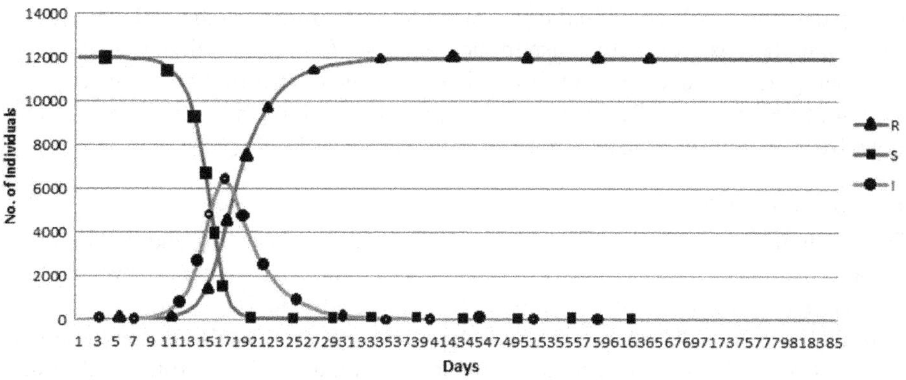

FIGURE 9.1 Rate of change in the size of sets *S, I,* and *R* for recovery rate ν = 0:25 and transmission rate β = 0:0001.

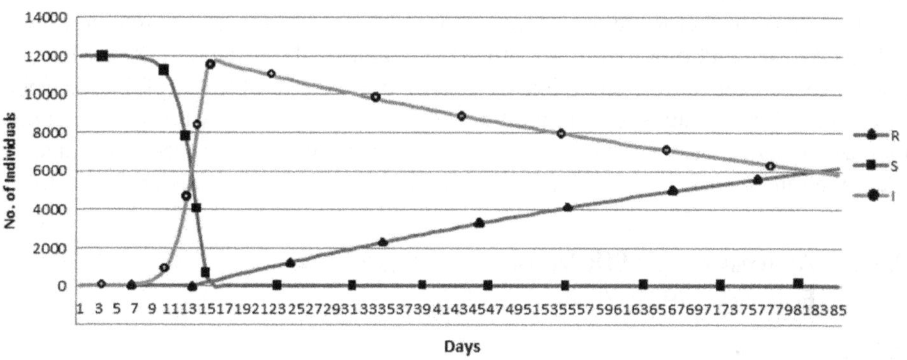

FIGURE 9.2 Rate of change in the size of sets *S, I,* and *R* for recovery rate ν = 0:01 and transmission rate β = 0:0001.

the 10th day onwards, a sharp decrease is observed in the size of set *S*, and this trend continues until the 20th day. Simultaneously, a notable increase in the size of set *R* is observed which is seen converging to the size of set *N* by the 35th day. The size of the set *I* increased from day 9 and reached its maximum value of 6,493 on the 17th day, followed by a subsequent decrease. The size of set *I* follows a normal distribution along the x-axis representing the days.

9.5.1.2 Scenario 2

The graph in Figure 9.2 shows the trends in the sizes of set S, I, and set R. The value of the transmission rate β was set to 0.0001 while the value of the recovery rate ν was set to 0.01. The size of the population was set to 12,000 individuals.

It may be observed that the size of set *S* remains the same as the size of the population set *N* for the initial 9 days, while during this period, the size of set *I* is zero, and for the initial 14 days, the size of set *R* remains zero. From the 10th day onwards a sharp decrease is observed in the size of set S, continuing until the 15th day. At the same time, there is a sharp increase in the size of set I until the 17th day. The size of set I then gradually decreases until it reaches a value of 0. Simultaneously, the size of set R increases gradually from day 15, the day from which individuals recover and move from set I to set R, until it reaches the size of set N.

9.5.1.3 Scenario 3

The graph in Figure 9.3 illustrates the trends in the sizes of sets S, I, and R. The value of the transmission rate β was set to 0.0001, while the value of the recovery rate ν was set to 1. The population size was set to 12,000 individuals.

It may be observed that the size of set S remains the same as the size of the population set N, and sets I and R remain zero for the initial 33 days. From the 31st day onwards a decrease is observed in the size of set S, continuing until the 65th day. At the same time, a very low increase in the size of set I is observed until the 47th day, reaching the maximum value of 184. The size of the set I gradually decreases until it reaches the value of 0.

The size of the set R increases gradually from day 33, the day from which individuals recover and move from set I to set R, reaching the value of 4,000, which is lower than the size of the population set N. Due to the very high value of the recovery rate ν set to 1, individuals recover within a day. This does not allow the size of set I to increase beyond 184. Since the size of set I remains very low compared to the size of set S, the rate at which the size of set S decreases due to infection also remains low.

9.5.2 Analysis of the SIR Model Is Expressed in Equations (9.7), (9.8), and (9.9)

9.5.2.1 Scenario 1

The graph in Figure 9.4 illustrates the trends in the sizes of sets S, SS, SI, I, and R. The value of the transmission rate β was set to 0.0001, while the value of the

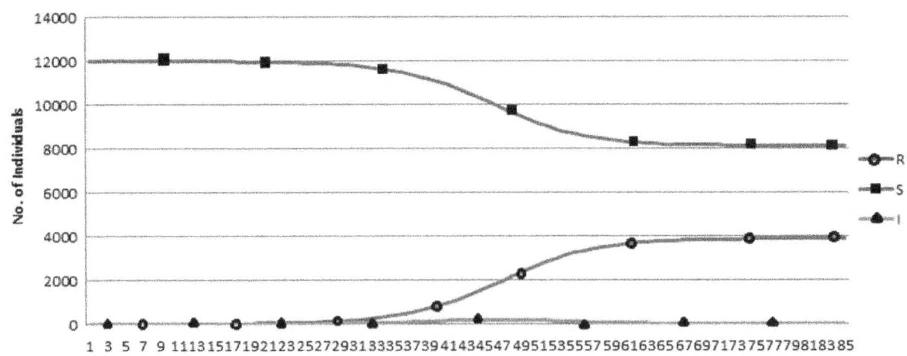

FIGURE 9.3 Rate of change in the size of sets S, I, and R for recovery rate $\nu = 1$ and transmission rate $\beta = 0:0001$.

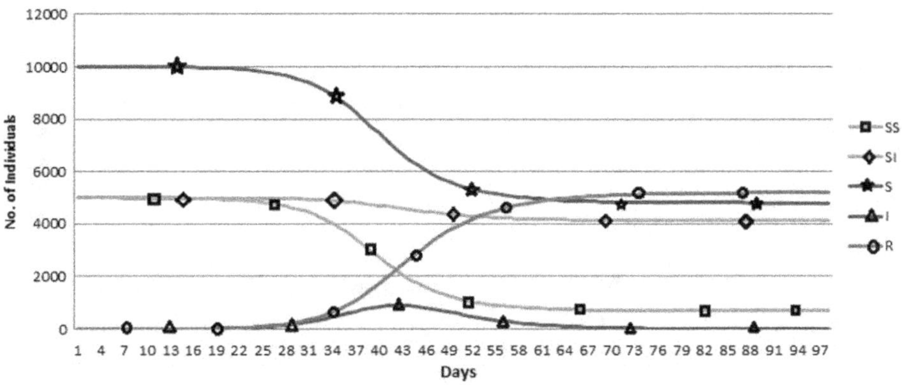

FIGURE 9.4 Rate of change in the size of sets S, S_S, S_I, I, and R for $\nu = 0{:}25$, $\gamma = 0{:}00001$, $\kappa = 0{:}00001$ and $\beta = 0{:}0001$.

recovery rate ν was set to 0.25. The values of γ and κ were set to 0.00001, respectively. The population size was set to 10,000 individuals, with the size of set S_S set to 5,000 individuals and the size of set S_I set to 5,000 individuals.

It may be observed that the size of all sets remained constant for the initial 24 days. Both sets S and S_S decrease from day 25 until day 65. Thereafter, the sizes of both sets remain almost constant. Similarly, the size of set R increases from day 25 until day 67, after which the size of set R almost remains constant.

The change in sizes of sets S, S_S, and R is due to the transition of individuals from set $S_S \subseteq S$ to set I due to the receipt and belief in fake news. And hate speech. The size of the set S_I remains constant followed by a small decrease and continues to remain constant further. This is because the number of individuals in set I is not sufficiently large to pass on fake news and hate speech to a large number of individuals in set S_I. Individuals from set S_I transit to set R upon the receipt of fake news and hate speech as they are already immune and unaffected by it. The size of the set I also remains constant with a slight increase during the period from day 28 to day 63, following a normal distribution.

9.5.2.2 Scenario 2

The graph in Figure 9.5 illustrates the trends in the sizes of sets S, SS, SI, I, and R. The value of the transmission rate β was set to 0.0001, while the value of the recovery rate ν was set to 0.25. The values of γ were set to 0.000, respectively. The population size was set to 10,000 individuals, with the size of set S_S set to 5,000 individuals and the size of set S_I set to 5,000 individuals.

It may be observed that the size of all sets remained constant for the initial 28 days. Both sets S and S_S decrease from day 28 until day 50. Thereafter, the sizes of both sets remain almost constant. Similarly, the size of set R increases from day 28 until day 47. Afterward, the size of set R slightly keeps on decreasing.

However, the size of the set I increase from day 30 until day 94 and then continues to remain almost constant. This situation implies that a large number of individuals

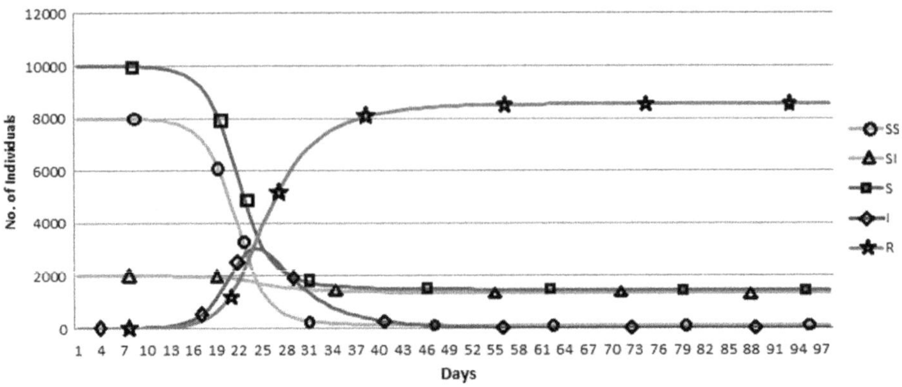

FIGURE 9.5 Rate of change in the size of sets S, S_S, S_I, I, and R for $\nu = 0{:}25$, $\gamma = 0{:}00001$, $\kappa = 0{:}0001$ and $\beta = 0{:}0001$.

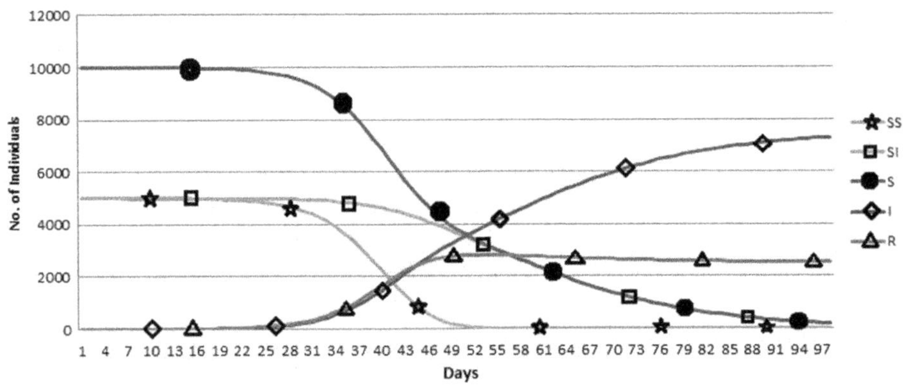

FIGURE 9.6 Rate of change in the size of sets S, S_S, S_I, I, and R for $\nu = 0{:}25$, $\gamma = 0{:}00001$, $\kappa = 0{:}00001$ and $\beta = 0{:}0001$.

remain infected, indicating that they continue to believe in the fake news and hate speech and spread it. This trend is observed due to the high value of the parameter κ, which is the transmission rate for the transition from the recovered set R to set I.

9.5.2.3 Scenario 3

The graph in Figure 9.6 illustrates the trends in the sizes of sets S, SS, SI, I, and R. The value of the transmission rate β was set to 0.0001, while the value of the recovery rate ν was set to 0.25. The values ofγ andκ were set to 0.00001, respectively. The population size was set to 10,000 individuals, with the size of set S_S set to 8,000 individuals and the size of set S_I set to 2,000 individuals.

It may be observed that the trends are similar to those described in scenario 1 of this subsection. However, the size of the set I remains constant with a larger increase during the period from day 13 to day 40 and follows a normal distribution. The increase is more pronounced as the number of susceptible individuals in the population is higher compared to that considered in scenario 1.

9.6 CONCLUSION

The diffusion of fake news and hate speech poses a significant challenge for policymakers. Successful attempts to curb their spread a comprehensive understanding of the framework of misinformation dissemination, as their impact extends to the economy, national security, and vulnerable communities.

This case study present case study employs an epidemiological model to elucidate the dissemination process. The similarities between the spread of disease and the propagation of fake news and hate speech lead us to adopt the Kermack–McKendrick SIR model. However, our study modifies the SIR model to incorporate aspects specific to fake news and hate speech, such as the intensity of impact on an individual's belief in the received information. This intensity is influenced by factors such as convincing ability, source credibility, sensitivity, exposure duration, and the reliability of the source of information.

The proposed model undergoes analysis to understand the trends in the sizes of sets S, S_S, S_I, I, and R over a set of days for different parameter values – transmission and recovery rates, and sizes of sets S_S and S_I.

From the analysis, it becomes evident that the modified SIR model is applicable for understanding the dynamics of fake news and hate speech spread. This model is valuable in designing effective policy interventions and strategies to either curb or reduce the velocity of misinformation spread.

In this case study, experiments were conducted solely to comprehend the trends in the size of sets of individuals, without real dataset analysis. Further plans include executing the model on real datasets. The proposed model assumes homogeneity among sets of individuals with no consideration of individual-level data. The study specifically focuses on the spread of fake news and hate speech within a population set, and the impact of cross-border spread remains unexplored. Future studies aim to investigate the spread of fake news in heterogeneous populations and across borders.

REFERENCES

Albright, J. 2016. "The election 2016 micro-propaganda machine." https://medium.com/@d1gi/the-election2016-micro-propaganda-machine-383449cc1fba.

Amballoor, R.G., and Naik, S.B. 2021. "Dissemination of Firm's market information: Application of Kermack-Mckendrick SIR model." In: Singh, M., Tyagi, V., Gupta, P.K., Flusser, J., Oren, T., and Sonawane, V.R. (eds.), *Advances in Computing and Data Sciences. ICACDS 2021. Communications in Computer and Information Science*, vol 1441. Springer. https://doi.org/10.1007/978-3-030-88244-0_3.

Baider, Fabienne, Millar, Sharon, and Assimakopoulos, Stavros. 2020. "Introduction: Developing, performing and countering hate speech." *Pragmatics and Society* 11(2), 171–176.

Beauvais, Catherine. 2022. "Fake news: Why do we believe it?." *Joint Bone Spine* 89(4). https://doi.org/10.1016/j.jbspin.2022.105371.

Chaffey, Dave. 2023. "Global social media statistics research Summary-2023." *Smartinsights.* https://www.smartinsights.com/social-media-marketing/social-media-strategy/new-global-social-media-research/.

Chetty, Naganna, and Alathur, Sreejith. 2018. "Hate speech review in the context of online social networks." *Aggression and Violent Behavior*40, 108–118.

Figueira, Alvaro, and Oliveira, Luciana. 2017. "The current state of fake news: Challenges and opportunities." *Procedia Computer Science* 121, 817–825.

Greenwood, Brad N., and Gopal, Anand. 2015. "Research note - Tigerblood: Newspapers, blogs, and the founding of information technology firms." *Information Systems Research* 26(4), 812–828.

Kawachi, K. 2008. "Deterministic models for rumour transmission." *Nonlinear Analysis: Real World Applications* 9(5), 1989–2028.

Kermack, W.O., and McKendrick, A.G. 1927. "A contribution to the mathematical theory of epidemics." *Proceedings of the Royal Society* 115(772), 367.

Khan, Tanveer, Michalas, Antonis, and Akhunzada, Adnan 2021. "Fake news outbreak 2021: Can we stop the viral spread?." *Journal of Network and Computer Applications* 190, 103–112.

Kim, B., Xiong, A., Lee, D., et al. 2021. "A systematic review on fake news research through the lens of news creation and consumption: Research efforts, challenges, and future directions." *PLoS One* 16(12), e0260080.

Kshetri, Nir, and Voas, J. 2017. "The economics of fake news." *IEEE It Professional* 19(6), 8–12.

Kubo, M., Naruse, K., and Matubara, T. 2007. "The possibility of an epidemic meme analogy for web community population analysis." In: Yin, H, Tino, P., Corchado, E., Byrne, W., and Yao, X. (eds.),*Intelligent Data Engineering and Automated Learning (IDEAL-2007)*, 1073–1080. Springer.

Lazer, D.M.J., Baum, M.A., Benkler, Y., et al. 2018. "The science of fake news." *Science* 359(6380), 1094–1096.

Mehra, Puja. 2019. "A good narrative is an economic remedy." *LiveMint.* https://www.livemint.com/news/india/a-good-narrative-is-an-economic-remedy-1568747096719.html.

Mokyr, Joel. 2016. *A Culture of Growth: The Origins of Modern Economy.* Princeton University Press.

Raj, Prateek. 2017. *The Role of Narratives in Economics.* University of Chicago Booth School of Business.

Seglow, J. 2016. "Hate speech, dignity and self-respect." *Ethical Theory and Moral Practice* 19(5), 1103–1116. https://doi.org/10.1007/s10677-016-9744-3.

Shahi, G.H., Dirkson, A., and Majchrzak, T.A. 2021. "An exploratory study of COVID-19 misinformation on Twitter." *Online Social Network*, 22, 100–104.

Shiller, Robert J. 2017. *Narrative Economics.* Cowles Foundation Discussion Paper 2069. Yale University Press.

Shirky, Clay. 2010. *Cognitive Surplus: How Technology Makes Consumers into Collaborators.* Penguin Books.

Wong, J.I. 2016. "Almost all the traffic to fake news sites is from Facebook. New data show." https://qz.com/848917/facebook-fb-fake-news-data-from-jumpshot-its-the-biggest-traffc-referrer-to-fake-and-hyperpartisan-news-sites/. (Accessed 1 January 2020).

Woo, J., and Chen, H. 2011. "A SIR model for violent topic diffusion in social media." IEEE International Conference on Intelligent & Security Informatics (ISI). IEEE.

Woo, Jiyoung, et al. 2016. "Epidemic model for information diffusion in web forums: Experiments in marketing exchange and political dialogue." *Springer Plus* 5(66), 1–19.

Zarocostas, J. 2020. "How to fight an infodemic." *The Lancet* 395(10225), 676.

10 Impact on Fake News in Social Media and Current Technology in Detection of Fake News

Rajeshwari B S, Jyothi S Nayak, and Namratha M

10.1 INTRODUCTION

10.1.1 Social Media

Social media's effects extend beyond its initial purpose of being a means to be in contact with friends and family, as it is now used in many methods that impact a variety of things, including politics, business, global culture, education, and innovation. Through social media, users can easily edit, create, and share content with the public, revealing enlightening and engaging materials to others, defining themselves, nourishing relationships, and promoting products and causes they believe in. [1].

Social media channels vary in their features and functionalities, with some such as X (formerly Twitter) being effective at distributing links and quick messages, while others such as Instagram and TikTok are designed for sharing photos and videos. Social media's widespread availability and mostly free nature make it unique. There is no denying the influence of social networks such as Facebook, X, WhatsApp, and MySpace, as people of all ages use social media in their daily routines. It is not surprising to see young people waking up and updating a "good-morning" message on Facebook or other appealing social networks, illustrating the extent of participation on these platforms.

In 2005, social media was a relatively new concept, and only 5% of US users were engaged in social media. However, by 2019, this quantity had risen significantly to 70%, as per the survey conducted by the Pew Research Center [1]. While YouTube and Facebook are some of the most widely used social networks for adults, younger users prefer Instagram and Snapchat, and TikTok is the social network with the highest rate of this demographic. Additionally, the Pew Research Center discovered 97% of teenagers use at least one of the major online platforms mentioned.

Social media has evolved into an everyday routine for people, providing a means to stay connected with family and friends, share happy moments, and even receive support from strangers when needed. While occasional utilize social media be

DOI: 10.1201/9781003409519-10

relaxing, excessive use can harm one's mental health, leading to feelings of inadequacy when comparing oneself to others on social media accounts.

Despite the fact that social media platforms were initially created For college pupils, they have grown in popularity and usage among people of all ages, including children and older adults. These sites have become a significant and integral part of people's lives, with users spending an average of 2 hours and 20 minutes on them daily. Social media platforms have also taken on different roles, such as being relied upon for communication, news consumption, and finding like-minded individuals.

10.1.2 How Do Social Network Platforms Work?

Creating a social media account is a simple process that requires an Internet connection. While developers establish the framework for these platforms, it is users who fill them with content by sharing their thoughts and media and engaging with others. To get started, a user typically needs to create a profile by entering one's name and email address. Once a profile has been established, users can generate and share content. For example, a new user on Instagram can take a photo and upload it to their feed with a caption. The customers can identify other users whose content they wish to follow or comment on and create satisfaction with their own profiles. Depending on the type of social media platform, a user can "follow" another user, "add" them as a friend, or "subscribe" to their page.

Social networking platforms frequently use "feeds" that allow users to browse through content. The content appears and its order is determined by algorithms based on user data. These feeds feature content from both followed users and organizations that pay to promote their content.

10.1.3 Various Forms of Social Media

Some of the major types of social media are:

- Social Networks
- Discussion Networks
- Review Networks
- Media Networks

Social Networks: They are highly effective at connecting users and enabling the exchange of ideas, content, and opinions, mostly connecting people with the same interests and preferences. Examples of social networks include popular platforms such as Facebook and X. While LinkedIn is more focused on professional networking, it can likewise be seen as a kind of social network.

Discussion Networks: Discussion platforms such as Reddit are ideal for sharing content that can spark meaningful conversations among users. Through the comment section, users can provide detailed responses, and other users can respond directly to those comments, facilitating the natural growth and progression of discussions.

Review Networks: There have been social media features added to review networks such as Yelp and TripAdvisor, allowing users and businesses to communicate directly with each other, enhancing the user review experience of goods and services.

Media Networks: Compared to social networks, media networks have a different focus on spreading visual content such as images and videos, rather than facilitating discussion among users. Examples of media networks include Instagram and YouTube. On YouTube, users can upload videos and receive engagement from other users in the form of likes, dislikes, and comments. If a user enjoys a particular creator's content, they can choose to subscribe to their channel and receive notifications of new videos posted if any.

10.1.4 Is Social Media Really Helpful?

Social media is essential in modern society, serving as a tool for decision-making, information access, and social interaction. Its ability to share and create content and connect people locally and globally is undeniable. However, like any social media and technology, both have both positive and also negative effects. While people rely on their smartphones and the internet for work, school, and personal connections, Social networking has also presented difficulties and risks to people's lives.

10.2 POSITIVE AND NEGATIVE IMPACTS OF NEWS IN SOCIAL MEDIA

The summary of the positive and negative impact of social media are shown in Figure 10.1.

10.2.1 Positive Effects of Social Media

Both positive and bad consequences of social media exist [2, 3]. These positive effects have brought about a new order in various fields such as academia, politics, arts, and charitable actions. Social networking has quickly grown in popularity, particularly among teenagers and college students.

Among the most crucial positive effects is that social media has introduced a new way of interacting with others. For people who struggle with face-to-face communication, social media provides a platform to overcome their fears and develop self-confidence while interacting with others. This has increased personal communication skills, which is a vital tool in maintaining an active and participatory society. The social media network also provided undergraduate students the chance to socialize with others from different races, backgrounds, religions, geographies, and more, leading to a wider knowledge spectrum. Some of the major benefits of social media are:

- Social media gives better connectivity and communication.
- Excellent stress reliever.
- Better learning by quick access to information and research.

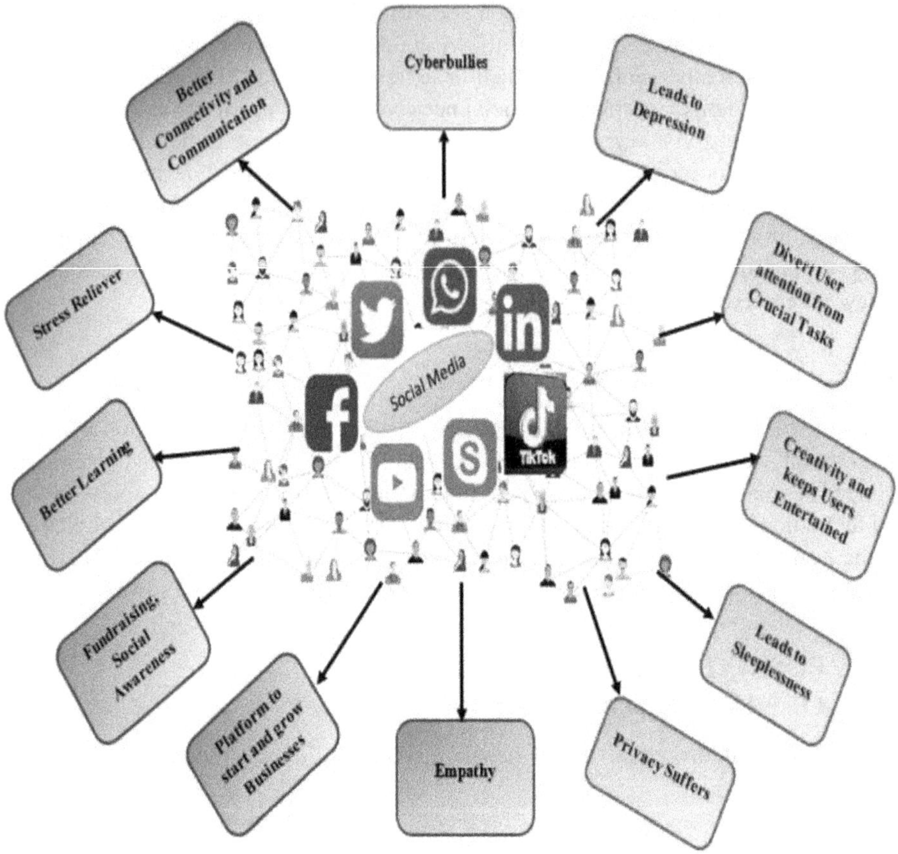

FIGURE 10.1 Summary of the positive and negative impact of social media.

- Allows individuals to participate in fundraising and social awareness.
- People with common interests get connected.
- It serves as a forum for people to start and grow their businesses.
- Showing empathy.
- Allows self-expression and expression of creativity and keeps users entertained.

Social media gives better connectivity and communication:

Communication has been changed by social media by enabling people to easily connect with their loved ones online, also facilitating new connections. In the past, communication was limited by distance, and could take a long time to reach remote areas. With the emergence of social media, one can instantly call distant family members or reconnect with long-lost friends from around the world. Additionally, people can share various aspects of their lives on social media, such as posts, content, thoughts, and experiences, which can lead to an increased number of global connections.

Excellent stress reliever:

Social media is an important tool for building meaningful contacts. Nevertheless, individuals recently who were infected by the COVID-19 pandemic found themselves isolated and lacking social interaction, leading to multiple mental health issues. However, social media platforms have been crucial in providing online communities and support to those affected.

Better learning by quick access to knowledge and research:

It is a valuable platform for learning new things, and it is not limited to just children and students. Individuals of all ages can utilize the wealth of information available on social media, including blog posts, tweets, videos, and articles, to acquire new skills and knowledge. Furthermore, the COVID-19 pandemic has shown how effective social media can be used to supplement physical learning. Students can access online seminars, free educational websites, and mentors to acquire new skills and advance their careers. YouTube is also a valuable resource for finding instructional videos to enhance their abilities.

Allows individuals to participate in fundraising and social awareness:

Social media provides a platform for individuals and groups to speak out on important issues, advocate for causes, and raise awareness. This has led to increased visibility and exposure to many critical topics. X and other social media sites such as Reddit and Facebook have developed into crucial instruments for activists, charity organizations, and advocates in their fight against injustice, disease, and other societal issues. They use these platforms to share information, educate others, and call attention to problems that require attention from the appropriate authorities and organizations.

People with common interests get connected:

Every individual has a distinctive passion or area of interest. Additionally, social media gives users the chance to communicate with various social groups on platforms such as Facebook, Instagram, Reddit, and others, such as book clubs, movie, fashion enthusiasts, and scientific communities, where like-minded people can find and connect with others who concur similar interests and ideas. Social media allows users to discover and interact with a diverse range of individuals from throughout the globe who share commonalities. This allows for the discovery of clubs, communities, and individuals that align with personal goals and interests. Social media can be utilized as a positive tool for like-minded individuals to network with each other and share their journeys.

It serves as a forum for people to start and grow their businesses:

Social media has developed into a significant platform for businesses to market and advertise their products. With various Facebook pages and Instagram posts dedicated to selling and purchasing products, using social media transformed the business potential. Social media advertising has attracted a huge number of customers. If utilized effectively, it can ensure a 24/7 business. Business organizations can expand their consumer reach and improve customer satisfaction.

Showing empathy:

Using social media has various positive impacts on people's lives. Users often share their personal struggles, successes, and journeys through social media. Through the supportive and encouraging messages that others leave in the comments section, users can feel motivated to improve their lives. It provides an avenue for users to show empathy by sharing their own experiences and offering support to others in need. Various support groups for concerns with mental health such as anxiety and depression, are available on social media, and these groups can offer a sense of community and belonging for individuals experiencing these difficulties.

Allows self-expression and expression of creativity and keeps users entertained:

Social media provides a setting for individuals to showcase their talents and creativity in areas such as fitness, beauty, and more, through blogs, videos, and tutorials. This has allowed for the growth of creativity and knowledge across the world. Additionally, it has evolved into a means of expressing oneself for teenagers and young adults. It has provided practical experience to students, helping them to upgrade their abilities and creativity while also expanding their knowledge base. Additionally, social media outlets have developed a hub of entertainment for individuals of all ages, providing various sources of amusement. It is undeniable that some social media posts have brought a smile to peoples' faces. From music to videos, games, and movies, social media provides entry to a plethora of entertainment options.

10.2.2 Negative Impacts of Social Media

Although social media offers numerous benefits such as global news dissemination, business development, and entertainment, it also has some drawbacks [4]. The harm caused by social networks is becoming more pronounced, as they seem to be reshaping society in ways that are difficult to fully comprehend [5, 6]. The influence of social media, which has had a significant impact on how people connect with one another, can be attributed to the degradation of social values and conventions. It is also clear that many young individuals, especially undergraduate students, struggle to regulate their use of social media and experience difficulties in their social, vocational, and personal lives as a result. As a consequence, these sites have a considerable impact on who and what they connect with, what they view, and how to make decisions. Some have developed such a strong dependence on the internet that they cannot abstain from checking their social media profiles for even a few hours, including during class time, negatively impacting their ability to focus on educational and career pursuits.

Some of the negative impacts of social media are:

- Lessens direct interaction with family and friends.
- Divert people's attention from crucial tasks.
- Leads to depression and anxiety disorders.

- Cyberbullies.
- Leads to sleeplessness.
- Reduces one's confidence.
- Privacy suffers.

Lessens direct interaction with family and friends:

Frequently social media consumption can result in people to resentful of you for not paying them your complete attention and quality time. Being physically in touch with relatives and friends provides a level of comfort that social media cannot provide. Though social media is really helpful for receiving assistance from those who are not physically nearby, online communication still lacks non-verbal cues and can lead to miscommunication, even among close friends.

Divert people's attention from crucial tasks:

Social media's demand for attention is a significant reason for its negative impact. Regular users may develop the habit of posting vague updates to gain attention from others. With the ability to upload content and images at any time, social media allows us to constantly seek attention, taking this demand to an extreme. This constant seeking of attention can lead to feelings of loneliness and isolation, which can have various negative consequences on our livelihood that may be linked to social media. Rather than pursuing a fulfilling career and developing practical skills, many people prioritize gaining internet popularity. Achieving goals requires dedication and hard work, but social media provides an easy escape from these responsibilities. As a result, individuals may find themselves struggling to complete tasks and lacking the motivation to achieve their dreams.

Leads to depression and anxiety disorders:

Recent studies indicate that the more social media a person uses, the more negative emotions they experience, including depression. This can be particularly harmful to those who have previous depression and anxiety issues. This is the main negative aspect of social media.

Cyberbullies:

Exposure to negative content and cyberbullying is a typical and concerning aspect of using social media. Even if users do not engage in such behavior themself, being exposed to it can have an adverse effect on his/her thoughts and attitudes toward others.

Leads to sleeplessness:

Using social media can have negative impacts on sleep patterns, as the blue light emitted from screens can disrupt circadian rhythms and suppress the release of the sleep hormone melatonin. This can lead to difficulty falling asleep and staying asleep, resulting in sleep deprivation and daytime fatigue. Studies have revealed that for both teenagers and adults, social media users more frequently have worse sleep patterns and are more inclined to experience sleep problems. It is important to establish healthy habits around technology use and prioritize getting enough sleep for overall health and well-being.

Reduces one's confidence:

Individuals who frequently use Facebook have lower self-esteem, which is linked to their increased subjection to social comparisons on social media. It follows that observing others' seemingly better lives using social media can lower our self-esteem. The constant comparison to others social media platforms can worsen this problem, leading to mental upset and anxiety, specifically among youngsters.

Privacy suffers:

The internet and privacy are often at odds, particularly the use of social media platforms that collect and sell personal data, including email, Zoom calls, website cookies, and more. Nowadays, potential employers are increasingly turning to utilizing social media to examine profiles of job applicants. If users share every thought online, he/she may create a negative impression, which can cost you opportunities.

10.3 IMPACT OF FAKE NEWS ON SOCIAL MEDIA IN DIFFERENT SECTORS

In this segment, the advantages of news on social media are illustrated with an example. Also, the impact of false news on social media in various sectors is discussed.

10.3.1 Advantages of Social Media

Participating in international platforms for collaboration can help educators and students promote positive learning. It also helps to improve skills by promoting knowledge and creativity. Keep up to date with events around the world or in the lives of others through social media. Social media, in contrast to media such as radio, television, or newspapers, enables individuals to accurately communicate information by providing a real image. They help present real news from around the world. Social media serves as an information channel, paving the way for innovation and success through the development of their familiarity and skills. Social media efficiently reports on international events, expanding people's awareness of their surroundings.

Social media may accustomed to spreading good deeds. It is one of the ideal tools to promote good causes, such as donations for cancer patients who need money for treatment. Social media is the simplest and quickest way to advance a great cause, and everyone can use it to help others financially.

10.3.2 Impact of Fake News in Social Media in Different Sectors

Impacts of fake information on social media on many sectors include:

i. **Social Media's Effect on Politics**

The main source of political news is social media. The study also demonstrates that individuals who primarily depend on social media for political news tend to be less informed and more inclined to be exposed to unverified claims. Social media now has a significantly greater impact on political campaigns than previous forms of media. Human society is being substantially changed by social media. Social media's increased freedom of communication is enabling once-marginalized groups to form surprisingly powerful social organizations.

ii. **Social Media's Effect on Society**

Anyone with radical opinions can understand they are not alone. If they communicate with one another through social media, they may also create periodicals, complete online universes, and memes that reflect their viewpoint. This will help them become more widely accepted. Without social media, it would be difficult to identify political, moral, environmental, and social inequalities. As a result of issues becoming more apparent, the public now holds a greater portion of the authority previously held by a select few. On the other side, as a result of social media, "slacktivism" is rapidly destroying genuine activism.

Social media activism does make people more aware of social concerns, but it is still not apparent if this awareness leads to real change. Some contend that, without actively taking part in campaigns, social sharing has made it simpler for people to voice their concerns about social issues online and through mobile devices. Simply by clicking the "like" button or sharing material, they show their support.

iii. **Social Media's Impact on Commerce**

Nowadays, almost every business interacts with its clients and potential clients through one social network or another. Businesses are becoming more conscious of how social media connects with consumers and produces income. Social media can be used by businesses to gather information, increase demand, and provide specialized product offers. These processes are necessary for both conventional brick-and-mortar retail and, inevitably, e-commerce. Social technology can help the growth of more highly skilled and informed employees by removing boundaries and silos, increasing contact, and fostering worker development.

iv. **Social Media's Impact on the World of Work**

Social media has a significant impact on hiring and recruitment. Anyone looking to make a name for themselves in their field should use professional social media platforms such as LinkedIn. They enable the development and promotion of personal brands. 19% of recruiting managers base their recruitment choices on information gathered through social media.

v. **Social Media's Impact on Training and Development**

Candidates for jobs who are up on the newest and most cutting-edge social media strategies are far more employable. Today, many educational institutions use wikis, blogs, LinkedIn, Facebook, X, and podcasts as standard teaching tools. Online, social media has been helpful in distance learning increase. In spite of privacy issues and some cases of cheating among distance learners, this has not stopped the utilizing of social platforms in education.

vi. **Social Media's Impact on Relationships**

One of the causes of social media is the creation and maintenance of "social media friendships" rather than actual friendships. The word "friend" as used on a social media channel is a hazy representation of true friendship. Real friends regularly speak in person, have a genuine relationship, and are well acquainted.

vii. **Social Media's Impact on Education**

Social networking is a cutting-edge method of educating people. Students need to be instructed on improved tool usage. Instead of educating students on how to use media responsibly, schools only use it for chatting or texting in their classrooms. Student collaboration has become more effective and efficient because of social media. Furthermore, students must complete actual work rather than paperwork. They can also publish blogs for themselves and their lecturers to further their understanding. Online exams are also conducted on social networks, which play a main role in improving students' knowledge.

viii. **Social Media's Impact on Youngsters**

Social media is a stylish new tool currently for engaging young people. The daily lives of many young people are permeated by social media. Young people entertain themselves and communicate every day with their peers and groups utilizing various media and gadgets. Young people used to solely communicate with their peers and groups from high school and university. Today, however, young people are not only in contact with both known friends and strangers via social networks, instant chatting, etc. Young people commonly utilize the internet, mobile devices, and online games to connect with one another and learn new things across the nation.

10.4 CURRENT TECHNOLOGY AND FAKE NEWS DETECTION SYSTEM

This section covers various current technologies in detecting whether news on social media is fake or real such as machine learning, data science, etc.

One of the most significant inventions is the Internet, which is used by a sizable population. Through these online platforms, any user can publish or disseminate news. The users or their posts are not reviewed by these platforms. As a result, some people attempt to distribute false information via these channels. This false information may be used to spread propaganda against a certain individual, group, company, or political party. A person cannot identify all of this fraudulent news. Therefore, checking the fake news is essential. A person can only recognize that it is fake news if he knows the complete story of the issue. Because most people do not know the whole story and start believing fake news without any proof, this is a challenging task. Here, the issue is how to manage fake news. Fake news cannot be stopped by a human [7]. Machine learning is the solution. Therefore, currently machine learning that can detect this fake news automatically is very much needed. This fake news can be quickly and automatically identified using machine learning [8, 9]. Tools such as Python, scikit-learn, and natural language processing for text analysis can be used to categorize fake news as real or false using a supervised machine learning algorithm [10]. Once fake news is posted, machine learning algorithms review the post's content to determine whether it is fake or not. To identify bogus news, various academics are competing to develop the best machine learning classifier. The classifier's accuracy must be taken into account since if it is unable to accurately identify fake news, it may hurt a variety of individuals. The classifier's training determines how accurate it will be. A model with more experience will be more accurate. Several machine learning classifiers can be used to identify fake news [11, 12].

10.4.1 Naïve Bayes

Naïve Bayes employs the Bayes theorem in the area of probability. This classifier presupposes that changes to one feature have no impact on changes to the other features or that all features are conditionally independent. It determines the cumulative likelihood of all other events occurring in order to compute the likelihood of one event occurring. When trained inexpensively and with ease of use, the Naïve Bayes classifier produces good classification results.

10.4.2 Logistic Regression

Logistic regression is a statistical method for linear categorization. The sigmoid function is applied to the incoming data, and returns a probability value which can be used for the classification of data. Depending on the worth of the sigmoid function, a classification limit or threshold is computed for the data points. It is predicated on the notion that the attributes of a sample can be combined linearly to determine how likely it is for it to belong to a given class.

10.4.3 Support Vector Machines

A decision hyperplane is a component of the support vector machine's classification process in order to divide samples into different classes. The hyperplane is positioned in hyperspace to optimize the distance between the various classes. Since the training samples do not need to be converted into other spaces, the support vector machine can work on a broad feature subset. The support vector machine, one of the most effective classifiers with good classification performance, has been used by various researchers.

10.4.4 Decision Tree

Another of the most well-liked machine learning models for text classification is the decision tree. A classifier is represented as a tree data structure. The test to be applied to a particular feature is depicted by the internal nodes of the tree, for each outcome of the test is depicted by the subtree, and the label of a target class is depicted by the leaf node of the tree. Moving from the tree's root, to the leaf node, reflects the sample's target class, and classifies the dataset sample.

10.4.5 Random Forests

Random forests is a collection of different decision trees that can be used for both classification and regression issues. The elective process is used to determine the conclusion. The sample with the most votes receives the class designation. The leaf node of each decision tree is divided into a random subcategory of features. To produce the value K of a decision tree, this process is repeated. The decision trees are programmed to give the bulk of their votes to the class of the instance.

10.4.6 K-nearest Neighbor

One of the simplest techniques for resolving categorization issues is the K-nearest neighbor (KNN). By comparing it to the training data that is the closest match, the KNN model determines the class of a sample. A point in an n-dimensional space serves as the representation for each sample in the dataset. This area contains all training data. By looking for the K training data that are near the test data point in this area, the class of the test data point is ascertained. K-nearest neighbors are the nearest training data points. By computing the separation between the space's training data and test data, the closest neighbors are identified.

10.4.7 Convolutional Neural Network (CNN or ConvNet)

CNN is a supervised, discriminatory deep learning model that automatically extracts features from input data. The CNN is a development of conventional artificial neural networks. Every layer of the CNN takes into account the ideal hyperparameter parameters to get decent outcomes. Additionally, the CNN provides a model overfitting handling mechanism not present in traditional neural networks. Pattern recognition, language processing, and the use of CNNs have tremendously helped all aspects of natural language processing.

10.4.8 Long Short-Term Memory (LSTM)

The recurrent neural network that has the capacity to selectively retain patterns across time is LSTM. The recurrent cell state of the LSTM functions as a long-term memory with the ability to store the past. The statuses of the cells are modified by the forget gates placed beneath them. Whether or not the data should be retained depends on the forget gate's output. Data entry into the cells is managed by the input gate. Which information must be transferred to the following state is determined by the output gate. Traditional machine learning methods are not as effective as the LSTM but they have an advantage where it can infer class labels from multi-word strings.

10.5 OPEN ISSUES IN DETECTION OF FAKE NEWS AND FUTURE RESEARCH DIRECTIONS

The difficulties in identifying fake news and the upcoming directions for this field of study are discussed. This information gives researchers, designers, and experts the knowledge they need to make the best and most suitable model for figuring out whether news on social media is phony or true.

In the real world, spotting false news is a severe problem, thus there are unique challenges that must be taken into consideration. Additionally, recent developments in machine learning techniques such as tensor factorization, deep neural networks, and probabilistic models enable researchers to deal with specific settings to detect whether news in social media is fake or real and better extract useful features of news from auxiliary data.

It is essential to recognize fake news as soon as possible in order to prevent it from going further on social media. Because gathering the facts about fake news is time and labor-intensive, it is essential to study fake news detection in a weakly supervised setting. It is necessary to comprehend why a particular item of news is classified as fake by machine learning models. [13]

The media landscape, the public sphere, and the journalism industry are experiencing a dramatic and subtle scenario that warrants discussion and investigation, highlighting two essential aspects: The first is based on the notion that news publishers no longer have any influence over how news is presented to Internet users, who now receive it through enigmatic and unpredictable algorithms. Furthermore, by embracing these technologies, newcomers to the news industry have made their presence known while challenging the long-standing dominance of more conventional news publishers. The second pillar is reliant on the expanding control that social media behemoths such as Apple, Google, Facebook, and Amazon have over who can read what and how it is monetized.

It is also evident that contemporary firms face the issue of having their staff tricked into disclosing their credentials in addition to the danger of malware being introduced into their information management systems. Some experts claim that a specific group of content writers is increasingly using clickbait to advance their phishing objectives. After clicking the link and viewing the website's content, a person who also happens to be an employee of the target company is persuaded to provide sensitive information, albeit covertly. The user might, for example, be deceived into believing they are promoting the spread of the news when, in reality, they are giving the perpetrators access to their email [14, 15].

On the one hand, individuals use social media as a source of news since it is free, accessible, and information is shared quickly. On the other side, it makes it easier for "fake news", or bad news that contains deceptive facts on purpose, to spread widely. Fake news' capacity to spread widely has the potential to be exceedingly harmful to people and society. The detection of fake news on social media is thus a new area of study that is attracting a lot of attention. Social media presents unique aspects and challenges for the detection of false news, rendering traditional news media identification algorithms redundant or worthless. Because fake news is initially written with the intent of deceiving readers into believing false information, the user must include auxiliary information, such as social engagements on social media, to aid in making a decision. As a result, detecting it purely on the basis of news content is challenging and nontrivial. Second, because of the massive, sparse, disorderly, and noisy data that users' social interactions with fake news create, using this supplementary data is challenging in and of itself. The difficult and urgent problem of spotting fake news on social media. A complete examination of fake news on social media using assessment criteria, current data mining algorithms, descriptions of false news based on psychological and sociological theories, and other methods.

The identification of bogus news on social media presents several innovative and challenging research difficulties. Although it is nothing new for governments or other groups to use the news media for propaganda or influence campaigns, the rise of web-generated news on social media has strengthened fake news as a force that challenges long-standing journalistic standards. The quirks that this problem presents make automatic detection very challenging. First, it can be challenging to distinguish fake news from legitimate news since it is prepared with the intention of misleading readers. Fake news makes fun of legitimate news while attempting to misrepresent the facts using a range of linguistic techniques. Fake news has a wide range of themes, writing philosophies, and media outlets. For instance, fake news may back an inaccurate claim with legitimate evidence that is used in an inappropriate situation. Therefore, current hand-made and data-specific textual features are frequently insufficient to identify fake news. Additional data must also be used, such as knowledge bases and user social interactions, to improve detection. Second, using this auxiliary data actually has a severe issue with the quality of the data. Fake news frequently refers to recent, urgent occurrences that may not have been sufficiently validated by existing knowledge bases since there wasn't enough evidence to back up the claims. Additionally, users' social interactions with fake news generate large, sparse, chaotic, and noisy data. Although people react differently to real news and false news, there is still much to learn about how to identify useful behavioral patterns and extract relevant features from them. Assessing the validity of fake news is further complicated by the credibility of noisy social media posts [16].

The following is a summary of the main driving factors:

- Although the term "fake news" has been bandied about on social media for a while, no consensus on what it means exists. To better guide the future paths of false news detection research, appropriate explanations are needed.
- There are certain novel trends in social media that can be utilized to identify bogus news. Gaining a basic understanding of the most cutting-edge

fake news detection techniques will be made easier by reviewing the current false news detection techniques in various social media contexts.

The detection of fake news on social media is still in its early stages, and there are still many difficult problems that require further research. It is important to consider potential research directions that could enhance the ability to recognize and refute bogus news.

To summarize, the existing algorithm's primary weaknesses are [17]:

1. The inability to constantly monitor all posts for errors.
2. The entity recognition NLP libraries.
3. The ability to compare facts and determine whether or not they agree.

- ***Reputation of the sources***

A source must be given a score value in order to be tracked and kept in a history record that can be used for cross-referencing. That value ought to fluctuate dynamically in response to regular assessments made by the system or by a centralized, reliable server system run by a third party. The source is deemed untrustworthy if this score falls below a predetermined cutoff point; otherwise, it can be trusted.

- ***Synthesis***

Despite the fact that they are deserving, some recent approaches to fake news detection still rely on a very crude technique that involves seeing if the preferred site is on a blacklist. Consequently, these techniques are not: 1) cross-checking is available, 2) source reputation histories are not used, and frequently 3) dynamic reputation is not even used.

The present COVID-19 epidemic has shown the grave consequences of the spread of erroneous information. The continuing epidemic is currently one of the major public health catastrophes, affecting millions of people in various ways. False news has been epidemic spreading on digital platforms, alarming the public during the epidemic. The epidemic has already irreparably disrupted people's lives. Misinformation about the condition led to a large quantity of COVID-19 patients who were diagnosed to commit themselves. An effort must be taken to stop incorrect information about COVID-19 from propagating on social media because the disease is still considered to be a worldwide epidemic in many countries. Therefore, scientists are working to contain this threat and developing intelligent and automated techniques for identifying whether the content is fake or real. In order to perform this goal, Techniques for machine learning are utilized to forecast the substance of false news.

10.5.1 Deep Learning – Identify Fake News

By utilizing a range of algorithms and machine learning (ML) techniques, a computer system may automatically identify patterns and correlations in incoming data and resolve issues without being explicitly programmed [18, 19]. Deep learning, a specialized kind of machine learning, employs artificial neural networks to simulate the numerous layers of neurons in the human brain in order to tackle complicated issues. Deep learning models have been demonstrated to outperform machine learning models in a variety of challenging problems.

Using the classification supervised machine learning technique, the tagged data may be categorized. More research is needed to determine how successfully the classification models can identify fake news, despite the fact that many academics have attempted to increase classification accuracy across numerous datasets. A text classification task might be used to describe this circumstance. A binary classification problem, the COVID-19 false news detection challenge. The goal of the current study is to select the classification model that will be most successful at identifying false news on COVID-19 from a wide range of competing models. This can be accomplished using both traditional machine learning models and more recent deep learning techniques [20, 21].

- *Social Media and Suicide*

Sadly, young people may experience the drawbacks of social networking. Suicide continues to be one of the leading causes of death for children under the age of 14. Most young individuals who hang themselves die.

- Over the past years, the suicide rate among 10 to 14-year-olds has climbed by more than 50%, according to the study.
- The study says that although suicide rates among kids aged 10 and 14 are extremely low, they are gradually rising.

- *How can parents help?*

As parents, there are things that they can do to progress their children's lives online and in actual life.

- Put out an attempt to model the behavior that they desire [22].
- When parents give their first phone to their child, set limits in the appropriate way. Having access to their credentials, set parental controls on their phone. When charging at night, phones should be taken out of the room and turned off an hour or two before bed.
- Talk to the kids about why certain topics should be kept private.
- Spend some time interacting actively with the children in person. They learn how to read social cues through this interaction, both vocal and nonverbal.
- Without looking at a phone, converse with the children.
- Look for chances to engage in real conversations rather than lectures.
- Be mindful of difficulties with cybersecurity and privacy.

People now live, work, and socialize in a different way because of technology. But it can't take the place of parenting.

10.6 CONCLUSION

The chapter discusses the influence of news on social media, both positive and bad, false news on social media, existing technology for identifying fake news, some difficulties, and future research possibilities. This will assist experts, academics, and designers in creating the best and most suitable model for calculating if news on social media is fake or true. As technology advances, social media has been ingrained in everyone's daily routine, and we see more and more people becoming dependent on it. People are affected differently by different fields. Student collaboration has improved in both quality and quantity because of social media. Children are frequently observed interacting with these mediums. Social media offers many benefits, but it also has drawbacks that have an adverse effect on people. False information may cause the educational system to fail, bad advertising can reduce productivity in an organization. Social media usage is advantageous but should be moderate to avoid addiction.

REFERENCES

1. https://www.simplilearn.com/real-impact-social-media-article.
2. Edikan Ukpong. 2014. *The Positive and Negative Effects of Social Media*. Munich: GRIN Verlag. https://www.grin.com/document/508570.
3. https://www.lifespan.org/lifespan-living/social-media-good-bad-and-ugly.
4. Shabnoor Siddiqui, and Tajinder Singh. 2016. "Social Media Its Impact with Positive and Negative Aspects." *International Journal of Computer Applications Technology and Research*. 5(2): 71–75.
5. https://studentlesson.com/understanding-social-media-and-the-common-positive-and -neg ative-effects-it-has-on-human-beings/.
6. https://montarebehavioralhealth.com/social-media-and-mental-health-what-are-the -positi ve -and-negative-effects.
7. Alim Al Ayub Ahmed, Ayman Aljabouh, Praveen Kumar Donepudi, and Myung Suh Choi. 2021. "Detecting Fake News Using Machine Learning: A Systematic Literature Review." *arXiv-2102*. DOI: 10.48550/arXiv.2102.04458.
8. Iftikhar Ahmad, Muhammad Yousaf, Suhail Yousaf, and Muhammad Ovais Ahmad. 2020. "Fake News Detection Using Machine Learning Ensemble Methods." *Complexity. Hindawi*. 8885861: 1–11. DOI: 10.1155/2020/8885861.
9. Z. Khanam, B. N Alwasel, H. Sirafi, and Mamoon Rashid. 2021. "Fake News Detection using Machine Learning Approaches." *IOP Conference Series: Materials Science and Engineering*. 1099(1). DOI: 10.1088/1757-899X/1099/1/012040.
10. Ray Oshikawa, Jing Qian, and William Yang Wang. 2018. "A Survey on Natural Language Processing for Fake News Detection." *Proceedings of the 12th Language Resources and Evaluation Conference*: 6086–6093. DOI: 10.48550/arXiv.1811.00770.
11. Eliza Shoemaker. 2019. "Using Data Science to Detect Fake News." *Senior Honors Projects. 2010-Current*, 714. https://commons.lib.jmu.edu/honors201019/714.
12. Alhakami Hosam, Wajdi Alhakami, Abdullah Baz, Mohd Faizan, Mohd Waris Khan, and Alka Agrawal. 2022. "Evaluating Intelligent Methods for Detecting COVID-19 Fake News on Social Media Platforms." *Electronics*. 11(15). DOI: 10.3390/electronics 11152417.
13. Kai Shu, and Huan Liu. 2019. "Challenging Problems of Fake News Detection." In: *Detecting Fake News on Social Media. Synthesis Lectures on Data Mining and Knowledge Discovery*. Cham: Springer. 55–77. DOI: 10.1007/978-3-031-01915-9_4.

14. Monther Aldwairi, and Ali Alwahedi. 2018. “Detecting Fake News in Social Media Networks.” *Procedia Computer Science*. 141: 215–222. DOI: 10.1016/j.procs.2018.10.171.
15. Wajiha Shahid, Bahman Jamshidi, Saqib Hakak, Haruna Isah, Wazir Zada Khan, and Muhammad Khurram Khan. 2022. “Detecting and Mitigating the Dissemination of Fake News: Challenges and Future Research Opportunities.” *IEEE Transactions on Computational Social Systems*: 1–14. DOI: 10.1109/TCSS.2022.3177359.
16. Kai Shu, Amy Sliva, Suhang Wang, Jiliang Tang, and Huan Liu. 2018. “Fake News Detection on Social Media: A Data Mining Perspective.” *ACM SIGKDD Explorations Newsletter*. 19(1): 22–36.
17. Álvaro Figueira, and Luciana Oliveira. 2017. “The Current State of Fake News: Challenges and Opportunities.” Procedia Computer Science. *ACM SIGKDD Explorations Newsletter*. 19(1). 22–36. DOI: 10.1145/3137597.3137600.
18. Shaban Shabani, and Maria Sokhn. 2018. “Hybrid Machine-Crowd Approach for Fake News Detection.” 4th IEEE International Conference on Collaboration and Internet Computing. 299–306. DOI: 10.1109/CIC.2018.00048.
19. Sebastian Kula, Michał Choraś, Rafał Kozik, Paweł Ksieniewicz, and Michał Woźniak. 2020. “Sentiment Analysis for Fake News Detection by Means of Neural Networks.” 20th International Conference on Computational Science. Springer. 653–666. DOI: 10.1007/978-3-030-50423-6_49.
20. Aswini Thota, Priyanka Tilak, Simrat Ahluwalia, and Nibrat Lohia. 2018. “Fake News Detection: A Deep Learning Approach.” *SMU Data Science Review*. 1(3): 10.
21. Dibyajyoti Baishya, Joon Jyoti Deka, Gaurav Dey, and Pranav Kumar Singh. 2021. “SAFER: Sentiment Analysis-Based Fake Review Detection in E-commerce Using Deep Learning.” *Computer Science SN*. 2(479). DOI: 10.1007/s42979-021-00918-9.
22. M. Munk, A. Barushka, and P. Hajek. 2020. “Deep Neural Networks Integrated with Word Embeddings and Emotion Mining Are Used to Detect Fake Customer Reviews.” *Neural Computer and Application*: 17259–17274. DOI: 10.1007/s00521-020-04757-2.

11 Connotative Meaning of Political Emotive Expressions in Arab Spring Fake News

Abderrahim Bouderbane

11.1 INTRODUCTION

Nowadays, politics is to some extent a dominant activity in the world. Political events become a major part of our lives all across the world. Also, changes in world powers representations have been made easy with the help of the media. These rapid and ongoing changes in representations have had a direct impact on political discourse in fact, it has contributed to making political discourse a powerful tool to be used between different rivals. In this perspective, politics and language have become strong allies, especially in deploying the power of language along with the influence of politics.

Some Arab countries have been witnessing massive demonstrations and even civil wars over the last ten years. This has resulted in many changes at different levels. People conquered the streets chanting freedom, democracy, and more rights. This situation has created a conflict in political terminology; that is to say, political emotive expressions are used with negative and positive connotations. For instance, an expression such as "revolutionaries" has a positive connotation, which means it connotes people who are fighting for their rights and facing colonial powers and tyranny; this is on one hand. On the other hand, expressions are used to describe the same people, yet with negative connotations such as the words "rebellions, anti-government protestors" which imply negative connotations.

Before we start investigating and studying the main questions of this chapter, we have to provide the reader with some discussions of the main points. We will discuss the notion of political discourse briefly, connotative meaning, and emotive expressions. The second part of this chapter analyzes a number of selected expressions in order to determine their positive or negative connotations. We aim to see how these lexical expressions are used with specific political connotations in order to serve given goals.

DOI: 10.1201/9781003409519-11

11.2 ORGANIZATION OF THE CHAPTER

The chapter is organized coherently from general to specific as it starts in Section 11.3 by introducing political discourse with some fundamental theories introduced and the claims discussed in the domains of politics in relation to language and their communicative purposes. Section 11.4 delves into the notion of connotative meaning and emotive expressions when it explores the definitions of emotive expressions and the emotional use of words, and phrases with particular meanings in different contexts. Meanwhile, Section 11.5 deals with the most representative emotive expressions, their origins, and their meaning in news media. It also deals with fake news and the broadcasting of emotive expressions in Arab Spring countries, and it presents some of the most common emotive expressions before the Arab Spring and during the Arab Spring to compare the connection between their intended meanings in Arab Spring countries. Section 11.6 deals with research methodology and mainly presents the aim of the study, the procedure of analysis, and the definition of the context. After that, Section 11.7 presents the data and analyses them, while Section 11.8 discusses the results of the data. The conclusion in Section 11.9 wraps up the whole chapter.

11.3 POLITICAL DISCOURSE

Thompson claims, "The fundamental patterns of political institutions arise out of words that people exert on behalf of their interests" (1987: 24). Politics is a war with words, and accordingly Chilton claims that:

> "At every stage of politics comes up against the questions of language and these questions range from the choice of words to the choice of Language: from fine detail of phrasing and wording to large scale issues of national language policy."
>
> **(2004: 14).**

In this perspective, the linguistic-political dimension results in how those in power deploy language in order to achieve their aims through either power or cooperation; in other words, this indicates how important language is when it comes to political issues. According to Joseph, "the study of language and politics is aimed at understanding the role of linguistic communication in the functioning of social units and how these social units shape language itself" (2004: 347). In light of what Chilton and Schaffner (2002: 05) claim, political communication between the social units is divided into two levels, micro and macro. The micro level concerns the conflicts of interests, struggle for dominance, and efforts for co-operation between individuals, genders, and social groups. However, the macro level includes the power struggle or cooperation between political institutions, social groups, or individuals on a state level.

As stated byJoseph (2004), the connection between language and politics was first brought to general attention in 1946, in an essay by George Orwell "Politics and the English Language". It is mentioned,

> "People dislike one thing and want to express solidarity with another, but they are not interested in the detail of what they are saying. You can shirk it by simply throwing

> your mind open and letting the ready-made phrases come crowding in. They will construct your sentences for you, even think your thoughts for you (…). It is at this point the connection between politics and language becomes clear" (Joseph 2004: 352)

In light of this, we can say that language shapes our reality and defines us. In other words, what we are is what we say. In his book, *Words that Work* Luntz claims that "people will not understand what is happening to them, and they cannot rebel against what they do not understand" (2007: 49). Therefore, unveiling the hidden ideological structures behind political discourse has been the concern of discourse analysts who apply different methods in analyzing political discourse.

Political discourse analysis is rather an interesting field in linguistics. Its main concerns are how politicians promote their authority and ideology in an implicit way, by successfully employing linguistic means. Therefore, political analysis has much to do with credibility and legitimization of one's deeds according to the ideology one is supporting. Research in this field is mostly rooted in communication and linguistic theories, which are used to disclose the politician's intentions and analyze the effects of their speeches. One of the first to address the question of implied meaning and credibility of linguistic communication was Paul Grice. His "Theory of Implicature" has inspired many scholars in this field. Grice proposed four conversation maxims: The maxim of quantity (give information as required), quality (be truthful), relation (be relevant), and manner (avoid obscurity). So, when a speaker follows all four maxims, there is no implicature. However, when the speaker "flouts" one of the maxims, the situation results in conversational implicature (implied pragmatic meaning) (Vine 2004: 47). According to Chilton, the usage of implicatures in political language enables politicians to convey more than they say through intended meaning which is only recognizable to the hearer if he/she adopts a particular ideology or set of attitudes and values (2004: 37). Hence, the modern approach to political discourse is a critical study of signs of deception and authority in the language of politicians.

11.4 CONNOTATIVE MEANING AND EMOTIVE EXPRESSIONS

Nida and Taber (1969: 91) indicate that the connotative meaning of a sign, which is called "associative" or "emotive", is "the aspect of the meaning which deals with our emotional reactions to words". Connotative meaning refers to the non-criterion properties of a word. It is associative, subjective, and affective. Leech (1981: 12) defines it as "the communicative value an expression has by virtue of what refers to over and above its purely conceptual contents." According to Waard and Nida (1986: 146), connotative meaning consists of certain features derived primarily from the practical contexts in which such a term is used; including people who habitually use such expressions and the circumstances in which such words frequently occur. Newmark (1988: 16) also maintains that "all texts have connotations, an aura of ideas and feelings suggested by lexical words (e.g. 'run' may suggest 'haste' and 'sofa' may suggest 'comfort')."

Nida (1969: 91) states that we do not only understand the references of words, but also "react to them emotionally, sometimes strongly, sometimes weakly, sometimes affirmatively, and sometimes negatively." Unlike the conceptual meaning, the connotative is culture-specific. Different languages frequently articulate different connotations and associations of feeling, because of differences in cultural roots. As far as political concepts are concerned, connotations play an important role in determining word usage in certain contexts. For example, the words 'm**unadil'** (fighter) and **'thawri'** (rebellion) have positive connotations in a given political context as they may have negative connotations in a different context.

Taking the present period as an example, certain concepts could be analyzed according to their communicative value, evaluative meaning, and connotations; that is to say, what messages do they communicate, and what sorts of results are to be evaluated? Lakoff (1972: 221–271) points out that to be able to measure the communicative value and evaluative meaning of "a concept or signified", its connotation in a given culture with a certain historical period to be the indicators. For relevance to the present investigation, it would be convenient to measure political terms and concepts according to their positive and negative connotations and investigate what is being communicated with a given expression. Hence, the connotations of particular political concepts differ from one speech community to another according to the adopted political systems and the policy of their media, for instance, the word "jihadist" has positive connotations in some Islamic states, while negative connotations in all non-Islamic states. In addition to this, a word such as "revolutionaries" may have a positive connotation in one setting as it may have a negative connotation in a different setting according to the context and the circumstances of the events.

Furthermore, in situations of conflict, political connotative words or expressions are likely to be used in order to legitimize given actions. Rival parties engage in real lexical battles with each other; as a result, everyone is trying to depict a good picture of himself and a bad picture of his rival. Hence, deploying powerful lexical items in their discourse is often influential.

11.5 THE LANGUAGE OF FAKE NEWS IN ARAB SPRING COUNTRIES

The language of fake news has always been a misleading instrument to give false news and data and incorporate wrong information during high stakes in political or military conflicts (Lazer et al.2018). News agencies and channels start broadcasting events up-to-the-minute and spread them quickly. However, the words used to describe people involved in conflicts are particularly sensitive and vulnerable according to viewers and their backgrounds towards the ideology and their involvement in the conflict. Therefore, researchers including Grieve and Woodfield (2023) and Cull, et al., (2017) state that fake news are misleading for countries and governments, and this may cause some undesirable political conflicts. For example in the Cold War, the Soviet Union spread numerous rumors against the United States for allegedly starting experiments which may had caused the spread of deadly diseases in India. As a result, Egelhofer and Lecheler (2019) differentiated between the fake news genre as the deliberate creation of disinformation and the fake news label, which is the use of

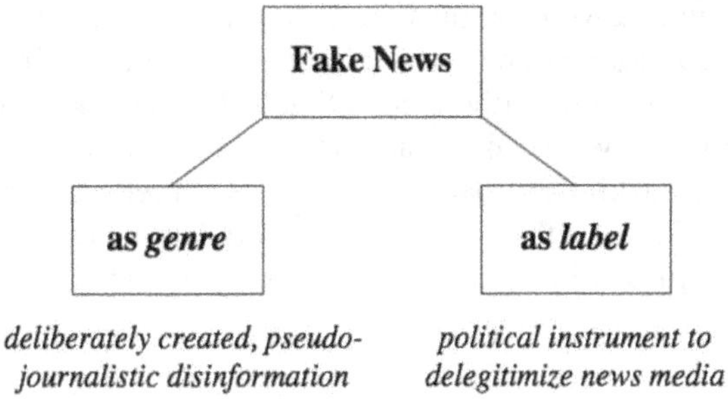

FIGURE 11.1 Fake news differences.

political instruments to legitimize news media. Figure 11.1 'fake news differences' illustrates the distinction between fake news.

In the case of the Arab Spring, social media played a great role in shaping viewers' opinions and misleading them into false propaganda, which created chaos and confusion. Due to the influence of news on social media, populations in the Arabic world gather in public places, protest against their governments and corruption, and even start riots and destroy public and government facilities (Giselle and Althiyabi 2019). Since the beginning of the Arab Spring, many studies tried to discuss the effects of fake news on cultural aspects among Arabic populations such as Egypt (Attiaet al.2011) and Tunisia(Marzoukiet al.2012). These studies tried to explore the cultural backgrounds of fake news on social media in different Arabic uprisings. However, other studies such as Alian (2016), Mellor (2005), and Howard and Hussain (2011) explored the representation of news in English and Arabic news in terms of its vocabulary, collocations, and slogans. In fact, a growing interest in foreign news has been the center of analysis in the first decade of the twenty-first century when foreign policies of the superpowers (the United States, Russia, Israel, NATO countries, and China) started to interfere in the internal affairs and political conflicts of Arab countries. Many events took place in this era including the Gulf War (Iraq's invasion of Kuwait), the Algerian Civil War, the invasion of Iraq in 2003, and the Palestinian-Israeli conflict over the Gaza Strip. Many connotative meanings introduced in foreign news have become particularly widespread after the 9/11 attacks on the World Trade Center in the United States including Al-Qaeda, Hezbollah, WMDs (Weapons of Mass Destruction), and Bin Laden. Meanwhile, other connotations were coined during the Arab Spring including ISIS, Ennahda, Al-Assed, Gaddafi, and the October 25 revolution. The following table summarizes different connotative meaning and their connotations as they were used in the pre-Arab spring era.

It is obvious how culturally the connotations during the Arab Spring are in misinforming and enlightening public opinion in foreign news. Most of the connotative meanings in the Arab Spring are traced back to approximately two decades before when the West started to interfere in events. Therefore, the connotative meanings in the news collocate directly with what had happened and what is happening in the Arabic world either politically, militarily, or even socially. Mohammad Alian (2016) investigated how connotative meanings are collocated with political events according to their historical backgrounds. For example, the conflict in the Gulf area is always supported by an alliance (the United States, Russia, and China) and opposed by a regional dominant power such as Iraq, in the case of Kuwait, and Iran in the case of Saudi Arabia. Meanwhile, Al-Qaeda collocates with terrorist organizations such as the Houthis or ISIS, while the tyranny of Saddam Hussein's regime is also collocated with other regimes in the Arab Spring such as Gaddafi in Libya and Al-Assed in Syria.

11.6 RESEARCH METHODOLOGY

11.6.1 Procedure of Analysis

The analysis is carried out as follows, we take a number of selected expressions and analyze them in the light of their positive and negative connotations. First, we assign the features of positive or negative connotations to each expression. Second, we provide the connotative meaning of each expression. Third, a link is made between a given used expression, its connotative meaning, and the course of events. This is done in order to shed light on the strong relationship between language and political conflicts in the Arab Spring countries, mainly Tunisia, Egypt, Libya, and Syria. Here, we consider the selected expressions as political emotive expressions for they are used in a very sensitive setting which is the political conflict in many Arab countries. This setting constitutes political speeches, statements in news channels, and statements made by the rival parties. From all of this, we collected and selected our small corpus for this study.

11.6.2 Defining the Context

More than a decade ago, massive demonstrations covered by almost all news channels were seen in some Arab countries successively. It started with Tunisia and then moved to Egypt, Yemen, Libya, and Syria. People went out to the streets asking for freedom and democracy from what they considered totalitarian and corrupt regimes. It was unprecedented and unpredicted. Those demonstrators have succeeded in forcing many presidents to step down; some of them have been even killed. This was a never-before-seen event in the history of the Arab nations.

These unprecedented events have been named "The Arab Spring". This expression has become a key notion for describing the situation afterward. The aim of this chapter is to study the use of emotive expressions in this political conflict and try to identify their connotative meanings whether negative or positive based on a linguistic-political view.

11.7 DATA ANALYSIS

In the following table, we have collected the most used expressions in relation to the events. The table follows a chronological order with respect to the events; that is to say, from the starting point to the current situation. Therefore, we select expressions and list and analyze them respectively. First, we assign the features positive or negative connotations to each expression. Second, we provide the political connotative meaning of each expression. Third, we provide the results by making a link between the use of a given expression and the escalation of events. Therefore, our aim is to shed light on how influential is adopting a given emotive, connotative expression in a given political setting.

Table 11.2 provides a number of positive used emotive expressions in the Arab Spring countries. It illustrates in this specific setting the effect of political emotive expressions in the course of events; that is to say, what is the relationship between the linguistic and the political dimensions of events, and which one led to the other?

The table shows that there is a strong relationship between the linguistic side and the political one, which means the political results on the ground are guided by a specific linguistic terminology that is the use of emotive and connotative expressions. In other words, the more connotative and emotive an expression is, the more deteriorating the situation becomes. Let us consider the two first expressions from the table "freedom protestors and democracy protestors". These two expressions are less emotive and connotative than the others, and there is no sign of violence or clashes. If we provide a degree of how much are these expressions emotive and connotative, it is less emotive and the words carry positive connotations. As a result, the situation is not violent. However, things start to change with "anti-government protestors and pro-democracy protestors" which are more emotive and carry different connotations. Here, it is clear from Table 11.2 that the situation is starting to escalate. Generally speaking, in situations like this the news assesses the situation on the ground and takes information from different sources and witnesses because a wrong choice of emotive expressions shows the affiliation of the channel (that is, for or against) and it may have different communicative purposes Chilton (2004). In this context, the situation determines the extent to which news uses positive emotive meaning to express the degree of the situation at hand.

Some of the channels try to hide affiliation (which side they support much) by using a kind of neutral emotive expressions even in escalating situations. The fact is that, the use of such expressions to maintain neutrality against all odds, hide affiliation behind the scenes, and achieve the discretion of information and news towards the viewers. Therefore, the neutral connotative expressions used are often simple and express the intended meaning without any other denotations. As an example, the first emotive expression in Table 1.3"people" refers neutrally to civilians or casualties on both sides of the conflict and, whether they are victims or perpetrators, the channels always use a balanced meaning. In the preceding two emotive expressions "ceasefire" and "truce", the expressions collocate with the expression "call for" which expresses concern towards the conflicting situation and does not indicate any support or affiliation on both sides of the conflict. The situation on the ground does not always refer to emotive expressions, but it is sometimes a question of the relationship between the viewers and the news itself.

Table 11.4 demonstrates the most important and the most broadcasted negative emotive expressions in the Arab Spring. Henceforth, the words "pro-government forces and rebellions" carry negative connotations and they are highly emotive. In light of this, it is clear that this is the turning point of events, and these two expressions connote with split and division in the country. As a result, the degree of violence is increasing due to the use of more connotative and emotive words. Furthermore, "conspirators, terrorists" are extremely emotive and they portray negative connotations such as traitors and a threat that must be eradicated. Here, the situation has gone out of control resulting in massive killings and arrests.

If we take the last three expressions, which are "Extremists, Jihadists, and Takfirists", it is noticed first that they are highly emotive and have extremely negative connotations. These connotative meanings vary from ideology no way for any dialogue, and holly war leaves no way but the way of war. They have played a vital role in the course of events until almost every country is a war zone.

11.8 DISCUSSION

The analysis of the connotative meanings of the emotive expressions shows a great variance in terms of the use of specific expressions to achieve communicative purposes. At first, most of the emotive expressions are negative connotations of some vulgarized words, such as takfirists, jihadists, extremists, and terrorists convey anti-government, dangerous, and threatening ideologies against governments and civilians, which are, in turn, negative emotive expressions. Some news refers to terrorist organizations in their news headlines, specifically when the channel supports the regime and hides this affiliation by using different neutral emotive expressions in the climax of political or military clashes. The remaining words (see Table 11.2) are used to maintain a balance between the political parties and the rivals on the one hand, and how to broadcast the information to viewers on the other hand. Macagno and Walton (2019) concluded that words, which are repeated in the news or speeches, are referred to as "emotive" and that they are used to represent emotive involvement and the misuse of these words may involve the manipulative risks of the presupposed meaning of the interlocutors' commitment.

Concerning the positive emotive expressions, they are formulaic expressions and they are generally collocated with authorities and governments specifically when reference is made to hostile situations. Hence, news in the media is broadcasted with careful considerations of all the emotive expressions. The words collocated with government in Table 11.1 Pre-Arab Spring and During Arab Spring Connotations and Their Denotative Meanings are "anti-government protesters and anti-democracy protesters" which make these emotive expressions basic in terms of their meaning and use in news media. To clarify the point, referred to words such as "anger", "fear", and "sadness" as the basic concepts in terms of expressing emotional meaning, that is they are more basic than other words such as pride or hope. Emotional words in English have a core meaning (the basic connotative meaning) and peripheral meanings (other denotations which are collocated with the word to express the exact meaning. The word "angry" has other peripheral meanings on the superordinate level which express emotions such as "agitated" and "furious". Besides, at the subordinate level, it has other peripheral meanings, which express "annoyance", "boredom", and "anxiety" as these meanings are less emotional.

TABLE 11.1
Pre-Arab Spring and During Arab Spring Connotations and Their Denotative Meanings

Pre-Arab Spring connotations	1. Al-Qaeda 2. Hezbollah 3. WMDs 4. Bin Laden 5. 9/11	1. Terrorist organization located in Afghanistan 2. Shi'it Lebanese militant group • Weapons of Mass Destruction (nuclear, biological…) 4. The most wanted man in the United States and leader of Al-Qaeda 5. The terrorist attacks on the World Trade Center
During Arab Spring connotations	1. ISIS 2. Ennahda 3. Al- Assed 4. Gaddafi 5. Mobarak 6. October 25 revolution 7. Iran's Nuclear programme 8. Huthis	1. A militant Sunni–Salafi jihadist organization in Iraq and Syria 2. Tunisian Renaissance Party after the revolution 3. The Syrian regime 4. The Libyan regime 5. The Egyptian regime 6. The start of the Egyptian Revolution 7. The proliferation of nuclear weapons in Iran and the embargo by the United States 8. A YameniSh'ite political party

TABLE 11.2
Positive Emotive Expressions and Their Connotations According to the Situation

The Expression	Positive Connotation	Negative Connotation	What Is Being Communicated? (Implied Meaning)	The Situation on the Ground
Freedom protestors	+		Freedom of speech/personal freedom	Protestors on the streets
Democracy protestors	+		More personal rights and justice	Protestors on the streets
Anti-government protestors		-	Illegal activity, no legal ground to assemble	Clashes begin
Pro-democracy protestors	+		Have the right to protest	Violence and escalation

The emotional words (referred to as emotive expressions in this section) in the Arab Spring are collocated in the news media by virtue of their communicative purposes, conventions, shared background knowledge, and context. The emotive expressions convey basic meanings with positive connotative meanings at the subordinate

TABLE 11.3
Neutral Emotive Expressions and Their Connotations According to News Channels Affiliation

The Expression	Positive Connotation	Neutral Connotation	Negative Connotation	What is Being Communicated? (implied meaning)	The Situation on The Ground
Five people were killed		+		Civilians/soldiers/ rebellions	People killed on both sides
Both parties are calling for a truce	+			Conflicting parties are seeking atruce	Truce is mandatory to avoid conflicts
The UN is calling for an immediate and unconditional ceasefire			-	The UN tries to calm down the escalating situation	The situation requires immediate ceasefire from both sides
	+			Have the right to protest	Violence and escalation

TABLE 11.4
Negative Emotive Expressions and Their Connotations According to the Situation

The Expression	Positive Connotation	Negative Connotation	What Is Being Communicated? (Implied Meaning)	The Situation on the Ground
Pro-government forces		-	Split and division	More violent actions
Rebellions		-	Outlaw/ looters	Things go out of control
Revolutionaries	+		Freedom fighters	Things go out of control
Conspirators		-	Traitors	Use of weapons resulted in death cases
Terrorists		-	A threat that must be eliminated	Massive killings and arrests
Extremists		-	Ideological concept.	The country is a war zone
Jihadists		-	Very dangerous; no way for any solution.	A civil war and thousands of victims
Takfirists		-	Ideology and religion are included	More fighting and killing; bloodshed

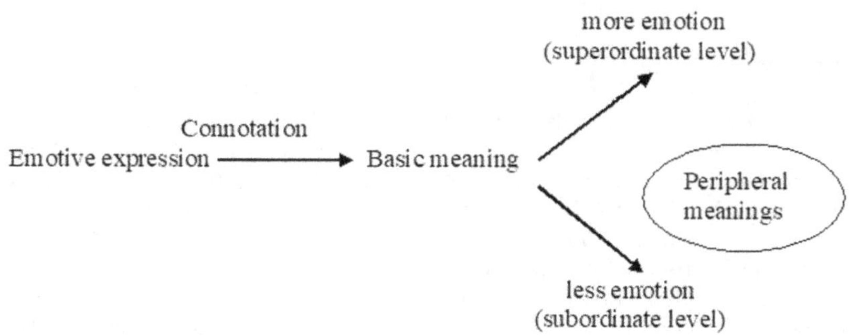

FIGURE 11.2 Core meaning and peripheral meanings of emotive expressions.

level. The situation here is hostile and less violent. However, when there is a turnout in the events with tensions and clashes and even gunfire, the connotative meanings are used to express emotions with different peripheral meanings such as in the case of the word "democracy protester" which can be expressed negatively as "revolutionists" and "rioters". The word "rebellions" also has other peripheral meanings in escalating situations which could be expressed in "Baltagiya","conspirators", and "extremists". Figure 11.2 explains the levels of emotional expressions in Arab Spring emotiveness:

11.9 CONCLUSION

To conclude, the study in this chapter is an attempt to spotlight the link between language and politics, but from a narrowed-down perspective, which is the role of the connotative meaning of emotive political expressions in political conflicts. We have tried to follow the course of events by making a link between the linguistic and the political dimensions of events. Moreover, it is noticed that the more a given expression is emotive and connotative, the more escalating the situation becomes. Here, we can say that these expressions are the first actors in the events and they have played an effective role as well; therefore, prior to any act of violence, there is an expression that lies behind. In addition to this, it is noticed that the connotative meaning and the communicative value of any expression have a vital role in determining the situation on the ground; that is to say, there is a strong relation between what is said and what is happening. Here, it is likely to say that political emotive expressions do play a role in shaping political conflicts. So, in politically sensitive settings such as the one discussed here. It is noticed that emotive connotative expressions play a vital role in the course of events in any country having a political problem. So, the more emotive and connotative the used expressions are, the more problematic the situation becomes. Take for instance Tunisia and Syria. Both countries have witnessed power change demonstrations, but in Syria, things are tragic. Any follower of the events would easily notice that there is a big difference in the language used in both countries. Unless we choose our lexis carefully, our political problems can never be solved easily and this is of course as far as language is concerned.

REFERENCES

Attia, A. M., Aziz, N., Friedman, B., & Elhusseiny, M. F. Commentary: The impact of social networking tools on political change in Egypt's "Revolution 2.0". *Electronic Commerce Research and Applications*, 10(4) (2011): 369–374. DOI: 10.1016/j.elerap.2011.05.003.

Chilton, P. *Analysing Political Discourse. Theory and Practice.* London: Routledge, 2004.

Chilton, P., & Schäffner, C. *Politics as Text and Talk.* Amsterdam/Philadelphia: John Benjamins Publishing Company, 2002.

Cull, N. J., Gatov, V., Pomerantsev, P., Applebaum, A., & Shawcross, A. *Soviet Subversion, Disinformation and Propaganda: How the West Fought against It.* London, UK: LSE Consulting, 2017.

Giselle, R. & Althiyabi, T Fake news: Acceptance by demographics and culture on social media. *Journal of Information Technology & Politics*, 3 (2019). DOI: 10.1080/19331681.2019.1686676.

Grieve, J., & Woodfield, H. *The Language of Fake News.* Jack Grieve and Helena Woodfield, 2023. E-book. DOI: 10.1017/9781009349161.

Howard, P. N., &Hussain, M. The upheavals in Egypt and Tunisia: The role of digital media. *Journal of Democracy*, 22(3) (2011): 35–48.

Joseph, E. J. Language and politics. In: A. Davies & C. Elder (eds.), *The Handbook of Applied Linguistics.* Oxford: Blackwell Publishing, 2004.

Lakoff, R. Hedges: A study in meaning criteria and the logic of fuzzy concepts. In: D. Hockney, et al. (eds.), *Contemporary Linguistic Semantics.* Dorecht: D. Reidel, 1972.

Leech, G. *Semantics: The Study of Meaning.* 2nd ed. Harmondsworth/Middlesex, England: Penguin Books Ltd, 1981.

Lazer, D., Baum, M., Benkler, J., Berinsky, A., Greenhill, K., Metzger, M., Zittrain, J. The science of fake news. *Science*, 359(6380) (2018): 1094–1096.

Luntz, F. *Words That Work*. New York: Hyperion, 2007.

Macagno, F., &Walton, D. Emotive meaning in political argumentation., 39(3) (2019): 229–261. DOI: 10.22329/il.v39i3.5493.

Marzouki, Y., Skandrani-Marzouki, I., Béjaoui, M., Hammoudi, H., & Bellaj, T. The contribution of Facebook to the 2011 Tunisian revolution: A cyberpsychological insight. *Cyberpsychology, Behavior, and Social Networking*, 15(5) (2012): 237–244. DOI: 10.1089/ cyber.2011.0177.

Mellor, N. *The Making of Arab News*. Lanham: Rowman and Littlefield Publishers, 2005.

Mohammed, Alian N. H. *The Representation of the Arab Spring Narratives in English and Arabic News Media*. Doctoral dissertation. School of English, University of Leeds, 2016.

Newmark, P.*A Textbook of Translation*. Hertfordshire: Prentice Hall, 1988.

Nida, E. Linguistics and ethnology in translation-problems. In Dell Hymes (ed.), *Language in Culture and Society*. New York: Harper and Row, 1969.

Nida, E. & Charles, T. *The Theory and Practice of Translation*. Leiden: E. J. Brill, 1969.

Thompson, W. K. *The History and Philosophy of Rhetoric and Political Discourse*, vol. I. Boston: University Press of America, 1987.

Vine, B. *Getting Things Done at Work: The Discourse of Power in Workplace Interaction*. Philadelphia: John Benjamins Publishing Company, 2004.

Waard, D., &Eugene, N. *From One Language to Another: Functional Equivalence in Bible Translating*. Nashville: Thomas Nelson Publishers, 1986.

12 Detecting Fake News and Hate Speech Using Machine Learning
An Overview of Frameworks

Bahubali Shiragapur, Nishikant Surwade,
Kaustubh Sakhare, Vijaylaxmi Jain,
and Maheshwari Biradar

12.1 INTRODUCTION

12.1.1 The Proliferation of Fake News and Hate Speech Online

The proliferation of fake news and hate speech online is a complex and multifaceted issue that poses significant challenges for individuals, organizations, and societies. Fake news refers to intentionally false information presented as if it were true. At the same time, hate speech seeks to denigrate, demean, or harm individuals or groups based on race, religion, gender, sexual orientation, or ethnicity (Garbe et al. 2021).

One of the primary drivers of the proliferation of fake news and hate speech online is the ease with which information can be shared and disseminated through social media platforms and other online channels. This has created a situation where false or misleading information can be spread quickly and easily, often without fact-checking or verification (Addawood et al. 2019).

Another factor contributing to the problem is the ability of individuals and organizations to manipulate algorithms and search engine results to promote their agendas or viewpoints. This can result in the amplification of extremist or divisive messages and the suppression of more moderate or balanced perspectives.

Addressing the problem of fake news and hate speech online will require a multifaceted approach that includes education, media literacy, regulation, and enforcement. It will also require cooperation and collaboration between governments, technology companies, and civil society organizations to develop effective strategies for identifying and countering false information and hate speech while protecting freedom of speech and expression ("Political Leadership, Voter Education, and Collective Action" 2023).

Efforts to combat the problem must also be grounded in respect for diversity, inclusivity, and human rights and should aim to promote a culture of dialogue,

 DOI: 10.1201/9781003409519-12

empathy, and mutual understanding. Ultimately, the fight against fake news and hate speech online will require a sustained and collaborative effort from all stakeholders involved.

12.1.2 Importance of Detecting and Combating Fake News and Hate Speech

The detection and combating of fake news and hate speech are essential for several reasons:

Protecting democracy: Fake news and hate speech can manipulate public opinion and interfere with democratic processes such as elections, referenda, and political decision-making. By detecting and combating fake news and hate speech, we can help ensure that citizens can access accurate information and make informed decisions.

Preserving social cohesion: Hate speech can create social divisions and tensions, leading to conflict and violence. By detecting and combating hate speech, we can help maintain social cohesion and promote mutual understanding and respect between different groups.

Promoting human rights: Hate speech can also be used to violate the human rights of individuals and groups, including the right to dignity, freedom from discrimination, and freedom of expression. By detecting and combating hate speech, we can help to protect these fundamental rights.

Ensuring quality journalism: The proliferation of fake news can undermine the credibility of journalism and erode public trust in the media. By detecting and combating fake news, we can promote quality journalism and ensure citizens can access accurate and reliable information.

Preventing harm: Fake news and hate speech can have real-world consequences, such as inciting violence, promoting discrimination, or undermining public health efforts. By detecting and combating fake news and hate speech, we can help to prevent harm and promote public safety.

In short, detecting and combating fake news and hate speech are essential for promoting democracy, preserving social cohesion, protecting human rights, ensuring quality journalism, and preventing harm.

12.2 APPLICATION OF MACHINE LEARNING TO DETECT FAKE NEWS AND HATE SPEECH

Machine learning can be a powerful tool for detecting fake news and hate speech online. Here are some of how machine learning can be applied to this problem (Ai et al. 2022):

Natural language processing (NLP): NLP is a branch of machine learning that analyzes and understands human language. It can be used to develop algorithms to analyze text and identify patterns and features characteristic of fake news and hate speech (Sjoding and Liu 2016, 1443).

Sentiment analysis: Sentiment analysis is a subfield of NLP that determines the sentiment or emotion expressed in a text. By analyzing the sentiment of online content, machine learning algorithms can identify instances of hate speech and other harmful content.

Network analysis: Machine learning algorithms can analyze social media networks and identify behavior patterns that are characteristic of fake news and hate speech. For example, network analysis can be used to identify clusters of users who are sharing false or divisive content.

Content-based filtering: Content-based filtering is a machine learning technique that analyzes the content of online posts to identify keywords, topics, and other features associated with fake news and hate speech. This can be used to develop algorithms that automatically filter out or flag inappropriate content.

Hybrid approaches: Machine learning algorithms can also be combined with other techniques, such as crowd-sourcing and human moderators, to improve their accuracy and effectiveness in detecting fake news and hate speech.

Overall, machine learning has the potential to be a valuable tool in the fight against fake news and hate speech online. However, it is essential to note that these algorithms are imperfect and susceptible to bias and errors. Therefore, it is necessary to continue developing and refining these techniques to improve their accuracy and effectiveness.

12.3 OVERVIEW OF FAKE NEWS DETECTION FRAMEWORKS

12.3.1 Fake News: Definition, Types, and Manifestations

Fake news refers to intentionally false or misleading information presented as if it were true, often disseminated through traditional or social media. The term "fake news" has been popularized in recent years due to its widespread use in political discourse, particularly in elections and other high-profile events.

Here are some types and manifestations of fake news:

- **Satire or parody:** Some fake news stories are written as satire or parody, often using humor or irony to highlight absurdity or hypocrisy. While these stories may be intended to be humorous or thought-provoking, they can sometimes be mistaken for real news.
- **Propaganda:** Fake news can be used as propaganda to promote a particular political agenda or ideology. This can involve spreading false or misleading information about political opponents or issues to sway public opinion.
- **Hoaxes:** Fake news can also take the form of scams, such as stories about celebrity deaths or other sensational events that are entirely fabricated.

- **Clickbait:** Clickbait refers to headlines or stories designed to attract clicks and generate advertising revenue, often using sensational or misleading headlines.
- **Deepfakes:** Deepfakes are fake news that use artificial intelligence to create videos or images that appear natural but are manipulated or altered.

  Fake news can take many forms and be used for various purposes, from satire and entertainment to political propaganda and disinformation. As such, it is essential for individuals to be vigilant and critical consumers of news and to verify the information before sharing it with others.

12.3.2 Overview of Machine Learning Techniques for Fake News Detection

Machine learning techniques can detect and combat fake news by analyzing patterns and characteristics in the data. Here are some standard machine-learning methods used for counterfeit news detection.

Natural language processing (NLP): NLP is a machine learning subfield that analyzes human language. Using NLP techniques, machine learning algorithms can analyze text to identify patterns and features associated with fake news.

Sentiment Analysis: Sentiment analysis involves determining the sentiment expressed in a text, such as whether it is positive, negative, or neutral. This can identify fake news stories that contain sensationalized or inflammatory language.

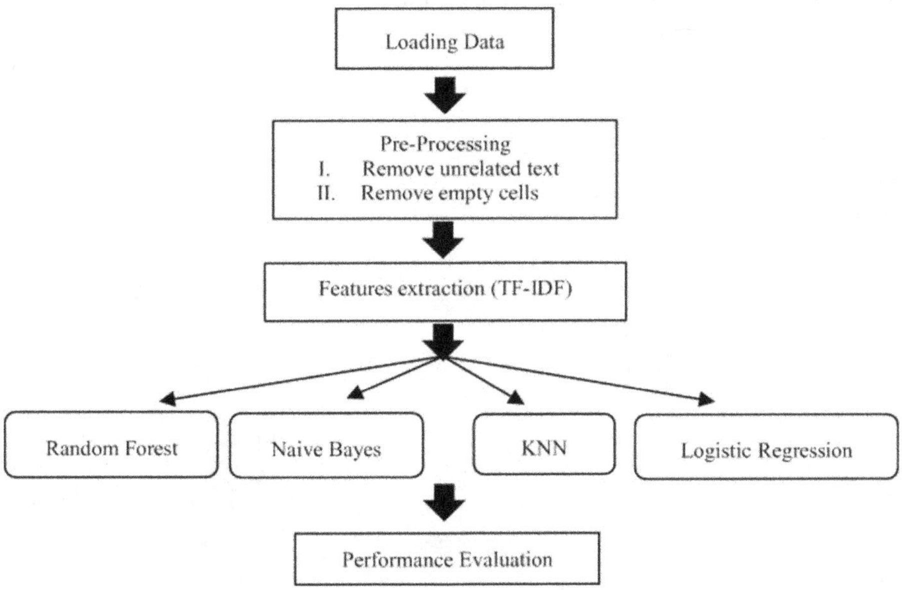

FIGURE 12.1 Overall framework for Fake news detection.

Machine learning classification: Machine learning classification algorithms can be trained to differentiate between fake and real news articles. These algorithms can use features such as the language used in the report, the sources cited, and other factors to make this distinction.

Network analysis: Network analysis involves analyzing the structure of social media networks and identifying patterns of behavior associated with fake news. For example, it can be used to identify groups of users who are sharing fake news stories.

Clustering analysis: Clustering analysis involves grouping similar data points based on their characteristics. Machine learning algorithms can be trained to cluster news articles based on their topic, source, and other factors. This can identify clusters of pieces more likely to contain fake news.

Hybrid approaches involve combining multiple machine-learning techniques to improve the accuracy of fake news detection. For example, sentiment analysis and machine learning classification algorithms can be connected to develop more effective classifiers.

Overall, machine learning techniques can be powerful tools for detecting fake news. However, it is essential to note that these algorithms are imperfect and susceptible to bias and errors. Therefore, it is necessary to continue developing and refining these techniques to improve their accuracy and effectiveness.

12.4 STRENGTHS AND LIMITATIONS OF DIFFERENT FRAMEWORKS

There are various frameworks and approaches for detecting fake news, each with strengths and limitations. Here are some examples:

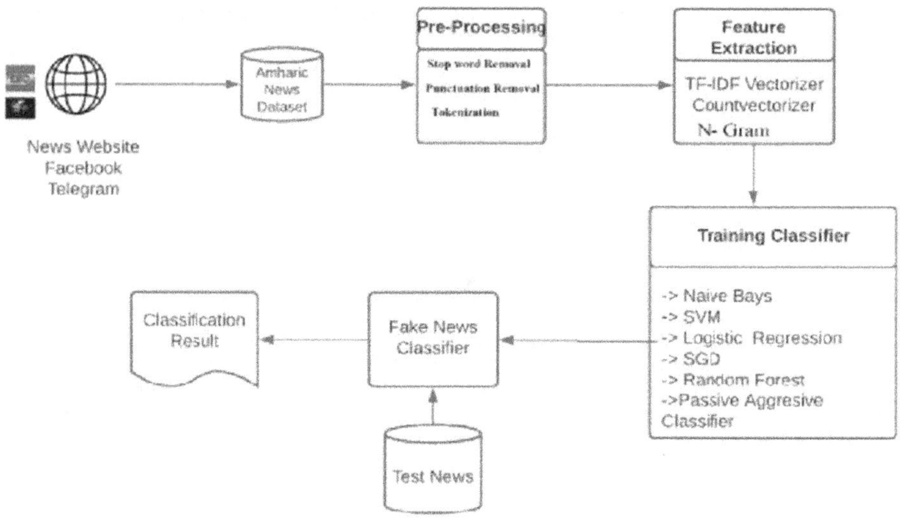

FIGURE 12.2 Fake news detection using classifier.

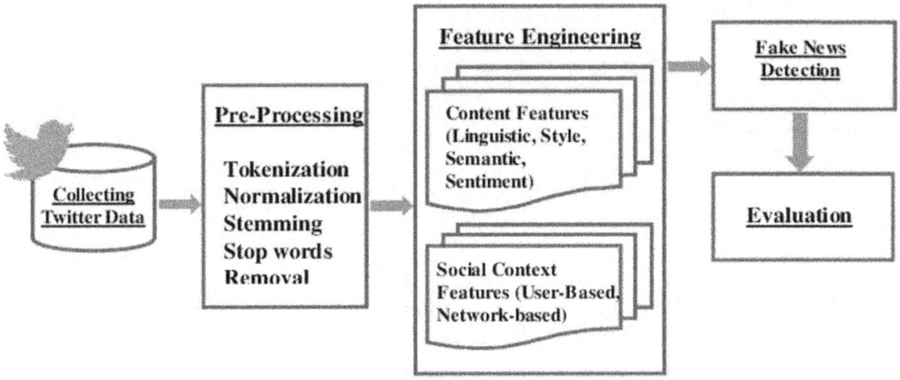

FIGURE 12.3 Fake news detection for X data.

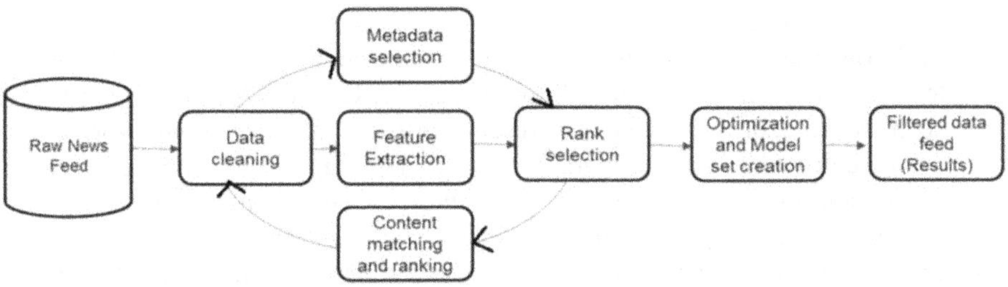

FIGURE 12.4 Data processing for fake news.

Natural language processing (NLP): NLP is a robust framework for detecting fake news as it can analyze the content of news articles to identify patterns and features associated with fake news. NLP can see phony information by exploring the use of specific words or phrases, the article's tone, the structure of the sentences, and other linguistic features. However, NLP has some limitations, such as being biased toward certain types of news, and it can be hard to identify fake news in articles with a neutral tone.

Machine learning classification: Machine learning classification algorithms can be used to differentiate between fake and real news articles. This approach works well with large datasets and can be used to build highly accurate models for detecting fake news. However, machine learning classification algorithms require large amounts of labeled data to be trained and can be prone to overfitting, leading to lower accuracy in detecting fake news.

Network analysis: Network analysis can be used to identify clusters of users who are sharing fake news stories. This approach can effectively detect coordinated campaigns to spread fake news. However, network analysis requires access to social media data and can be limited by the available quality and quantity of data.

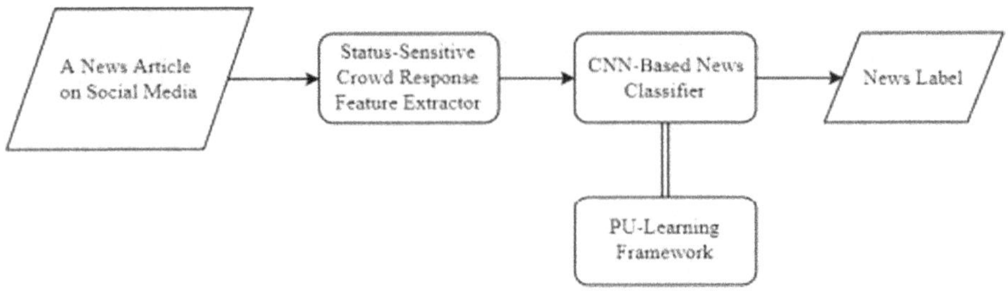

FIGURE 12.5 Early detection fake news machine learning (ML) model.

Hybrid approaches: Hybrid approaches combine multiple frameworks to improve fake news detection accuracy. For example, combining NLP and machine learning classification can lead to more effective classifiers. However, these approaches can be complex and require significant computational resources.

Crowd-sourcing: Crowd-sourcing can detect fake news by leveraging the collective intelligence of large groups of people. Crowd-sourcing platforms such as Amazon Mechanical Turk can be used to have human workers evaluate news articles and identify those that contain fake news. However, crowd-sourcing can be expensive and time-consuming, and the quality of the results may vary based on the workers' skills and experience.

Overall, each framework for detecting fake news has its strengths and limitations, and it is essential to use a combination of approaches to develop more effective detection methods.

12.5 OVERVIEW OF HATE SPEECH DETECTION FRAMEWORKS

12.5.1 Explanation of the Concept of Hate Speech and Its Various Forms

Hate speech is any speech or expression that attacks or dehumanizes a person or a group based on race, ethnicity, national origin, religion, gender, sexual orientation, or another characteristic. The purpose of hate speech is often to spread a message of intolerance, discrimination, and violence toward a particular group.

There are various forms of hate speech, including:

- **Verbal assault:** Verbal assaults involve using language to attack or intimidate an individual or group based on their identity. Examples of verbal assaults include derogatory terms, slurs, and hate speech.
- **Threats:** Threats involve using language to suggest or imply that harm will come to an individual or group based on their identity. Hazards can be explicit or implicit, including physical, emotional, or psychological damage.
- **Harassment:** Harassment involves behavior intended to intimidate, degrade, or humiliate an individual or group based on their identity. Examples of harassment can include following, stalking, and persistent insults or taunts.

- **Incitement:** Incitement involves using language to encourage or promote violence or discrimination against an individual or group based on their identity. Examples of incitement can include encouraging others to commit hate crimes or engaging in violent behavior towards a particular group.
- **Denial of rights:** Denial of rights involves using language to justify or promote denying rights or opportunities to an individual or group based on their identity. Examples of deprivation of ownership can include advocating for discriminatory policies or practices that limit access to education, employment, or housing.

It is important to note that hate speech is not protected under free speech laws in many countries and can have serious consequences, including physical harm, psychological trauma, and social exclusion. Therefore, it is essential to identify and combat hate speech to promote a more inclusive and equitable society.

12.5.2 A Brief Overview of Machine Learning Methods for Detecting Fake News

Machine learning methods are becoming increasingly popular for detecting fake news because they can process large amounts of data and learn patterns from it. Here are some standard machine learning methods used for detecting fake news:

- **Supervised learning:** This approach involves training a machine learning model on a labeled real and fake news article dataset. The model learns to differentiate between the two based on the features and patterns present in the dataset. Once trained, the model can classify new articles as real or fake (Chakravorty and Lam 2017, 1139).
- **Unsupervised learning:** Unsupervised learning involves training a machine learning model on an unlabelled dataset of news articles. The model learns to identify common patterns and features in the dataset, which can then be used to identify themes likely to be fake news (He et al. 2019).
- **Deep learning:** Deep learning involves using neural networks to analyze and classify news articles. Deep learning models can learn complex patterns and features from large amounts of data and accurately detect fake news. However, deep learning models can be computationally expensive and require training extensive data.
- **Natural language processing (NLP):** NLP is a branch of machine learning focused on understanding and processing human language. NLP techniques can be used to analyze the content of news articles, including the words used, sentence structure, and tone. By analyzing these features, NLP models can identify pieces likely to be fake news.

Ensemble Learning: Ensemble learning involves combining multiple machine learning models to improve the accuracy of fake news detection. This approach can be highly effective as it can mitigate the weaknesses of individual models and provide more robust results.

Overall, machine learning methods are a powerful tool for detecting fake news. By analyzing large amounts of data and learning patterns and features associated with fake news, these methods can help to identify and combat the spread of misinformation.

12.5.3 The Strengths and Weaknesses of Different Frameworks

Different machine learning frameworks have their strengths and weaknesses in detecting fake news. Here are some examples:

- **Naïve Bayes:** Naïve Bayes is a simple and efficient algorithm that can be trained quickly on large datasets. It works by calculating the probability that a news article is fake or real based on the frequency of certain words or features. However, Naïve Bayes assumes that all features are independent, which may not be true in real-world scenarios (Muchene and Safari 2021).
- **Support vector machines (SVMs):** SVMs are robust and accurate classifiers that can work well on small datasets. They are handy for separating complex datasets into different classes. However, SVMs can be computationally expensive and require significant tuning to achieve optimal performance.
- **Random forest:** Random forest is an ensemble learning algorithm that combines multiple decision trees to improve classification accuracy. It can handle categorical and continuous data and is robust to noisy and missing data. However, random forests can be prone to overfitting on small datasets and may not perform as well on larger datasets (Nesheiwat et al. 2020, 652).
- **Recurrent neural networks (RNNs):** RNNs are deep learning models that can learn complex patterns in sequential data, such as news articles. They are handy for detecting fake news disguised as real news. However, RNNs can be computationally expensive and require significant tuning to achieve optimal performance.
- **Convolutional neural networks (CNNs):** CNNs are deep learning models that can learn hierarchical representations of data, such as images or text. They can be used to identify specific patterns in news articles that are associated with fake news. However, CNNs may require large amounts of training data and can be sensitive to noise in the data.

Each framework has its strengths and weaknesses, and the best approach depends on the problem and dataset. Combining different frameworks or ensemble learning can improve the accuracy of fake news detection.

12.6 EVALUATION METRICS FOR FAKE NEWS AND HATE SPEECH DETECTION

12.6.1 Performance Evaluation Metrics for Fake News Detection

Performance evaluation metrics are essential to assess the effectiveness of machine learning models for counterfeit news detection. Here are some commonly used metrics:

- **Accuracy:** Accuracy measures the proportion of correctly classified news articles from the total number of pieces. While accuracy is a standard metric, there may be other appropriate measures for imbalanced datasets where the number of fake news articles is much lower than accurate news articles.
- **Precision:** Precision measures the proportion of true positives (i.e., correctly classified fake news articles) out of all articles classified as fake news. It can be used to assess the balance of false positives and the model's effectiveness in detecting fake news.
- **Recall:** Recall measures the proportion of true positives (i.e., correctly classified fake news articles) out of all fake news articles. It can be used to assess the balance of false negatives and the model's effectiveness in detecting all instances of fake news.
- **F1 score:** F1 score is the harmonic mean of precision and recall and provides a balanced measure of both. It helps evaluate models when both precision and recall are essential.
- **AUC–ROC:** AUC–ROC (area under the receiver operating characteristic curve) is a metric that measures the model's overall performance across different classification thresholds. It provides a good measure of the model's ability to distinguish between real and fake news (Celliers and Hattingh 2020)
- **Confusion matrix:** A confusion matrix is a table that shows the number of true positives, true negatives, false positives, and false negatives for a model's predictions. It can be used to calculate other performance metrics and identify specific areas of the model that need improvement (Sharma et al. 2022, 31–51).

Overall, combining these metrics can provide a more comprehensive assessment of the performance of machine learning models for fake news detection. Choosing the appropriate metrics based on the specific problem and dataset is essential to accurately evaluate the model's effectiveness.

12.6.2 Performance Evaluation Metrics for Hate Speech Detection

Performance evaluation metrics are essential to assess the effectiveness of machine learning models for hate speech detection. Here are some commonly used metrics:

- **Accuracy:** Accuracy measures the proportion of correctly classified instances of hate speech out of the total number of cases. While accuracy is a standard metric, there may be other appropriate measures for imbalanced datasets where the number of instances of hate speech is much lower than non-hate speech instances.
- **Precision:** Precision measures the proportion of true positives (i.e., correctly classified instances of hate speech) out of all the cases classified as hate speech. It can be used to assess the proportion of false positives and the model's effectiveness in detecting hate speech.

- **Recall:** Recall measures the proportion of true positives (i.e., correctly classified instances of hate speech) out of all actual cases of hate speech. It can be used to assess the proportion of false negatives and the model's effectiveness in detecting all instances of hate speech.
- **F1 score:** F1 score is the harmonic mean of precision and recall and provides a balanced measure of both. It helps evaluate models when both precision and recall are essential.
- **AUC–ROC:** AUC–ROC (area under the receiver operating characteristic curve) is a metric that measures the model's overall performance across different classification thresholds. It provides a good measure of the model's ability to distinguish between hate speech and non-hate speech.
- **Confusion matrix:** A confusion matrix is a table that shows the number of true positives, true negatives, false positives, and false negatives for a model's predictions. It can be used to calculate other performance metrics and identify specific areas of the model that need improvement.

Overall, combining these metrics can provide a more comprehensive assessment of the performance of machine learning models for hate speech detection. Choosing the appropriate metrics based on the specific problem and dataset is essential to accurately evaluate the model's effectiveness.

12.7 CONCLUSION

Here is a recap of the essential findings and conclusions regarding the application of machine learning for fake news and hate speech detection:

Machine learning techniques have shown promising results in detecting fake news and hate speech. However, there are still limitations in accuracy and the ability to see nuanced or subtle forms of fake news and hate speech.

Different frameworks, such as supervised learning, unsupervised learning, and deep learning, have strengths and weaknesses in terms of their effectiveness and efficiency in detecting fake news and hate speech.

Performance evaluation metrics such as accuracy, precision, recall, F1 score, AUC–ROC, and confusion matrix are commonly used to assess the effectiveness of machine learning models for fake news and hate speech detection.

To improve the accuracy and effectiveness of machine learning models for fake news and hate speech detection, it is essential to consider factors such as the quality and diversity of the training data, the use of explainable AI techniques, and the incorporation of human experts to validate and refine the results.

Overall, using machine learning techniques for fake news and hate speech detection is a promising area of research and development. Still, it requires ongoing refinement and improvement to address these issues' complexity and evolving nature.

12.7.1 Insights into Future Directions in Fake News and Hate Speech Detection

Here are some insights into future directions in fake news and hate speech detection:

Multimodal detection: Using multiple modalities such as text, images, and videos can provide a more comprehensive and accurate detection of fake news and hate speech.

Explainable AI: There is a growing need for machine learning models to be transparent and interpretable to address concerns around bias and ethics. Explainable AI techniques can provide insights into how machine learning models make decisions and increase trust in the results.

Adversarial attacks: Adversarial attacks aim to deceive machine learning models by introducing subtle changes to the input data. Developing robust models that can detect and prevent malicious attacks is an important direction for future research.

Online context: Detecting fake news and hate speech in online social networks and platforms is a complex and dynamic problem that requires the consideration of the social and cultural context of the content. Future research can focus on developing models that capture the context and dynamics of online communication.

Human–machine collaboration: Combining the strengths of machine learning models with the expertise and judgment of human experts can provide more accurate and nuanced detection of fake news and hate speech. Future research can explore how to design effective human-machine collaboration systems for fake news and hate speech detection.

Overall, fake news and hate speech detection are evolving and advancing rapidly. There is a need for ongoing research and development to address these issues' complex and nuanced nature.

REFERENCES

Addawood, Abdulrahman, Ahmed Badawy, Kristina Lerman, and Emilio Ferrara. "Linguistic Cues to Deception: Identifying Political Trolls on Social Media." *Proceedings of the International AAAI Conference on Web and Social Media* 13 (2019): 15–25. https://doi.org/10.1609/icwsm.v13i01.3205.

Ai, Yuehan, et al. "Application of Machine Learning for Multi-community COVID-19 Outbreak Predictions with Wastewater Surveillance." *PLoS One* 17, no. 11 (November 2022): e0277154.

Celliers, M., and M. Hattingh. "A Systematic Review on Fake News Themes Reported in Literature." In *Responsible Design, Implementation and Use of Information and Communication Technology. I3E 2020*, edited by M. Hattingh, M. Matthee, H. Smuts, I. Pappas, Y.K. Dwivedi, and M. Mäntymäki, Lecture Notes in Computer Science, vol. 12067. Springer, Cham, 2020. https://doi.org/10.1007/978-3-030-45002-1_19.

Chakravorty, Shiladitya, and Sarah Lam. "Decision Analysis with Limited Information: Designing Dispatching Algorithms for Automation." IIE Annual Conference Proceedings, Institute of Industrial and Systems Engineers (IISE), January 2017, p. 1139.

Garbe, Lisa et al. "How African Countries Respond to Fake News and Hate Speech." *Africa at LSE.* Accessed March 29, 2023. https://blogs.lse.ac.uk/africaatlse/2021/11/25/how-african-countries-respond-fake-news-and-hate-speech-tech-regulation/.

He, Kaiming, Haoqi Fan, Yuxin Wu, Saining Xie, and Ross Girshick. "Momentum Contrast for Unsupervised Visual Representation Learning." *arXiv preprint arXiv:1911.05722v3* (2019). https://doi.org/10.48550/ARXIV.1911.05722.

Muchene, Leacky, and Wende Safari. "Two-Stage Topic Modelling of Scientific Publications: A Case Study of University of Nairobi, Kenya." *PLoS One* 16, no. 1 (2021): e0243208.

Nesheiwat, Joseph, et al. “Prediction of Lower Back Pain Abnormality Using Machine Learning Algorithms.” IIE Annual Conference. Proceedings, Institute of Industrial and Systems Engineers (IISE), January 2020, p. 652.

“Political Leadership, Voter Education, and Collective Action.” Accessed March 29, 2023. https://www.dailynews.lk/2023/03/25/features/300055/political-leadership-voter-education-and-collective-action.

Sharma, D. K., M. Chatterjee, G. Kaur, and S. Vavilala. “Deep Learning Applications for Disease Diagnosis.” In *Deep Learning for Medical Applications with Unique Data*, edited by S. Vavilala, pp. 31–51. Elsevier, 2022. https://doi.org/10.1016/b978-0-12-824145-5.00005-8.

Sjoding, Michael, and Vincent Liu. “Can You Read Me Now? Unlocking Narrative Data with Natural Language Processing.” *Annals of the American Thoracic Society* 13, no. 9 (2016): 1443.

13 Hate Content Identification in Code-mixed Social Media Data

Supriya Chanda and Sukomal Pal

13.1 INTRODUCTION

Rapid digitalization has made social media more common than ever before. Globally, the Internet is accessed by a substantial proportion of the global population, exceeding 5.16 billion individuals, which accounts for approximately 64.4% of the total population worldwide. This represents more than half of all people on Earth who identify as social beings (Petrosyan 2023). Social media has firmly established itself in our daily lives. Given their extensive user populations, social media platforms serve as a means for individuals to establish connections with friends and family, express their perspectives and personal encounters, stay informed about current trends in news, and serve as a global arena for deliberation. Globally, social media is accessed by approximately 4.76 billion individuals, which constitutes around 59.4% of the global population.

In contemporary times, individuals with diverse racial and educational backgrounds have increasingly come together on social media platforms, primarily facilitated by the widespread availability and accessibility of the Internet. People and groups are demonized using offensive and unparliamentary language, by the users while expressing their opinions and displeasure. The content generated by users has emerged as a fertile environment for the propagation of offensive language and hate speech, notably within the realm of social media. User morale is going down. It can lead to a user suffering from trauma, PTSD, anxiety, etc., such mental suffering is avoidable. Consequently, the extraction of information from social media data and the subsequent identification of abusive language are of utmost importance. It helps to foster civil dialogue, adherence to rules of conduct, safety, inclusion, and respect in online communities.

Code-mixing is a spoken phenomenon where speakers use more than two languages within the same conversation. This phenomenon is particularly common in informal settings, such as social media, where people may feel more relaxed and

DOI: 10.1201/9781003409519-13

comfortable using a mix of languages to communicate with their friends and family. In a linguistically diverse nation such as India, individuals employ regional languages for the purpose of text messaging or posting on social media platforms.

Hindi[1] is spoken by approximately 50% of the population. The research conducted by (Grover et al. 2017) examined the patterns of English–Hindi code-mixing and slang usage on social networks by individuals with multilingual abilities. The study used a sizable dataset of Hindi and English tweets, where the tweet was monolingual in nature, as well as code-switched tweets from Indian users, to conduct a thorough investigation of the swearing behavior displayed by multilingual users. The findings unveiled a strong inclination towards a specific language among bilingual individuals, while also highlighting that the presence of profanity and swearing can act as influential factors motivating code-switching behaviors.

The domain of hate speech identification has been extensively researched and explored; on which both academia and researchers have worked tirelessly for many years. Most of the work is explored in a monolingual setup. Processing and analyzing code-mixed data might be more challenging than processing and analyzing monolingual data since it incorporates various languages and linguistic variations. Multiple languages and scripts can also bring forth new obstacles, including problems with tokenization and part-of-speech tagging. thus, it is crucial for academics and practitioners to provide tools and approaches to efficiently analyze and handle this sort of data, especially in the context of hate speech identification, given the ubiquity of code-mixed data in social media.

Considering these challenges, there has been a rise in interest in creating automated systems for identifying hate content in social media code-mixed data. Creating such tools might greatly impact the battle against hate speech and advance an inclusive and courteous online community.

This chapter focuses on identifying hate content in code-mixed social media data. We explore all possible ways to solve hate speech identification and give an overview of the current state-of-the-art hate content identification in social media data. We then discuss the challenges of identifying hate speech in code-mixed social media data and review the existing approaches for addressing these challenges. Finally, we offer some suggestions for further research in this field.

The subsequent sections of this chapter are structured as follows: In Section 13.2, an extensive examination of previous research pertaining to hate speech identification is presented. Section 13.3 presents a comprehensive overview of the relevant task concerning the identification of hate content in social media data. The methodology employed for identifying hate speech in code-mixed social media data is detailed in Section 13.4. Section 13.5 encompasses a thorough analysis and discussion of the outcomes obtained through various methods. Lastly, Section 13.6 offers a conclusive summary of the chapter.

13.2 RELATED WORK

Identification of hate and offensive content is a well-defined issue in both academia and business. The majority of the studies focusing on hate speech identification have focused primarily on English as it is considered to be a language that is globally spoken and there is a scarcity of relevant corpora for other languages. Hate speech has been categorized into many types, based on the nature of the text and different datasets exist for each of these different types of hate speech, Several studies have delved into the varied aspects of offensive content, such as *abusive language* (Nobata et al. 2016; Mubarak, Darwish, and Magdy 2017), *cyber-aggression* (Kumar et al. 2018), *cyber-bullying* (Xu et al. 2012; Dadvar et al. 2013), and *toxic comments* or *hate speech* (Djuric et al. 2015; Davidson et al. 2017; Kwok and Wang 2013). We provide a brief overview of some notable works in these areas.

- **Aggressive content identification:** About 15,000 annotated Facebook posts and comments in Hindi and English were used in the first shared assignment on aggression content identification (Kumar et al. 2018), which Trolling, Aggression and Cyberbullying (TRAC) organized at the Conference on Computational Linguistics (COLING) 2018. The goal was to divide the posts into three groups: Overtly aggressive, covertly aggressive, and non-aggressive. The best performance was achieved by deep learning techniques based on convolutional neural networks (CNNs), recurrent neural networks (RNNs), and long short-term memory (LSTM) (Aroyehun and Gelbukh 2018; Modha, Majumder, and Mandl 2018).
- **Bullying content identification:** Peer victimization, often known as bullying, has been acknowledged as a serious national health problem by a number of institutions, including the White House (2011), the American Academy of Paediatrics (2009), and the American Psychological Association (2004). Techniques for sentiment analysis and topic modeling have been used in earlier investigations (Xu et al. 2012) along with user-related features (Dadvar et al. 2013) to address this problem.
- **Hate speech identification:** Hate speech involves making offensive statements with the intent to offend or use cruel and abusive language based on an individual's perceived or actual group membership[2]. The study's main goal is to create a lexical baseline for identifying hate speech and profanity using a common dataset (Malmasi and Zampieri 2017). This task has received significant attention in the field of Abusive Language Detection (Djuric et al. 2015; Kwok and Wang 2013; Burnap and Williams 2015). A recent work by Davidson et al. (2017) utilized a dataset of nearly 24,000 labeled tweets for this purpose.
- **Toxic comment identification:** A Kaggle open competition[3] was conducted to classify toxic comments into six distinct categories utilizing an external dataset (Georgakopoulos et al. 2018).

Numerous academic and professional organizations frequently hold workshops and seminars (Kumar et al. 2018) such as Text Analytics for Cybersecurity and Online Safety (TA-COS)[4], TRAC[5], and Abusive Language Online (ALW)[6]. In the research community, there were some popular datasets available such as TRAC-1 (Kumar et al. 2018), OLID, and HateEval (Basile et al. 2019). Datasets are available not only in the English language, but there are also some attempts in German (Mandl et al. 2019; Ross et al. 2017), Spanish, Arabic (Mubarak, Darwish, and Magdy 2017; Mubarak et al. 2020), Greek (Pitenis, Zampieri, and Ranasinghe 2020), Slovene (Fišer, Erjavec, and Ljubešić 2017), and Chinese (Su et al. 2017). Mubarak, Darwish, and Magdy (2017) generated a collection of profane terms referred to as SeedWords (SW) and calculated the Log Odds Ratio (LOR) for individual word unigrams and bigrams. Saroj, Chanda, and Pal (2020) employed a support vector machine (SVM) approach along with term frequency–inverse document frequency (TF–IDF) features to detect and classify instances of hate speech and offensive language in social media, specifically focusing on two languages: Arabic and Greek. In 2019, the introduction of hate speech and offensive content identification in English and Indo-Aryan languages (HASOC) shared task (Mandl et al. 2019) resulted in the development of a substantial multilingual dataset for the purpose of identifying hate speech. The initial HASOC shared task centered around the detection of hate speech within Indo-European languages, namely Hindi, English, and German (Mandl et al. 2019). In HASOC 2020, there were two sub-tasks, the second sub-task was for Tamil and Malayalam languages and the first track was similar to HASOC 2019. The SemEval 2019 Task-5 (Basile et al. 2019) was dedicated to identifying hate speech targeting immigrants and women by analyzing messages in Spanish and English sourced from X (formerly Twitter). Similar to SemEval, GermEval was coordinated by Wiegand, Siegel, and Ruppenhofer (2018) emphasizing the importance of addressing hate speech detection in different languages and contexts. Two studies conducted by Schmitdt and Wiegand (2017) and Fortuna and Nunes (2018), which demonstrate the process of categorizing offensive tweets using various features such as sentiment analysis, linguistic characteristics, and diverse lexical resources. One notable initiative in this domain is Task 6 of SemEval 2019, spearheaded by Zampieri et al. (2019) which specifically addresses three sub-tasks pertaining to Twitter data, limited to the English language.

Since communication in social media is performed in an informal setting, the identification of hate speech becomes a challenging task. Mathur et al. (2018) attempted hate speech recognition on Hinglish data, a more challenging case of code mixed language. In India, most research is reported on Hindi–English code-mixed language, as Hindi is the most commonly spoken language. Apart from Hindi–English, Odia–English (Mohapatra et al. 2021), Tamil–English, Urdu–English, Malayalam–English, and Kannada–English datasets are also used for hate speech identification. The shared task of Dravidian LangTech (Chakravarthi et al. 2021) focused on the detection of offensive language content in a code-mixed dataset consisting of comments and posts from three closely related Dravidian Languages: Tamil–English, Malayalam–English, and Kannada–English, which were collected from social media. This provides an excellent opportunity to utilize multilingual models for identifying offensive language in these data. Nevertheless, it is important to acknowledge that the linguistic resemblances between these languages frequently present difficulties for natural language processing (NLP) pipelines, as exemplified in the recent Dravidian language identification (DLI) shared task held at VarDial (Chakravarthi et al. 2021). Within the domain of Dravidian LangTech, several high-performing systems made use of neural network architectures that relied on pre-trained transformer models, including multilingual bidirectional encoder representations from transformers (BERT), XLM-RoBERTa, and IndicBERT. Interestingly, none of these systems explored the potential advantages of transfer learning across different languages to enhance performance. The datasets employed in this study for Tamil–English and Kannada–English were obtained from the aforementioned shared task. Limited research has been conducted regarding the impact of transfer learning on offensive language identification in Indian languages, as mentioned by Ranasinghe and Zampieri (2020), By utilizing transfer learning on the English OLID dataset, Sai and Sharma (2021) enhanced offensive language recognition for code-mixed Kannada, Malayalam, and Tamil (Zampieri et al. 2019). Additionally, by applying transfer learning from English, Ranasinghe et al. (2020) improved offensive language recognition for a code-mixed Malayalam dataset.

A challenging scenario arises when dealing with conversational code-mixed data, which has become increasingly prevalent on social media platforms. Specifically, our focus lies on the task of identifying hate speech in conversational Hindi–English code-mixed data, as organized by the HASOC 2021 team. The detection of hate speech in conversational code-mixed contexts introduces additional complexities due to the conversational nature of the data. Conversational posts found on social media platforms exhibit a hierarchical structure, consisting of a tuple that comprises a post, comment, and reply, as illustrated in Figure 13.1. Multiple comments can be associated with each post, and each comment may have several replies. In the case of English–Hindi data, each component of the tuple can exhibit code-mixing between Hindi and English, be exclusively in English, exclusively in Hindi, in the form of Romanized Hindi, or a combination thereof. As a result, complex input patterns emerge. The labels assigned to replies or comments are significantly influenced by the contextual information provided by the parent text. An example of this can be observed in Figure 13.2, although the second comment content seems neutral, it actually reinforces the post's hateful and offensive (HOF) tone, making it deserving of the HOF designation. Furthermore, in a sequence of several <post, comment, reply> tuples, identifying the relevant context becomes crucial and poses a challenge. To address this, Chanda et al. (2021) treated all the posts, comments, and replies as a single unified text and applied a pre-trained multilingual BERT model. To maintain the context of posts, comments, and replies, Chanda, Sheth, and Pal (2022) concatenated the data. Bagora et al. (2022) proposed a novel hierarchical neural network architecture, while Madhu et al. (2023) employed a pipeline consisting of an LSTM classifier followed by a fine-tuned SentBERT model.

13.3 TASKS AND DATASETS

In order to detect offensive language, various conferences have organized "shared task" competitions such as HatEval, HASOC, OffensEval, and TRAC. These initiatives have primarily focused on English, with some attention given to high-resource languages such as German and Arabic, aiming to generate new datasets and tools. Notably, recent competitions have made significant contributions to the

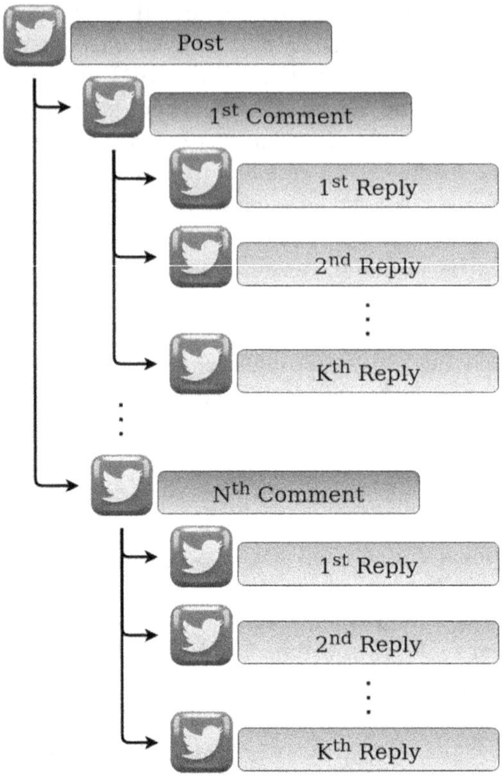

FIGURE 13.1 The structure of conversational code-mixed tweets.

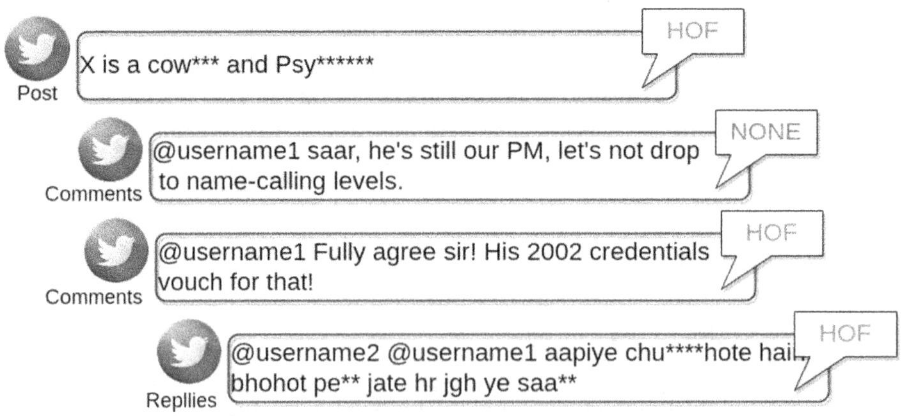

FIGURE 13.2 Example of conversational code-mixed data from Twitter.

development of multilingual datasets for Indian languages. The HASOC shared task and the TRAC shared task were conducted in separate years, while the shared task on offensive language identification in Dravidian languages was held at the Dravidian LangTech workshop in 2021. The main aim of the Dravidian LangTech shared task was to detect offensive language in code-mixed datasets that consisted of comments and posts in three Dravidian Languages: Tamil–English, Malayalam–English, and Kannada–English, which were gathered from social media. Due to their close linguistic relationship, these languages offer the potential to utilize multilingual models for the identification of offensive language in the aforementioned datasets. Nevertheless, the linguistic similarities between these languages present challenges for natural language processing (NLP) pipelines, as demonstrated by the recent Dravidian language identification (DLI) shared task conducted at VarDial. The shared task at Dravidian LangTech encompassed various subtasks, as illustrated in Figure 13.3.

The initial task within the shared challenge revolves around offensive language detection, entailing the classification of the dataset into two primary categories: Offensive (OFF) and non-hate-offensive (NOT). Subsequently, the subsequent task pertains to offensive language categorization. In this stage, posts identified as OFF undergo further classification into two distinct classes: Targeted insult (TIN) and untargeted (UNT). The final phase of the task involves offense target identification. For posts classified as TIN, a further categorization is performed, dividing them into three classes: Individual (IND), group (GRP), and other (OTH).

The aim of the European chapter of the association for computational linguistics (EACL) 2021[7] assignment is to identify abusive language in a code-mixed dataset of social media comments and postings in Dravidian languages (Tamil–English, Malayalam–English, and Kannada–English). The comments/posts may consist of multiple sentences, but on average, the corpora have a sentence length of one. Each comment/post is annotated at the comment/post level. The dataset exhibits class imbalance issues, which accurately reflect real-world scenarios. Mohapatra et al.

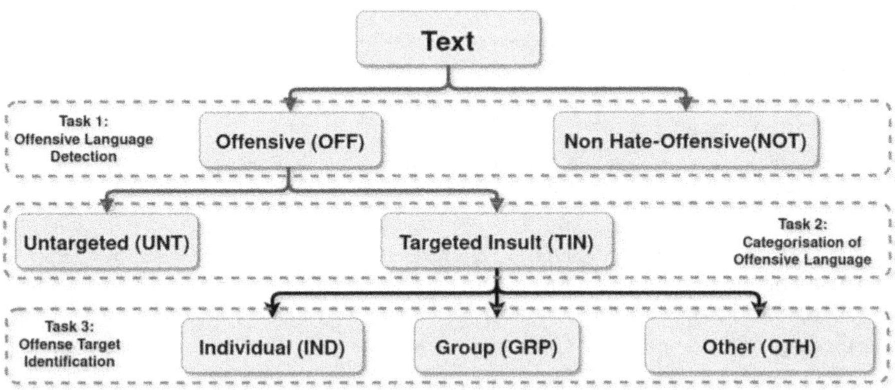

FIGURE 13.3 Classes of all task and their relation.

(2021) created a total of 5,000 Odia–English datasets, and the distribution of the three classes in the dataset is presented in Table 13.1.

Anbukkarasi and Varadhaganapathy (2022) collected a dataset of 10,000 code-mixed tweets in Tamil–English from various domains. The dataset statistics are provided in Table 13.1. Akhter et al. (2020) introduced the first offensive dataset in Urdu, which includes user-generated comments from social media. The study focuses on detecting offensive language in the resource-poor languages Urdu and Roman Urdu. The Table 13.1 illustrates the statistics of this database. Khan, Shahzad, and Malik (2021) released a dataset of 5,000 tweets annotated into three categories: Hate, offensive, and neutral. The dataset statistics are illustrated in Table 13.1. Bohra et al. (2018) created Hindi–English code-mixed a corpus comprising 4,575 tweets annotated for hate speech and normal speech.

In HASOC 2021, the shared task was divided into two parts as shown in Figure 13.4.

TABLE 13.1
Statistical Overview of the Datasets

Odia–English Dataset				
Language	# of Sentence	OFS	HS	OK
OR–EN	5000	2299	1193	1508
Hindi–English Dataset				
Language	# of Sentence	Hate Speech	Normal Speech	
HI–EN	4575	1661	2914	
Tamil–English Dataset				
Language	# of Sentence	Hate Speech	Non-hate Speech	
TA–EN	10000	5000	5000	
Urdu–English Dataset				
Language	# of Sentence	Offensive	Non-Offensive	
UR–EN	10000	5000	5000	
UR–EN	5000	3570	1430	
HASOC 2021 SubTask-2				
Language	# of Sentence	NONE	HOF	
HI–EN (train)	5740	2899	2841	
HI–EN (test)	1348	653	695	
HASOC 2022 Task-1				
Language	# of Sentence	NOT	HOF	
German (train)	307	219	88	
German (test)	81	-	-	
HI–EN (train)	4914	2390	2524	
HI–EN (test)	996	-	-	
HASOC 2022 Task-2				
Language	# of Sentence	NONE	SHOF	CHOF
HI–EN (train)	4914	2390	1636	888
HI–EN (test)	996	-	-	

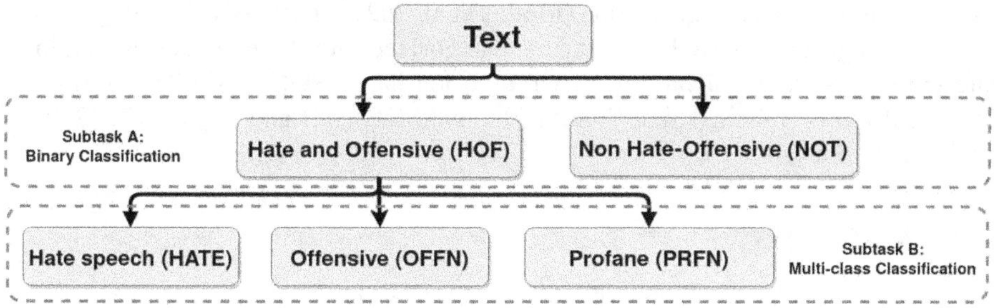

FIGURE 13.4 All tasks of HASOC 2021 shared task.

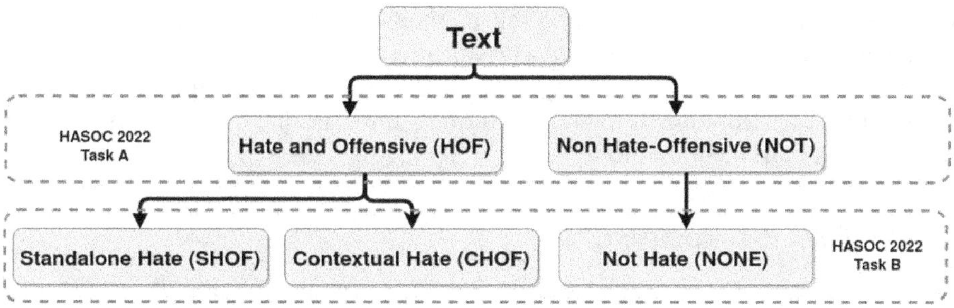

FIGURE 13.5 The categorization of HASOC 2022 shared task.

Sub-task A focuses on the identification of hate and offensive language, which involves a binary classification task. The system is required to classify the data into two primary classes: hate and offensive (HOF) and non hate-offensive (NOT). Moving forward, sub-task B entails a multi-class categorization of offensive language. Once a post is classified as HOF, it undergoes further categorization into three distinct classes: Hate speech (HATE), offensive (OFFN), and profane (PRFN).

13.3.1 Conversational Hate Speech Identification

The challenge of hate speech detection increases exponentially when multilingualism is introduced. Apart from that conversational code-mixed data presents another challenging scenario, which in the present scenario is common for almost all social media, such as X, Facebook, etc. There are two datasets available from HASOC 2021 and HASOC 2022 named the identification of conversational hate-speech in code-mixed languages (ICHCL). In HASOC 2021, there was only one sub-task (Task 1) and HASOC 2022 introduced two shared tasks. Task 1 was similar to previous years but in addition to that a new dataset was introduced along with Hindi–English and German code-mix data. The task categorization is shown in Figure 13.5.

Task 1 is hate and offensive language identification, which is a binary classification task (Modha et al. 2019, 2022). The system needs to classify into two basic classes: Hate and offensive (HOF) and non hate-offensive (NOT). In the next step, task 2 is a multi-class categorization (Modha et al. 2022) of offensive language. After a post is categorized as HOF, it is further categorized into three classes: Standalone hate (SHOF), contextual hate (CHOF), and non-hate (NONE) similar to Task 1. Table 13.2 shows some example Tweets from HASOC 2021 and HASOC 2022 dataset for all classes.

13.4 METHODS

The process of text representation or text understanding plays a pivotal role in enabling machines to comprehend textual data. In recent times, numerous algorithms have emerged with a specific emphasis on text representation. These algorithms encompass a range of approaches, including statistical methods, lexicon-based methods, and deep learning methods, all geared towards effectively representing text data. For any text classification problem, there are a few steps involved. Figure 13.6 indicates a typical classification block diagram. Data preprocessing, representation of data (embedding), and classifier are the main component of a text classification model.

13.4.1 Data Pre-processing

Text pre-processing is a crucial step in handling complex natural language processing tasks, such as hate speech detection. It aims to transform the text into a

TABLE 13.2
Example Tweets from HASOC 2021 and HASOC 2022 Dataset for All Classes (HI for Hindi, EN for English, and Lang for Language)

Language	Sample Tweet from HASOC 2022	Task 1	Task 2
HI–EN	@Joydas @NSaina 2 rs k liye tweet kiya isne samjho bhai national hero hogi phle ab to izzat gawa di.. Andhbhakt ban gayi didi	HOF	CHOF
HI–EN	@itsoutrageeyash @NSaina Yet another man telling a woman what to do and yet another telling her to #shutup. Shame on you Yash! #Feminism #Mansplaining #shethepeople	HOF	SHOF
HI–EN	#Islamophobia Harish Ramkali, leader of the Bajrang Dal in Jind, Haryana posted a video descreating a Muslim mazar on the same land where a temple was built. As seen in the video he is using hateful and violent language against Muslims and the religion. https://t.co/q9dCjdFpne	NOT	NONE
Language	**Sample tweet from HASOC 2021**	**SubTask 2**	
HI–EN	@Samriddhi0809 We can count bewakoof, berozagar , anpad, jhahil, chu*** ya ss in the clip	HOF	
HI–EN	@Samriddhi0809 @police_haryana plzz sir look into this matter and do something to right BCOZ they spread hate	NONE	

FIGURE 13.6 Block diagram of a classification task.

more coherent and consistent format, reducing noise and inconsistencies. This pre-processing facilitates the modeling process for machine learning and deep learning algorithms. The following pre-processing steps were undertaken to prepare the code-mixed text for feature extraction in the classification task:

- **URL removal:** All links and URLs were eliminated from the tweets or comments since they do not contribute to the classification task and are considered noise.
- **Username replacement:** In tweets, it is common to mention other users by including an "@" symbol followed by their Twitter username. All user information such as username is substituted with a fixed word.
- **Elimination of extra white spaces:** Additional spaces and line breaks were removed from the tweets or comments to enhance readability and consistency.
- **Emoji and symbol removal:** Appropriate textual expressions were employed to remove emojis and symbols from the text. This step ensures that the focus remains on the textual content itself.
- **Removal of long repetitions:** Instances where characters are repeated multiple times were addressed by retaining only two consecutive occurrences. This helps in reducing noise caused by excessive character repetition.
- **Handling hashtags:** If a hashtag is present in the text, it can be removed altogether or processed using Python packages to break it down into meaningful words. For example, the hashtag "\#BlackLivesMatter" can be transformed into "Black Lives Matter" to extract the intended meaning.
- **Lowercasing:** Convert all the text to lowercase. This step ensures that the text is case-insensitive, preventing the duplication of words with different capitalization forms and improving consistency in the data.
- **Numeric and special characters:** Exclude numbers and special characters that may not carry substantial semantic meaning in the context of the classification task.

The above-mentioned pre-processing steps contribute to a cleaner and more standardized representation of the text data, enabling more effective analysis and modeling for the classification task.

13.4.2 Features for Text Representation

There are several methods used to extract features for text representation. Some commonly used techniques include:

13.4.2.1 n-Gram Feature

In many studies, a word n-gram feature extraction technique was employed, exploring various values of n ranging from one to three. Here, n represents the number of words used in the probability sequences. The feature extraction process involved utilizing unigrams, bigrams, trigrams, as well as combinations of n-grams. The performance of the n-gram approach greatly relies on selecting an appropriate value for n. Furthermore, this method offers distinct feature models that enable training and comparison of the n-gram features against each other. (Mohapatra et al. 2021).

13.4.2.2 Bag-of-Word (BoW)

This method represents text as a collection of unique words, ignoring the order and context of the words. Each document is represented by a vector where each dimension corresponds to a specific word, and the value in each dimension represents the frequency or occurrence of that word in the document.

13.4.2.3 TF–IDF

The TF–IDF (term frequency–inverse document frequency) method is employed to determine the significance of a word within a document, taking into account its frequency in comparison to its occurrence in the entire corpus. It assigns greater weights to words that appear frequently in a particular document but are infrequent in other documents. By combining TF and IDF, TF–IDF generates a numerical representation of the text. The significance of a word within a dataset can be assessed by calculating its IDF value in relation to the dataset. This particular model offers classifiers that utilize both the word frequency and its importance, which are transformed into a feature vector for the purpose of training. (Mohapatra et al. 2021).

13.4.2.4 Word2vec

Word2vec is a popular method for learning word embedding, which are dense vector representations of words that capture semantic relationships and contextual information. Word2vec is trained on large amounts of text data to generate these embeddings. Each word in a text document is replaced by its corresponding word embedding. Depending on the task and level of granularity desired, different strategies can be employed to generate document-level or sentence-level representations. For example, averaging the word embedding within a document or using weighted sums based on word importance.

13.4.2.5 FastText

FastText is a widely used variant of contemporary word embeddings that exhibits great suitability for processing text originating from social media platforms. It generates embeddings, or representations, for each word, typically ranging in dimensionality from 50 to 300. These embeddings are trained on extensive collections of text, ensuring that words appearing in similar contexts acquire similar embeddings. An advantage of FastText lies in its capacity to capture information at the subword level, which proves advantageous in dealing with words that are not present in the vocabulary. To provide an example, let us consider an unfamiliar word such as "happy" within the FastText lexicon. FastText can tokenize this word into multiple subwords, such as "ha", "hap", "ppy", and "py", among others. This feature of FastText enables the representation of words at the subword and even character level, making it highly advantageous for identifying patterns, particularly in code-mixed tweets.

13.4.2.6 GloVe

GloVe (global vectors for word representation) embeddings are widely employed for generating word embeddings. Although these embeddings are not specifically tailored for code-mixed data, they can still be advantageous for generating features in code-mixed text representation. By utilizing GloVe embeddings, one can capture contextual, semantic, and cross-lingual information embedded within the embeddings, which contributes to the creation of meaningful features for code-mixed data. Despite the fact that GloVe embeddings are not explicitly trained on code-mixed data, they provide valuable insights into word representations that assist in comprehending and processing code-mixed text.

13.4.2.7 Transformer-based

Transformer-based embeddings offer contextual understanding, handle subword information, and are language-agnostic, making them effective for generating features in code-mixed data representation. Fine-tuning on code-mixed datasets and leveraging transfer learning from pre-trained models further enhance their performance in capturing code-mixed language patterns and structures. The attention mechanism in transformers aids in effectively extracting relevant features from code-mixed text. Based on the transformer architecture, there are many models which were used to extract embeddings.

1. BERT
2. M-BERT
3. Indic-BERT
4. MuRIL
5. XLM-RoBERTa

13.4.3 Classification Models Based on ML

A range of conventional classifier models, including logistic regression, Naïve Bayes, k-nearest neighbors, support vector machine, and random forest were extensively explored in this study with the tuning of hyperparameters. The prominent utilization of the scikit-learn library facilitated the experiments on machine learning classifiers. In the case of multiple class classifications, the One-vs-Rest (OVR) strategy of the SVM classifier was employed, while the simpler version of SVM, commonly used for binary classification, was also examined. Additionally, a random forest, comprising numerous individual decision trees operating as an ensemble of separate models, was incorporated in the analysis (Mohapatra et al. 2021).

13.4.4 Classification Models Based on Neural Models

Neural models have been extensively utilized for classification tasks, offering advanced capabilities in capturing complex patterns and relationships within data. Several neural-based classification models have been explored, including:

13.4.4.1 Feed-forward Neural Networks

Feed-forward neural networks, also known as multilayer perceptron (MLP), are a fundamental neural model for classification. These networks consist of multiple layers of interconnected nodes, or neurons, with each neuron applying a non-linear activation function. Training these networks involves optimizing weights through backpropagation, enabling them to learn complex decision boundaries and classify input data.

13.4.4.2 Convolution Neural Network (CNN)

The convolution neural network (CNN) architecture encompasses an input layer, an output layer, and multiple hidden layers. Within the hidden layers of a CNN, essential components include convolution layers, pooling layers, and fully connected layers. Convolution layers perform convolution operations on the input, while the resulting output is then passed to pooling layers, which can be either max pooling or min pooling. The fully connected layer of the CNN connects every neuron in one layer to every neuron in another layer, facilitating comprehensive neural connectivity and information flow.

13.4.4.3 Bidirectional long short-term memory (BiLSTM)

BiLSTM refers to a bidirectional long short-term memory (LSTM) architecture that enables signal propagation in both forward and backward directions in time. It is a variant of recurrent neural networks (RNNs) that enhances learning by processing the original data sequentially from both ends. This bidirectional approach is generally faster than the unidirectional approach, although its efficiency may vary depending on the task at hand. The architecture of BiLSTM comprises a bidirectional LSTM layer followed by a word embedding layer. The output from the bidirectional LSTM is subsequently passed through two distinct pooling layers, namely global average pooling and global maximum pooling, which effectively capture and extract important features from the text. These extracted features are then concatenated and fed into three consecutive fully connected layers, which further reduce their dimensionality. The final fully connected layer serves as the output layer for the BiLSTM model. During model training, proper setting of parameters and hyperparameters is essential, and techniques such as dropout and early stopping are employed to mitigate overfitting. To generate predictions, the “softmax” function is applied to ensure that the probabilities of all output classes sum up to 1, providing a normalized probability distribution.

13.4.4.4 TabNet

TabNet (Chopra et al. 2023) is a specialized architecture developed to leverage the combination of feature attention and neural networks for tabular data. In our case, the feature set can be considered as tabular data since all the collected data points possess feature vectors of the same length, enabling comparability among different data points. TabNet primarily functions as a classifier architecture, harnessing the capabilities of neural networks while incorporating sequential attention to determine which features to focus on at each step. This approach is reminiscent of tree-based architectures, where decisions or splits are made based on specific features.

13.4.5 Ensemble Model

Ensemble learning is a methodology in which multiple machine learning or deep learning techniques are integrated into a single predictive model to mitigate variance, bias, or enhance the predictive quality. By amalgamating the strengths of diverse techniques, ensemble learning aims to achieve more robust and accurate predictions .

13.4.5.1 Ensemble of CNN and BiLSTM

To detect hate speech, an ensemble approach combining CNN and BiLSTM with a multi-layer perceptron (MLP) is employed. CNN has demonstrated effectiveness in text classification tasks with limited data, including spam classification and sentiment analysis. It excels at capturing crucial text information without relying on sequential assumptions. On the other hand, the BiLSTM model considers sequential dependencies in the text, incorporating the benefits of sequential assumptions. By combining these models within an ensemble framework, a comprehensive approach is developed for hate speech detection.

13.4.6 Transfer Learning-based

Transfer learning-based models play a pivotal role in the identification of hate speech within code-mixed data. This approach involves harnessing the power of pre-trained models that have been extensively trained on large-scale datasets from related domains. These pre-trained models possess a comprehensive understanding of language patterns, contextual cues, and semantic representations, which prove advantageous for hate speech detection. Specifically, in the case of code-mixed data, transfer learning models such as BERT (bidirectional Encoder representations from transformers) have demonstrated exceptional efficacy. By virtue of being pre-trained on vast text corpora, BERT exhibits a profound comprehension of language semantics and can effectively encode code-mixed text while preserving contextual information. Fine-tuning the pre-trained BERT model on a smaller labeled dataset that specifically pertains to hate speech in code-mixed data enables the model to learn and identify hate speech patterns within this unique context. During the fine-tuning process, the model's parameters are updated based on the target dataset while retaining the knowledge acquired during pre-training. Leveraging the general language understanding captured during pre-training, the transfer learning-based model adeptly captures the intricacies and complexities of code-mixed text. A notable advantage of this approach is its ability to achieve satisfactory performance with a reduced requirement for labeled training data, as the model generalizes from the pre-training stage and seamlessly adapts to the task of hate speech detection in code-mixed data. To further enhance the granularity of classification, artificial neural network (ANN) and XGBoost models were employed, utilizing feature representations derived from BERT. The hate and offensive content identification task benefited from representations extracted from models such as XLM-RoBERTa, mBERT, and MuRIL.

13.4.7 Conversational Contextual

The domain of hate speech detection in conversational text has received limited attention thus far. As an initial approach, one could treat each individual post, comment, and reply as separate standalone texts and employ transformer-based models to enhance textual representation, considering the code-mixed nature of the data. Models such as mBERT, XLM-RoBERTa, and MuRIL are expected to outperform other alternatives due to their multilingual capabilities. However, this approach fails to capture the contextual relationship between posts, comments, and replies, hindering the transfer of relevant information. To address this limitation, a promising solution involves concatenating the posts, comments, and replies, which has the potential to yield significant improvements. Subsequently, a multilingual pre-trained model can be utilized for further analysis. Nevertheless, even concatenation does not consistently yield the desired results. To address this challenge, Bagora et al. (2022) proposed a hierarchical model that focuses on natural abstraction and context selection to effectively capture the underlying patterns. In addition, a cross-lingual transfer learning approach is proposed, wherein a model trained on a high-resource language such as English is applied to low-resource languages, thereby reducing the substantial time required to create annotated datasets. This bilingual embedding-based classifier leverages zero-shot learning techniques to enhance its performance and generalization capabilities.

13.5 RESULTS

Hate speech identification can be viewed as a classification problem, which can be a binary classification or multi-class classification. To discuss the results of different methods, we need to know the possible evaluation matrices for this task.

13.5.1 Evaluation Metrics

Each model is trained on the training dataset and evaluated by predicting the labels for the test dataset. The maximum dataset is a highly imbalanced label distribution that is why it is a standard way to evaluate and compare each and every model's performance in terms of precision, recall, F1-score, and accuracy. The definitions of metrics are given below.

$$Precision\left(P\right)=\frac{\{TP\}}{\{TP+FP\}} \tag{13.1}$$

$$Recall(R) = \frac{\{TP\}}{\{TP + FN\}} \tag{13.2}$$

where, TP = True Positive, FN = False Negative, FP = False Positive,

$$F1 = \frac{\{2 * R * P\}}{\{R + P\}} \tag{13.3}$$

$$Accuracy = \frac{\#correct\ predictions}{\#test - instances} \tag{13.4}$$

13.5.2 Odia–English (Mohapatra et al. 2021)

Three feature extraction techniques were used: n-gram; TF–IDF, and word2vec. Support vector machine (SVM), Naïve Bayes (NB), and random forest (RF) classifier were used. Table 13.3 and Table 13.4 show that RF with word2vec resulted in better accuracy than both the SVM and NB models on Odia–English code-mixed data for both tasks: Binary and ternary classification.

13.5.3 Tamil–English (Anbukkarasi and Varadhaganapathy 2022)

The author of the study employed several recurrent neural networks (RNNs) models, including LSTM, bi-directional LSTM, and 1DConv, for the purpose of classifying the provided input sequences. According to the presented Table 13.5, it is evident that the bi-LSTM model exhibited favorable outcomes in terms of overall accuracy.

13.5.4 Tamil–English (Chakravarthi et al. 2021)

Vasantharajan and Thayasivam (2021) proposed an idea where they used ULMFiT, mBERT–BiLSTM model, and various multilingual transformers. They finally reached the conclusion that the ULMFiT model and mBERT–BiLSTM model performed better than fine-tuning pre-trained models such as BERT, XLM-RoBERTa for Tamil–English low-resourced language.

TABLE 13.3
The Result of Different Models (accuracy) for Binary Classification

	Word Unigram	Word Bigram	Word Trigram	Combined n-Grams	TF–IDF	TF–IDF + Combined n-Grams	Word2vec
SVM	71.4	72	71.9	71.5	69.8	69.9	72.6
NB	74.4	74.4	74.5	74.6	72.2	73.7	70.7
RF	73.1	72.7	72.9	72.9	72.8	71.4	75.4

TABLE 13.4
The Result of Different Models (Accuracy) for Ternary Classification

	Word Unigram	Word Bigram	Word Trigram	Combined n-Grams	TF–IDF	TF–IDF + Combined n-Grams	Word2vec
SVM	51	52	52	52	48	49	54
NB	42	44	44	49	47	48	49
RF	51	50	51	51	50	50	55

TABLE 13.5
Performance Measures of Models Used by (Anbukkarasi and Varadhaganapathy 2022)

Model	Precision	Recall	Accuracy	F1-Score
1DConv	0.72	0.72	0.72	0.72
LSTM	0.81	0.81	0.81	0.81
BiLSTM	0.82	0.81	0.82	0.82

13.5.5 Hindi–English (Bohra et al. 2018)

The author performed two experiments with SVM and RF with character n-gram and word n-gram. They found that character n-gram performs better with SVM, but RF outperformed when they used the word n-gram. On the same dataset, Kamble and Joshi (2018) applied a deep learning model (CNN-1D, LSTM, BiLSTM) with domain-specific embedding, and they observed that their model improved by 12% from the previous approach. CNN-1D model performed better than LSTM and BiLSTM model in terms of F1-score and accuracy. If we look at Santosh and Aravind's (2019) work on the same dataset, they used two different models. One is a sub-word level LSTM model and another is a hierarchical LSTM model with attention. They observed that although their second method's accuracy was less than the SVM model the F1-score was better than the previous model.

13.5.6 Conversational Contextual (HASOC 2021 Dataset)

Chanda et al. (2021) treated all the posts, comments, and replies as a single unified text applied a pre-trained mBERT model, fine-tuned the model, and scored 0.6795 (Macro F1). To maintain the context of posts to comments and replies, Chanda, Sheth, and Pal (2022) concatenated posts, comments, and replies. But on the HASOC 2022 dataset, the performance was not that good because of the concatenation. When model read the data in which post concatenating with comments, or posts with comments and replies, the model appears to struggle in grasping contextual nuances during training. In instances where the post contains hateful content, the learning process tends to heavily prioritize the detection of hate, thereby hindering the model's ability to discern hierarchical relationships between posts, comments, and replies. Bagora et al. (2022) proposed a novel hierarchical neural network architecture and scored 0.72 (Macro F1). Madhu et al. (2023) proposed a novel idea and tried many combinations of context-capturing methods. They employed a pipeline consisting of an LSTM classifier followed by a fine-tuned SentBERT model which outperformed all the models proposed on the HASOC 2021 dataset. They applied the sentBERT on a word level and created a matrix of $m \times n$, where m is the number of words present in the sentence and n is the embedding size of sentBERT.

13.6 CONCLUSION

In this chapter, our exploration focused on a novel domain of hate speech identification. While significant progress has been made in identifying hate speech in monolingual languages, particularly in high-resource languages such as English, the recognition of hate speech in code-mixed languages has lagged behind. Consequently, the presence of user-generated code-mixed language poses a significant challenge in hate speech identification. We provided a comprehensive overview of the available datasets and various shared tasks organized by academic and research institutions. Based on the existing work and datasets, it is evident that we do not currently possess a benchmark dataset capable of evaluating models across all language pairs. Each dataset exhibits its own class distribution, and the classification scheme differs among language pairs. Some language pairs involve a primary classification of hate or non-hate, while others further classify hate speech into fine-grained categories. We observed varying model performances across different language pairs and even within the same language pair but with different datasets. Throughout our analysis, it became clear that transformer-based pre-trained models offer distinct advantages in hate speech identification. We also delved into the challenges and state-of-the-art methods of handling code-mixed data within conversational contexts. The absence of suitable datasets, benchmark results, and the unique characteristics of code-mixed data contribute to the increased difficulty of this hate speech identification task, thereby opening up potential avenues for future research.
References:

NOTES

1. https://www.censusindia.gov.in/Census_Data_2001/Census_Data_Online/Language/Statement4.html
2. https://www.britannica.com/topic/hate-speech
3. https://kaggle.com/c/jigsaw-toxic-comment-classification-challenge
4. https://ta-cos.org/
5. https://sites.google.com/view/trac1/home
6. https://sites.google.com/view/alw3/
7. https://competitions.codalab.org/competitions/27654

REFERENCES

Akhter, Muhammad Pervez, Zheng Jiangbin, Irfan Raza Naqvi, Mohammed Abdelmajeed, and Muhammad Tariq Sadiq. 2020. "Automatic Detection of Offensive Language for Urdu and Roman Urdu." *IEEE Access* 8: 91213–26. https://doi.org/10.1109/ACCESS.2020.2994950.

Anbukkarasi, S., and S. Varadhaganapathy. 2022. "Deep Learning-Based Hate Speech Detection in Code-Mixed Tamil Text." *IETE Journal of Research*: 1–6. https://doi.org/10.1080/03772063.2022.2043786.

Aroyehun, Segun Taofeek, and Alexander Gelbukh. 2018. "Aggression Detection in Social Media: Using Deep Neural Networks, Data Augmentation, and Pseudo Labeling." In *Proceedings of the First Workshop on Trolling, Aggression and Cyberbullying (TRAC-2018)*, 90–97. Santa Fe, NM: Association for Computational Linguistics. https://www.aclweb.org/anthology/W18-4411.

Bagora, Aditi, Kamal Shrestha, Kaushal Maurya, and Maunendra Sankar Desarkar. 2022. "Hostility Detection in Online Hindi-English Code-Mixed Conversations." In *14th ACM Web Science Conference 2022*, 390–400. Barcelona, Spain: Association for Computing Machinery.

Basile, Valerio, Cristina Bosco, Elisabetta Fersini, Debora Nozza, Viviana Patti, Francisco Manuel Rangel Pardo, Paolo Rosso, and Manuela Sanguinetti. 2019. "SemEval-2019 Task 5: Multilingual Detection of Hate Speech Against Immigrants and Women in Twitter." In *Proceedings of the 13th International Workshop on Semantic Evaluation*, 54–63. Minneapolis, MN: Association for Computational Linguistics. https://doi.org/10.18653/v1/S19-2007.

Bohra, Aditya, Deepanshu Vijay, Vinay Singh, Syed Sarfaraz Akhtar, and Manish Shrivastava. 2018. "A Dataset of Hindi-English Code-Mixed Social Media Text for Hate Speech Detection." In *Proceedings of the Second Workshop on Computational Modeling of People's Opinions, Personality, and Emotions in Social Media*, 36–41. New Orleans, LA: Association for Computational Linguistics. https://doi.org/10.18653/v1/W18-1105.

Burnap, Pete, and Matthew L Williams. 2015. "Cyber Hate Speech on Twitter: An Application of Machine Classification and Statistical Modeling for Policy and Decision Making." *Policy & Internet* 7 (2): 223–42. https://doi.org/10.1002/poi3.85.

Chakravarthi, Bharathi Raja, Gaman Mihaela, Radu Tudor Ionescu, Heidi Jauhiainen, Tommi Jauhiainen, Krister Lindén, Nikola Ljubešić, et al. 2021. "Findings of the VarDial Evaluation Campaign 2021." In *Proceedings of the Eighth Workshop on NLP for Similar Languages, Varieties and Dialects*, 1–11. Kiyv, Ukraine: Association for Computational Linguistics. https://aclanthology.org/2021.vardial-1.1.

Chakravarthi, Bharathi Raja, Ruba Priyadharshini, Navya Jose, M. Anand Kumar, Thomas Mandl, Prasanna Kumar Kumaresan, Rahul Ponnusamy, R. L. Hariharan, John P. McCrae, and Elizabeth Sherly. 2021. "Findings of the Shared Task on Offensive Language Identification in Tamil, Malayalam, and Kannada." In *Proceedings of the First Workshop on Speech and Language Technologies for Dravidian Languages*, 133–45. Kyiv: Association for Computational Linguistics. https://aclanthology.org/2021.dravidianlangtech-1.17.

Chanda, Supriya, Sacchit Sheth, and Sukomal Pal. 2022. *Coarse and Fine-Grained Conversational Hate Speech and Offensive Content Identification in Code-Mixed Languages Using Fine-Tuned Multilingual Embedding.* Forum for Information Retrieval Evaluation (FIRE) 2021, Virtual Event. *CEUR-WS. org.*

Chanda, Supriya, S. Ujjwal, Shayak Das, and Sukomal Pal. 2021. *Fine-Tuning Pre-Trained Transformer Based Model for Hate Speech and Offensive Content Identification in*

English, Indo-Aryan and Code-Mixed (English-Hindi) Languages. Kolkata, India: Forum for Information Retrieval Evaluation (FIRE) 2022. *CEUR-WS. org*.

Chopra, Abhishek, Deepak Kumar Sharma, Aashna Jha, and Uttam Ghosh. 2023. "A Framework for Online Hate Speech Detection on Code-Mixed Hindi-English Text and Hindi Text in Devanagari." *ACM Transactions on Asian and Low-Resource Language Information Processing* 22 (5). https://doi.org/10.1145/3568673.

Dadvar Maraland, Trieschnigg, Dolfand Ordelman Roelandand, and de Jong Franciska. 2013. "Improving Cyberbullying Detection with User Context." In *Advances in Information Retrieval*, edited by P. Serdyukov, P. Braslavski, S. Kuznetsov, J. Kamps, S. Rüger, E. Agichtein I. Segalovich, and E. Yilmaz, 693–96. Berlin, Heidelberg: Springer Berlin Heidelberg.

Davidson, Thomas, Dana Warmsley, Michael W Macy, and Ingmar Weber. 2017. "Automated Hate Speech Detection and the Problem of Offensive Language." *CoRR abs/1703.04009*. http://arxiv.org/abs/1703.04009.

Djuric, Nemanja, Jing Zhou, Robin Morris, Mihajlo Grbovic, Vladan Radosavljevic, and Narayan Bhamidipati. 2015. "Hate Speech Detection with Comment Embeddings." In *Proceedings of the 24th International Conference on World Wide Web*, 29–30. WWW '15 Companion. New York, NY: Association for Computing Machinery. https://doi.org/10.1145/2740908.2742760.

Fišer, Darja, Tomaž Erjavec, and Nikola Ljubešić. 2017. "Legal Framework, Dataset and Annotation Schema for Socially Unacceptable Online Discourse Practices in Slovene." In *Proceedings of the First Workshop on Abusive Language Online*, 46–51. Vancouver, BC: Association for Computational Linguistics. https://doi.org/10.18653/v1/W17-3007.

Fortuna, Paula, and Sérgio Nunes. 2018. "A Survey on Automatic Detection of Hate Speech in Text." *ACM Computing Surveys* 51 (4). https://doi.org/10.1145/3232676.

Georgakopoulos, Spiros V., Sotiris K. Tasoulis, Aristidis G. Vrahatis, and Vassilis P. Plagianakos. 2018. "Convolutional Neural Networks for Toxic Comment Classification." In *Proceedings of the 10th Hellenic Conference on Artificial Intelligence*, 1–6. Patras, Greece: Association for Computing Machinery.

Grover, Jeenu, Prabhat Agarwal, Ashish Sharma, Mayank Sikka, Koustav Rudra, and Monojit Choudhury. 2017. *I May Talk in English but Gaali Toh Hindi Mein Hi Denge: A Study of English-Hindi Code-Switching and Swearing Pattern on Social Networks*. In *Proceedings of the Social Networking Workshop, COMSNETS 2017*. Bengaluru, India.

Kamble, Satyajit, and Aditya Joshi. 2018. "Hate Speech Detection from Code-Mixed Hindi-English Tweets Using Deep Learning Models." *ArXiv E-Prints*, arXiv:1811.05145, November. https://doi.org/10.48550/arXiv.1811.05145.

Khan, Muhammad Moin, Khurram Shahzad, and Muhammad Kamran Malik. 2021. "Hate Speech Detection in Roman Urdu." *ACM Transactions on Asian and Low-Resource Language Information Processing* 20 (1). https://doi.org/10.1145/3414524.

Kumar, Ritesh, Ojha, Atul Kr., Malmasi, Shervin, and Zampieri, Marcos. 2018. "Benchmarking Aggression Identification in Social Media." In *Proceedings of the First Workshop on Trolling, Aggression and Cyberbullying (TRAC-2018)*, 1–11. Santa Fe, NM: Association for Computational Linguistics. https://www.aclweb.org/anthology/W18-4401.

Kwok, Irene, and Yuzhou Wang. 2013. "Locate the Hate: Detecting Tweets against Blacks." In *Proceedings of the Twenty-Seventh AAAI Conference on Artificial Intelligence*, 1621–22. Bellevue, Washington, USA: AAAI Press, AAAI'13.

Madhu, Hiren, Shrey Satapara, Sandip Modha, Thomas Mandl, and Prasenjit Majumder. 2023. "Detecting Offensive Speech in Conversational Code-Mixed Dialogue on Social Media: A Contextual Dataset and Benchmark Experiments." *Expert Systems with Applications* 215: 119342. https://doi.org/https://doi.org/10.1016/j.eswa.2022.119342.

Malmasi, Shervin, and Marcos Zampieri. 2017. "Detecting Hate Speech in Social Media." In *Proceedings of the International Conference Recent Advances in Natural Language Processing, RANLP 2017*, 467–72. Varna, Bulgaria: INCOMA Ltd. https://doi.org/10.26615/978-954-452-049-6_062.

Mandl, Thomas, Sandip Modha, Prasenjit Majumder, Daksh Patel, Mohana Dave, Chintak Mandlia, and Aditya Patel. 2019. "Overview of the HASOC Track at FIRE 2019: Hate Speech and Offensive Content Identification in Indo-European Languages." In *Proceedings of the 11th Annual Meeting of the Forum for Information Retrieval Evaluation*, 14–17. FIRE '19. New York, NY: Association for Computing Machinery. https://doi.org/10.1145/3368567.3368584.

Mathur, Puneet, Rajiv Shah, Ramit Sawhney, and Debanjan Mahata. 2018. "Detecting Offensive Tweets in Hindi-English Code-Switched Language." In *Proceedings of the Sixth International Workshop on Natural Language Processing for Social Media*, 18–26. Melbourne, Australia: Association for Computational Linguistics. https://doi.org/10.18653/v1/W18-3504.

Modha, Sandip, Prasenjit Majumder, and Thomas Mandl. 2018. "Filtering Aggression from the Multilingual Social Media Feed." In *Proceedings of the First Workshop on Trolling, Aggression and Cyberbullying (TRAC-2018)*, 199–207. Santa Fe, NM: Association for Computational Linguistics. https://www.aclweb.org/anthology/W18-4423.

Modha, Sandip, Thomas Mandl, Prasenjit Majumder, and Daksh Patel. 2019. "Overview of the HASOC Track at FIRE 2019: Hate Speech and Offensive Content Identification in Indo-European Languages." In *FIRE '19 - Forum for Information Retrieval Evaluation*, 14–17. Kolkata, India: Association for Computing Machinery, CEUR-WS.org.

Modha, Sandip, Thomas Mandl, Prasenjit Majumder, Satapara Shrey, Tithi Patel, and Hiren Madhu. 2022. "Overview of the HASOC Subtrack at FIRE 2022: Identification of Conversational Hate-Speech in Hindi-English Code-Mixed and German Language." In *Working Notes of FIRE 2022 - Forum for Information Retrieval*, 4–7. Association for Computing Machinery, CEUR-WS.org.

Mohapatra, Sudhir, Srinivas Prasad, Dwiti Bebarta, Tapan Das, Kathiravan Srinivasan, and Yuh-Chung Hu. 2021. "Automatic Hate Speech Detection in English-Odia Code Mixed Social Media Data Using Machine Learning Techniques." *Applied Sciences* 11 (September): 8575. https://doi.org/10.3390/app11188575.

Mubarak, Hamdy, Kareem Darwish, and Walid Magdy. 2017. "Abusive Language Detection on Arabic Social Media." In *Proceedings of the First Workshop on Abusive Language Online*, 52–56. Vancouver, BC: Association for Computational Linguistics. https://doi.org/10.18653/v1/W17-3008.

Mubarak, Hamdy, Ammar Rashed, Kareem Darwish, Younes Samih, and Ahmed Abdelali. 2020. "Arabic Offensive Language on Twitter: Analysis and Experiments." *ArXiv Preprint ArXiv:2004.02192.*

Nobata, Chikashi, Joel Tetreault, Achint Thomas, Yashar Mehdad, and Yi Chang. 2016. "Abusive Language Detection in Online User Content." In *Proceedings of the 25th International Conference on World Wide Web*, 145–53. WWW '16. Republic and Canton of Geneva, CHE. Geneva: International World Wide Web Conferences Steering Committee. https://doi.org/10.1145/2872427.2883062.

Petrosyan, Ani. 2023. "Number of Internet and Social Media Users Worldwide as of January 2023." https://www.statista.com/statistics/617136/digital-population-worldwide/.

Pitenis, Zeses, Marcos Zampieri, and Tharindu Ranasinghe. 2020. "Offensive Language Identification in Greek." In *Proceedings of the 12th Language Resources and Evaluation Conference*. Marseille, France: European Language Resources Association.

Ranasinghe, Tharindu, Sarthak Gupte, Marcos Zampieri, and Ifeoma Nwogu. 2020. "WLV-RIT at HASOC-Dravidian-CodeMix-FIRE2020: Offensive Language in

Code-Switched YouTube Comments." *CoRR abs/2011.00559*. https://arxiv.org/abs/2011.00559.

Ranasinghe, Tharindu, and Marcos Zampieri. 2020. "Multilingual Offensive Language Identification with Cross-Lingual Embeddings." In *Proceedings of the 2020 Conference on Empirical Methods in Natural Language Processing (EMNLP)*, 5838–44. Association for Computational Linguistics. https://doi.org/10.18653/v1/2020.emnlp-main.470.

Ross, Björn, Michael Rist, Guillermo Carbonell, Benjamin Cabrera, Nils Kurowsky, and Michael Wojatzki. 2017. "Measuring the Reliability of Hate Speech Annotations: The Case ofthe European Refugee Crisis." *CoRR abs/1701.08118*. http://arxiv.org/abs/1701.08118.

Sai, Siva, and Yashvardhan Sharma. 2021. "Towards Offensive Language Identification for Dravidian Languages." In *Proceedings of the First Workshop on Speech and Language Technologies for Dravidian Languages*, 18–27. Kyiv: Association for Computational Linguistics. https://aclanthology.org/2021.dravidianlangtech-1.3.

Santosh, T. Y. S. S., and K. V. S. Aravind. 2019. "Hate Speech Detection in Hindi-English Code-Mixed Social Media Text." In *Proceedings of the ACM India Joint International Conference on Data Science and Management of Data*, 310–13. CODS-COMAD '19. New York, NY: Association for Computing Machinery. https://doi.org/10.1145/3297001.3297048.

Saroj, Anita, Supriya Chanda, and Sukomal Pal. 2020. "IRlab@IITV at SemEval-2020 Task 12: Multilingual Offensive Language Identification in Social Media Using SVM." In *Proceedings of the Fourteenth Workshop on Semantic Evaluation*, 2012–16. Barcelona: International Committee for Computational Linguistics. https://doi.org/10.18653/v1/2020.semeval-1.265.

Schmidt, Anna, and Michael Wiegand. 2017. "A Survey on Hate Speech Detection Using Natural Language Processing." In *Proceedings of the Fifth International Workshop on Natural Language Processing for Social Media*, 1–10. Valencia, Spain: Association for Computational Linguistics. https://doi.org/10.18653/v1/W17-1101.

Su, Hui-Po, Zhen-Jie Huang, Hao-Tsung Chang, and Chuan-Jie Lin. 2017. "Rephrasing Profanity in Chinese Text." In *Proceedings of the First Workshop on Abusive Language Online*, 18–24. Vancouver, BC: Association for Computational Linguistics. https://doi.org/10.18653/v1/W17-3003.

Vasantharajan, Charangan, and Uthayasanker Thayasivam. 2021. "Towards Offensive Language Identification for Tamil Code-Mixed YouTube and Posts." *CoRR abs/2108.10939*. https://arxiv.org/abs/2108.10939.

Wiegand, Michael, Melanie Siegel, and Josef Ruppenhofer. 2018. "Overview of the GermEval 2018 Shared Task on the Identification of Offensive Language." In *Proceedings of GermEval 2018, 14th Conference on Natural Language Processing (KONVENS 2018)*, 1 –10. Vienna, Austria: Austrian Academy of Sciences, September 21. http://nbn-resolving.de/urn:nbn:de:bsz:mh39-84935.

Xu, Jun-Ming, Kwang-Sung Jun, Xiaojin Zhu, and Amy Bellmore. 2012. "Learning from Bullying Traces in Social Media." In *Proceedings of the 2012 Conference of the North American Chapter of the Association for Computational Linguistics: Human Language Technologies*, 656–66. NAACL HLT '12. Montreal, Canada.: Association for Computational Linguistics.

Zampieri, Marcos, Shervin Malmasi, Preslav Nakov, Sara Rosenthal, Noura Farra, and Ritesh Kumar. 2019. "SemEval-2019 Task 6: Identifying and Categorizing Offensive Language in Social Media (OffensEval)." In *Proceedings of the 13th International Workshop on Semantic Evaluation*, 75–86. Minneapolis, Minnesota, USA: Association for Computational Linguistics.

14 Social Media Skirmish

Dealing With Fake News and Propaganda Using AI and ML

C S Raghuvanshi, Hari Om Sharan, and Hemant Kumar Soni

14.1 INTRODUCTION

False information that is deliberately disseminated to deceive others is referred to as fake news, also known as disinformation or misinformation. Fake news is now a serious issue due to the growth of social media and how fast and easily it can reach a big audience. Because fake news is so prevalent on social media, there is a lot of worry about how it can affect people, society, and even democratic institutions.

Social networks have evolved into a vital tool for disseminating knowledge throughout time because of advancements in technology and smart devices. They can broadcast them, which are made up of texts, images, and videos and utilized to gather data and information, as well as streamline the inquiry process. The speed of information transmission through social networks is typically significantly faster than that of traditional media, which focuses on the dissemination of breaking news.

False information spreads to a huge audience on social networks without limitations and without being able to pinpoint its exact source because the dissemination of content there cannot be controlled. Both X (formerly Twitter) and Facebook are typically used to facilitate communication, information sharing, and the distribution of content to a large audience.

The head of the US National Academy of Sciences, Marcia McNutt, was quoted as saying that fake news, false information, and propaganda are worse than an epidemic in an apparent reference to the COVID-19 pandemic. It propagates at the speed of light throughout the globe and has the potential to be fatal when it reinforces biased opinions in the face of reliable evidence; its widespread use and popularity have accelerated the transmission of fake news by enhancing its reach.

As a result, social media is now a significant platform for the spread of false information (Goot 1991; Micallef et al. 2020). According to the Pew Research Center's study of news use across social media platforms, more than half of US adults will receive news via social media at least occasionally in 2020, up from just one-fifth in 2018. As distorted and inaccurate content gets easier to make and harder to spot

DOI: 10.1201/9781003409519-14

(Vosoughi, Roy, and Aral 2018) fake news can therefore have a large impact on society as disinformation actors modify their tactics.

By 2022, most people in advanced economies will consume more false information than true, according to a Snow prediction published in the MIT Technology Review in 2017. For example, online articles purporting to offer various COVID-19 "cures"—such as consuming boiling garlic or consuming chlorine dioxide, an industrial bleach—were found to be false, in some cases hazardous, and ineffective.

Additionally, a lot of fake news is produced online for a variety of reasons because it is easier to develop and distribute news there than through traditional media or face-to-face interactions (Micallef et al. 2020). Furthermore, it was discovered that 70% of users could not tell the difference between the two due to the novelty of the latter's appeal during the dissemination of online news on X. False news spreads six times more quickly than truthful content online.

Over 1 million tweets were estimated to include fake news by the time the 2016 US presidential election was over. In 2017, in relation to the extraordinary spread of misleading information on social media, a government spokeswoman in Germany said "We are dealing with a phenomenon of a dimension that we have not seen before."

Artificial intelligence (AI) algorithms must be quickly developed by IT professionals to handle fake news and alternative realities. However, spotting fake news is a difficult issue. The researchers also questioned if AI could defeat false news.

Experts also concurred that fake news cannot be detected by artificial intelligence, regardless of how good it is. Furthermore, current research suggests that AI systems are more adept at creating false information than they are at identifying it.

Even worse, by producing and sharing fake content, AI systems such as machine learning and deep learning are used to deceive people. Because the content is created to closely mimic reality, it is frequently difficult to establish its veracity by AI alone without additional information from third parties. As a result, automatic fake news identification continues to be a big difficulty. This chapter's goal is to examine how fake news affects people, society, and democratic institutions. We will look at the factors that contribute to fake news being so pervasive on social media, the effects of its dissemination, and the steps that may be taken to stop it. It is critical to comprehend the seriousness of this situation and take action.

14.2 IMPACT OF FAKE NEWS ON INDIVIDUALS, SOCIETY, AND DEMOCRATIC SETUP

Fake news and information disorders endanger democracy and effective government. By influencing opinions and altering the normal processes of public opinion creation, fake news can have an impact on behaviors, such as voting and adopting a position on a variety of public issues. Fake news ultimately promotes negative narratives, creates polarization and uncertainty in society, and threatens freedom of choice.

In recent years, there have been many instances of how false information may travel quickly and seriously affect people, communities, and a country's democratic system. Fake news has the ability to spread chaos and uncertainty, from debunked claims about election fraud to conspiracy theories about the COVID-19 epidemic.

In addition to having an impact on society as a whole, fake news also has a big effect on people and groups. False information can cause people to become confused, anxious, or even afraid. This is particularly risky when correct information is essential for the public's health and safety, such as during a pandemic or natural disaster. For instance, misleading information about potential treatments and preventative measures was swiftly disseminated on social media during the COVID-19 pandemic, leading some people to take risky acts such as consuming bleach or refusing to wear masks. Fake news can also encourage prejudice and discrimination since it frequently targets particular groups and reinforces negative stereotypes. In some instances, this might result in societal unrest and even violence. Communities are also affected, with certain regions seeing an upsurge in prejudice against Asian Americans as a result of untrue allegations tying them to the virus. These instances highlight the negative effects of fake news on people and communities in the real world.

Political ramifications can also result from confusion and misinformation, as misleading information has the power to impact public opinion and affect elections. In 2016, during the US presidential election, fake news articles were broadly dispersed on social media, which may have had an impact on the outcome. Furthermore, the proliferation of false information can erode public confidence in the media and institutions, further undermining democratic principles. People must be informed of the effects of fake news and take steps to stop it from spreading, such as fact-checking and promoting dependable sources of information (Weedon, Nuland, and Stamod 2017).

Fake news can also cause societal polarization and the emergence of echo chambers when people only read news that supports their viewpoints. This can set off a hazardous cycle where people grow less open to hearing different viewpoints and more firmly committed to their own beliefs.

As evidenced by the emergence of extremist organizations and the dissemination of conspiracy theories, in severe circumstances, this can result in violence and conflict. To counteract the damaging impacts of fake news, people must actively seek out a variety of information sources and engage in civic conversation. We can encourage a more educated and tolerant society by doing this. It also emphasizes the importance of teaching media literacy to assist people in differentiating between trustworthy and dependable sources of information.

The polarization and division we are seeing today are also a result of a loss of faith in institutions and the media. Social media and the internet have grown in popularity, making it easier than ever to access a variety of information sources, but it is also more challenging to determine which ones are trustworthy. This has caused a profusion of false information and conspiracy theories, which can further weaken trust in existing institutions and aggravate societal tensions. We can start to repair trust and move towards a more cohesive and informed society, though, by approaching the information we consume critically and looking for trustworthy sources.

Fake news can cause societal norms and values to disintegrate, which can make society more fractious and unstable. In order to stop the spread of false information and promote reliable and accurate sources of information, it is imperative that individuals, media organizations, and organizations collaborate.

We can only guarantee an educated and healthy society by working together. For instance, false information was quickly disseminated on social media during the 2016 US presidential election, intensifying political polarization and stoking social unrest. False information being spread about candidates and issues has also resulted in a decline in public participation in civic affairs and confidence in democratic institutions. To prevent the negative consequences of fake news on society, it is evident that media literacy training and ethical journalistic practices are required.

14.3 THE DIGITAL MEDIA LANDSCAPE'S CHALLENGES

There have been a number of worrying developments as the media landscape as a whole has transformed. Some users have misused social media and online platforms by creating and disseminating false information. and misinformation in an effort to confuse, mislead, or hurt others, as opposed to using digital tools to educate people and enhance civic conversation. These activities become misinformation campaigns with the potential to undercut elections and the administration in entire countries when they progress from being irregular and random to organized and planned actions.

The dissemination of false information has presented social media firms with a number of difficulties. Misinformation has been made worse by the way their algorithms are set up and how they make use of human prejudices. The spread of false information has increased significantly in spite of the efforts of social media corporations, even endangering lives during the pandemic. In addition to providing a venue for cybercrime on social media, the issues with privacy, surveillance, and control have exacerbated societal divisiveness (Meserole 2018). Social media can serve as a fertile ground for false information due to technological factors such as algorithms and cognitive biases like how human brains perceive information. The relationship between these two factors makes it more difficult to control false information.

14.3.1 The Challenge of Algorithms

Misinformation is largely transmitted via social media because of the way it works and how it is structured. Because social media corporations have not been open about their algorithms, it is challenging to determine how much of an impact their amplification systems have had.

They have, however, admitted that because their platforms' algorithms favor content that garners the greatest attention, they allow for widespread engagement of false information. High-view content is prioritized as "relevant", and its distribution is boosted (Loader 1997).

However, they have acknowledged that because their platforms' algorithms encourage content that gets the most attention, extensive engagement with erroneous information is permitted. Content with a high number of views is regarded as "relevant", and its dissemination is encouraged.

14.3.2 The Challenge of Cognitive Biases

Although social media firms' amplification technologies contribute significantly to the spread of false information, the methods by which human brains can be tricked account for a greater portion of its impact and influence on such a vast audience. Misinformation can have different effects depending on how the brain interprets information. Confirmation bias is one thing that affects these processes. The algorithms help disinformation propagators take advantage of users' confirmation bias. The emotional overtones of articles easily evoke strong feelings in readers, and marketing technologies are designed to target content to people who are more likely to believe them (Meserole 2018). People are more likely to accept or trust information that confirms their beliefs or preconceptions and ignore any evidence that contradicts them. For instance, following comments made by a spokesperson for the Chinese foreign ministry during the pandemic, a number of social media posts circulated false information about the US Army's involvement in the virus' introduction to China. Such stuff is more likely to be believed by those who oppose the US.

14.4 FATE NEWS DETECTION

Today, news and advertising drive Internet traffic. Disinformation on the Internet is intentionally shaped to harm or mislead the public. Misinformation may cause harm to many people, false information has been shown to incite conflict, sway public opinion, and, most crucially, heighten societal hatred. People who hold similar religious beliefs or who support the same party will distribute information without conducting enough fact-checking. Cognitive theories claim that people are gullible and therefore prone to false information. The newest social media platform to suffer from the dissemination of fake information is WhatsApp. In order to combat the rise of fake news, the central government is compelled to make a significant move. According to research, spreading inaccurate information harms society. Today, there are numerous ways to identify fake news, together with knowledge-based, linguistic, machine learning–based, hybrid, and topic-independent approaches.

The community as a whole is significantly impacted by the large, diverse, and heterogeneous information flow that occurs on social media platforms (Guimarães et al. 2021). The topic of the content and social context of the news item under review is the focus of the cutting-edge research on fake news detection discussed in this part (Zhou et al. 2019).

14.4.1 Content-based

The content-based fake news recognition strategy (Revez and Corujo 2020) seeks to identify fake news by looking at the text, the photos, or any combination of these aspects. Researchers frequently rely on latent (Raza and Ding 2022) or handcrafted (Apuke and Omar 2021) features of the material to automatically detect fake news.

14.4.2 Knowledge-based

Knowledge-based systems use the fact-checking method, which involves comparing the supplied claim to data gathered from outside sources, to verify the veracity of a given claim. There are already manual fact-checking methods (using experts or the public) and automated fact-checking methods (using artificial intelligence).

1. **Manual fact-checking:** Manual fact-checking comes in two flavors: Both expert-based and crowdsourced methods. Expert-based approaches are tactics that rely on real people with training in particular fields to make decisions and take an export-oriented stance.
2. **Automated fact-checking:** Automated fact-checking systems have been developed to address the problem of labor-intensive fact-checking not scaling successfully with a large amount of data, especially those provided by social media. These solutions generally rely on methods from natural language processing (NLP), machine learning, graph/network theory, data mining, and many other fields rather than human brains.

14.4.3 Style-based

The style-based method, which is similar to the knowledge-based false news identification, can be used to detect false news. This method (Silva et al. 2021) evaluates the writer's intent to deceive the reader rather than the accuracy of the news report. The majority of the time, those who spread false and misleading information are doing so out of a desire to exert influence over big populations.

14.4.4 Linguistic-based

Twenty-six lexical textual features were offered by Varma et al. (2021) for examination. A better set of linguistic standards was offered by several academics to discern between false and accurate news (Pilkevych et al. 2021), they created a model for social article fusion (SAF) that takes linguistic components and social engagement aspects into account The authors Bhavani and Kumar (2021) have distinguished between true and fake news sources using linguistic characteristics as well as syntactic and semantic elements.

14.4.5 Visual-based

Producers of fake news frequently employ controversial graphics to draw in and mislead viewers because it is widely believed that visual content may boost the trustworthiness of a news piece (Guimarães et al. 2021). Using a statistical modeling approach, Orabi et. al. (2020) gather a noteworthy number of visual and statistical image attributes for news credibility from a variety of photographs.

14.4.6 Social Context-based

User profiles, publishing and replying by users, and network architecture have all been highlighted as three crucial components of the social environment (Qasim et al. 2022). It provides important information for judging the reliability and political stance of news items and serves as a visual picture of how news spreads over time. Recently, many context-based methods for identifying fake news have been studied (Qasim et al. 2022).

14.4.7 Temporal-based

According to studies, news stories on the Internet are dynamic and constantly change when new details are added or the veracity of the initial claim is called into question. This is especially clear when speculations persist after the first news item has been published. A rumor lifecycle study is helpful in understanding this phenomenon and Varma et al.'s (2021) examination of the recurrent rumors at the message level through time offers more insight.

14.4.8 Credibility-based.

According to a number of sources, a claim's newsworthiness and trustworthiness/credibility are signs of a spreader's credibility. Pilkevych et al. (2021) employ the concept of credibility to identify people who are disseminating false information. Bhavani and Kumar's (2021)credibility analysis approach is recommended for evaluating a tweet's dependability, which prevents the spread of erroneous or damaging information on the social media network.

14.5 MECHANISMS/TECHNIQUES FOR DETECTING FAKE NEWS AND THEIR CHALLENGES

We will talk about different false news detecting techniques and strategies, as well as the difficulties in applying them. False news detection methods fall into two basic categories: Those based on machine learning and those based on deep learning.

14.5.1 Machine Learning–based Techniques

The literature is plentiful for research articles about false detection. They focus on machine learning algorithms that use supervised learning to distinguish between real news and misinformation. Machine learning (ML) is an application of artificial intelligence (AI) that uses a variety of algorithms on datasets to educate computers to conduct actions without being explicitly instructed to do so. Supervised, unsupervised, semi-supervised, and reinforcement learning are the four primary categories of machine learning (ML). The detection process in machine learning falls under supervised learning, where the set contains the appropriate output labels. Semantic analysis, Naïve Bayes, support vector machine (SVM), and other classifiers are only a few of the many techniques that have been developed specifically to handle detection difficulties.

14.5.2 Naïve Bayes Classifier

Naïve Bayes, a technique for supervised learning, is a type of classifier (Silva et al. 2021). It belongs to the machine language class since it predicts "membership probability" for each class. It determines, among other things, the probability that a certain piece of information or evidence belongs to a certain category (Hutto and Gilbert 2014). It is possible that the Naïve Bayes classifier's appeal stems in part from how rapid and accessible it is. It is a fantastic choice for "text classification issues" due to its versatility. It can be applied to multiclass or binary classifications (Alonso et al. 2021). The Naïve Bayes classifier requires a small number of counts to get its results because it is so simple to use. As a result, training on a small dataset is straightforward, as suggested by the name (Drif and Giordano 2019).

Some of the challenges of the naïve Bayes classifier are the following:

(i) Naïve Bayes makes the assumption that all predictors (or qualities) are independent, which is rarely the case in practice. This technology's application is therefore constrained.
(ii) By making a little contribution to a categorical variable whose category was missing from the training dataset, this method avoids the "zero-frequency problem". You must employ a smoothing approach to solve this problem (Drif and Giordano 2019). The likelihood it generates should not rely upon much because there is a chance that its predictions will be off.

14.5.3 Support Vector Machine (SVM)

The SVM's ultimate purpose is to identify a hyperplane that divides the dataset into two separate groups. In order to change where their dividing hyperplane is positioned, "support vectors", or the data points nearest to the hyperplane, must be removed (Shahnawaz and Astya 2017).

The support vectors are crucial because of this. As a result, using the SVM technique is a fantastic option because it is very accurate and performs well on small, concise datasets. This method's broad variety of applications can be used to determine classification and even quantity. Contrarily, support vector machines use less memory and can handle huge, multidimensional spaces (Ting et al. 2021). Conversely, SVMs have the downside of performing worse on noisy (meaningless) datasets with overlapping classes since "the training time with SVMs might be substantial" (Zhang and Su 2004). The SVM algorithm does not, in addition, "directly provide probability estimates".

14.5.4 Semantic Analysis

Semantics is the ancestor of the area of natural language processing (NLP), a branch of computer science. A "content" profile "formed from a collection of comparable facts" may be equated to a "personal experience" in the semantic analysis technique, which examines the "degree of compatibility between personal experiences" (Murphy 2007).

One of the key arguments in favor of semantic analysis is its ability to classify texts accurately by utilizing association and collocation, two of the best existing techniques (Dai et al. 2022). This is especially useful for the speaker when speaking in languages such as English, where many words have many meanings and are nearly synonyms.

The use of semantic analysis has two potential limitations, which may be considered in the context of both the aforementioned "description of the writer's personal experience" and the scenario of comparing profiles (Lin 2007). There must be sufficient previously uncovered content for profiles to even "assess the alignment between traits and descriptions", which is the first and most important need. There is also the challenge of correctly linking "descriptors with retrieved properties", which is a challenging process.

Due to these difficulties, "comparative and objective sentences, classification accuracy, and sarcasm are all considered problems in sentiment analysis", is a claim that may be made. A significant part of opinionated data is incorrectly classified as neutral by the majority of sentiment analysis algorithms (Segura-Bedmar and Alonso-Bartolome 2022; Micallef et al. 2020), even if it is not.

14.6 TEXTUAL CONTENT-BASED FAKE NEWS DETECTION

This section will examine the detection of "fake news" using textual content. We explore the key features at the content, user, and social levels. Each level is thoroughly detailed in the subsections that follow.

14.6.1 Content-level

Using news content, it is possible to compare real versus fake news. In general, verbal and visual information are the most useful components extracted from news items. The following can grow into many different kinds of linguistic traits.

(i) Word counts, character counts inside words, the frequency of huge words, and the number of distinct terms are examples of lexical features.
(ii) Use of part of speech (POS) tagging, functional phrases, n-grams, and other syntactic elements such as the bag of words approach (Varma et al. 2021). Additionally, visual cues play a crucial role in the spread of false information (Guimarães et al. 2021).

The component takes content in the news ecosystem. The news body (content) and supporting materials make up a news piece. Generally speaking, the style of writing a news report reveals the author's perspective on the issue. We include the following news-related supplemental data: Political news, links, title, authors, and publishing date.

14.6.2 User-level

Participating in news-related activities on social media has certain user characteristics. In order to determine each user's dependability and trustworthiness, these user-level variables are generated from user-level data, such as the user's age at registration, their number of follows and followers, and the overall number of tweets sent (Hoy and Koulouri 2021). Numerous studies have demonstrated that key perceptual and behavioral factors strongly encourage user participation in the spread of false information.

14.6.3 Social-level

This is what we mean when we talk about social dimensions—the ties that bind different social groups together, even if they may be quite different and have nothing in common. Social media connections may have a major impact on how people understand misleading news items, albeit the extent to which this is true differs across different social dimensions (Guimarães et al. 2021). Therefore, it is important to look at the reasons and sociocultural elements that facilitate the dissemination of false information. Recent research suggests (Abu Arqoub et al. 2022) that Facebook users frequently select material in ways that are congruent with their worldview, resulting in the growth of polarized groups sometimes referred to as echo chambers. Users frequently follow others who share their interests on social media sites such as Facebook, for example, which causes them to get news that supports their preferred established narratives (Segura-Bedmar and Alonso-Bartolome 2022). Numerous psychological elements have an impact on the method by which individuals absorb and trust incorrect information that causes the echo chamber effect.

14.7 OTHER APPROACHES

There are a number of strategies that different organizations might use to combat incorrect information and misinformation. Many of these solutions aim to combat incorrect and misleading information without endangering free expression or investigative journalism.

14.7.1 Government Responsibilities

One of the most important things that governments can do is to support the development of professional, independent media. There is a need for journalists who can help the public understand complicated changes and navigate the constantly altering nature of social, economic, and political events.

Governments must hold online platforms accountable for spreading incorrect information without prohibiting them. This has the potential to stifle free speech by making people afraid to express their political opinions for fear of being labeled as false news.

14.7.2 News Industry Actions

The media should continue to highlight reliable content that attracts greater audiences. A benefit is that many news organizations have enjoyed considerable growth in readership and viewership over the past several years, which has improved the financial situation of major news organizations. The world needs powerful and efficient news media that can enlighten people about current events and long-term patterns at a time of immense upheaval and confusion.

Without supporting it, news organizations must expose erroneous information and disinformation. They might achieve this by utilizing their internal specialists and reliable fact-checkers. In order to educate readers about news sources that are intended to mislead them, non-profit organizations such as Factcheck.org, PolitiFact, and Snopes examine the truthfulness of prominent claims and offer articles that explain the truth or lack thereof of specific occurrences.

14.7.3 Technology Companies Responsibilities

Technology firms should invest in technologies that use crowdsourcing and analytics to find fake news and expose it to users. Advancements in hoax and false news identification can help media outlets. Businesses in the social media space should invest in their ability to automate processes like spotting fake news. Former FCC commissioner Tom Wheeler claims that "public interest algorithms" can assist in identifying and highlighting fake news stories, making them a valuable tool for protecting consumers.

These organizations ought to prohibit the creation of false information and make it difficult to profit from hoaxes. Reducing financial incentives for damaging content, especially false news and disinformation, is vital since the production of fake news is typically motivated by financial concerns, false information can be beneficial owing to ad sales or general brand-building, like any clickbait. In fact, trolls in nations such as North Macedonia claimed to have made large amounts of money during the 2016 presidential campaign by disseminating false information. Despite the fact that social media platforms such as Facebook have made it more difficult for users to profit from false information, ad networks can still do much more to prevent the commercialization of fake news, and publishers should stop using ad networks that will not do so.

Enforce laws against fake accounts and establish stronger real-name rules to strengthen online responsibility. Businesses may achieve this by using "real-name registration", which asks Internet users to provide the hosting platform with their true identities. This makes it simpler to hold users accountable for the content they publish or share online and deters users from using fictitious names to conceal their abusive words or illegal actions.

14.7.4 Educational Institutions

Governments should give funding projects to increase news literacy their top priority. Those who are just beginning to use the Internet in particular frequently encounter this. Instead of taking everything they read on social media or online news channels at face value because these individuals find it difficult to distinguish between the real from the phony, students should learn how to assess news sources. Helping people use Internet information more effectively is crucial as the world moves closer to total digital immersion. Funding should be made available to encourage partnerships between journalists, businesses, academic institutions, and non-profit organizations in order to foster news literacy.

14.8 HOW CAN THE PUBLIC PROTECT ITSELF?

Users may protect themselves against false information and disinformation by following a diversity of people and opinions. The range of information available to people is constrained, and there is a higher chance they may fall for hoaxes or false rumors if they only rely on a small group of news sources that share their viewpoints. Although not fully foolproof, this approach raises the likelihood of hearing a variety of well-rounded and opposing opinions.

When choosing news sources online, readers and viewers should use caution. In an effort to increase traffic, several websites on the internet utilize deceptive or inflammatory headlines. They emphasize the provocative or attention-grabbing even when the news hook is untrue. News consumers should use caution and be aware that not all of the information they get is accurate and that many online publications deliberately spread false information. Learning to analyze news sources and protect against misleading information is essential in the digital age.

14.9 CONCLUSION

In this chapter, we looked at the problem of fake news. Our inquiry focuses on the impact of fake news and false news detecting methods/techniques in the context of news, users, and social levels. Also carefully considered techniques for identifying and detecting fake news, including those based on content, credibility, time, and social context. When we were given the duty of identifying fake news, we looked at the various approaches that are presently being used from a data mining perspective. We recommended these techniques, which comprised feature extraction and model development, in light of our findings.

BIBLIOGRAPHY

A. Bhavani, B. Santhosh Kumar A. Bhavani and B. Santhosh Kumar, "A review of state art of text classification algorithms," 2021 5th International Conference on Computing Methodologies and Communication (ICCMC), pp. 1484–1490, Erode, India, 2021.

A. Bovet and H. A. Makse, "Influence of fake news in Twitter during the 2016 US presidential election," *Nature Communications*, vol. 10, no. 1, January 2019, doi: 10.1038/s41467-018-07761-2.

A. A. Ahmed et al., "Detecting fake news using machine learning: A systematic literature review," *Journal of Educational Psychology*, vol. 58, no. 1, pp. 1932–1939, 2021.

B. Loader, *The governance of cyberspace: Politics, technology and global restructuring*. Routledge, 1997, pp. 1–35.

C. Lin, "Support vector machine solvers," *Large Scale Kernel Machines*, vol. 3, no. 1, pp. 301–320, 2007.

C. Meserole, "How misinformation spreads on social media—And what to do about it," *Brookings*, May 9, 2018.

C. V. Meneses Silva et al., "Intelligent fake news detection: A systematic mapping," *Journal of Applied Security Research*, vol. 16, no. 2, pp. 168–189, 2021.

Drif and S. Giordano, "Fake news detection method based on text-features," *International Academy, Research, and Industry Association (IARIA)*, vol. 23, no. 3, pp. 26–31, France 2019.

G. Ciampaglia, and F. Menczer, *Biases make people vulnerable to misinformation spread by social media*. Scientific American, n.d..

H. Zhang and J. Su, "Naive Bayesian Classifiers for Ranking," in *Machine Learning: ECML 2004*, eds., J. F. Boulicaut, F. Esposito, F. Giannotti, and D. Pedreschi, vol. 3201. Lecture Notes in Computer Science, Berlin, Heidelberg: Springer, 2004.

I. Pilkevych et al., "Fake news detection in the framework of decision-making system through graph neural network," 2021 IEEE 4th International Conference on Advanced Information and Communication Technologies (AICT), Lviv, Ukraine, pp. 153–157, 2021.

I. Sánchez-Torné, J. C. Morán-Álvarez, and J. A. Pérez-López, "The importance of corporate social responsibility in achieving high corporate reputation, " *Corporate Social Responsibility and Environmental Management*, vol. 27, no. 6, pp. 2692–2700, 2020.

I. Segura-Bedmar and S. Alonso-Bartolome, "Multimodal fake news detection," *Information*, vol. 13, no. 6, p. 284, 2022.

J. Hutto and E. Gilbert, "Vader: A parsimonious rule-based model for sentiment analysis of social media text," in *Proceedings of the International AAAI Conference on Web and Social Media*, vol. 4, no. 3, pp. 216–225, Ann Arbor, MI: AAAI Press, 2014.

J. Revez and L. Corujo, "Librarians against fake news: A systematic literature review of library practices (Jan. 2018–Sept. 2020)," *The Journal of Academic Librarianship*, vol. 47, no. 2, 2021, article pages 102304.

J. Weedon, William Nuland, and Alex Stamos, "Information Operations," *Facebook*, April 27, 2017.

K. Sharma, F. Qian, H. Jiang, N. Ruchansky, M. Zhang, and Y. Liu, "Combating fake news," *ACM Transactions on Intelligent Systems and Technology*, vol. 10, no. 3, pp. 1–42, April 2019, doi: 10.1145/3305260.

K. Shu, A. Sliva, S. Wang, J. Tang, and H. Liu, "Fake news detection on social media," *ACM SIGKDD Explorations Newsletter*, vol. 19, no. 1, pp. 22–36, September 2017, doi: 10.1145/3137597.3137600.

L. Zhang, W. Zhou, and L. Jiao, "Wavelet support vector machine," *IEEE Transactions on Systems, Man, and Cybernetics—Part B*, vol. 34, no. 1, pp. 34–39, 2004.

M. Orabi et al., "Detection of bots in social media: A systematic review," *Information Processing & Management*, vol. 57, no. 4, 2020.

M. Goot, "Review: National social science survey report," *Media Information Australia*, vol. 60, no. 1, pp. 72–73, May 1991, doi: 10.1177/1329878x9106000113.

M. A. Alonso et al., "Sentiment analysis for fake news detection," *Electron*, vol. 10, no. 11, 2021.

N. Guimarães et al., "Can fake news detection models maintain the performance through time? A longitudinal evaluation of twitter publications," *Mathematics*, vol. 9, no. 22, 2988, 2021.

N. Guimarãeset al., "An organized review of key factors for fake news detection," 2021, http://arxiv.org/ abs/2102.13433

N. Hoy and T. Koulouri, "A systematic review on the detection of fake news articles," 2021, http://arxiv.org/abs/2110.11240

N. Lomas, "Facebook's latest 'transparency' tool doesn't offer much — So we went digging," *Techcrunch*, February 25, 2020.

N. Micallef, B. He, S. Kumar, M. Ahamad, and N. Memon, "The role of the crowd in countering misinformation: A case study of the COVID-19 infodemic," *arXiv (Cornell University)*, November 2020, doi: 10.48550/arxiv.2011.05773.

O. Abu Arqoub et al., "Mapping the scholarship of fake news research: A systematic review," *Journalism Practice*, vol. 16, no. 1, pp. 56–86, 2022.

O. D. Apuke and B. Omar, "Fake news and COVID-19: Modelling the predictors of fake news sharing among social media users," *Telematics and Informatics*, vol. 56, 2021, article 101475.

P. Murphy, "Naive Bayes classifiers generative classifiers," *Bernoulli*, vol. 4701, pp. 1–8, October 2007.

R. Biswas et al., "Sentiment analysis on national education policy change 2020," *Turkish Journal of Computer and Mathematics Education*, vol. 12, no. 11, pp. 1480–1488, 2020.

R. Britt, "Why people won't change their minds on Covid-19," *Medium*, June 1, 2020.

R. Oshikawa R. Oshikawa, J. Qian, and W. Y. Wang, "A survey on natural language processing for fake news detection," 2020, https:// arxiv.org/abs/1811.00770.

R. Qasim et al., "A fine-tuned BERT-based transfer learning approach for text classification," *Journal of Healthcare Engineering*, vol. 2022, 17 pages, 2022, Article ID 3498123.

R. Varma et al., "A systematic survey on deep learning and machine learning approaches of fake news detection in the pre- and postCOVID-19 pandemic," *International Journal of Intelligent Computing and Cybernetics*, vol. 14, no. 4, pp. 617–646, 2021.

S. Khan et al, "Detecting COVID-19-related fake news using feature extraction," *Frontiers in Public Health*, vol. 9, pp. 1–9, January 2021.

S. Raza and C. Ding, "Fake news detection based on news content and social contexts: A transformer-based approach," *International Journal of Data Science and Analytics*, vol. 13, no. 4, pp. 335–362, 2022.

S. Shahnawaz, P. Astya, S. Shahnawaz, and P. Astya, "Sentiment analysis: Approaches and open issues," 2017 International Conference on computing, Communication and automation (ICCCA), vol. 2017– January, pp. 154–158, Greater Noida, India, 2017.

S. Vosoughi, D. Roy, and S. Aral, "The spread of true and false news online," *Science*, vol. 359, no. 6380, pp. 1146–1151, March 2018, doi: 10.1126/science.aap9559.

S. L. Ting, W. H. Ip, and A. H. C. Tsang, "Is Naïve Bayes a good classifier for document classification?," *International Journal of Software Engineering and Its Applications*, vol. 5, no. 3, pp. 37–46, 2021.

W. Dai et al., "Transferring naive Bayes classifiers for text classification," *Proceedings of the AAAI Conference on Artificial Intelligence*, vol. 1, pp. 540–545, 2022.

X. Zhang et al., "An overview of online fake news: Characterization, detection, and discussion," *Information Processing and Management*, vol. 57, no. 2, 2020, article 102025.

X. Zhou et al., "Fake news early detection: An interdisciplinary study," pp. 3207–3208, 2019, http://arxiv.org/abs/1904.11679.

15 Detection and Prevention of Fake News and Hate Speech through Machine Learning and Natural Language Processing

Aaryan Barde, Veena Kaimal, Snehlata Barde, and Sanjiv Sharma

15.1 INTRODUCTION

Fake news and hate speech messages are those messages that spread negativity in society about castes, religions, politics, race, disabilities, sexual orientations, and many more. Hate speech detection is the process of automatic identification and flagging this content, that is considered to be hateful or discriminatory towards a particular group of people based on their race, ethnicity, gender, religion, sexual orientation, or other characteristic.

This process involves using natural language processing (NLP) techniques, such as text classification and sentiment analysis, to analyze the content and identify patterns that suggest hateful or discriminatory language. The goal of hate speech detection is to identify and remove harmful content from online platforms, such as social media networks, that contributes to the spread of hate and discrimination.

The vulnerability of social media platforms and the rapid development of mobile computing and web technologies, especially the younger generation, has led to serious offline consequences. These platforms provide anonymity and easy access to online communities. The importance of the Internet today is palpable, it opens the gateway to vast amounts of information and enables socio-political participation in any type of social group is unquestionable, the radical advancement in digital and communication technologies has posed dire problems to companies, political bodies, government organizations, and all socio-economic bodies. These issues have become more intricate with the development of social media platforms and search engine algorithms, which curate and proliferate content based on the preferences of users. The anonymity of social networks makes it attractive for hate speech to mask their criminal activities online posing a challenge to the world. With this

 DOI: 10.1201/9781003409519-15

ever-increasing volume of social media data, hate speech identification becomes a challenge in aggravating conflict between citizens of nations.

Hate speech gets generated in many different places, including online platforms, social media platforms, news articles, blogs, forums, and even in-person interactions. People can easily create and spread harmful content on social media platforms, chat rooms, and discussion forums, often anonymously or under a pseudonym. This can lead to the rapid spread of hate speech and misinformation across the internet. As India is a secular state, many languages are spoken in the country. Indian languages have a rich cultural and social context. Therefore, many words and expressions may have multiple meanings depending on the context in which they are used (Zhou et al. 2020).

Moreover, Indian languages have very complex grammar, syntax, and vocabulary, and the use of slang and colloquialisms can vary widely across different regions and communities. This makes the task of hate speech detection in India even more difficult. Hate speech can also be generated in offline settings. These are public speeches, rallies, and protests. In some cases, political leaders or media outlets may use hate speech to stir up emotions and gain support, which can further exacerbate existing tensions and lead to social unrest. Regardless of where hate speech is generated, it creates a negative impact on individuals and communities, contributing to feelings of fear, division, and discrimination. The explosive growth in fake news and its erosion of democracy, justice, and public trust has increased the demand for fake news detection and intervention.

Abusive language and behavior in social media platforms constitute a significant problem that affects online platforms, as well as the communities in which they are employed. The problems laid down due to hate speech are serious and most importantly it escapes the virtual boundaries of social media platforms (Mossie et al. 2020).

Here is an illustration of fake news:

Breaking News: NASA Confirms 15 Days of Total Darkness on Earth in November 2023

The idea that the Earth would endure 15 days of total darkness in November 2023 is false, according to science, hence this is an example of fake news. This report is a fraud that came from a website that publishes fake news, and it has been thoroughly discredited by reliable sources.

Such fake news articles frequently aim to get people's attention and encourage social media clicks, shares, and likes. Due to the spread of false information and the potential for public confusion, fear, and mistrust, they may be harmful. The information must be fact-checked and the news sources' reliability must be confirmed (Velankar et al. 2022).

A significant difficulty that can be met by the application of machine learning and natural language processing techniques is the detection and prevention of fake news and hate speech. The procedure generally consists of two steps:

1. Determining whether a piece of information comprises fake news or hate speech.
2. Taking the necessary steps to stop its dissemination.

15.2 RECOGNIZING FALSE INFORMATION AND HATE SPEECH

Predicting fake news jointly from multiple perspectives is encouraged if we are able to combine their strengths. Based on fake news characteristics and the current state of fake news research, we highlight the following potential research tasks that can facilitate a deeper understanding of fake news, and improve the interpretability and performance of current fake news detection studies:

1. Detection of non-traditional fake news.
2. Fake news early detection.
3. Identifying check-worthy content.
4. Cross-domain fake news analysis.
5. Explainable fake news detection.
6. Fake news intervention.

15.2.1 Various ML Techniques in Hate Speech Detection

Machine learning (ML) techniques have shown promise in the detection of hate speech in various forms of digital content, including text, audio, and visual media. The use of ML algorithms for hate speech detection involves training a model to recognize patterns and features in the data that are indicative of hate speech. Here are some ML techniques that can be used for hate speech detection (Mossie et al. 2020):

- **Supervised learning:** This approach involves training a machine learning model on a large dataset of annotated text, where each sample is labeled as either hate speech or not. The model learns to recognize patterns and features in the data and can then predict whether new text contains hate speech or not (Barde et al. 2020)
- **Unsupervised learning:** Unsupervised learning demands using clustering algorithms to group similar documents or text fragments based on their features. This can help identify patterns in the data that may indicate hate speech, even if the training data doesn't contain explicit labels for hate speech.
- **Deep learning:** This requires using deep neural networks to automatically learn features and patterns from text data. This can be particularly effective for detecting subtle variations in language use and context that may be indicative of hate speech.
- **Transfer learning:** Transfer learning uses pre-trained models on large datasets for natural language processing tasks, such as sentiment analysis or topic classification, and then fine-tuning the model on a smaller dataset of annotated hate speech to adapt it to the task of hate speech detection.
- **Hybrid learning:** Hybrid learning is a machine learning approach that combines more than one technique such as supervised and unsupervised learning, to improve the performance and accuracy of a model. In the context of hate speech detection (HSD), hybrid learning can be used to leverage

the strengths of different techniques and models to improve the detection of hate speech.

15.3 APPLICATION OF ML TECHNIQUES IN HATE SPEECH DETECTION

- **Predictive learning**

Supervised learning is a popular ML technique that involves training a model on a large dataset of labeled data to classify new data points. For hate speech detection, the labeled data would consist of examples of hate speech and non-hate speech content. The model would learn to recognize patterns and features in the data that are associated with hate speech, such as specific words or phrases, and use this knowledge to classify new content as hate speech or not. The most common algorithms used for supervised learning are support vector machine (SVM), Naïve Bayes, decision tree algorithms, etc., which are highly effective in separating two classes of data points (Buzea et al. 2022).

To train a predictive model for hate speech detection:

- The first step is to create a labeled dataset of hate speech and non-hate speech content.
- This dataset should be diverse and representative of the range of hate speech that can exist online.
- The dataset needs to be pre-processed, which involves cleaning and standardizing the text data, removing stop words, and converting the text into numerical features.
- Once the dataset is ready, it can be split into training and testing sets, with the majority of the data used for training the model and the rest used for testing its accuracy.
- Ultimately, the model can be trained using the training data.
- The performance can be evaluated using the testing data.
- The model can then be used to classify new content as hate speech or not.

- **Self-organized learning**

Self-organized learning is an ML technique used for identifying patterns in data that do not have labeled examples. For hate speech detection, unsupervised learning can be used to group or associate similar pieces of content together based on their features. This can be useful for identifying new types of hate speech that may not be present in the labeled dataset.

To train an unsupervised learning model:

- The first step is to pre-process the data and convert it into numerical features.
- Next, the data can be fed into an algorithm such as k-means clustering, which groups similar data points together based on their distance from each other.

- The clusters can then be analyzed to identify patterns and features that are associated with hate speech. For example, if a particular word or phrase is present in many of the data points in a cluster, it may be indicative of hate speech.

- **Deep learning**

Deep learning is a subset of machine learning that involves training a neural network to recognize patterns and features in data. For hate speech detection, deep learning can be used to analyze the context and semantics of the text and identify subtle variations in language used, that may indicate hate speech.

To train a deep learning model for hate speech detection:

- The first step is to create a labeled dataset of hate speech and non-hate speech content.
- Next, the dataset needs to be pre-processed, which involves cleaning and standardizing the text data, removing stop words, and converting the text into numerical features.
- Once the dataset is ready, it can be used to train a neural network, such as a convolutional neural network (CNN) or a recurrent neural network (RNN).
- The neural network is trained on the features extracted from the text data, and its performance is evaluated using the testing data.
- The neural network can then be used to classify new content as hate speech or not.

- **Transfer learning**

Transfer learning is an ML technique that involves using a pre-trained model on a large dataset to perform a similar task on a smaller dataset. This approach can be particularly useful when there is limited labeled data available for a specific task and can help improve the accuracy of the model by leveraging the knowledge gained from the pre-trained model. The knowledge of an already trained machine learning model is transferred to a different but closely linked problem throughout transfer learning.

In the context of hate speech detection, transfer learning involves using a pre-trained model that has already learned to recognize language patterns and features to classify hate speech in a different language or domain. For example, a pre-trained model on English text can be used to classify hate speech in Hindi text, even though the training data for the pre-trained model did not contain any Hindi text.

To perform transfer learning for hate speech detection:

- The first step is to obtain a pre-trained model that has been trained on a large dataset of text data. This can be done by using publicly available pre-trained models, or by training our own model on a large dataset.
- Then, the pre-trained model needs to be fine-tuned on a smaller labeled dataset, for the specific task of hate speech detection.
- This involves training the model on the labeled data while keeping the pre-trained weights fixed for the lower layers of the model, which are responsible for learning general language features.

- The higher layers of the model, which are responsible for learning task-specific features, are updated during training to adapt the model to the task of hate speech detection.

- **Hybrid learning**

One example of using hybrid learning in HSD is combining supervised and unsupervised learning techniques. Unsupervised learning techniques can be used to identify patterns and clusters of words or phrases that are indicative of hate speech, while supervised learning techniques can be used to label and classify the identified instances of hate speech. This approach can improve the accuracy of the hate speech detection model by reducing the number of false positives and false negatives.

Another example of using hybrid learning in HSD is combining deep learning models with traditional machine learning models. Deep learning models, such as convolutional neural networks (CNNs) and recurrent neural networks (RNNs), can be used to extract complex features from text data and learn complex patterns, while traditional machine learning models, such as logistic regression or support vector machines (SVMs), can be used for classification and prediction. This approach can improve the accuracy and efficiency of the hate speech detection model by leveraging the strengths of both types of models (Perifanos et al. 2021).

Hybrid learning can also be used in transfer learning approaches for HSD. For example, a hybrid approach can combine a pre-trained language model, such as BERT or GPT, with additional supervised or unsupervised learning techniques to fine-tune the model for hate speech detection. This approach can improve the performance of the transfer learning model and adapt it to the specific task and domain of HSD.

The application of hybrid learning in HSD can improve the accuracy and efficiency of hate speech detection models by capitalizing on the strengths of multiple techniques and models. The choice and combination of techniques and models should be carefully evaluated and tailored to suit the specific dataset of HSD.

The fine-tuning process typically involves several iterations of training the model on the labeled data and evaluating its performance on a validation set. The hyperparameters of the model, such as the learning rate and batch size, can be tuned during this process to improve the performance of the model. Once the model has been fine-tuned, its performance can be evaluated on a separate test set to measure its accuracy in classifying hate speech.

15.4 CONTROLLING THE DISSEMINATION OF FALSE INFORMATION AND HATE SPEECH

- **Content filtering:** Content filtering is the process of monitoring and restricting access to specific types of content, such as websites, restricted access to online media, etc. This technique is commonly used in various settings, such as corporate networks, schools, and public spaces, to enforce policies and guidelines for appropriate usage of resources and to protect users from harmful or unwanted content.

Content filtering is usually performed using the following methods: URL filtering, keyword filtering, image and video filtering, application and protocol filtering, etc. To apply these methods content filtering is implemented using techniques such as hardware-based appliances, software-based solutions, and cloud-based services (Arango et al. 2022).

Content filtering can be proven to be effective in preventing access to inappropriate or harmful content if it is carefully designed to evaluate content filtering policies and techniques to ensure their effectiveness and compliance with legal and ethical standards.

- **User behavior monitoring:** It involves collecting and analyzing data on user interactions with online platforms, such as social media or messaging apps, to identify specific patterns of behavior that may indicate hate speech or fake news.

Machine learning algorithms can be trained on such data to detect and classify instances of hate speech or fake news, based on various features and characteristics, such as the use of specific words or phrases, frequency of posting, and social network analysis. Natural language processing (NLP) techniques are used to analyze the text of user posts and identify patterns of hate speech or fake news based on linguistic and semantic features.

Since this process involves privacy concerns, its implementation should be practiced in a transparent and accountable manner, with clear guidelines and safeguards in order to protect user rights and interests.

- **Education and awareness:** Education and awareness is one of the crucial components in combating hate speech and fake news. Users can benefit greatly from learning how to recognize and stay away from such content, and how to verify information that they come across online.

These awareness initiatives must cover topics such as media literacy, critical thinking, fact-checking, and digital citizenship. It can provide users with practical tools and resources to verify information, such as fact-checking websites or browser plugins.

Education and awareness efforts should be targeted to various user groups, such as students, teachers, journalists, or members of the general public. It must be customized to address specific cultural, linguistic, or regional contexts, in order to ensure maximum relevance and effectiveness.

15.5 NLP-BASED MODELS FOR HSD

15.5.1 Implementing a Predictive Learning Model

Supervised learning is a type of machine learning in which an algorithm is trained on a labeled dataset to learn a mapping function from input variables (features) to output variables (labels). In the context of hate speech detection (HSD), a supervised learning method can be used to classify text as either hate speech or not.

The working of a predictive learning method for HSD is shown in Figure 15.1. It can be broken down into several steps:

Data Collection: The first step in the process is to collect a large amount of data containing examples of hate speech and non-hate speech text. This data can be collected from various sources such as social media platforms, forums, blogs, or news articles.

Data is collected from various sources such as X (formerly Twitter), Facebook, Instagram, search history, etc. Data collection from social media for HSD contains the following steps shown in figure 15.2.

Data pre-processing: This involves cleaning and transforming the raw data into a format that can be easily used by the machine learning algorithm. Figure 15.3 shows the steps involved in data pre-processing in supervised learning for HSD:

a. **Data cleaning:** It removes any irrelevant or redundant data such as punctuation and numbers. Data correction for spelling errors and typos is also done in this step.

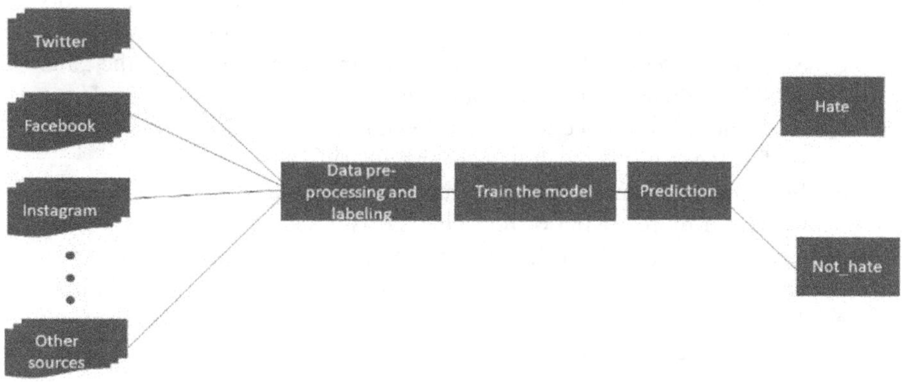

FIGURE 15.1 Block diagram of a predictive learning model for HSD.

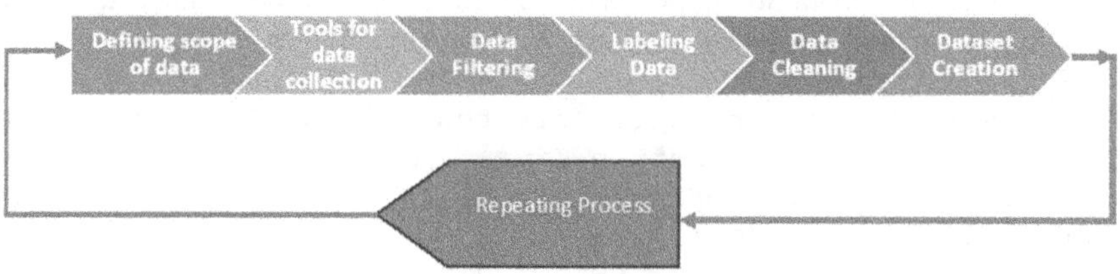

FIGURE 15.2 Data collection steps.

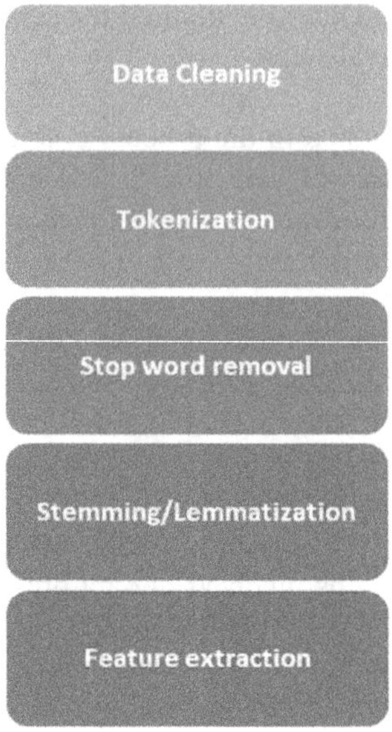

FIGURE 15.3 Data pre-processing steps.

b. **Tokenization:** This is the process of splitting the text into smaller units that can be analyzed by the machine learning algorithm.
c. **Stop word removal:** Commonly occurring words such as "the" and "and" that do not carry significant meaning are called stop words. These are removed to reduce the dimensionality of the data and improve the performance of the machine learning algorithm.
d. **Stemming/Lemmatization:** Stemming converts a word to the common root form by removing or replacing suffixes such as "looking" will be stemmed as "look" and lemmatization identifies the inflected form of a word and returns its base form such as "least" gets lemmatized as "little".
e. **Feature extraction:** The final step is to extract relevant features from the pre-processed data.

Splitting the data: The next step is to split the data into two parts: the training set and the test set. The training set is used to train the machine learning model, while the test set is used to evaluate its performance. Example code in Figure 15.4 shows the splitting of a dataset into train and test from a tweet dataset.

```
train2, test2=train_test_split(df, test_size=0.3,random_
            state=10, shuffle=True)
train2=train2[['id','label','tweet']]
test2=test2[['id','tweet']]
x_train, x_test, y_train, y_test=train_test_split(x, y_hate,
test_size=0.30, random_state=1)
```

```
train2, test2 = train_test_split(df, test_size=0.3,random_state=10, shuffle=True)

train2 = train2[['id','label','tweet']]

test2 = test2[['id','tweet']]

x_train, x_test, y_train, y_test = train_test_split(x, y_hate, test_size = 0.30, random_state = 1)
```

FIGURE 15.4 Splitting of dataset.

15.5.2 Selection of a Model

There are various supervised learning algorithms that can be used for HSD such as logistic regression, Naïve Bayes, decision trees, random forest, and support vector machines. The appropriate algorithm is selected based on the characteristics of the data and the problem at hand. Machine learning algorithms are addressed as a combination of methods to automatically detect the potential patterns in the given set of data. It learns from previous data to explore unknown patterns or to predict future data for decision-making under uncertainty.

- The most commonly used classical algorithms are random forests (RF) and gradient-boosted decision trees (GBDT).
- For these classifiers, feature selection takes time while the neural network approaches are supposed to automatically learn abstract features.
- The deep neural network approaches appear to be more effective for learning text sequences while feature-based approaches preserve some sort of explanation. Deep recurrent neural networks (RNN) such as long short-term memory (LSTM), and gated recurrent units (GRU) are also employed as shown in Figure 15.5 (Mossie and Wang 2020).

15.5.3 Training the Model

The selected algorithm is trained on the training set by adjusting the model's parameters to minimize the error between the predicted and actual labels, Table 15.1 shows the training and test performed on a Kaggle dataset.

Training on an example dataset:

```
train1=pd.read_csv('/kaggle/input/twitter-hate-speech/train_
E6oV3lV.csv')
print("Training Set 1 :"% train1.columns, train1.shape)
test1=pd.read_csv('/kaggle/input/twitter-hate-speech/test_twe
ets_anuFYb8.csv')
print("Test Set 1 :"% test1.columns, test1.shape)
print('Train Set 1 -----')
```

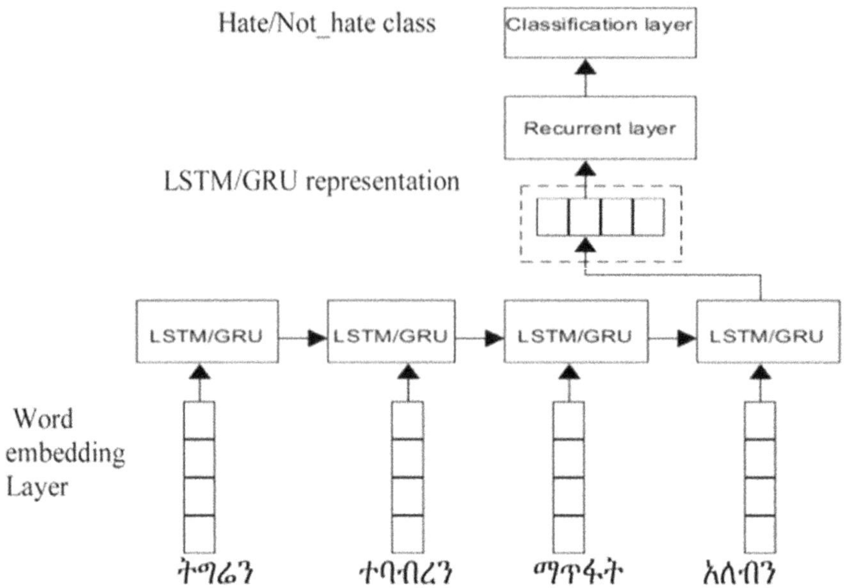

FIGURE 15.5 A deep (RNN) LSTM model.

TABLE 15.1
The Train and Test Performed on a Kaggle Dataset

S.No.	id	label	tweet
0	1	0	@user when a father is dysfunctional and is s...
1	2	0	@user @user thanks for #lyft credit i can't us...
2	3	0	bihday your majesty
3	4	0	#model i love u take with u all the time in ...
4	5	0	factsguide: society now #motivation

```
print(train1.isnull().sum())
print('Test Set 1 -----')
print(test1.isnull().sum())
train1.head()
```

Output:

```
Training Set 1 : (31962, 3)
Test Set 1 : (17197, 2)
Train Set 1 -----
id    0
label  0
```

```
tweet  0
dtype: int64
Test Set 1 -----
id    0
tweet  0
dtype: int64
```

15.5.4 Evaluating the Model

Once the model is trained, it is evaluated on the test set to measure its performance. Common metrics for evaluating classification models include accuracy, precision, recall, and F1-score.

The most common algorithms used are SVM, random forests, decision trees, logistic regression, Naïve Bayes, and deep learning respectively on the use of frequency by authors. The data classification is based on general hate speech, racism, sexism, religion, anti-Semitism, nationality, politics, and socio-economics status respectively on the categorization use of frequency.

For the accuracy of the model, the authors used cross-validation using a Spark evaluation tool namely binary class classification evaluator within the Spark ML. To evaluate the performance of the model classification in terms of quality or predictive effectiveness, different metrics appropriate for the work accuracy, ROC score, and area under curve F-measure (F1-score) shown in Table 15.2.

15.5.5 Fine-tuning the Model

If the performance of the model is not satisfactory, the model parameters can be fine-tuned by adjusting the hyperparameters such as learning rate, regularization, or number of iterations.

An Apache Spark-based model to classify Amharic Facebook posts and comments into hate and not hate. They employed random forest and Naïve Bayes for learning and Word2vec and term frequency–inverse document frequency (TF–IDF) for

TABLE 15.2
Various Classification Models Applied, Training Time, Accuracy, and F1-Score

Classification Algorithm used	Training time taken (seconds)	Evaluation Matrices Results	
		Accuracy	F1 score
Random Forest	63.106590	0.9816967472213725	0.9813176519567026
K-Nearest Neighbors	0.016990	0.8973182420719894	0.8865927135536911
Logistic Regression	39.988570	0.8774344855715306	0.8805347115241267
Decision Tree	233.756527	0.962182624655858	0.9606253234774992
Naïve Bayes	6.097073	0.7175486897114306	0.7755494783753671

feature selection. Tested by 10-fold cross-validation, the model based on Word2vec embedding performed best with 79.83% accuracy.

15.5.6 Deployment

Once the model is trained and fine-tuned, it can be deployed to classify new text as either hate speech or not.

Overall, a supervised learning method for HSD involves the collection and preprocessing of data, selection of an appropriate algorithm, training, and evaluation of the model, and fine-tuning to optimize its performance. The success of the method depends on the quality and quantity of the training data, the appropriateness of the algorithm, and the effectiveness of the pre-processing and fine-tuning techniques used.

15.6 IMPLEMENTING A SELF-ORGANIZED LEARNING MODEL

There are different unsupervised learning techniques that can be used for HSD, such as clustering, topic modeling, and anomaly detection.

Clustering: Clustering is one of the most common techniques used in implementing unsupervised learning. It groups similar data points together into clusters based on their features. In the context of HSD, this technique can be employed to identify groups of text that contain similar language or topics. For example, clustering can be used to identify clusters of text containing hate speech or fake news. The clusters can then be manually inspected to determine the specific features that define them.

Topic modeling: Topic modeling is another unsupervised learning technique that involves identifying the topics present in a large corpus of text data. In the context of HSD, this technique can be used to identify the topics that are associated with hate speech or fake news. Once the topics are identified, the model can be used to classify new text based on the presence of these topics.

Anomaly detection: Anomaly detection is another technique that is used in identifying unusual patterns or outliers in the data. This technique can be used to identify text that deviates significantly from the norm. This technique can be used to identify tweets or posts that contain unusual language or are written in a style that is not normal for a particular user.

Self-organized learning techniques can be useful for HSD, particularly when there is a lack of labeled datasets. But, the success rate of these techniques depends on the quality and quantity of the data, as well as the specific technique used.

15.7 IMPLEMENTING A HYBRID LEARNING MODEL

Implementing a hybrid learning model for HSD combines the strengths of both supervised and unsupervised learning techniques. This approach can be more effective where labeled data is limited or where the data is complex and difficult to classify using traditional supervised learning methods.

Pre-processing: The first step in implementing a hybrid learning model for HSD is to pre-process the data. This involves cleaning and preparing the data for analysis. Pre-processing can include tasks such as removing stop words, stemming, and tokenization.

Unsupervised learning: This step is to use unsupervised learning techniques to identify patterns or structures in the data. This can include techniques such as clustering, topic modeling, or anomaly detection. The goal of this step is to identify groups of text that contain similar language or topics.

Labeling: Once patterns or structures have been identified using unsupervised learning techniques, the data can be labeled using human input or crowd-sourcing. This step involves manually reviewing the data and assigning labels to each text based on its content. The labeled data can then be used to train a supervised learning model.

Supervised learning: The labeled data is then used to train a supervised learning model such as a decision tree, random forest, or neural network. The model is trained to recognize patterns in the data and make predictions based on those patterns. The model is then evaluated using a hold-out set of data to determine its performance.

Fine-tuning: Finally, the model can be fine-tuned to improve its performance. This can involve adjusting hyperparameters, re-sampling the data, or using ensemble techniques to combine multiple models.

15.8 RESULT ANALYSIS

The success rate of a predictive learning model in hate speech detection depends on various factors, such as the quality and quantity of the training data, the choice of features and algorithms, and the evaluation metrics used. In general, supervised learning models can achieve high accuracy in hate speech detection, especially when trained on large, diverse datasets and using advanced algorithms and techniques (Deng et al. 2010).

The success rate of a supervised learning model in hate speech detection can vary depending on the specific dataset and task, and there may be cases where the model's performance is lower due to the complexity of the language or the diversity of the data. Additionally, it is important to consider the potential biases in the training data and to regularly evaluate the model's performance on new data to ensure its accuracy and effectiveness. According to a study published in ScienceDirect, despite the apparent difficulty of the hate speech detection problem evidenced by social media providers, current state-of-the-art approaches reported in the literature show near-perfect performance. Within dataset experiments on labeled hate speech datasets using supervised learning achieve F1 scores above 93%. Figure 15.6 shows the result of the classification modal in terms of precision-recall and ROC curves.

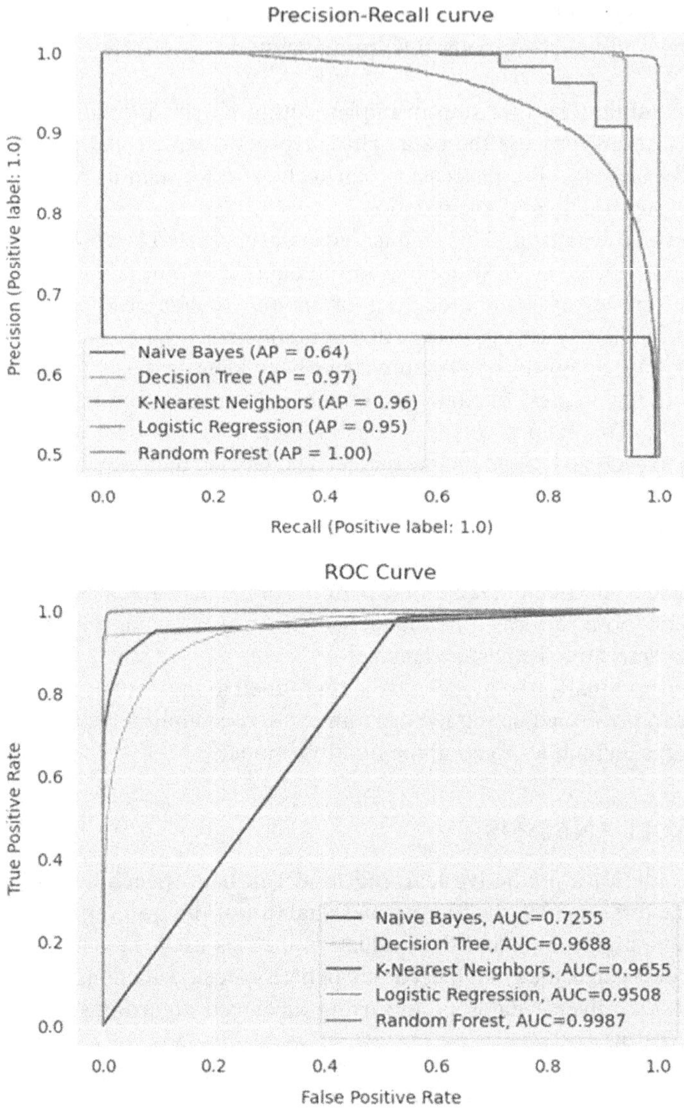

FIGURE 15.6 Result of classification modal in terms of precision-recall and ROC curve.

An example using the Kaggle dataset:

```
from sklearn.metrics import plot_precision_recall_curve
plot_precision_recall_curve (classifier_np, x_test, y_test, ax
= plt.gca(),name = "Naive Bayes")
plot_precision_recall_curve (classifier_dt, x_test, y_test, ax
= plt.gca(),name = "Decision Tree")
```

```
  plot_precision_recall_curve (classifier_knn, x_test, y_test,
ax = plt.gca(),name = "K-Nearest Neighbors")
  plot_precision_recall_curve (classifier_lr, x_test, y_test,
ax = plt.gca(),name = "Logistic Regression")
  plot_precision_recall_curve (classifier_rf, x_test, y_test,
ax = plt.gca(),name = "Random Forest")
  plt.title('Precision-Recall curve')
       plt.plot(fpr_np,tpr_np,label="Naive Bayes,
AUC="+str(auc_np))
  plt.plot(fpr_dt,tpr_dt,label="Decision Tree,
AUC="+str(auc_dt))
  plt.plot(fpr_knn,tpr_knn,label="K-Nearest Neighbors,
AUC="+str(auc_knn))
  plt.plot(fpr_lr,tpr_lr,label="Logistic Regression,
AUC="+str(auc_lr))
  plt.plot(fpr_rf,tpr_rf,label="Random Forest,
AUC="+str(auc_rf))
  plt.ylabel('True Positive Rate')
  plt.xlabel('False Positive Rate')
  plt.title('ROC Curve')
     plt.legend()
```

The success rate of a self-organized learning model in hate speech detection is generally lower than that of predictive learning models. This is because self-organized learning models do not rely on labeled data, which can be crucial for accurately detecting hate speech.

Self-organized learning models for hate speech detection involve clustering or topic modeling techniques to identify patterns and clusters of words or phrases that are indicative of hate speech. While these techniques can be effective in identifying potential hate speech, they may also produce false positives or miss some instances of hate speech.

While self-organized learning models have lower accuracy rates than supervised learning models, they can still be useful for identifying potential instances of hate speech or for identifying trends and patterns in a large dataset.

Transfer learning models have also shown promising results in hate speech detection and can achieve high accuracy rates, especially when combined with deep learning models.

Transfer learning involves using pre-trained models, such as BERT or GPT, that have been trained on large, general-purpose datasets, and then fine-tuning them on a specific task, such as hate speech detection.

This approach allows the model to leverage the knowledge and patterns learned from the pre-training stage to improve its performance on the target task with less training data.

The success rate of a transfer learning model in hate speech detection can vary depending on the quality and quantity of the training data and the specific task and language being analyzed. Transfer learning models have shown promising results in hate speech detection and can achieve high accuracy rates when carefully fine-tuned and trained on appropriate datasets (Allcott et al. 2017).

15.9 CONCLUSION

Machine learning is pertinent for the development of hate speech detection models. In our experiment, machine learning algorithms such as support vector classifier, logistic regression, and random forest classifier were applied to hate speech detection prototypes for X.

Nowadays, governments and public institutions are using different machine learning algorithms to automate the important processes of several departments, such as human resources and claims revenue, with it being necessary to follow several ethical rules such as transparency, responsibility, or fairness and to avoid epistemic and normative concerns.

The exclusive use of algorithms and AI systems may encounter errors or have insufficient data for selecting the best ways to work, but these systems should deliver socially good outcomes, and ethical and technological analyses are mandatory.

Even if the results are promising for hate detection, researchers are far from perfect. A lot of work ahead of us to work on technical improvements that can be made for the language in terms of (Kaimal and Barde 2021):

1. Expand the datasets that would reduce the risk of overfitting and improve the statistical significance of the results.
2. Analyzing the different aspects of the category of hate, either hate with politics, ethnicity, religion, or socio-economy.
3. Utilize the information provided by Facebook so that classification can be improved by expanding the feature space with profile information, list of followers, geolocation, etc.
4. Crawl through other sources to improve the feature space for such under-resourced language for computational purposes by adding synonyms from other sources such as Twitter, forums, and other homepages.

REFERENCES

Allcott, Hunt, and Matthew Gentzkow. "Social media and fake news in the 2016 election." 31, no. 2 (2017): 211–236.

Arango, Aymé, Jorge Pérez, and Barbara Poblete. "Hate speech detection is not as easy as you may think: A closer look at model validation (extended version)." *Information Systems* 105 (2022): 101584. ISSN 0306-4379. https://doi.org/10.1016/j.is.2020.101584.

Barde, S., and V. Kaimal. "Speech recognition technique for identification of raga." *Cognitive Informatics, Computer Modelling, and Cognitive Science* (2020): 101–117. ISBN 9780128194454. https://doi.org/10.1016/B978-0-12-819445-4.00005-9.

Buzea, Marius Cristian, Stefan Trausan-Matu, and Traian Rebedea. "Automatic fake news detection for Romanian online news." *Information* 13, no. 3 (2022): 151.

Deng, Jiabin, JuanLi Hu, Hehua Chi, and Juebo Wu. "An improved fuzzy clustering method for text mining." 2010 Second International Conference on Networks Security, Wireless Communications and Trusted Computing. IEEE, 2010, vol. 1, no. 5, 65–69.

Kaimal, V., and S. Barde. "Implementation of a supervised learning model for raga identification in Carnatic music," 2021 Asian Conference on Innovation in Technology (ASIANCON), 2021, 1–6. https://doi.org/10.1109 / ASIANCON 51346.

Mossie, Z., and H. Wang. "Social network hate speech detection for Amharic language." *Computer Science and Information Technology* 3, no. 1 (2018): 41–55. https://doi.org /10.5121 /csit. 2018.8060.

Mossie, Zewdie, and Jenq-Haur Wang, "Vulnerable community identification using hate speech detection on social media." *Information Processing and Management* 57, no. 3 (2020). https://doi.org/10.1016/j.ipm.2019.102087.

Perifanos, Konstantinos, and Dionysis Goutsos. "Multimodal hate speech detection in Greek social media." *Multimodal Technologies and Interaction* 5, no. 7 (2021): 34.

Velankar, A., H. Patil, and R. Joshi. "Mono vs multilingual Bert for hate speech detection and text classification: A case study in Marathi.". Artificial Neural Networks in Pattern Recognition: 10th IAPR TC3 Workshop, ANNPR. Springer, Dubai, United Arab Emirates, 2022, 121–128. https://doi.org/10.1007/978-3-031-20650-4_10.

Zhou, X., and R. Zafarani. "A survey of fake news: Fundamental theories, detection methods, and opportunities." *ACM Computing Surveys (CSUR)*, 53, no. 5 (2020): 1–40.

16 Fake News and Hate Speech

Influence on Society and Detection by Machine Learning

Bishakha Mandal, Pragya Goswami, and Hemant Kumar Soni

16.1 INTRODUCTION: BACKGROUND ON FAKE NEWS AND HATE SPEECH

16.1.1 FAKE NEWS

Fake news is a broadcasted or published report that has misleading information or the content in the information is not true to the word. Fake news often has the aim of damaging the reputation of a person or entity, or making money through advertising revenue (Schlesinger 2017; Hunt 2016). The term is a neologism (a new or re-purposed expression that is entering the language, driven by culture or technology changes) (Ember and Mihailidis 2017). Fake news, or fake news websites, have no basis in fact but are presented as being factually accurate (Allcott and Gentzkow 2017). Although false news has always been spread throughout history, the term "fake news" was first used in the 1890s when sensational reports in newspapers were common (Kadakas 2017).

Further, disinformation may turn out to have harmful intent if it is intentionally spread by a foreign hostile party during some infamous event or elections in a country. In some definitions, fake news includes satirical articles misinterpreted as genuine, and articles that employ sensationalist or clickbait headlines that are not supported in the text (Hunt 2016).

The frequency of fake news has risen on social media sites, such as Facebook, Youtube, and X (formerly Twitter). Even the mainstream media is no longer immune to the effects of fake news. Several factors have been implicated in the spread of fake news, such as political polarization, post-truth politics, motivated reasoning, confirmation bias, and social media algorithms (Hunt 2016).

 DOI: 10.1201/9781003409519-16

Fake news in India (Grover et al. 2019) spread through word of mouth and traditional media and more recently through digital forms of communication such as edited videos, memes, unverified advertisements, and social media propagated rumors (Krishnan 2019). In the recent past, fake news spread through social media posed a threat to democracy and peace in the country as it instigated mob violence in the name of social justice, religion, personal beliefs, and suspicion. For example, more than 22 people had been killed by mobs since May 10, 2018, on the suspicion of being child-lifters or involved in cow slaughter in different parts of the country. Police had blamed rumor mongers and fake messages spread through social media for the lynchings (Dutta 2018). The Indian government had to face serious accusations from the opposition and Home Minister Rajnath Singh had to make a speech in the Lok Sabha that the government was taking the matter seriously and had asked social sites for regulation (Times now digital 2018).

However, fake news did not spear animals that appeared in pictures. India Today's Anti Fake News War Room (AFWA) found that the pictures and reports of dead cows in several cow shelters in Rajasthan were being published to earn votes in the election were misleading claims and were pictures from Kenya, East Africa, posted in 2014 (Kundu 2019).

Fake news spread during the Citizenship (Amendment) Act 2019, targeted the Delhi police and the protesters causing serious harm to them. Even the members of the ruling BJP were seen to be sharing videos, falsely insinuating that the students at Aligarh Muslim University, Aligarh, India, were raising anti-Hindu slogans (Goel 2019). It was, subsequently, found that a few BJP leaders had circulated a phone number via social media, X handles, asking people to give a missed call to show support for the act. The number was widely shared on X, with fake claims luring people with companionship with lonely women and free subscriptions to streaming platforms such as Netflix (Chatterji 2020). Later, the central government of India was asked by the Supreme Court of India to consider "a plea for publicising aims, objectives and the benefits of the Citizenship Amendment Act (CAA) to weed out fake news that was being circulated on the issue" (Hindu 2019). Subsequently, Indian security and intelligence agencies reportedly identified around 5,000 social media handles from Pakistan which were "spreading fake and false propaganda" about the CAA, some using "deep fake videos" in the process (IANS 2019). Further, old pictures, images, and videos were shared on social media, even by prominent personalities, giving a communal spin to the protests, such as old clips involving police brutality were reposted and falsely purported to be linked with a crackdown on CAA protesters (Goel 2019).

Fake news was very prevalent during the 2019 Indian general election (News 2019a, 2019b). The elections were called by some as "India's first WhatsApp elections", with WhatsApp being used by many as a tool of propaganda (Perrigo 2019).

Fake news related to the COVID-19 pandemic was spread in the form of social media messages related to non-verified home remedies, fake advisories, and conspiracy theories, and the government had to step in to issue an advisory to put an end to such atrocious rumors which were not only harmful to the health of people but also the image of the country (Purohit 2020; Sutaria 2020).

Fake news and its types: (Social Media 2020; Manzoor, Singla, and Nikita 2019)

a) **Targeted misinformation:** The fictitious information is shared with susceptible and gullible groups over social media for personal gains, as the information is accepted easily and shared without verifying its authenticity.
b) **Fake headlines:** The fictitious content or "clickbait headlines" is usually used by tabloid newspapers to generate attention. Only knowledgeable readers grasp the falseness of the content.
c) **Viral posts:** Social media has become a soup bowl for information on various topics and has a vast fan base. The large social media following groups spread favors and shares, likes and dislikes, fan followers, and popular posts without checking the authenticity of the content.
d) **Satire:** Satirical content on current affairs and politics of a country often employed to raise awareness of social issues or criticize political wrongdoings, if amalgamated with fictitious content, often goes undetected as they are considered as true.
e) **Visual-based:** Fictitious content which uses graphics by including morphed images, doctored video, or a combination of both to instigate strong opinions or hatred towards a person or belief system.
f) **User-based:** Fictitious content created by faux accounts to target a specific audience of certain age groups, gender, culture, and political affiliations to insinuate a thought or philosophy or to brainwash.
g) **Knowledge-based:** Content which claims to be authentic and scientific and gives explanations to solve issues and mysteries in life, health, natural processes, environmental issues, politics, and the world. For example, natural remedies for increased sugar levels in the human body, exercises, and diet plans for a slim or younger look, or the famous crop circles related to UFO sightings.
h) **Style-based:** This type of content is written by pseudo-journalists who pretend and copy the style of some accredited journalists to post fictitious news which is considered authentic due to the writing style used.
i) **Stance-based:** When a true incident, news, or statement is represented negatively or inappropriately by changing the meaning and purpose of the original content.

16.1.1.1 Fundamental Human Cognition and Behavior Theories

Fundamental human cognition and behavior theories can be used for qualitative and quantitative studies of big fake news data which could be I. News-related theories and II. User-related theories (Zhou and Zafarani 2018).

I. **News-related theories:** These theories reveal the possible characteristics of fake news content compared to true news content via writing style and quality such as word counts and expression of sentiments (Zhou and Zafarani 2018).

II. **User-related theories:** These theories probe the traits and activities of the users involved in spreading misinformed content on social media. e.g., posting, forwarding, liking, commenting, and trolling. Fake news could be welcomed by both malicious and normal users (Shao et al. 2018). Malicious users (e.g., some social bots (Ferrara et al. 2014) spread fake news, often intentionally, to earn benefits, while some vulnerable normal users frequently and unintentionally spread fake news without recognizing the falsehood due to social impacts and self-impact (Zhou and Zafarani 2018).

16.1.2 Hate Speech

Hate speech is commonly defined as any communication that disparages a person or a group based on some characteristics such as race, color, ethnicity, gender, sexual orientation, nationality, religion, or some other characteristics (Schmidt and Wiegand 2017).

The rise of social media usage and user-generated web content has increased online hate speech. From misogyny and homophobia to xenophobia and racism, online hate speech has become a topic of greater concern as the Internet matures, particularly as its offline impacts become more widely known (Alsagheer, Mansourifar, and Shi 2022). Over the past few years, interest in online hate speech detection, particularly the automatization of this task, has continuously grown, along with the societal impact of the phenomenon (Schmidt and Wiegand 2017).

Hate speech in news and social media has provoked violence in many countries, Such as the attacks on refugees provoked by Facebook in Germany;; in South Carolina the Charleston church shooter, who killed nine black clergy and worshippers in June 2015, who had engaged in a "self-learning process" online that led him to believe that the goal of white supremacy required violent action; in a Pittsburgh synagogue a shooter espoused the conspiracy that Jews sought to bring immigrants into the United States, and render whites a minority, before killing 11 worshippers at a refugee-themed Shabbat service; and the 2019 New Zealand mosque shootings, the perpetrator who killed 49 Muslims at prayer and sought to broadcast the attack on YouTube (Zachary Laub 2019).

Hate speech has provoked violence in India as well as lynch mobs and other types of communal violence, in many cases originating with rumors on WhatsApp groups, which have been on the rise since the Hindu-nationalist Bharatiya Janata Party (BJP) came to power in 2014 (News 2021; Laub 2019).

Hate speech on online platforms has led to extremist violence in India (The Listening Post 2022). As Muslim people were targeted by cyber perpetrators in order to increase social unrest in India.

Hate news and its types: (Hoyt 2008)

a) **Racism:** News such as slave trade, racial profiling, and countless hate crimes highlight racial prejudice or discrimination with the intention to increase tension among a targeted population or country. According to Merriam-Webster "prejudice" is defined as "an irrational attitude of hostility directed toward an individual, a group, a race or their supposed characteristics." Such news often gives rise to hostility and insecurity and instigates fear in people leading them to make heinous errors in human judgment and take lawless or illegal actions.

b) **Extreme nationalism:** Like any other emotion hatred or love for one's nation is a learned emotion rather than innate. Nationalism means to love one's country but there have been numerous incidences since the historical past where civilizations adopted the "us vs. them" theory, which is based on territorial love rather than racial hatred due to less exposure to other populations. Much psychological research proves that humans are innately programmed to judge, classify, and differentiate people around them. The same has been mentioned by author Michael Shermer on ethics and evolutionary psychology, in his book *The Science of Good and Evil* (Holt Paperback 2004). According to Shermer—if humans have no distinctive skin colors, they will find other traits to gossip, chat, and judge each other on, such as age, gender, or habit.
c) **Religious and politically based hatred:** Throughout history populations and civilizations have been threatened and annihilated due to religious and political reasons, inspired by greed, envy, and fear. For example, the famous bloody wars of Protestants and Catholics which killed many in the name of religion, the extermination or slavery of the two branches of the Maori tribe and Moriori tribe in New Zealand, the unforgettable holocaust and Nazi extermination of the Jewish population in the name of religion, and presently most terrorist attacks are related to political and religious arguments or disagreements or both.
d) **Hatred based on sexual orientation:** The rampant homophobia that persists in present society and countries which according to the American Psychological Association has subjected homosexuals and bisexuals to become social stigmas to such an extent that they often become victims of prejudice, violence (mob lynching and domestic violence), discrimination, and crimes.
e) **Political greed:** Political parties use hate speech and spread hate news to provoke mob lynching or extremist violence (The Listening Post 2022; News 2021; Laub 2019).

Counter speech to detect hate speech: (Alsagheer et al. 2022)

Counter speech can be used to detect hate speech in social media, such as—hard counter hate speech and soft counter hate speech.

I. **Hard counter:** Globalization and advanced communication systems paved the way for the fast spread of information (good or bad) and the same technology has become a tool to spread hate speech on online platforms. To cope with the scenario most companies in the global market had to pass strict laws against such publications to prevent tension within the employees and communities. Such hard counter measures are fast and focused and have been accepted worldwide to put a stop to extremist activities or behavior.

II. **Soft counter:** Public speech sometimes expounds or reduces mob violence while protecting the rights to freedom of speech and expression of thought. The rise in Internet activity accelerated the spread of hate speech, via X, Facebook, etc. Thus, in soft counter, automatically generated counter hate speech is posted as a set of new comments in order to provide an extra positive voice to keep the overall language less dominated by hateful comments or attempts to insert new positive comments automatically.

16.2 SIGNIFICANCE OF FAKE NEWS AND HATE SPEECH DETECTION

In today's globalized world, people commonly rely on news and social media to keep themselves updated with the events happening within their country and abroad, since each incidence triggers changes in the thoughts and lives of people. Hence, it becomes imminent to check for fake news and hate speeches, as it would:

1. Put a stop to extremist violence against innocent people.
2. Reduce mob lynching.
3. Reduce negative vote banking.
4. Reduce manslaughter in the name of religion, creed, and gender.
5. Reduce rumors about false and invalid medical therapies for various diseases.
6. Reduce cult-related crimes.
7. Reduce child slaughter, female infanticide, and mass massacres.
8. Reduce economic and trade losses, etc.

16.2.1 Threats of Fake News (Fake News 2022; Tarran 2017; Lewandowsky, Ecker, and Cook 2017)

i. Representation of inaccurate facts.
ii. Enticing style of writing optimizes online activity such as sharing and giving likes and dislikes.
iii. Preys on prejudice and instigates hatred in online users.

16.2.2 Threats of Hate Speech (Zannettou et al. 2020)

i. Includes interplay of words in articles or write-ups related to politics and journalism via linguistic styles and hate remarks.
ii. Includes subjects which showcase high clout or hit score (most likes or comments) and the lower tone scores.
iii. Includes topics with .a high reference to social and religious effects on online users.
iv. Includes use of first- and third-person singular pronouns to trap online users.

v. Includes references symbolic of the highest anger and anxiety references.
vi. Includes a minimum number of words to hint at inconsistency, uncertainty, connections, segregation, and achievement.
vii. Include maximum references linked to connections between people, events, politics, and global affairs.

16.3 DISCUSSIONS

16.3.1 Techniques for Fake News Detection (Zhou and Zafarani 2018)

I. **Knowledge-based fake news detection:** This process is used to check the authenticity of news in journalism.

a. **Manual fact-checking:** The method is not efficient enough to check the latest or newly added information but is still workable. It is of two types—expert-based and crowd-based:
   i. **Expert-based manual fact-checking:** It is used for less amount of information and relies on a small expert group of fact-checkers, thus is manageable, accurate, and expensive.
   ii. **Expert-based fact-checking websites:** Websites (refer to the table in the referenced paper; Dong et al. 2014) which provide statistical scorecards to present the authenticity of the statements in articles published online. For example, PolitiFact provides facts related to politics and its aspects, such as the scorecard on Donald Trump, the former President of the United States (Dong et al. 2014).
   iii. **Crowd-sourced manual fact-checking:** Data is checked via collective intelligence of regular fact-checkers such as the Amazon Mechanical Turk and CREDBANK (Mitra and Gilbert 2021), a news dataset. This provides detailed feedback but is inaccurate and hard to control and manage.. Hence, it requires a second-time filtration of non-credible users.
   iv. **Crowd-sourced fact-checking websites:** These websites provide more choices to fact-checkers. These websites can scrutinize content in news and blog posts accurately. For instance, Fiskkit, is very user-friendly since it allows users to post articles, rate sentences within articles, and choose categories that most accurately describe the uploaded content.

b. **Automatic fact-checking:** Scalability has led to the development of automatic fact-checking methods, which mainly rely on network/graph theory, information retrieval (IR), natural language processing (NLP), and machine learning (ML) approaches (Cohen, Hamilton, and Turner 2011). A unified standard representation of knowledge is used to evaluate the techniques that are automatically processed by machines and has been widely adopted in related studies given below (Nickel et al. 2016). For example, the knowledge (a set of subject, predicate, object (SPO) triples) within the sentence "Donald Trump is the president of

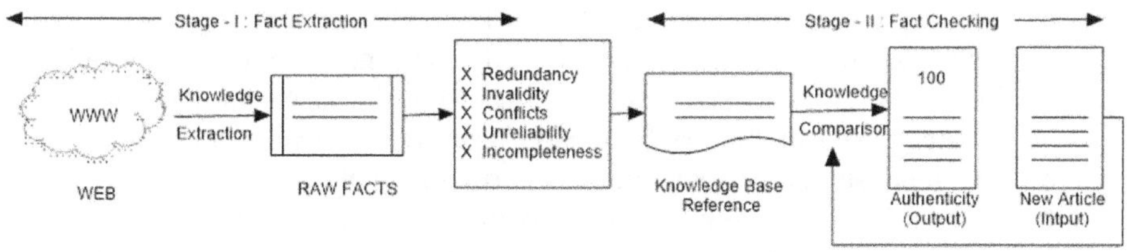

FIGURE 16.1 Automatic news fact-finding process.

the U.S." can be (DonaldTrump, Profession, President) can be extracted (Figure 16.1) (Ciampaglia et al. 2015; Shi and Weninger 2016).

II. **Style-based fake news detection:** Similar to knowledge-based fake news detection (refer to Table-4 in Zhou and Zafarani (2018)), style-based fake news detection also focuses on analyzing the news content. Though style-based approaches can evaluate news purpose, i.e., whether or not there is an aim to mislead the audience, knowledge-based methods primarily analyze the veracity of the supplied news. The underlying premise and intuition of style-based approaches is that hostile actors would rather publish fake news in a "special" way to get readers to read it and be persuaded to believe it. We first describe fake news styles in a way that makes machine learning easier to utilize before talking about how such "special" content styles may be automatically identified.

III. **Propagation-based fake news detection:** When approaching the detection of false news from a propagation-based standpoint, it is possible to investigate and make use of data pertaining to its distribution, such as user-generated content. Propagation-based false news identification is frequently stated as a binary (or multi-label) classification problem but with a different input than style-based fake news detection. In general, the input of a propagation-based approach can be one of two types: (I) A self-defined graph, which is an indirect representation that captures extra information on news propagation, or (II) a news cascade, which is a direct representation of news propagation. Thus, the identification of false news by propagation essentially consists of categorizing either (I) news cascades or (II) self-defined graphs.

IV. **Source-based fake news detection:** The best way to identify false news is to evaluate its source's credibility, which is commonly described as "offering reasonable grounds for being believed" in the sense of quality and plausibility (Castillo, Mendoza, and Poblete 2011; Viviani and Pasi 2017). A [false] news story has three steps (refer to the paper Castillo, Mendoza, and Poblete (2011)), which are creation, online publication, and social media propagation. This section will explain how news stories' credibility may be evaluated at each level depending on the reliability of their sources. Stated differently, we define "sources" as a broad concept that encompasses (I) the news writers and publishers who create the news stories, (II) the news publishers who publish the news stories, and (III) the social media accounts that share the news stories. For two reasons, we consolidate (I) and (II) into a single subsection: Because (i) not much research has looked at news authors and (ii) news authors and publishers frequently have an employee–employer connection, there should be some intuitive correlation between their credibility. Because of this, evaluating the reliability of news sources is sometimes seen as an oblique method of identifying false information. That is, news stories from untrustworthy sources may be seen as fake news even when it is possible for them to provide accurate information. Although it may appear random, this method of identifying fake news is effective (Horne, Nørregaard, and Adalı 2019). Research has shown that many false news articles originate from hyper-partisan websites that pose as news sources or from fake news websites that only produce hoaxes (Silverman 2016).

16.3.2 Techniques for Hate Speech Detection (MacAvaney et al. 2019)

The majority of social media sites contain user guidelines that forbid hate speech; nonetheless, implementing these guidelines involves a lot of manual effort because each report must be reviewed. Recently, a few platforms— such as Facebook—have boosted the number of content moderators. Automated methods and instruments have the potential to expedite the evaluation process or assign human resources to positions that need meticulous scrutiny. This section provides an overview of automated methods for textual hate speech identification.

A. **Keyword-based approaches:** A keyword-based approach is a fundamental method for detecting hate speech. Text that contains potentially hostile terms is found using a dictionary or ontology. For example, Hatebase keeps a collection of disparaging words for several groups in 95 different languages. These carefully kept resources are important since language might change over time. But as we saw in our investigation of the criteria of hate speech, it is not always sufficient to merely use a derogatory term for it to qualify as hate speech.
B. **Source metadata:** Further social media data can aid in understanding the post features and may even result in a more effective identification strategy. Details such as the publishing user's demographics, geography, date, and even social involvement on the site can all provide further context for comprehending the message at various levels of detail. However, because releasing data that contains sensitive user information creates privacy concerns, this information is frequently not easily accessible to outside researchers. It is possible that outside researchers have access to none or very little of the user data. As a result, they could answer the incorrect problem or draw incorrect conclusions from the data. For example, depending on incidental dataset features, a system trained on this data may naturally be biased towards classifying information flagged as hate speech by specific people or groups.

C. **Machine learning classifiers:** Using labels annotated by content reviewers, machine learning models generate a classifier that can identify hate speech from samples of tagged text. Numerous models were put out and shown to be effective in the past. We provide an overview of a few open-sourced systems that were featured in the most current study.
D. **Content preprocessing and feature selection:** Hate-indicating text characteristics need to be extracted in order to categorize or identify user-generated material. Individual words or phrases (also known as n-grams, or sequences of n consecutive words) are obvious characteristics. Words can be stemmed to get simply the root, eliminating morphological distinctions, to enhance feature matching. When classifying texts, the bag-of-words assumption is frequently applied. This presumption states that a post is just an unordered collection of words or n-grams. This assumption, while it leaves out a significant feature of languages, has shown to be effective in a variety of tasks. There are several methods, such as term frequency-inverse document frequency (TF–IDF), for allocating weights to the phrases that could be more significant in this context.

Word embeddings, or the act of assigning a vector to a word (e.g., Word2vec)—along with distributional features—are frequently used in conjunction with deep learning techniques in text mining and natural language processing. The bag-of-words assumption is contested by certain deep learning architectures, such as transformer and recurrent neural networks, which simulate word ordering by processing over a series of word embeddings.

16.3.3 Hate Speech Detection Approaches and Baselines

Support vector machine, Naïve Bayes, and logistic regression. These approaches are frequently applied to the classification of texts. With the presumption that features do not interact, Naïve Bayes models explicitly label probabilities. Linear classifiers such as support vector machines (SVMs) and logistic regression determine classes by combining the scores of individual features. These models have open-source implementations, such as the well-known scikit-learn machine learning package for Python.

A. **N-gram model:** N-gram modeling is a well-liked feature identification and analysis technique in the domains of natural language processing and language modeling. An n-gram is a continuous series of n-elements. It could consist of a string of characters, bytes, syllables, or words. Word-based and character-based n-gram models are the most often utilized n-gram models in text classification. In this study, we construct features to categorize the content and reflect its context using word-based n-grams. We create a basic classifier based on n-grams to distinguish between authentic and fraudulent news items. The goal is to use the training data to create different sets of n-gram frequency profiles that reflect authentic and fraudulent news stories.

We looked at how the n-gram length affected the accuracy of several classification algorithms using a variety of baseline n-gram features that were based on words.

- **Data Pre-processing:** The data must undergo a number of improvements, including stop-word removal, tokenization, lowercasing, sentence segmentation, and punctuation removal, before being represented using an n-gram and vector-based model. Eliminating unnecessary information from the data will assist us in reducing the amount of the real data.

  We decreased the document's letter case after developing a general processing method to eliminate punctuation and non-letter characters for every document. Furthermore, a word-based tokenizer based on n-grams was developed to segment the text according to the length of n.
- **Stop word removal:** Stop words are unimportant words in a language that make a sound when they are utilized as text classification characteristics. These are terms that are frequently used in sentences to support sentence structure or to help link ideas. Stop words include articles, prepositions, conjunctions, and some pronouns. Common terms such as "a", "about", "an", "are", "as", "at", "be", "by", "for", "from", "how", "in", "is", "of", "on", "or", "that", "the", "these", "this", "too", "what", "when", "where", "who", "will", etc., were eliminated. Each document that had those terms deleted was processed, saved, and carried on to the next phase.
- **Stemming:** The next stage is to convert the tokens into a standard form after tokenizing the data. Reverting words to their original forms and reducing the number of word classes or kinds in the data is known as stemming. For instance, the terms "run", "run", and "runner" will all be combined to form the word "run". Stemming allows us to classify data more quickly and effectively. In addition, we employ the Porter stemmer, the most popular stemming method because of its precision. (Ahmed, Traore, and Saad 2017).

B. **Features extraction**

Learning from high-dimensional data is one of the issues in text classification. Documents include a large number of keywords, words, and phrases that increase the computational load on the learning process. Moreover, superfluous and unnecessary features might negatively impact the classifiers' performance and accuracy. In order to minimize the size of the text features and prevent huge feature space dimensions, feature reduction is the ideal method. In this study, two distinct feature selection techniques—term frequency (TF) and term frequency–inverted document frequency (TF–IDF)—were investigated.

- **Term Frequency (TF):** Term frequency is a method for determining the degree of similarity between papers by counting the number of terms that appear in each document. The word counts are included in an equal-length vector that represents each document. Each vector is then normalized so that the total of its components equals one. After that, each word count is translated into the likelihood that it will appear in the texts. For instance, a word will be set to zero if it is not found in a document and will be represented as one if it is. As a result, word groupings reflect each document.

- **TF–IDF:** Term frequency counts the terms that appear in each text to determine how similar two papers are to one another. Each document is represented by an equal-length vector containing the word counts. Next, each vector is normalized so that the sum of its parts is one. The possibility that each word will appear in the texts is then calculated based on its word count. For example, if a word is not discovered in a document, it will be set to zero, and if it is, it will be represented as one. Word clusters therefore represent each document.

C. **Dataset for hate news:** (MacAvaney et al. 2019)

It is difficult to gather and annotate data in order to train computer classifiers to identify hate speech. In particular, it might be challenging to determine if a certain text qualifies as hate speech since, as was previously indicated, there is no accepted definition of the term. According to research on the validity of hate speech annotations by Ross et al annotators are not trustworthy. As determined by Krippendorff's α, there was extremely little agreement (as little as 0.29), among the annotators. However, they discovered a significant association when they contrasted annotations made according to their personal beliefs with those made according to X's criteria.

In addition, hate speech thrives on social media platforms, even though many of them have highly stringent guidelines for data sharing and usage. Because of this, there are just a few datasets that are available for public analysis, the majority of which are from X (which has a laxer policy on data usage). Though the X resources are useful, the character restriction makes them less applicable to a wider audience; this leads to brief, to-the-point material. Posts from other platforms, on the other hand, are usually lengthier and can contribute to a broader conversation on a certain subject. This adds further context, which might change the text's meaning.

The fact that there are so few well-selected, publicly accessible datasets that label offensive, hostile, and abusive material presents another difficulty. The public datasets (refer to Table-1 in MacAvaney et al. 2019) that are accessible for training and evaluation are as follows:

- **HatebaseX:** A collection of 24,802 tweets from Davidson et al. constitutes one X dataset. They followed the following process to create the dataset. Initially, using a Hatebase hate speech vocabulary, they looked for tweets from around 33,000 individuals that contained these phrases. After that, they extracted a chronology from each of these individuals, yielding a collection of almost 85 million tweets. A randomized sample of 25,000 tweets containing terms from the lexicon was selected from the dataset including around 85 million tweets. They annotated each tweet using crowdsourcing, classifying it as either objectionable (but not hate speech), hate speech, or neither. A tweet was removed from the collection if the annotators' agreement was too low. There is also a widely used subset of 14,510 tweets in this dataset accessible.

- **Waseem A:** Waseem and Hovy offer a X dataset with 16,914 tweets classified as either sexist, racist, or neither. Approximately 136,000 tweets that contain derogatory remarks concerning sexual, gender, religious, and ethnic minorities were first assembled into a corpus by the researchers. 16,914 tweets from this corpus were annotated (classified) by the authors, who then had a gender studies major examine their work.
- **Waseem B:** By selecting a fresh group of tweets from the corpus of 136,000 tweets, Waseem generates a new dataset in a subsequent publication. Waseem used crowdsourcing and feminists and anti-racism activists to annotate the tweets in this collection. There are three designations in there: sexist, racist, or neither.
- **Stormfront:** A dataset of postings from the white nationalist forum Stormfront is made available by de Gilbert et al. 10,568 sentences have been categorized as Hate, NoHate, Relation, or Skip as a consequence of their sentence-level annotation of the postings. The labels "Hate" and "NoHate" designate whether hate speech is present in each statement or not. When paired with the other lines, the label "Relation" denotes that the statement constitutes hate speech. Lastly, sentences that are not in English or do not include information pertaining to hate speech or non-hate speech are classified as "Skip". They also record the extent to which an annotator classified the text using context, or earlier sentences.
- **TRAC:** The shared goal of identifying hostile writing in both Hindi and English was organized by the 2018 Workshop on Trolling, Aggression, and Cyberbullying (TRAC). Hate speech frequently includes aggressive wording. 15,869 Facebook comments classified as overtly hostile, covertly aggressive, or non-aggressive make up the publicly accessible dataset from this job. Additionally, a small 1,253-tweet X dataset with the same labels exists.
- **HatEval:** This dataset is from the SemEval 2019 competition (Task 5), which focused on multilingual hate speech identification in tweets directed towards immigrants and women. It is made up of many label sets. The first one shows if the tweet is hostile against immigrants or women; the second one shows if the message is aggressive; and the third one shows if the tweet is meant for a specific person or for a group as a whole. Be aware that not all definitions of hate speech classify targeting someone as such.
- **Kaggle:** There was a shared job on Kaggle.com to identify offensive remarks. 8,832 social media comments that have been classified as offensive or not make up the dataset. Insulting text could be a sign of hate speech, even though it's not always the case.

- **GermanX:** Ross et al. produced a X dataset in German about the European refugee crisis as part of their investigation of annotator dependability. It is made up of 541 German tweets that are classified as either hate speech or not.

16.4 CONCLUSION

The chapter concludes that the globalized world and easy access to the internet have increased social media usage, which will only grow in the future. With the growing social media usage, the user, size, choice, and data accessed have become immeasurable. The data accessed and reuse of the information via various social media handles have become more obscure and keeping track of the flow of information has become even more relevant with the increase in fake news and hate speech. The highest number of social media users or Internet users in any country is its youth. The youth, furthermore, are influenced by the information good or bad on the internet or social media applications. Hence, it becomes necessary to study fake news and hate speech and its effect on the youth and society.

The chapter differentiates between fake news and hate speech, makes a detailed description of problems caused by them and their types, and discusses the significance of detecting fake news and hate speech via the use of the latest computer techniques (using online and offline modes) and varied datasets.

Therefore, the chapter makes a literary survey and qualitative study of fake news and hate speech and discusses the aspects behind the spread and containment of both to safeguard the internet user from becoming victims or misusing the unauthentic information or data available online.

REFERENCES

Ahmed, Hadeer, Issa Traore, and Sherif Saad. 2017. *Detection of Online Fake News Using N-Gram Analysis and Machine Learning Techniques*, 127–38. doi:10.1007/978-3-319-69155-8_9.

Allcott, Hunt, and Matthew Gentzkow. 2017. 'Social Media and Fake News in the 2016 Election'. *Journal of Economic Perspectives* 31 (2): 211–36. doi:10.1257/jep.31.2.211.

Alsagheer, Dana, Hadi Mansourifar, and Weidong Shi. 2022. 'Counter Hate Speech in Social Media: A Survey'. February. http://arxiv.org/abs/2203.03584.

Castillo, Carlos, Marcelo Mendoza, and Barbara Poblete. 2011. 'Information Credibility on Twitter'. In *Proceedings of the 20th International Conference on World Wide Web*, 675–84. New York, NY: ACM. doi:10.1145/1963405.1963500.

Chatterji, Rohini. 2020. 'BJP Resorts To Fake 'Lonely Woman' On Twitter To Drum Up Support For CAA'. *Huffpost News*. January 4. https://www.huffpost.com/archive/in/entry/bjp-lonely-woman-twitter-caa-support_in_5e10660cc5b6b5a713ba970b.

Ciampaglia, Giovanni Luca, Prashant Shiralkar, Luis M. Rocha, Johan Bollen, Filippo Menczer, and Alessandro Flammini. 2015. 'Computational Fact Checking from Knowledge Networks'. January. doi:10.1371/journal.pone.0128193.

Cohen, Sarah, James T. Hamilton, and Fred Turner. 2011. 'Computational Journalism'. *Communications of the ACM* 54 (10): 66–71. doi:10.1145/2001269.2001288.

Davidson, T., Warmsley, D., Macy, M. W., Weber, I.,. 2017. 'Automated Hate Speech Detection and the Problem of Offensive Language'. ICWSM

de Gibert, O.. Perez, N., Garc'ia-Pablos, A., Cuadros, M.2018. 'Hate Speech Dataset from a White Supremacy Forum'. In: 2nd Workshop on Abusive Language Online @ EMNLP.

Dong, Xin Luna, Evgeniy Gabrilovich, Geremy Heitz, Wilko Horn, Ni Lao, Kevin Murphy, Thomas Strohmann, Shaohua Sun, and Wei Zhang. 2014. 'Knowledge Vault: A Web-Scale Approach to Probabilistic Knowledge Fusion'. The 20th ACM SIGKDD International Conference on Knowledge Discovery and Data Mining, August, 601–10. https://storage.googleapis.com/pub-tools-public-publication-data/pdf/45634.pdf.

Dutta, Prabhash K. 2018. '16 Lynchings in 2 Months. Is Social Media the New Serial Killer?' *India Today*. July 2. https://www.indiatoday.in/india/story/16-lynchings-in-2-months-is-social-media-the-new-serial-killer-1275182-2018-07-02.

Ember, Sydney, and Paul Mihailidis. 2017. 'This Is Not Fake News (but Don't Go by the Headline)'. *The New York Times*. April 3.

Fake News. 2022. 'Characteristics of Fake News & Media Bias'. *Thompson Rivers University Library*. August 2. https://libguides.tru.ca/fakenews/characteristics#:~:text=In%20the%20most%20general%20form%2C%20fake%20news%20has,distort%20with%20emotions%3B%20preying%20on%20prejudice%20or%20bias.

Ferrara, Emilio, Onur Varol, Clayton Davis, Filippo Menczer, and Alessandro Flammini. 2014. 'The Rise of Social Bots'. July. doi:10.1145/2818717.

Goel, Kritika. 2019. 'Here's Your Round-Up of All the Fake News Around CAA Protests'. *The Quint*. December 18. https://www.thequint.com/news/webqoof/round-up-of-fake-news-around-caa-protests-students-police.

Grover, Gurshabad, Elonnai Hickok, Arindrajit Basu, Akriti Bopanna, Torsha Sarkar, Research Assistance, Vedika Pareek, and Shweta Mohandas. 2019. 'Response to the Draft of The Information Technology [Intermediary Guidelines (Amendment) Rules] 2018'. https://en.unesco.org/fightfakenews.

Himma-Kadakas, Marju. 2017. 'Alternative Facts and Fake News Entering Journalistic Content Production Cycle'. *Cosmopolitan Civil Societies: An Interdisciplinary Journal* 9 (2): 25–40. doi:10.5130/ccs.v9i2.5469.

Hindu. 2019. 'Supreme Court Asks Centre to Consider Publicising Info about CAA to Curb Circulation of Fake News'. *Hindu*. December 18. https://www.thehindu.com/news/national/supreme-court-asks-centre-to-consider-publicising-info-about-caa-to-curb-circulation-of-fake-news/article61604760.ece.

Horne, Benjamin D., Jeppe Nørregaard, and Sibel Adalı. 2019. 'Different Spirals of Sameness: A Study of Content Sharing in Mainstream and Alternative Media'. *Proceedings of the International AAAI Conference on Web and Social Media* 13 (July): 257–66. doi:10.1609/icwsm.v13i01.3227.

Hoyt, Alia. 2008. 'How Do You Define Hate?' *StuffWorks.Com*. June 24. https://science.howstuffworks.com/life/inside-the-mind/emotions/define-hate.htm.

Hunt, Elle. 2016. 'What Is Fake News? How to Spot It and What You Can Do to Stop It.' *The Guardian*. December. https://www.theguardian.com/media/2016/dec/18/what-is-fake-news-pizzagate.

IANS. 2019. 'Around 5,000 Pak Social Media Handles Spread Fake News on CAA'. Newsd. In. December 16. https://newsd.in/around-5-000-pak-social-media-handles-spread-fake-news-on-caa/#:~:text=New%20Delhi%2C%20Dec%2016%20%28IANS%29%20Security%20and%20intelligence,protests%20to%20incite%20communal%20violence%20in%20the%20country.

Krishnan, Murali. 2019. 'Social Media in India Fans Fake News', https://www.nationalheraldindia.com/india/social-media-in-india-fans-fake-news.

Kundu, Chanyan. 2019. 'Fact Check: Misleading Picture of Cow Deaths Goes Viral Again on Social Media'. *India Today*. May 12. https://www.indiatoday.in/fact-check/story/fact-check-misleading-picture-cow-deaths-rajasthan-1523386-2019-05-12.

Laub, Zachary. 2019. 'Hate Speech on Social Media: Global Comparisons'. *Council on Foreign Relations*. June 7. https://www.cfr.org/backgrounder/hate-speech-social-media-global-comparisons.

Lewandowsky, Stephan, Ullrich K. H. Ecker, and John Cook. 2017. 'Beyond Misinformation: Understanding and Coping with the 'Post-Truth' Era.' *Journal of Applied Research in Memory and Cognition* 6 (4): 353–69. doi:10.1016/j.jarmac.2017.07.008.

MacAvaney, Sean, Hao-Ren Yao, Eugene Yang, Katina Russell, Nazli Goharian, and Ophir Frieder. 2019. 'Hate Speech Detection: Challenges and Solutions'. *PLoS One* 14 (8): e0221152. doi:10.1371/journal.pone.0221152.

Manzoor, Syed Ishfaq, Jimmy Singla, and Nikita. 2019. 'Fake News Detection Using Machine Learning Approaches: A Systematic Review'. 2019 3rd International Conference on Trends in Electronics and Informatics (ICOEI), 230–34. IEEE. doi:10.1109/ICOEI.2019.8862770.

Mitra, Tanushree, and Eric Gilbert. 2021. 'CREDBANK: A Large-Scale Social Media Corpus With Associated Credibility Annotations'. *Proceedings of the International AAAI Conference on Web and Social Media* 9 (1): 258–67. doi:10.1609/icwsm.v9i1.14625.

News. 2019a. 'Junk News and Misinformation Prevalent in Indian Election Campaign'. *University of Oxford*. May 13. https://www.ox.ac.uk/news/2019-05-13-junk-news-and-misinformation-prevalent-indian-election-campaign.

News. 2019b. 'Clip, Flip and Photoshop: Anatomy of Fakes in Indian Elections'. *India Today*. May 28. https://www.indiatoday.in/elections/story/india-lok-sabha-elections-fake-news-photoshop-lie-truth-1537053-2019-05-28.

News. 2021. 'The Interplay between Social Media and Hate Speech in India'. *Sabrang India*. January 16. https://sabrangindia.in/article/interplay-between-social-media-and-hate-speech-india.

Nickel, M., and Murphy K., Tresp, V.Gabrilovich, E.. 2016. 'A review of relational machine learning for knowledge graphs'. *Proceedings of the IEEE* 104 (1): 11–33.

Perrigo, Billy. 2019. 'How Volunteers for India's Ruling Party Are Using WhatsApp to Fuel Fake News Ahead of Elections'. *Time*. January 25. https://time.com/5512032/whatsapp-india-election-2019/.

Purohit, Kunal. 2020. 'Misinformation, Fake News Spark India Coronavirus Fears'. *ALJAZEERA*. March 10. https://www.aljazeera.com/news/2020/3/10/misinformation-fake-news-spark-india-coronavirus-fears.

Ross, B., Rist, M., Carbonell, G., Cabrera, B., Kurowsky, N., and Wojatzki, M., 2016. 'Measuring the Reliability of Hate Speech Annotations: The Case of the European Refugee Crisis'. In *The 3rd Workshop on Natural Language Processing for Computer-Mediated Communication @ Conference on Natural Language Processing.*

Schlesinger, Robert. 2017. 'Fake News in Reality'. *U.S. News and World Report*. April 14. https://www.usnews.com/opinion/thomas-jefferson-street/articles/2017-04-14/what-is-fake-news-maybe-not-what-you-think.

Schmidt, Anna, and Michael Wiegand. 2017. 'A Survey on Hate Speech Detection Using Natural Language Processing'. In *Proceedings of the Fifth International Workshop on Natural Language … Processing for Social Media*, 1–10. Stroudsburg, PA: Association for Computational Linguistics. doi:10.18653/v1/W17-1101.

Shao, Chengcheng, Giovanni Luca Ciampaglia, Onur Varol, Kai-Cheng Yang, Alessandro Flammini, and Filippo Menczer. 2018. 'The Spread of Low-Credibility Content by Social Bots'. *Nature Communications* 9 (1): 4787. doi:10.1038/s41467-018-06930-7.

Shi, Baoxu, and Tim Weninger. 2016. 'Discriminative Predicate Path Mining for Fact Checking in Knowledge Graphs'. *Knowledge-Based Systems* 104 (July): 123–33. doi:10.1016/j.knosys.2016.04.015.

Silverman, Craig. 2016. 'This Analysis Shows How Viral Fake Election News Stories Outperformed Real News On Facebook'. *BuzzFeed News.* November 17.

Social Media. 2020. 'What Is Fake News? Definition, Types, and How to Detect Them'. *Digital Guide IONOS.* July 27. https://www.ionos.com/digitalguide/online-marketing/social-media/what-is-fake-news/.

Sutaria, Shachi. 2020. 'Boiled Garlic Water For Treating Coronavirus? Not Really'. *Boomlive.* February 1. https://www.boomlive.in/health/boiled-garlic-water-for-treating-coronavirus-not-really-6737.

Tarran, Brian. 2017. 'Why Facts Are Not Enough in the Fight against Fake News'. *Significance* 14 (5): 6–7. doi:10.1111/j.1740-9713.2017.01066.x.

The Listening Post. 2022. 'Hate Speech and Online Abuse: India's Growing Extremism Problem'. *Al Jazeera English.* January 8. https://www.bing.com/videos/riverview/relatedvideo?&q=hate+speech+in+social+media+in+India&qpvt=hate+speech+in+social+media+in+India&mid=DF538B1E9196371245FBDF538B1E9196371245FB&&FORM=VRDGAR.

Times Now Digital. 2018. 'Fake News, Rumour Mongering Leading to Lynchings; Have Asked Social Media Sites for Regulation: Rajnath Singh'. *Times Now.* July 19. https://www.timesnownews.com/india/article/mob-lynchings-cow-vigilantism-vigilante-groups-cattle-slaughter-fake-news-social-media-rumour-mongering-rajnath-singh-parliament-monsoon-session/256639.

Viviani, Marco, and Gabriella Pasi. 2017. 'Credibility in Social Media: Opinions, News, and Health Information—A Survey'. *WIREs Data Mining and Knowledge Discovery* 7 (5). doi:10.1002/widm.1209.

Waseem, Z and Hovy D. 2016. 'Hateful Symbols or Hateful People? Predictive Features for Hate Speech Detection on Twitter'. In *SRW@HLT-NAACL*

Zannettou, Savvas, Mai Elsherief, Elizabeth Belding, Shirin Nilizadeh, and Gianluca Stringhini. 2020. 'Measuring and Characterizing Hate Speech on News Websites'. In *12th ACM Conference on Web Science*, 125–34. New York, NY: ACM. doi:10.1145/3394231.3397902.

Zhou, Xinyi, and Reza Zafarani. 2018. *A Survey of Fake News: Fundamental Theories, Detection Methods, and Opportunities*, 1–10. Association for Computational Linguistics, December. doi:10.1145/3395046.

Index

D

E

F

G

H

I

J

K

S

T

For Product Safety Concerns and Information please contact our EU
representative GPSR@taylorandfrancis.com
Taylor & Francis Verlag GmbH, Kaufingerstraße 24, 80331 München, Germany

www.ingramcontent.com/pod-product-compliance
Lightning Source LLC
LaVergne TN
LVHW011114300926
849160LV00008B/377
9781032529752